7-10-93

To Dad,

From Suzi & Deaver
for Your '93 Birthday

P.S. thanx for the
fun Sailing!

The Civil War

Through The Camera

The Civil War

Through The Camera

A Complete Illustrated History
of
THE CIVIL WAR

HENRY W. ELSON

ARNO PRESS
New York / 1979

Publisher's Note:
This volume is reprinted from the edition ©1912
by Patriot Publishing Company, Springfield, Mass.;
Published by McKinlay, Stone and Mackenzie, New York.

Reprint edition 1979 by Arno Press Inc.

Library of Congress Cataloging in Publication Data

Main entry under title:

The Civil War through the camera.

  Reprint of the 1912 ed. published by McKinlay,
Stone & Mackenzie, New York.
  Partly illustrated by the Brady photos.
  1. United States—History—Civil War, 1861-1865.
I. Elson, Henry William, 1857-   II. Brady,
Matthew B., 1823-1896.
E468.C65 1979   973.7   79-15382
ISBN 0-405-12294-2

Manufactured in the United States of America.

THE CIVIL WAR
THROUGH THE CAMERA

Hundreds of Vivid Photographs
Actually Taken in Civil War Times

Sixteen Reproductions in Color of Famous War Paintings

The New Text History

By

HENRY W. ELSON

Professor of History, Ohio University

A Complete Illustrated History of the
CIVIL WAR

⊞

NEW YORK

McKinlay, Stone & Mackenzie

MAJOR ROBERT ANDERSON AND FAMILY

This Federal major of artillery was summoned on April 11, 1861, to surrender Fort Sumter and the property of the government whose uniform he wore. At half-past four the following morning the boom of the first gun from Fort Johnson in Charleston Harbor notified the breathless, waiting world that war was on. The flag had been fired on, and hundreds of thousands of lives were to be sacrificed ere the echoes of the great guns died away at the end of four years into the sobs of a nation whose best and bravest, North and South, had strewn the many battlefields. No wonder that the attention of the civilized world was focussed on the man who provoked the first blow in the greatest conflict the world has ever known. He was the man who handled the situation at the breaking point. To him the North looked to preserve the Federal property in Charleston Harbor, and the honor of the National flag. The action of the South depended upon his decision. He played the part of a true soldier, and two days after the first shot was fired he led his little garrison of the First United States Artillery out of Sumter with the honors of war.

SCENES OF '61
THAT QUICKLY
FOLLOWED
"BROTHER JONA-
THAN" (PAGE 44)

The upper photograph
shows Confederates on
Monday the fifteenth of
April, 1861—one day
after the momentous
event which Holmes
dimly prophesied in
" Brother Jonathan "
(page 44). The picture
below, with the two fol-
lowing, were made on
the 16th. As April wore
on, North and South
alil had been reluctant
to strike first. When
Major Robert Anderson,
on December 26, 1860,
removed to Fort Sumter,
on an island at the
entrance to Charleston

TERRE PLEIN OF THE GORGE.
Showing the Guns, "en barbette." April 15, 1861.

CONFEDERATES IN SUMTER THE DAY AFTER ANDERSON LEFT

NORTH-EASTERN ANGLE AND EASTERN FACE OF FORT SUMTER
Barbett Columbiad in position as a Mortar—pointing towards the City.

A GUN TRAINED ON CHARLESTON BY ANDERSON

Harbor, he placed him-
self in a position to withstand long attack. But
he needed supplies. The
Confederates would al-
low none to be landed.
When at length rumors
of a powerful naval force
to relieve the fort
reached Charleston, the
Confederates demanded
the surrender of the gar-
rison. Anderson prom-
ised to evacuate by April
15th if he received no
additional supplies. His
terms were rejected. At
half-past four on the
morning of April 12th a
shell from Fort Johnson
"rose high in air, and
curving in its course,
burst almost directly
over the fort." The
mighty war had begun.

TWO DAYS AFTER THE BOMBARDMENT OF SUMTER, APRIL 16, 1861

Wade Hampton (the tallest figure) and other leading South Carolinians inspecting the effects of the cannonading that had forced Major Anderson to evacuate, and had precipitated the mightiest conflict of modern times—two days before.

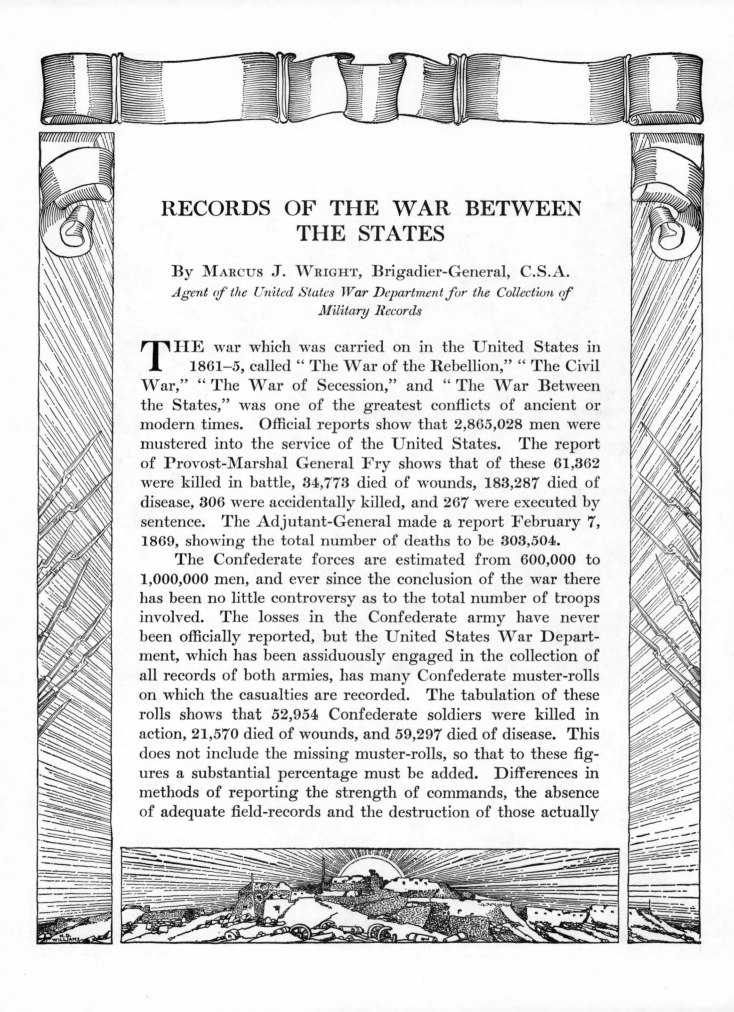

RECORDS OF THE WAR BETWEEN THE STATES

By MARCUS J. WRIGHT, Brigadier-General, C.S.A.
*Agent of the United States War Department for the Collection of
Military Records*

THE war which was carried on in the United States in 1861–5, called "The War of the Rebellion," "The Civil War," "The War of Secession," and "The War Between the States," was one of the greatest conflicts of ancient or modern times. Official reports show that 2,865,028 men were mustered into the service of the United States. The report of Provost-Marshal General Fry shows that of these 61,362 were killed in battle, 34,773 died of wounds, 183,287 died of disease, 306 were accidentally killed, and 267 were executed by sentence. The Adjutant-General made a report February 7, 1869, showing the total number of deaths to be 303,504.

The Confederate forces are estimated from 600,000 to 1,000,000 men, and ever since the conclusion of the war there has been no little controversy as to the total number of troops involved. The losses in the Confederate army have never been officially reported, but the United States War Department, which has been assiduously engaged in the collection of all records of both armies, has many Confederate muster-rolls on which the casualties are recorded. The tabulation of these rolls shows that 52,954 Confederate soldiers were killed in action, 21,570 died of wounds, and 59,297 died of disease. This does not include the missing muster-rolls, so that to these figures a substantial percentage must be added. Differences in methods of reporting the strength of commands, the absence of adequate field-records and the destruction of those actually

AFTER THE GREAT MASS MEETING IN UNION SQUARE, NEW YORK, APRIL 20, 1861

Knots of citizens still linger around the stands where Anderson, who had abandoned Sumter only six days before, had just roused the multitude to wild enthusiasm. Of this gathering in support of the Government the *New York Herald* said at the time: "Such a mighty uprising of the people has never before been witnessed in New York, nor throughout the whole length and breadth of the Union. Five stands were erected, from which some of the most able speakers of the city and state addressed the multitude on the necessity of rallying around the flag of the Republic in this hour of its danger. A series of resolutions was proposed and unanimously adopted, pledging the meeting to use every means to preserve the Union intact and inviolate. Great unanimity prevailed throughout the whole proceedings; party politics were ignored, and the entire meeting—speakers and listeners—were a unit in maintaining the national honor unsullied. Major Anderson, the hero of Fort Sumter, was present, and showed himself at the various stands, at each of which he was most enthusiastically received. An impressive feature of the occasion was the flag of Sumter, hoisted on the stump of the staff that had been shot away, placed in the hand of the equestrian statue of Washington."

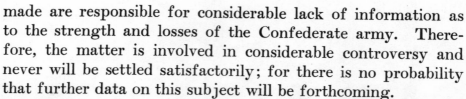

made are responsible for considerable lack of information as to the strength and losses of the Confederate army. Therefore, the matter is involved in considerable controversy and never will be settled satisfactorily; for there is no probability that further data on this subject will be forthcoming.

The immensity and extent of our great Civil War are shown by the fact that there were fought 2,261 battles and engagements, which took place in the following named States: In New York, 1; Pennsylvania, 9; Maryland, 30; District of Columbia, 1; West Virginia, 80; Virginia, 519; North Carolina, 85; South Carolina, 60; Georgia, 108; Florida, 32; Alabama, 78; Mississippi, 186; Louisiana, 118; Texas, 14; Arkansas, 167; Tennessee, 298; Kentucky, 138; Ohio, 3; Indiana, 4; Illinois, 1; Missouri, 244; Minnesota, 6; California, 6; Kansas, 7; Oregon, 4; Nevada, 2; Washington Territory, 1; Utah, 1; New Mexico, 19; Nebraska, 2; Colorado, 4; Indian Territory, 17; Dakota, 11; Arizona, 4; and Idaho, 1.

It soon became evident that the official record of the War of 1861–5 must be compiled for the purposes of Government administration, as well as in the interest of history, and this work was projected near the close of the first administration of President Lincoln. It has continued during the tenure of succeeding Presidents, under the direction of the Secretaries of War, from Edwin M. Stanton, under whom it began, to Secretary Elihu Root, under whose direction it was completed. As a successor to and complement of this Government publication, nothing could be more useful or interesting than the present publication. The text does not aim at a statistical record, but is an impartial narrative supplementing the pictures. Nothing gives so clear a conception of a person or an event as a picture. The more intelligent people of the country, North and South, desire the truth put on record, and all bitter feeling eliminated. This work, with its text and pictures, it is believed, will add greatly to that end.

RECRUITING ON BROADWAY, 1861

Looking north on Broadway from "The Park" (later City Hall Park) in war time, one sees the Stars and Stripes waving above the recruiting station, p a s t which the soldiers stroll. There is a convenient booth with liquid refreshments. To the right of the picture the rear end of a street car is visible, but passenger travel on Broadway itself is by stage. On the left is the Astor House, then one of the foremost hostelries of the city. In the lower photograph the view is from the

balcony of the Metropolitan looking north on Broadway. The twin towers on the left are those of St. Thomas's Church. The lumbering stages, with the deafening noise of their rattling windows as they drive over the cobblestones, are here in force. More hoop-skirts are retreating in the distance, and a gentleman in the tall hat of the period is on his way down town. Few of the buildings seen here remained half a century later. The time is summer, as the awnings attest.

EDWIN M. STANTON
Secretary of War.

MONTGOMERY BLAIR
Postmaster-General.

GIDEON WELLES
Secretary of the Navy.

SALMON P. CHASE
Secretary of the Treasury.

HANNIBAL HAMLIN
Vice-President.

WILLIAM H. SEWARD
Secretary of State.

CALEB B. SMITH
Secretary of the Interior.

MEMBERS OF PRESIDENT LINCOLN'S OFFICIAL FAMILY

Other members were: War, Simon Cameron (1861); Treasury, W. P. Fessenden, July 1, 1864, and Hugh McCulloch, March 4, 1865; Interior, John P. Usher, January 8, 1863; Attorney-General, James Speed, December 2, 1864; Postmaster-General, William Dennison, September 24, 1864.

EDWARD BATES
Attorney-General.

JAMES A. SEDDON
Secretary of War.

CHRISTOPHER G. MEMMINGER
Secretary of the Treasury.

STEPHEN R. MALLORY
Secretary of the Navy.

JOHN H. REAGAN
Postmaster-General.

ALEXANDER H. STEPHENS
Vice-President.

JUDAH P. BENJAMIN
Secretary of State.

MEN WHO HELPED PRESI-
DENT DAVIS GUIDE THE
SHIP OF STATE

The members of the Cabinet were
chosen not from intimate friends of
the President, but from the men preferred by the States they represented.
There was no Secretary of the Interior in the Confederate Cabinet.

GEORGE DAVIS
Attorney-General.

VICE–PRESIDENT STEPHENS
AND MEMBERS OF THE
CONFEDERATE CABINET

Judah P. Benjamin, Secretary of
State, has been called the brain of
the Confederacy. President Davis
wished to appoint the Honorable
Robert Barnwell, Secretary of State,
but Mr. Barnwell declined the honor.

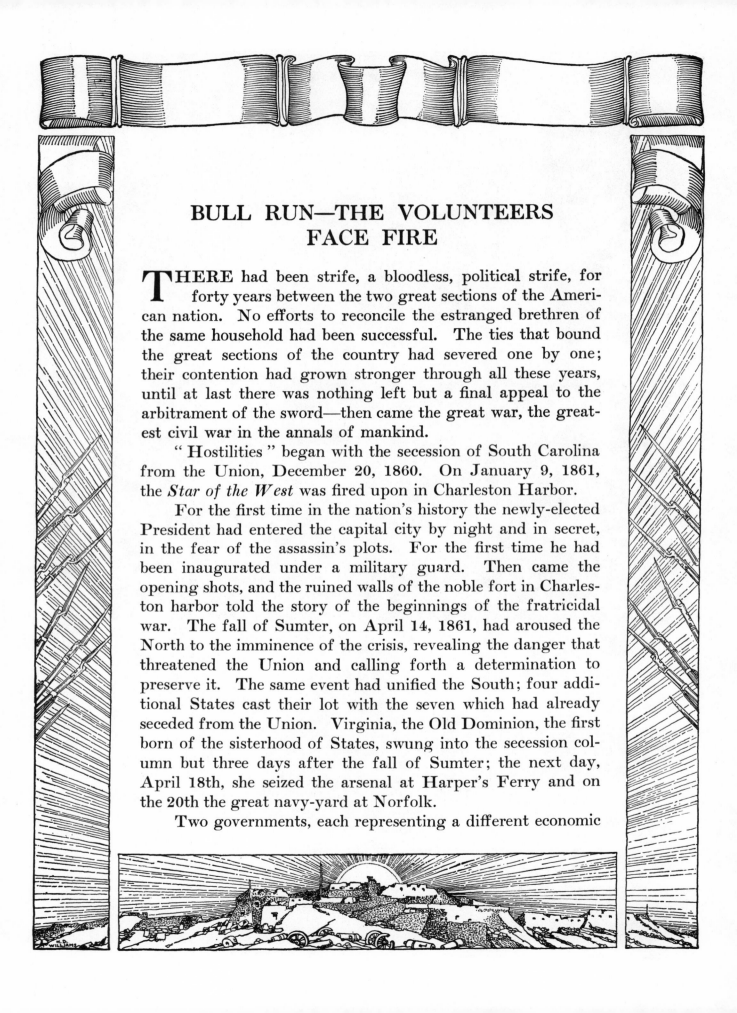

BULL RUN—THE VOLUNTEERS
FACE FIRE

THERE had been strife, a bloodless, political strife, for forty years between the two great sections of the American nation. No efforts to reconcile the estranged brethren of the same household had been successful. The ties that bound the great sections of the country had severed one by one; their contention had grown stronger through all these years, until at last there was nothing left but a final appeal to the arbitrament of the sword—then came the great war, the greatest civil war in the annals of mankind.

"Hostilities" began with the secession of South Carolina from the Union, December 20, 1860. On January 9, 1861, the *Star of the West* was fired upon in Charleston Harbor.

For the first time in the nation's history the newly-elected President had entered the capital city by night and in secret, in the fear of the assassin's plots. For the first time he had been inaugurated under a military guard. Then came the opening shots, and the ruined walls of the noble fort in Charleston harbor told the story of the beginnings of the fratricidal war. The fall of Sumter, on April 14, 1861, had aroused the North to the imminence of the crisis, revealing the danger that threatened the Union and calling forth a determination to preserve it. The same event had unified the South; four additional States cast their lot with the seven which had already seceded from the Union. Virginia, the Old Dominion, the first born of the sisterhood of States, swung into the secession column but three days after the fall of Sumter; the next day, April 18th, she seized the arsenal at Harper's Ferry and on the 20th the great navy-yard at Norfolk.

Two governments, each representing a different economic

THE DEFENDER OF WASHINGTON—GENERAL IRVIN McDOWELL AND HIS STAFF.

The man who planned the battle of Bull Run for the Northern Army was Brigadier-General Irvin McDowell, then in command of the forces before Washington. When assured that Patterson would hold Johnston in the Shenandoah, he undertook to advance with his raw and unorganized troops on Beauregard at Manassas. The plan for the battle which he adopted on the night of July 18th was. according to General Sherman, one of the best formed during the entire war. But it failed because, even before he began his attack, Johnston with a good part of his troops had already joined Beauregard at Manassas. After the defeat McDowell was placed in charge of the defenses of Washington on the Virginia side of the Potomac. This picture was taken the next year at General Robert E. Lee's former home in Arlington.

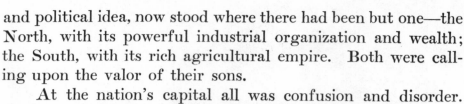

and political idea, now stood where there had been but one—the North, with its powerful industrial organization and wealth; the South, with its rich agricultural empire. Both were calling upon the valor of their sons.

At the nation's capital all was confusion and disorder. The tramp of infantry and the galloping of horsemen through the streets could be heard day and night. Throughout the country anxiety and uncertainty reigned on all sides. Would the South return to its allegiance, would the Union be divided, or would there be war? The religious world called unto the heavens in earnest prayer for peace; but the rushing torrent of events swept on toward war, to dreadful internecine war.

The first call of the President for troops, for seventy-five thousand men, was answered with surprising alacrity. Citizens left their farms, their workshops, their counting rooms, and hurried to the nation's capital to take up arms in defense of the Union. A similar call by the Southern President was answered with equal eagerness. Each side believed itself in the right. Both were profoundly sincere and deeply in earnest. Both have won the respect of history.

After the fall of Fort Sumter, the two sides spent the spring months marshaling their forces for the fierce conflict that was to follow. President Lincoln had called for three-months' volunteers; at the beginning of July some thirty thousand of these men were encamped along the Potomac about the heights of Arlington. As the weeks passed, the great Northern public grew impatient at the inaction and demanded that Sumter be avenged, that a blow be struck for the Union.

The " call to arms " rang through the nation and aroused the people. No less earnest was the feeling of the South, and soon two formidable armies were arrayed against each other, only a hundred miles apart—at Washington and at Richmond.

The commander of the United States Army was Lieut.-General Winfield Scott, whose military career had begun before most of the men of '61 had been born. Aged and infirm,

G. T. Beauregard

THE SOUTHERNER OF THE HOUR IN '61.

Born in New Orleans on May 28, 1818, the Southern leader upon whom **at** first all eyes were turned, Pierre Gustave Toutant Beauregard, was graduated from the U. S. Military Academy in 1838. Gallant and dashing, he won the brevets of Captain and Major in the war with Mexico and was wounded at Chapultepec. Early in '61 he resigned from the army, and joined the Confederacy, being in command of the Confederate forces in the firing on Fort Sumter in April. Owing to his forceful personality, he became a popular and noted leader in the Confederacy. After the Union defeat at Manassas, he was looked upon as the coming Napoleon. He was confirmed as Major-General in the Confederate army on July 30, 1861, but he had held the provisional rank of Brigadier-General since February 20th, before a shot was fired. After his promotion to Major-General, he commanded the Army of the Mississippi under General A. S. Johnston, whom he succeeded at Shiloh. He defended Charleston, S. C., in 1862–3 and afterward commanded the Department of North Carolina and Southeastern Virginia. He died at New Orleans in 1893.

he remained in Washington. The immediate command of the army was entrusted to Brigadier-General Irvin McDowell.

Another Union army, twenty thousand strong, lay at Martinsburg, Virginia, under the command of Major-General Patterson, who, like General Scott, was a veteran of the War of 1812 and of the Mexican War.

Opposite McDowell, at Manassas Junction, about thirty miles from Washington, lay a Confederate army under Brigadier-General Beauregard who, three months before, had won the homage of the South by reducing Fort Sumter. Opposed to Patterson in the Shenandoah valley was Joseph E. Johnston with a force of nine thousand men. The plans of the President and General Scott were to send McDowell against Beauregard, while Patterson was to detain Johnston in the Valley and prevent him from joining Beauregard. It was confidently believed that, if the two Confederate forces could be kept apart, the " Grand Army " could win a signal victory over the force at Manassas; and on July 16th, with waving banners and lively hopes of victory, amid the cheers of the multitude, it moved out from the banks of the Potomac toward the interior of Virginia. It was a motley crowd, dressed in the varied uniforms of the different State militias. The best disciplined troops were those of the regular army, represented by infantry, cavalry, and artillery. Even the navy was drawn upon and a battalion of marines was included in the Union forces. In addition to the regulars were volunteers from all the New England States, from New York and Pennsylvania and from Ohio, Michigan, and Minnesota, organizations which, in answer to the President's call for troops, had volunteered for three months' service. Many were boys in their teens with the fresh glow of youth on their cheeks, wholly ignorant of the exhilaration, the fear, the horrors of the battle-field. Onward through the Virginia plains and uplands they marched to the strains of martial music. Unused to the rigid discipline of war, many of the men would drop out of line to gather

ONE OF THE FIRST UNION VOLUNTEER REGIMENTS.

The First Minnesota, a regiment that fought in the flanking column at Bull Run. On April 14, 1861, the day after Sumter's surrender, the Federal Government received an offer of a volunteer regiment from Minnesota, and on April 29, the First Minnesota was mustered into service by Lieutenant W. W. Sanders, U. S. A. Under Colonel William O. Gorman the regiment proceeded to Washington in June and, attached to Franklin's Brigade, Heintzelman's Division of McDowell's Army, at Bull Run gave an excellent account of itself, finally retiring from the field in good order. A record for conspicuous bravery was sustained by the First Minnesota throughout the war, notably its famous charge on the field of Gettysburg, July 2, 1863.

The photograph was taken just before the regiment left Fort Snelling in 1861. In the front line the first from the left is Lieut. Colonel Stephen Miller, the next is Colonel Gorman. On his left hand is Major Dyke and next to him is Adjutant W. B. Leach. Between the last two and behind them is Captain William Colvill, while at the left hand of Adjutant Leach is Captain Mark Downie. At the extreme right of the picture stands General J. B. Sanborn with Lieutenant Sanders (mustering officer) on his right hand, and on Sanders' right is the Honorable Morton S. Wilkinson. Colvill, as Colonel, led the regiment in its Gettysburg charge.

berries or tempting fruits along the roadside, or to, refill their canteens at every fresh stream of water, and frequent halts were necessary to allow the stragglers to regain their lines.

After a two days' march, with "On to Richmond" as their battle-cry, the army halted at the quiet hamlet of Centreville, twenty-seven miles from Washington and seven miles from Manassas Junction where lay the waiting Confederate army of similar composition—untrained men and boys. Men from Virginia, from North and South Carolina, from the mountains of Tennessee, from Alabama, Mississippi, and Georgia, even from distant Arkansas, had gathered on the soil of the Old Dominion State to do battle for the Southern cause. Between the two armies flowed the stream of Bull Run, destined to give its name to the first great battle of the impending conflict. The opposing commanders, McDowell and Beauregard, had been long-time friends; twenty-three years before, they had been graduated in the same class at West Point.

Beauregard knew of the coming of the Federal army. The news had been conveyed to him by a young man, a former government clerk at Washington, whose sympathies, however, lay with the cause of the South. He won the confidence of Beauregard. The latter sent him to the capital city bearing a paper with two words in cipher, "Trust Bearer." With this he was to call at a certain house, present it to the lady within, and wait a reply. Traveling all night, he crossed the Potomac below Alexandria, and reached the city at dawn, when the newsboys were calling out in the empty streets the latest intelligence of the army. The messenger rang the doorbell at a house within a stone's throw of the White House and delivered the scrap of paper to the only one in the city to whom it was intelligible. She hurriedly gave the youth his breakfast, wrote in cipher the words, "Order issued for McDowell to march upon Manassas to-night," and giving him the scrap of paper, sent him on his way. That night the momentous bit of news was in the hands of General Beauregard. He instantly wired

MRS. GREENHOW, THE CONFEDERATE SPY, WITH HER DAUGHTER, IN THE OLD CAPITOL PRISON

Mrs. Rose O'Neal Greenhow, a zealous and trusted friend of the Confederacy, lived in Washington at the opening of the war. It was she who, on July 16, 1861, sent the famous cipher message to Beauregard, "Order issued for McDowell to move on Manassas to-night." Acting on this, Beauregard promptly arranged his army for the expected attack, while Johnston and "Stonewall" Jackson hastened from the Valley to aid in repelling the Federal advance. Mrs. Greenhow's secret-service work was cut short on August 26th, when Allan Pinkerton, the Federal detective, arrested her and put her under military guard at her home, 398 Sixteenth Street. Afterward she was transferred to the Old Capitol Prison. She remained there until April, 1862. On June 2d, after pledging her word not to come north of the Potomac until the war was over, Mrs. Greenhow was escorted beyond the lines of the Union army and set at liberty. It was later discovered that she had, even while in prison, corresponded extensively with Colonel Thomas Jordan, of General Beauregard's staff.

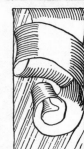

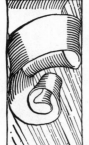

President Davis at Richmond and asked that he be reenforced by Johnston's army.

As we have seen, General Scott had arranged that Patterson detain Johnston in the Valley. He had even advised McDowell that "if Johnston joins Beauregard he shall have Patterson on his heels." But the aged Patterson was unequal to the task before him. Believing false reports, he was convinced that Johnston had an army of thirty-five thousand men, and instead of marching upon Johnston at Winchester he led his army to Charlestown, twenty miles in the opposite direction. Johnston thereupon was free to join Beauregard at Manassas, and he promptly proceeded to do so.

McDowell's eager troops had rested at Centreville for two days. The time for them to test their mettle in a general engagement was at hand. Sunday, July 21st, was selected as the day on which to offer battle. At half-past two in the morning the sleeping men were roused for the coming conflict. Their dream of an easy victory had already received a rude shock, for on the day after their arrival a skirmish between two minor divisions of the opposing armies had resulted in the retreat of the Union forces after nineteen of their number lay dead upon the plain. The Confederates, too, had suffered and fifteen of their army were killed. But patriotic enthusiasm was too ardent to be quenched by such an incident, and eagerly, in the early dawn of the sultry July morning, they marched toward the banks of the stream on which they were to offer their lives in the cause of their country.

The army moved out in three divisions commanded by Generals Daniel Tyler, David Hunter, and S. P. Heintzelman. Among the subordinate officers was Ambrose E. Burnside, who, a year and five months later, was to figure in a far greater and far more disastrous battle, not many miles from this same spot; and William T. Sherman, who was to achieve a greater renown in the coming war.

On the Southern side we find equally striking characters.

TROOPS THAT FOUGHT AT BULL RUN—A THREE MONTHS' COMPANY.

When Lincoln issued his call for volunteers on the evacuation of Sumter, Rhode Island was one of the first to respond. We here see Company "D" of the First Regiment (organized April, 1861), as it looked during its encampment at Camp Sprague, Washington, from April 24th to July 16th, 1861. The care-free faces of the men lack all the gravity of veterans. In the famous first battle of the war, the regiment was in Burnside's Brigade of Hunter's Division, which marched some miles to the north, crossed Bull Run at Sudley Ford, met the Confederates north of Young's Branch, and drove them south across the stream to the Henry house plateau. Later it yielded to the panic which seized upon the Union army. On August 2, 1861, Company "D" closed its brief career in the conflict that was to fill four years with continuous combat.

General Joseph E. Johnston was not held by Patterson in the Valley and with a portion of his army had reached Manassas on the afternoon of the 20th. In the Indian wars of Jackson's time Johnston had served his country; like McDowell and Beauregard, he had battled at the gates of Mexico; and like the latter he chose to cast his lot with the fortunes of the South. There, too, was Longstreet, who after the war was over, was to spend many years in the service of the country he was now seeking to divide. Most striking of all was "Stonewall" Jackson, whose brilliant military career was to astonish the world.

The Union plan for this fateful July day was that Tyler should lead his division westward by way of the Warrenton turnpike to a stone bridge that crossed Bull Run, about four miles from Centreville. At the same time the main army under Hunter and Heintzelman was to make a detour of several miles northward through a dense forest to a ford of Bull Run, known as Sudley's Ford. Here they were to cross the stream, march down its right bank and, while Tyler guarded the Stone Bridge, engage the foe on the west side of Bull Run. The plan of the battle was admirably drawn, but the march around to Sudley's Ford was slower than had been expected, and it was ten o'clock before the main army reached the point west of the Stone Bridge. While the Federals were making their plans to attack the Confederate left wing, Generals Beauregard and Johnston were planning an aggressive movement against the left wing of the Federal army. They were to cross Bull Run by fords several miles below the Stone Bridge and attack the Northern troops on the weaker wing of the Union force in an effort to rout them before relief could be sent from the Federal right. The Confederate attack was planned to take place a few hours later than McDowell had decided to move. The Southern troops were preparing to cross the stream when the boom of cannon at the Stone Bridge told that the Federals had taken the aggressive and that the

THE FOURTH NEW JERSEY ON THE BANKS OF THE POTOMAC, 1861

THE RAW MATERIAL

The faces of these untried soldiers from New Jersey and Vermont show the enthusiasm with which men flocked from every state to form an army for the Union.   Nor was that enthusiasm chilled by the long tedious unfamiliar beating into shape that McClellan was giving them in '61.   War's tedious rudiments had to be learned, but when the time came for fighting, fighting qualities were not lacking and our citizen soldiers gave an account of themselves that startled the world.   The Green Mountain Boys that first came to Washington were among the troops that made the first warlike move from the city to extend the Federal lines into Virginia.   It was on these advanced defences of the Capital that a Green Mountain Boy was found one night asleep on post.   His life was forfeit, but the great heart of Father Abraham interposed.   Lincoln knew the stuff of which these country lads were made, and this one a few months later on the battlefield nobly laid down the life he owed to his Commander-in-Chief.   Vermont was lavish of her sons and sent 35,262, nearly 60 per cent. of her male population between the ages of 18 and 45, to the nation's aid.   The State of New Jersey sent 76,814 men, 61.2 per cent. of her military population.   The first raw New Jersey soldiers in Washington were among the troops that occupied Arlington Heights, one of the advance positions in the defences.   About one-eighth of New Jersey's troops laid down their lives for their country, while nearly one-fourth of the Vermonters that went to the War never returned.

THE SIXTH VERMONT AT CAMP GRIFFIN, VIRGINIA

weak Confederate left was in danger of being overwhelmed by the superior numbers of the Union right wing. Orders countermanding the command to attack were quickly sent to the Southerners at the lower fords, and preparations were hurriedly made to repulse the attack of the Northern force.

Tyler reached the Stone Bridge before six in the morning and opened fire on a Confederate force under Colonel Evans on the other side of the run. For some time this was kept up, and Evans was much puzzled that the Federals did not attempt to cross the bridge; they merely kept up a desultory fire. The failure of the Union troops to advance led Evans to believe that Tyler's attack was only a feint and that the real attacking force would approach from some other direction. This belief was confirmed when he descried a lengthening line of dust above the tree-tops far in the distance, north of the Warrenton turnpike. Evans was now convinced (and he was right) that the main Union army was marching to Sudley's Ford, three miles above the Stone Bridge, and would reach the field from that direction. Quickly then he turned about with six companies of brave South Carolinians and a battalion of "Louisiana Tigers" and posted them on a plateau overlooking the valley of Young's Branch, a small tributary of Bull Run. Here, not far from the Matthews and Carter houses, he awaited the coming of the Federals.

His force was stationed overlooking the Sudley and Newmarket road and an open field through which the Federal troops would be forced to pass to reach the higher ground held by the Confederates. Two 6-pound howitzers were placed to sweep the field of approach, one at each end of Evans' line of defense.

With guns loaded, and howitzers ready to pour their charges into an advancing force, the Southerners stood and watched the line of dust that arose above the trees. It moved slowly to the westward. Then, where the Sudley road turns to the southward to cross the Sudley Ford, it followed the

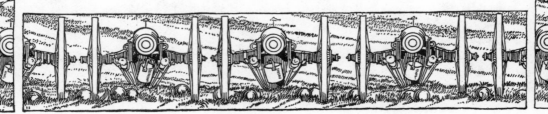

EVE OF THE CONFLICT.

Stone Church, Centreville, Virginia.—Past this little stone church on the night of July 20, 1861, and long into the morning of the twenty-first marched lines of hurrying troops. Their blue uniforms were new, their muskets bright and polished, and though some faces were pale their spirits were elated, for after their short training they were going to take part, for the first time, in the great game of war. It was the first move of the citizen soldier of the North toward actual conflict. Not one knew exactly what lay before him. The men were mostly from New England and the Middle States. They had left desk and shop and farm and forge, and with the thought in their minds that the war would last for three months the majority had been mustered in. Only the very wise and farseeing had prophe-sied the immensity of the struggle, and these were regarded as extremists. Their ideas were laughed at. So on they went in long lines down the road in the darkness of the night, chattering, laughing and talking carelessly, hardly realizing in the contagion of their patri-otic ardor the grim meaning of real war. The battle had been well planned, but who had had the experience, even among the leaders, to be sure of the details and the absolute carrying out of orders? With the exception of the veterans of the Mexican War, who were regulars, there was not one who had ever maneuvered a thousand men in the field. A lesson lay before them and it was soon to come. The surprising battle that opened early in the morning, and whose results spread such consternation through the North, was really the result of popular clamor. The press and the politicians demanded action, and throughout the South the same confident and reck-less spirit prevailed, the same urging to see something done.

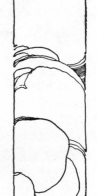

trend of the highway. It reached the crossing of Bull Run, and the line of dust faded as the Federals spread into battle-line behind the expanse of woodland that hid each column from the other's view.

It was nearing ten o'clock. The rays of the summer sun were beating in sweltering heat upon the waiting troops. Those who could find shelter beneath the trees moved from their places into the shade. Heavy banks of storm clouds were gathering on the horizon, giving promise of relief from oppressive warmth. A silence settled over the ranks of the Confederates as they watched the edge of the woodland for the first appearance of the approaching troops.

Suddenly there was a glimmer of the sunlight reflected from burnished steel among the trees. Then, in open battle array, the Federal advance guard, under the command of Colonel Burnside, emerged from the wood on a neighboring hill, and for the first time in the nation's history two hostile American armies faced each other in battle array. At Fort Sumter only the stone walls had suffered; not a drop of human blood was shed. But here was to be a gigantic conflict, and thousands of people believed that here on this field on this day would be decided the fate of the Union and the fate of the Confederacy. The whole country awaited in breathless expectancy the news of this initial conflict, to become known as the battle of Bull Run.

With little delay the battle opened. The Federals had a clear advantage in numbers as their outlying forces came up; but they met with a brave resistance. General Bee, of South Carolina, with two brigades, crossed a valley to the south of Evans in the face of a heavy artillery fire to a point within one hundred yards of the Federal lines. At this short range thousands of shots were fired and many brave men and boys were stretched upon the green. The outcome at this point was uncertain until the Union forces were joined by Heintzelman with heavy reenforcements and by Sherman with a portion of

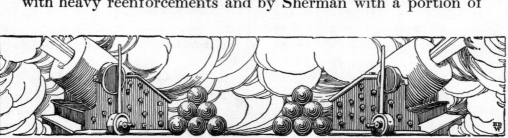

HERE "STONEWALL" JACKSON WON HIS NAME.

Robinson House, Bull Run.—"Stonewall" Jackson won his name near this house early in the afternoon of July 21st. Meeting General Bee's troops retreating in increasing disorder, he advanced with a battery to the ridge behind the Robinson House and held the position until Bee's troops had rallied in his rear. "Look at Jackson standing there like a stone wall," was the sentence that gave birth to his historic nickname. It was General Bee who uttered these words, just before he fell, adding, "Rally on the Virginians."

WHERE THE CONFEDERATES WAVERED.

Center of Battle of Morning—July 21, 1861.—North of this house, about a mile, the Confederate Colonel Evans met the columns of Burnside and Porter in their advance south from Sudley Ford. Though reinforced by General Bee, he was driven back at noon to this house in the valley near Young's Branch. Here a vigorous Union charge swept the whole battle to the hill south of the stream. General Bee sent for reinforcements, saying that unless he could be supported "all was lost."

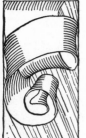

Tyler's division. Bee could now do nothing but withdraw, and in doing so his men fell into great disorder. Cheer after cheer arose from the ranks of the Union army.

Meanwhile, Generals Beauregard and Johnston had remained at the right of their line, near Manassas, nearly four miles from the scene of action, still determined to press their attack on the Federal left if the opportunity was offered. As the morning passed and the sounds of conflict became louder and extended further to the westward, it became evident to the Confederate leaders that the Federals were massing all their strength in an effort to crush the left of the Southern army. Plans for an aggressive movement were then abandoned, the commanders withdrawing all their reserve forces from the positions where they had been held to follow up the Confederate attack, and sending them to the support of the small force that was holding back the Federals. After dispatching troops to threaten the Union left, Johnston and Beauregard galloped at full speed to the scene of the battle. They arrived about noon—at the moment when Bee's brigade was fleeing across the valley from the hail of Federal bullets. As the frightened men were running in the utmost disorder, General Bee, seeing Thomas J. Jackson's brigade calmly waiting the onset, exclaimed to his men, "Look at Jackson; there he stands like a stone wall!" The expression spread to the army and to the world, and that invincible soldier has since been known as "Stonewall" Jackson.

Beauregard and Johnston found it a herculean task to rally the fleeing men and re-form the lines, but they succeeded at length; the battle was renewed, and from noon till nearly three o'clock it raged with greater fury than before. The fight was chiefly for the possession of the plateau called the Henry hill. Up and down the slopes the two armies surged in the broiling sun. Beauregard, like McDowell on the other side, led his men in the thickest of the fight. A bursting shell killed his horse under him and tore the heel from his boot; he mounted

AFTER BULL RUN—GUARDING THE PRISONERS.

Inside Castle Pinckney, Charleston Harbor, August, 1861.—In these hitherto unpublished Confederate photographs we see one of the earliest volunteer military organizations of South Carolina and some of the first Federal prisoners taken in the war. The Charleston Zouave Cadets were organized in the summer of 1860, and were recruited from among the patriotic young men of Charleston. We see in the picture how very young they were. The company first went into active service on Morris Island, January 1, 1861, and was there on the 9th when the guns of the battery turned back the *Star of the West* arriving with reinforcements for Sumter. The company was also stationed on Sullivan's Island during the bombardment of Sumter, April 12–13, 1861. After the first fateful clash at Bull Run, July 21, 1861, had taught the North that the war was on in earnest, a number of Federal prisoners were brought to Charleston and placed for safe-keeping in Castle Pinckney, then garrisoned by the Charleston Zouave Cadets. To break the monotony of guard duty Captain Chichester, some time in August, engaged a photographer to take some pictures about the fort showing his men. Gray uniforms with red stripes, red fatigue caps, and white cross belts were a novelty. The casemates of the fort had been fitted up with bunks and doors as sleeping quarters

THE PRISONERS—11TH NEW YORK ZOUAVES.

for the prisoners. Casemate No. 1 was occupied by prisoners from the 11th New York Zouaves, who had been recruited almost entirely from the New York Fire Department. The smaller picture is a nearer view of their quarters, over which they have placed the sign "Hotel de Zouave." We see them still wearing the uniform of the battlefield: wide dark-blue trousers with socks covering the bottoms, red flannel shirts with the silver badge of the New York Fire Department, blue jackets elaborately trimmed with braid, red fez caps with blue tassels, and a blue sash around the waist. Their regiment, the famous "Ellsworth's Zouaves," was posted at Bull Run as a support for Pickett's and Griffin's Batteries during the fierce fighting of the afternoon on the Henry House hill. They gave way before the charge of the Confederates, leaving 48 dead and 75 wounded on the field. About 65 of them were taken prisoners, some of whom we see here a month after the battle. The following October the prisoners were exchanged. At the beginning of the war the possession of prisoners did not mean as much to the South as it did later in the struggle, when exchanges became almost the last resource for recruiting the dwindling ranks. Almost every Southerner capable of bearing arms had already joined the colors.

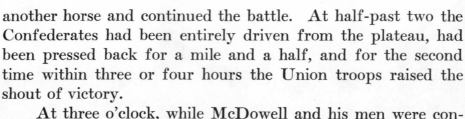

another horse and continued the battle. At half-past two the Confederates had been entirely driven from the plateau, had been pressed back for a mile and a half, and for the second time within three or four hours the Union troops raised the shout of victory.

At three o'clock, while McDowell and his men were congratulating themselves on having won the battle, a faint cheering was heard from a Confederate army far across the hills. It grew louder and nearer, and presently the gray lines were seen marching gallantly back toward the scene of the battle from which they had been driven. The thrilling cry then passed through the Union ranks, "Johnston has come, Johnston has come!" and there was terror in the cry. They did not know that Johnston, with two-thirds of his army, had arrived the day before; but it was true that the remaining third, twenty-three hundred fresh troops, had reached Manassas at noon by rail, and after a forced march of three hours, under the command of Kirby Smith, had just united with the army of Beauregard. It was this that caused the cheering and determined Beauregard to make another attack on the Henry plateau.

The Union men had fought valiantly in this, their first battle, untrained and unused to warfare as they were; they had braved the hail of lead and of bursting shells; they had witnessed their comrades, their friends, and neighbors fall at their feet to rise no more. They nevertheless rejoiced in their success. But with the long march and the five hours' fighting in the scorching July sun they were weary to exhaustion, and when they saw the Confederates again approaching, reenforced with fresh troops, their courage failed and they began to retreat down the hill. With waving colors the Confederates pressed on, opening a volley of musketry on the retreating Federals, and following it with another and another.

In vain McDowell and his officers attempted to rally his panic-stricken men and re-form his lines. Only the regulars,

THE CIVIL WAR SOLDIER AS HE REALLY LOOKED AND MARCHED

There is nothing to suggest military brilliancy about this squad. Attitudes are as prosaic as uniforms are unpicturesque. The only man standing with military correctness is the officer at the left-hand end. But this was the material out of which was developed the soldier who could average sixteen miles a day for weeks on end, and do, on occasion, his thirty miles through Virginia mud and his forty miles over a hard Pennsylvania highway. Sixteen miles a day does not seem far to a single pedestrian, but marching with a regiment bears but little relation to a solitary stroll along a sunny road. It is a far different matter to trudge along carrying a heavy burden, choked by the dust kicked up by hundreds of men tramping along in front, and sweltering in the sun—or trudge still more drearily along in a pelting rain which added pounds to a soaked and clinging uniform, and caused the soldiers to slip and stagger in the mud.

"RIGHT SHOULDER SHIFT"—COLUMN OF FOURS—THE TWENTY-SECOND NEW YORK ON THE ROAD

about sixteen hundred in number, were subject to the orders of their superiors, and they made a brave stand against the oncoming foe while they covered the retreat of the disorganized mass. On the Henry hill were the two powerful batteries of Griffin and Ricketts. They had done most valiant service while the tide of battle ebbed and flowed. But at last their hour had come. A Confederate regiment, dashing from a neighboring hill, poured in a deadly volley, cut down the cannoneers almost to a man, killed their horses, and captured the guns. A few minutes later General Beauregard rode up to the spot and noticed Captain Ricketts lying on the ground, desperately wounded. The two men had been friends in the years gone by. Beauregard, recognizing his old friend, asked him if he could be of any service. He then sent his own surgeons to care for the wounded captain and detailed one of his staff to make him comfortable when he was carried to Richmond as a prisoner of war.

There is little more to relate of the battle of Bull Run. In his report McDowell stated that after providing for the protection of the retreat from the battlefield by Porter's and Blenker's volunteer brigades, he took command in person of the force previously stationed for holding the road back to Centreville and made such disposition " as would best serve to check the enemy," at the Centreville ridge. Some hundreds of civilians, members of Congress and others, had come out from Washington to witness a victory for the Grand Army, and they saw that army scattered in wild flight to escape an imaginary pursuer. The Confederates made no serious effort to follow after them, for the routed Federals had destroyed the Stone Bridge as they passed it in their retreat, and had obstructed the other avenues of pursuit. As darkness settled over the field the Confederates returned to their camps.

McDowell made a desperate effort to check and reorganize his army at Centreville, but he was powerless. The troops refused to listen to any commands; they rushed on and

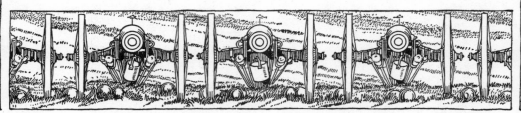

DRILLING THE 96TH PENNSYLVANIA AT CAMP NORTHUMBERLAND, NEAR WASHINGTON—1861

Along this sloping hillside, well suited for a camp, we see a Federal regiment at its full strength, before bullets and sickness had lowered its numbers to a mere skeleton of its former self. The band is out in front, the men are standing at "shoulder arms;" the Colonel and his Major and Adjutant, mounted on their sleek, well-fed horses, are grouped at one side, conscious that the eye of the camera is upon them. There is an old adage among military men that "a straight shot takes the best." When a freshly joined regiment, recruited to its full strength, reached the army corps to which it had been assigned and which had been for a long time actively engaged, it caused comment that well may be understood. "Hello, here comes a new brigade!" cried a veteran of the Potomac who had seen eight months' continuous service, calling the attention of a companion to a new regiment just marching into camp. "Brigade!" exclaimed the other, "I'll bet my hat it's a division!" There are instances in plenty where a company commander found himself at the head of less than a score of men; where regiments that had started a 1,000 strong could muster but some 200 odd, and where, in a single action, the loss in killed, wounded and missing was over sixty per cent. of those engaged. We begin to understand what war is when we stop to think of this.

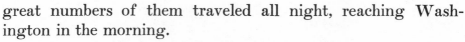
great numbers of them traveled all night, reaching Washington in the morning.

These raw troops had now received their first baptism of blood and fire. Nearly five hundred of their number were left dead on the field of battle, and fourteen hundred were wounded. The captured and missing brought the Federal loss to nearly three thousand men. The Confederate loss in killed, wounded, and missing was less than two thousand. The Federal forces engaged were nearly nineteen thousand, while the Confederates had more than eighteen thousand men on the field.

The Confederate victory at Bull Run did the South great injury in that it led vast numbers to believe the war was over and that the South had won. Many soldiers went home in this belief, and for months thereafter it was not easy to recruit the Southern armies. The North, on the other hand, was taught a needed lesson—was awakened to a sense of the magnitude of the task before it.

The first great battle of the American Civil War brought joy to the Confederacy and grief to the States of the North. As the Federal troops marched into Washington through a drenching downpour of rain, on July 22d, the North was shrouded in gloom. But the defeated army had not lost its courage. The remnants of the shattered forces were gathered, and from the fragments a mightier host was to be rallied under the Stars and Stripes to meet the now victorious foe on future battle-grounds.

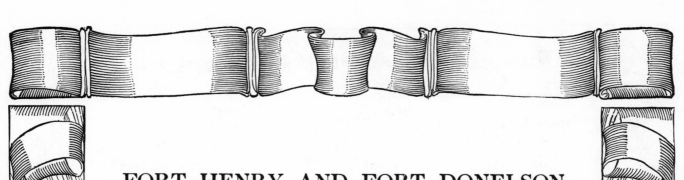

FORT HENRY AND FORT DONELSON

By this brilliant and important victory Grant's fame sprang suddenly into full and universal recognition. President Lincoln nominated him major-general of volunteers, and the Senate at once confirmed the appointment. The whole military service felt the inspiriting event.
—Nicolay and Hay, in "Life of Lincoln."

THE grasp of a great section of western Kentucky and Tennessee by the Northern armies, the capture of a stronghold that was thought impregnable, the forced surrender of a great army, and the bringing into public notice of a new commander who was destined to outshine all his fellows—these were the achievements of the short, vigorous campaign of Fort Donelson.

There were two great battle-grounds of the Civil War, nearly a thousand miles apart—Virginia and the valley of the great river that divides the continent—and the two definite objects of the Northern armies during the first half of the war period were to capture Richmond and to open the Mississippi. All other movements and engagements were subordinate to the dramas of these two great theaters, incidental and contributory. The South, on the other hand, except for the early threatening of Washington, the Gettysburg campaign, the raid of Morgan in Ohio, and the expeditions of Bragg and Hood into Kentucky and Tennessee, was on the defensive from the beginning of the war to the end.

In the East after the initial engagement at Bull Run "all was quiet along the Potomac" for some months. McClellan had loomed large as the rising hero of the war; but McClellan did not move with the celerity that was expected of him; the North became impatient and demanded that

something be done. But while the public was still waiting there were two occurrences in the West that riveted the attention of the nation, sending a thrill of gladness through the North and a wave of depression over the Southland. These were the fall of Fort Henry and of Fort Donelson.

After Missouri had been saved to the Union in spite of the disaster at Wilson's Creek in August, 1861, a Union army slowly gathered in southern Illinois. Its purpose was to dispute with the Confederates their hold on Kentucky, which had not seceded, and to regain control of the Mississippi. To secure the latter end a flank movement was decided upon—to open the mighty river by moving up the Cumberland and Tennessee—the greatest flanking movement in the history of warfare. It began at Fort Henry and ended at Vicksburg, covered a year and five months, and cost tens of thousands of human lives and millions of dollars' worth of property—but it was successful.

Eastern Kentucky, in the early days of 1862, was also in considerable ferment. Colonel James A. Garfield had driven the Confederate commander, General Humphrey Marshall, and a superior force into the Cumberland Mountains, after a series of slight encounters, terminating at Paintsville on the Big Sandy River, on January 10th. But one later event gave great encouragement to the North. It was the first substantial victory for the Union arms. General Zollicoffer held the extreme Confederate right at Cumberland Gap and he now joined General George B. Crittenden near Mill Springs in central Kentucky. General Buell, in charge of the Army of the Ohio, had placed General George H. Thomas at Lebanon, and the latter promptly moved against this threatening Confederate force. A sharp engagement took place at Logan's Cross Roads near Mill Springs on January 19th. The Confederate army was utterly routed and Zollicoffer was killed. The Union loss was about two hundred and sixty, and the Confederate over twice that number. It was not a great

CAPTAIN CLARK B. LAGOW.

DR. JAMES SIMONS.

WINNING HIS SPURS AT CAIRO.

Few will recognize in this early and unusual photograph the man who at Appomattox, wore plain fatigue dress in striking contrast with the fully uniformed Lee. Here Grant appears in his full-dress Brigadier-General's uniform as he came to Cairo to assume command of a military district including southern Illinois, September 4, 1861. Grasping at once the problems of his new post he began the work of reorganization, assisted by a well-chosen staff. Without waiting for permission from Frémont, his immediate superior, Commander of the Department of the West, Grant pushed forward a

BRIGADIER-GENERAL U. S. GRANT.

force and occupied Paducah, Kentucky, before the Confederates, approaching with the same purpose, could arrive. Grant was impatient to drive back the Confederate lines in Kentucky and Tennessee and began early to importune. Washington to be allowed to carry out maneuvers. His keen judgment convinced him that these must quickly be made in order to secure the advantage in this outlying arena of the war. Captain Rawlins was made Assistant Adjutant-General by Grant, and lifted from his shoulders much of the routine of the post. Captain Lagow and Captain Hillyer were two of the General's aides-de-camp. Dr. James Simons was Medical Director of the District.

CAPTAIN WILLIAM S. HILLYER.

CAPTAIN JOHN A. RAWLINS.

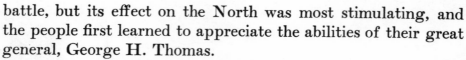

battle, but its effect on the North was most stimulating, and the people first learned to appreciate the abilities of their great general, George H. Thomas.

It was now February, 1862. General U. S. Grant was in command of the Union forces in western Kentucky and Tennessee. The opposing commander was Albert Sidney Johnston, then reputed the ablest general of the South. At Bowling Green, Kentucky, he had thirty thousand men. Believing, perhaps, that he could not hold Kentucky, he determined to save Tennessee for the South and took his stand at Nashville.

On February 2d, 1862, General Grant left Cairo with his army of seventeen thousand men and on transports moved up the Ohio and the Tennessee to attack Fort Henry. Accompanying him was Flag-Officer Foote with his fleet of seven gunboats, four of them ironclads.

Fort Henry was garrisoned by an army of about three thousand men under the command of General Lloyd Tilghman, a brave officer who was destined to give his life for the Confederate cause, the following year, near Vicksburg. It covered about three acres and mounted seventeen heavy guns. Grant's plan of attack was to land his army four miles below the fort, to move across the country and seize the road leading to Fort Donelson, while Foote should move up the river with his fleet and turn his guns on the Confederate batteries.

On February 6th, Foote formed his vessels into two lines, the ironclads—the *Cincinnati,* the *Carondelet,* the *Essex,* and the *St. Louis*—forming a front rank. Slowly and cautiously he approached the fort, firing as he went, the guns on the parapet answering those of the fleet. Several of the Confederate guns were disabled. The fleet was yet unhurt when the first hour had passed. Then a 24-pound shot struck the *Essex,* crashed through her side and penetrated her boiler, instantly killing both her pilots and flooding the vessel from stem to stern with scalding steam. The *Essex,* wholly disabled, drifted

CAIRO CITIZENS WHO MAY HAVE RECALLED THIS DAY.

With his hands thrust in his pockets stands General Grant, next to General McClernand, who is directly in front of the pillar of the Cairo post-office. The future military leader had yet his great name to make, for the photograph of this gathering was taken in September, 1861, and when, later, the whole world was ringing with his praises the citizens who chanced to be in the group must have recalled that day with pride. Young Al Sloo, the postmaster's son, leans against the doorway on Grant's right, and next to him is Bob Jennings; then comes Dr. Taggart, then Thomas, the mason, and Jaques, the butcher. On the extreme right, facing the camera, is young Bill Thomas. Up in the windows sit George Olmstead and Will Smith. In his shirt sleeves, on General McClernand's left, is C. C. Davidson. In the group about him are Benjamin Munn, Fred Theobold, John Maxey, and Phil. Howard. Perhaps these men told their children of the morning that Grant left his headquarters at the St. Charles Hotel and met them here. Who knows?

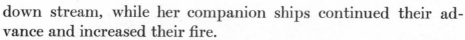

down stream, while her companion ships continued their advance and increased their fire.

Presently, a sound exceeding the roar of cannon was heard above the tumult. A great gun in the fort had exploded, killing or disabling every man who served it. A great 10-inch columbiad was also destroyed. Tilghman, seeing that he had no hope of holding the fort, decided to save his army by sending it to Fort Donelson, on the Cumberland River. This he did, reserving fewer than a hundred men to work the guns. He then raised the white flag and surrendered the seventy-eight that remained. Grant had failed to reach the road to Fort Donelson until the Confederates had escaped. The Southerners hastened across the country and added their numbers to the defenders of Donelson—and by so doing they deferred surrender for ten days.

Fort Donelson was a fortified enclosure of a hundred acres that crowned a plateau on the Cumberland River. It was just south of the boundary between Kentucky and Tennessee and close by the little village of Dover, consisting of a court-house, a two-story tavern, and a few houses scattered about. Beneath the bluff and on the river bank were two powerful batteries commanding the approach to the river. Outside the fort and stretching far along the ridges that enclosed it were rifle-pits, lines of logs covered with yellow clay. Farther beyond, the hillsides were covered with felled trees whose interlacing branches were supposed to render the approach of the foe impossible under fire.

At this moment Donelson was held by eighteen thousand men under the command of General John B. Floyd, late Secretary of War in the cabinet of Buchanan. Next to him were Gideon J. Pillow and Simon B. Buckner. The Union army under Grant was divided into three parts under the respective commands of Charles F. Smith, a veteran of the regular army; John A. McClernand, an Illinois lawyer and member of Congress, and Lew Wallace, the future author of " Ben Hur."

THE UNLUCKY *ESSEX* AFTER FORT HENRY.

The thousand-ton ironclad *Essex* received the severest punishment at Fort Henry. Fighting blood surged in the veins of Commander W. D. Porter, son of Admiral David Porter and brother of Admiral David D. Porter. The gunboat which he led into action at Fort Henry was named after the famous *Essex* which his father commanded in the War of 1812. Fifteen of the shots from Fort Henry struck and told upon the *Essex*, the last one penetrating her armor and piercing her middle boiler. Commander Porter, standing among his men directing the fight, was terribly scalded by the escaping steam,

COMMANDER W. D. PORTER.

as were twenty-seven others. Wrongly suspected of disloyalty at the outbreak of the war, Commander Porter's conduct during the struggle gave the lie to such calumny. He recovered after Fort Henry, and was made Commodore in July, 1862. Again in command of the *Essex* he attempted unsuccessfully to destroy the dread Confederate ram *Arkansas* at Vicksburg on July 22d. Porter and the *Essex* then joined Farragut's fleet. His shells helped the Union forces to repulse the Confederates at Baton Rouge, August 5th, and he witnessed the blowing up of the *Arkansas* the following day. He died May 1, 1864.

THE *ESSEX* TWO YEARS LATER.

With waving banners the divisions of Smith and McClernand marched across country on February 12th, arriving at noon and encircling the doomed fort ere nightfall. Smith was stationed on the left and McClernand on the extreme right, near the village of Dover. This left an open space in the center, to be filled by Lew Wallace, who arrived with his division the next day. On the 13th there was a continuous bombardment from morning till night, punctuated by the sharp crack of the sharpshooter's rifle.

The chief action of the day that involved the infantry was an attempt to capture a battery on a hill, near the center of the Confederate line of battle, known as Maney's Battery, commanded by Captain Maney, of Tennessee. This battery had annoyed McClernand greatly, and he delegated his third brigade to capture it. The charge was led by Colonel Morrison of Illinois, and a braver one never was made throughout the whole period of the war. The men who made it were chiefly youths from the farms and workshops of Illinois. With no apparent thought of danger they sallied forth, determined at all hazards to capture the battery on the hill, which stood out in relief against the sky. As they ran up the hill, firing as they went, their numbers were rapidly thinned by the terrific cross-fire from this battery and two others on adjoining hills. Still the survivors pushed on and their deadly fire thinned the ranks of the men at the battery. At length when they came within forty yards of the goal a long line of Confederate musketry beside the battery suddenly burst into flame and a storm of bullets cut down the brave boys of Illinois, with fearful slaughter. Even then they stood for fifteen minutes, returning volley for volley, before retreating. Reaching the foot of the hill, they rallied under the Stars and Stripes, and returned to the assault. Even a third time they charged, but the dry leaves on the ground now caught fire, the smoke stifled them, and they had to retreat. As they returned down the hill, Lew Wallace tells us, "their ears and souls were

THE GUNBOAT THAT FIRED THE FIRST SHOT AT FORT HENRY.

Here, riding at anchor, lies the flagship of Foote, which opened the attack on Fort Henry in the first movement to break the backbone of the Confederacy, and won a victory before the arrival of the army. This gunboat, the *Cincinnati*, was one of the seven flat-bottom iron-clads built by Captain Eads at Carondelet, Missouri, and Mound City, Illinois, during the latter half of 1861. When Grant finally obtained permission from General Halleck to advance the attack upon Fort Henry on the Tennessee River, near the border of Kentucky, Flag Officer Foote started up the river, February 2, 1862, convoying the transports, loaded with the advance detachment of Grant's seventeen thousand troops. Arriving before Fort Henry on

FLAG-OFFICER FOOTE.

February 6th, the intrepid naval commander at once began the bombardment with a well-aimed shot from the *Cincinnati*. The eleven heavy guns of the fort responded in chorus, and an iron rain began to fall with telling effect upon the *Cincinnati*, the *Essex*, the *Carondelet*, and the *St. Louis*, which were steaming forward half a mile in advance of the rear division of the squadron. At a range of 1,700 yards the *Cincinnati* opened the engagement. After a little over an hour of heavy firing the colors on Fort Henry were lowered and General Tilghman surrendered it to Flag-Officer Foote. When General Grant arrived an hour later, Foote turned over the fort to him and returned to Cairo with his disabled gunboats.

riven with the shrieks of their wounded comrades, upon whom the flames crept and smothered and charred where they lay."

Thus ended the 13th of February. That night the river gunboats, six in number, four of them ironclads, under the command of Andrew H. Foote, arrived. Grant had sent them down the Tennessee to the Ohio and up the Cumberland, to support his army at Fort Donelson. On the 14th, about three in the afternoon, Foote steamed with his four ironclads to a point in the river within four hundred yards of the two powerful batteries on the river bank under the fort and opened fire with his cannon while continuing to advance. The reply from the Confederate batteries was terrific and many of their shots struck home. In a short time the decks of the vessels were slippery with human blood. Foote himself was severely wounded. At length a solid shot struck the pilot house of the flagship and tore away the pilot wheel. At almost the same moment another gunboat was disabled. The two vessels, one of which had been struck fifty-nine times, could no longer be managed; they turned about with the eddies of the river and floated down with the current. The others followed.

The Confederates raised a wild shout of joy at this, their second victory since the coming of the Union army. But what will be the story of the morrow? With the reenforcements brought by Foote, Lew Wallace's division, Grant's army was now swelled to twenty-seven thousand, and in spite of the initial repulse the Federals felt confident of ultimate victory. But a dreary night was before them. The springlike weather had changed. All that fearful night of February 14th there was a fierce, pitiless wind with driving sleet and snow. Thousands of the men, weary of the burden of their overcoats and blankets during the warm preceding days, had thrown them away. Now they spent the night lying behind logs or in ditches or wherever they could find a little protection from the wintry blasts. General Floyd, knowing that Grant's army was much

A GALLANT GUNBOAT—THE *ST. LOUIS.*

With the shots from the Confederate batteries ringing and bounding off her iron plates, this gallant gunboat that Foote had chosen for his flagship, entered the zone of fire at Fort Donelson. In the confined space of her smoke-filled gun-deck, the river sailors were loading and firing the heavy broadsides as fast as the great guns could be run out and aimed at the frowning line of entrenchments on the river bank. From them the concentrated hail of iron was poured upon her and the marksmanship was good. Fifty-nine times was this brave vessel struck. But her armored sides withstood the heavy shocks although the plating, dented and bent, bore record of each impact. Nearer and nearer grew the forts as up the narrow channel the flag-ship led the way, the *Louisville*, the *Carondelet*, and the *Pittsburgh* belching their fire at the wooded heights, as though endeavoring to attract the attention of the Confederate gunners to themselves and save the flag-ship from receiving more than her share. Up in the pilot-house the brave man who knew the channel stood at the wheel, his eyes firmly fixed ahead; and on the "texas," as the upper deck was called, within speaking distance of him, stood Foote himself. A great shot, aimed accurately as a minie ball, struck the frail pilot-house. It was as if the vessel's heart was pierced. The wheel was swept away from the pilot's hand and the brave river guide was hurled into the corner, mangled, bleeding and soon to die. Flag Officer Foote did not escape. He fell badly wounded in the leg

THE FLAG-SHIP *ST. LOUIS* VIEWED
FROM ASTERN.

LOUISVILLE—A FIGHTER AT
THE FORT.

by a fragment of the shell—a wound from which he never fully recovered. Helpless now, the current swept the *St. Louis'* bow around, and past her consorts that were still fighting, she drifted down the stream and out of action; later, in convoy of the *Louisville*, she returned to Cairo, leaving the *Carondelet* and *Pittsburgh* to escort the transports. Meanwhile on shore, Grant was earning his first laurels as a soldier in a big battle. The disabling of the gunboats caused the Confederates to make the fatal attack that resulted so disastrously for them. Assailing Grant's right wing that held a strong position, on the 15th of February, 19,000 men were hurled against a force 8,000 greater in number. But the repulse was complete. Shattered they retreated to their works, and in the morning of the 16th, the Confederate general, Buckner, surrendered. About 14,000 prisoners were taken. The Federal loss was nearly 3,000, and that of the Southern cause about 1,000 less. For the capture of Fort Donelson Grant was made major-general. The first step to the conquest of the Mississippi had been achieved. In October, 1862, the river fleet was transferred from the Army to the Navy Department, and as there was another vessel in the service, bearing the same name the *St. Louis* was renamed the *Baron de Kalb.* At Fort Henry, she went into action lashed to the *Carondelet* on account of the narrowness of the stream; and later again, the gallant gunboat won laurels at Island No. 10, Fort Pillow, Memphis, and Vicksburg.

stronger than his own, decided, after consulting with Pillow and Buckner, to attack the Union right at dawn on the 15th.

The night was spent in preparing for this, and in the morning Pillow with ten thousand men fell upon McClernand, and Buckner soon joined him with an additional force. Toward noon many of McClernand's men ran short of powder and he was forced to recede from his position. Pillow seems then to have lost his head. He felt that the whole Union army was defeated, and though the road to Nashville was open, the Confederates made no attempt to escape. Just then General Grant rode upon the scene. He had been absent all morning down the river consulting Foote, not knowing that the Confederates had planned an escape. This moment, says Lew Wallace, was the crisis in the life of Grant.

Hearing the disastrous news, his face flushed for a moment; he crushed some papers in his hand. Next instant he was calm, and said in his ordinary tone, to McClernand and Wallace, "Gentlemen, the position on the right must be retaken." Then he galloped away to General Smith. In a short time the Union lines were in motion. General Smith made a grand assault on the Confederate outworks and rifle-pits. When his lines hesitated Smith waved his cap on the point of his sword and rode in front, up the hill, in the hottest fire of the foe, toward the rifle-pits—and they were carried. At the same moment Lew Wallace was leading his division up another slope with equal gallantry. Here again the Confederates retired, and the road to Nashville was no longer open. Furthermore, Smith held a position from which he could shell the fort on the inside, and nothing was left to the inmates but surrender or slaughter on the morrow.

A council was held by Floyd, Pillow, and Buckner. Buckner, who was a master in the art of warfare, declared that he could not hold his position for half an hour in the morning. The situation was hopeless. Floyd was under indictment at Washington for maladministration in the Buchanan cabinet.

THE ADVENTUROUS GUNBOAT *CONESTOGA*.

Lying at anchor in the Ohio River this little wooden gunboat is having the finishing touches put to her equipment while her officers and men are impatiently waiting for the opportunity to bring her into action. A side-wheel river steamer originally, she was purchased at Cincinnati by Commander John Rodgers in the spring of 1861 and speedily converted into a gunboat. Her boilers and steam pipes were lowered into the hold and the oaken bulwarks five inches thick which we see were put on her and pierced for guns. She got her first taste of fighting when, at Lucas Bend, she engaged the land batteries and a Confederate gunboat, September 10, 1861. She was present at Fort Henry in the second division of the attacking fleet, and also at Fort Donelson.

THE *TYLER*

A sister-ship of the *Conestoga*. She was present both at Fort Henry and Fort Donelson.

He declared that he must not be taken, and that with his Virginia troops he would escape on two little boats that were to arrive from Nashville in the morning. He passed the command to Pillow, and Pillow, declaring that he too would escape, passed it on to Buckner. Floyd and Pillow with their men made good their escape; so did Colonel Forrest, the cavalry leader, and his mounted force.

In the early morning Buckner sent a note to Grant offering to capitulate. The answer is well known. Grant demanded "unconditional surrender," and added, " I propose to move immediately on your works." Buckner was too good a soldier to sacrifice his men in needless slaughter. His men were so worn with eighty-four hours of fighting and watching that many of them had fallen asleep while standing in battle-line and under fire. He accepted the "ungenerous and unchivalrous terms," as he pronounced them, and surrendered Fort Donelson and the army, consisting of at least fourteen thousand men, with all its stores of ammunition. The Union loss was over twenty-eight hundred men. The Confederate loss, killed and wounded, was about two thousand.

The capture of Fort Donelson did three things. First, it opened up the way for the Federal army to penetrate the heart of the western South and gave it control of Kentucky and of western Tennessee. Second, it electrified the North with confident hopes of ultimate success. It was the first great victory for the North in the war. Bull Run had been a moral victory to the South, but the vanquished were weakened scarcely more than the victors. At Donelson, the victors gained control of an extensive territory and captured a noble army which could ill be spared by the South and which could not be replaced. Third, the capture of Donelson forced before the nation a new man—Ulysses S. Grant.

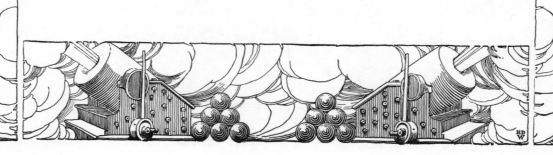

The Captured Commanders of Forts Henry and Donelson.—It requires as much moral courage to decide upon a surrender, even when odds are overwhelming, as it does physical bravery, in maintaining a useless fight to the death. Brigadier-General Tilghman, who commanded the Confederate Fort Henry on the Tennessee and General Simon Bolivar Buckner in command of the Confederate Fort Donelson—a much stronger position on the Cumberland only a few miles away—were men who possessed this kind of courage. Both had the misfortune to hold untenable positions. Each displayed generalship and sagacity and only gave up to the inevitable when holding out meant nothing but wasted slaughter and the sacrifice of men who had been called upon to exert every human effort. Fort Henry, on the banks of the Tennessee, was held by a few thousand men and strongly armed with twenty guns including one 10-inch Columbiad. But on the 6th of February it fairly lay in the possession of the Federals before a shot had actually been fired, for Grant with 17,000 men had gained the rear of the fortification after his move from Cairo on the 30th of the previous month. The actual reduction of the fort was left to the gunboat flotilla under Flag Officer Foote, whose heavy bombardment began early in the morning. • General Tilghman had seen from the first that the position could not be held. He was trapped on all sides, but he would not give way without a display of resistance. Before the firing began, he had sent off most of the garrison and maintained the unequal combat with the gunboats for an hour and a quarter with less than a hundred men, of whom he lost twenty-one. Well did this handful serve the guns on the river bank. One shot struck the gunboat *Essex*, piercing her boilers, and wounding and scalding twenty-eight men. But at last, enveloped on all sides, his retreat cut off —the troops who had been ordered to depart in the morning, some three thousand in number, had reached Fort Donelson, twelve miles away—General Tilghman hauled down his flag, surrendering himself and eighty-four men as prisoners of war. Here we see him—a brave figure of a man—clad in the uniform of a Southern Colonel. There was never the slightest doubt of his courage or of his proper discretion in making this surrender. Only for a short time was he held a prisoner, when he was exchanged and welcomed back with all honor into the ranks of the Confederacy, and given an important command. He did not, however, live long to serve his cause, for shortly after rejoining the army he was killed at the battle of Baker's Creek, Mississippi, on the 16th of May, 1863.

GENERAL FLOYD TILGHMAN.

TWO UNWILLING GUESTS OF THE NORTH.

BUCKNER, THE DEFENDER OF DONELSON.

It is not often that on the battlefield ties of friendship are cemented that last a lifetime, and especially is this so between conqueror and conquered. Fort Donelson, that was, in a measure, a repetition of Fort Henry, saw two fighting foes become thus united. It was impossible for the garrison of Fort Donelson to make its escape after the flotilla of gunboats had once appeared in the river, although General Floyd, its senior commander, the former Secretary of War under President Buchanan, had withdrawn himself from the scene tendering the command to General Pillow, who in his turn, after escaping with his own brigade, left the desperate situation to be coped with by General Buckner. Assailed in the rear by an army that outnumbered the defenders of the fort by nearly eight thousand and with the formidable gunboats hammering his entrenchments from the river, Buckner decided to cut his way out in a desperate charge, but being repulsed, saw his men flung back once more into the fort. There was nothing for it but to make terms. On February 16th, in a note to Grant he asked what might be granted him. Here, the coming leader won his nickname of "Unconditional Surrender" Grant. Buckner was informed that the Federal army was about to move upon his works. Hurt and smarting under his position, he sent back a reply that in a few short hours he would, perhaps, have been willing to recall. Yielding to circumstances he accepted what he bluntly pronounced, "ungenerous and unchivalrous terms." But when the capitulation had taken place and nearly fifteen thousand men had surrendered, a greater number than ever before laid down their arms upon the continent, Grant was so generous, that then and there began the friendship that grew as close as if the two men were brothers of the blood. Most of the prisoners were paroled. Each one was allowed to retain his personal baggage, and the officers to keep their side arms. Grant had known Buckner in the Mexican War, and received him after the battle as his guest. For a short time General Buckner was kept a prisoner at Fort Warren until he was exchanged. But the friendship between the two leaders continued. When General Grant, after having been twice President, failed in his business career, Buckner sent him a check, trusting that it might be of use in his time of trouble. Grant, shortly before his death, wrote his old-time comrade and antagonist requesting that Buckner do him the final honors by becoming one of his pallbearers.

SHILOH—THE FIRST GRAND BATTLE

No Confederate who fought at Shiloh has ever said that he found any point on that bloody field easy to assail.—Colonel William Preston Johnston (Son of the Confederate General, Albert Sidney Johnston, killed at Shiloh).

IN the history of America many battles had been fought, but the greatest of them were skirmishes compared with the gigantic conflicts of the Old World under Marlborough and Napoleon. On the field of Shiloh, for the first time, two great American armies were to engage in a mighty struggle that would measure up to the most important in the annals of Europe. And the pity of it was that the contestants were brethren of the same household, not hereditary and unrelenting enemies.

At Fort Donelson the western South was not slain—it was only wounded. The chief commander of that part of the country, Albert Sidney Johnston, determined to concentrate the scattered forces and to make a desperate effort to retrieve the disaster of Donelson. He had abandoned Bowling Green, had given up Nashville, and now decided to collect his troops at Corinth, Mississippi. Next in command to Johnston was General Beauregard who fought at Bull Run, and who had come from Virginia to aid Johnston. There also came Braxton Bragg, whose name had become famous through the laconic expression, "A little more grape, Captain Bragg," uttered by Zachary Taylor at Buena Vista; Leonidas Polk who, though a graduate of West Point, had entered the church and for twenty years before the war had been Episcopal bishop of Louisiana, and John C. Breckinridge, former Vice President of the United States. The legions of the South were gathered at Corinth until, by the 1st of April, 1862, they numbered forty thousand.

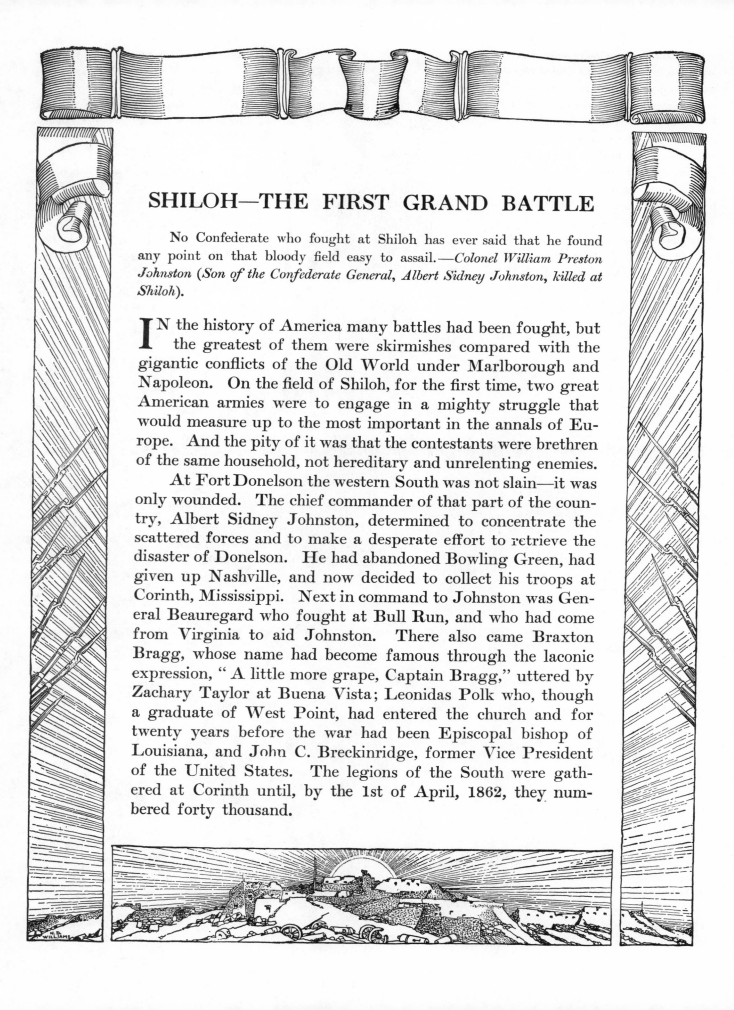

A brilliant Southern leader, whose early loss was a hard blow to the Confederacy. Albert Sidney Johnston was a born fighter with a natural genius for war. A West Pointer of the Class of '26, he had led a strenuous and adventurous life. In the early Indian wars, in the border conflicts in Texas, and in the advance into Mexico, he had always proved his worth, his bravery and his knowledge as a soldier. At the outbreak of the Civil War he had already been brevetted Brigadier-General, and had been commander of the military district of Utah. An ardent Southerner, he made his choice, dictated by heart and conscience, and the Federal authorities

GENERAL A. S. JOHNSTON, C. S. A.

knew the loss they would sustain and the gain that would be given to the cause of the Confederacy. In '61 he was assigned to a district including Kentucky and Tennessee with the rank of General. At once he displayed his gifts as an organizer, but Shiloh cut short a career that would have led him to a high place in fame and history. The early Confederate successes of the 6th of April were due to his leadership. His manner of death and his way of meeting it attested to his bravery. Struck by a minie ball, he kept in the saddle, falling exhausted and dying from the loss of blood. His death put the whole South into mourning.

CAMP OF THE NINTH MISSISSIPPI.
Southern soldiers in shirtsleeves a few months before they fought bravely at Shiloh.
General Chalmers, waving the flag of this regiment, led it in
a gallant charge on the second day.

To no one who was close to him in the stirring scenes of the early conflict in the West did Grant pay higher tribute than to this veteran of the Mexican War who was his Chief of Staff. He was a man to be relied upon in counsel and in emergency, a fact that the coming leader recognized from the very outset. An artillery officer and engineer, his military training and practical experience made him a most valuable executive. He had also the gift of leading men and inspiring confidence. Always cool and collected in the face of danger, and gifted with a personality that won friends everywhere, the reports of all of his superiors show the trust and confidence that were reposed in him. In

BRIG.-GEN. J. D. WEBSTER

April, 1861, he had taken charge of the fortifications at Cairo, Illinois. He was with Grant at Paducah, at Forts Henry and Donelson, and at Shiloh where he collected the artillery near the Landing that repelled the final Confederate attack on April 6th. He remained Chief of Staff until October, 1862. On October 14th, he was made a Brigadier-General of Volunteers, and was appointed superintendent of military railroads in the Department of Tennessee. Later he was Chief of Staff to General Sherman, and again proved his worth when he was with General Thomas at Hood's defeat before Nashville in December, 1864. On March 13, 1865, he received the brevet of Major-General of Volunteers.

Meantime, the Union army had moved southward and was concentrating at Pittsburg Landing, on the Tennessee River, an obscure stopping place for boats in southern Tennessee, and some twenty miles northeast from Corinth. The name means more now than merely a landing place for river craft. It was clear that two mighty, hostile forces were drawing together and that ere long there would be a battle of tremendous proportions, such as this Western hemisphere had not then known.

General Grant had no idea that the Confederates would meet him at Pittsburg Landing. He believed that they would wait for an attack on their entrenchments at Corinth. The position his army occupied at the Landing was a kind of quadrilateral, enclosed on three sides by the river and several small streams that flow into it. As the early days of April passed there were ominous rumors of the coming storm; but Grant was so sure that Johnston would not attack that he spent the night of the 5th of April at Savannah, some miles down the Tennessee River.

It was Saturday night. For two weeks the Union troops had occupied the undulating tableland that stretched away from the river at the Landing. There was the sound of the plashing streams overflowing from recent rains, there were revelry and mirth around the thousand camp-fires; but there was no sound to give warning of the coming of forty thousand men, who had for two days been drawing nearer with a steady tread, and during this night were deploying around the Union camp, only a mile away. There was nothing to indicate that the inevitable clash of arms was but a few hours in the future.

At the dawn of day on Sunday, April 6th, magnificent battle-lines, under the Confederate battle-flag, emerged from the woods on the neighboring hills within gunshot of the Federal camps. Whether the Union army was really surprised has been the subject of long controversy, which we need not

WAITING FOR THE SMELL OF POWDER—CONFEDERATES BEFORE SHILOH

Some very youthful Louisiana soldiers waiting for their first taste of battle, a few weeks before Shiloh. These are members of the Washington Artillery of New Orleans. We see them at Camp Louisiana proudly wearing their new boots and their uniforms as yet unfaded by the sun. Louisiana gave liberally of her sons, who distinguished themselves in the fighting throughout the West. The Fifth Company of the Washington Artillery took part in the closely contested Battle of Shiloh. The Confederates defeated Sherman's troops in the early morning, and by night were in possession of all the Federal camps save one. The Washington Artillery served their guns handsomely and helped materially in forcing the Federals back to the bank of the river. The timely arrival of Buell's army the next day at Pittsburg Landing enabled Grant to recover from the reverses suffered on that bloody "first day"—Sunday, April 6, 1862.

enter. Certainly, the attack on it was most sudden, and in consequence it fought on the defensive and at a disadvantage throughout the day.

General Hardee's corps, forming the first line of battle, moved against the outlying division of the Union army, which was commanded by General Benjamin Prentiss, of West Virginia. Before Prentiss could form his lines Hardee's shells began bursting around him, but he was soon ready and, though pressed back for half a mile in the next two or three hours, his men fought like heroes. Meanwhile the further Confederate advance under Bragg, Polk, and Breckinridge was extending all along the line in front of the Federal camps. The second Federal force to encounter the fury of the oncoming foe was the division of General W. T. Sherman, which was cut to pieces and disorganized, but only after it had inflicted frightful loss on the Confederate army.

General Grant, as we have noted, spent the night at Savannah, a town nine miles by way of the river from Pittsburg Landing. As he sat at breakfast, he heard the distant boom of cannon and he quickly realized that Johnston's army had attacked his own at the Landing. Instantly he took a boat and started for the scene of the conflict. At Crump's Landing, about half way between the two, General Lew Wallace was stationed with a division of seven thousand men. As Grant passed Crump's Landing, he met Wallace and ordered him to be ready for instant marching when he was called for. When Grant arrived at Pittsburg Landing, about eight o'clock in the morning, he found a tremendous battle raging, and he spent the day riding from one division commander to another, giving directions and cheering them on as best he could.

About two and a half miles from the Landing stood a little log church among the trees, in which for years the simple folk of the countryside had been wont to gather for worship every Sunday morning. But on this fateful Sunday, the demon of war reigned supreme. The little church was known

"ON THE SLOPES OF SHILOH FIELD"

PITTSBURG LANDING—A FEW DAYS AFTER THE BATTLE

By the name of "Pittsburg Landing," this Tennessee River point, Southerners designate the conflict of April 6 and 7, 1862. The building upon the left and one farther up the bank were the only ones standing at the time of the battle. Of the six steamers, the name of the *Tycoon*, which brought hospital supplies from the Cincinnati branch of the Sanitary Commission, is visible. Johnston's plan in the attack on the Federal forces was to pound away on their left until they were driven away from the Landing and huddled in the angle between the Tennessee River and Snake Creek. The onset of the Confederates was full of dash. Sherman was at length driven from Shiloh Church, and the command of Prentiss was surrounded and forced to surrender. It looked as if Johnston would crush the left. Just at this point he was struck down by a minie-ball from the last line of a Federal force that he had victoriously driven back. The success of the day now begins to tell on the Confederate army. Many of the lines show great gaps. But the men in gray push vigorously toward the point where these boats lie anchored. Some heavy guns are massed near this point. Reënforcements are arriving across the river, but General Beauregard, who succeeds Johnston in command, suspends the battle till the morrow. During the night 24,000 fresh troops are taken across the river by the transports here pictured. They successfully withstand the attempt of Beauregard, and with the arrival of Lew Wallace from up the river victory shifts to the Stars and Stripes.

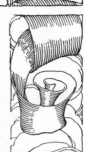

as Shiloh to all the country around, and it gave its name to the great battle that raged near it on that memorable day.

General Prentiss had borne the first onset of the morning. He had been pressed back half a mile. But about nine o'clock, after being reenforced, he made a stand on a wooded spot with a dense undergrowth, and here he held his ground for eight long hours, until five in the afternoon, when he and a large portion of his division were surrounded and compelled to surrender. Time after time the Confederates rushed upon his position, but only to be repulsed with fearful slaughter. This spot came to be known as the "Hornet's Nest." It was not far from here that the Confederates suffered the irreparable loss of the day. Their noble commander, Albert Sidney Johnston, received his death wound as he was urging his troops to force back Hurlbut's men. He was riding in the center of the fight, cheering his men, when a minie ball cut an artery of his thigh. The wound was not necessarily fatal. A surgeon could easily have saved him. But he thought only of victory and continued in the saddle, raising his voice in encouragement above the din of battle. Presently his voice became faint, a deadly pallor blanched his cheek. He was lifted from his horse, but it was too late. In a few minutes the great commander was dead, from loss of blood.

The death of Johnston, in the belief of many, changed the result at Shiloh and prevented the utter rout or capture of Grant's army. One of Johnston's subordinates wrote: "Johnston's death was a tremendous catastrophe. Sometimes the hopes of millions of people depend upon one head and one arm. The West perished with Albert Sidney Johnston and the Southern country followed." Jefferson Davis afterward declared that "the fortunes of a country hung by a single thread on the life that was yielded on the field of Shiloh."

Beauregard succeeded to the command on the fall of Johnston and the carnage continued all the day—till darkness was falling over the valleys and the hills. The final charge

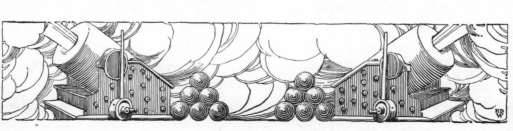

THE *LEXINGTON*

THE GUNBOATS AT SHILOH

In the river near Pittsburg Landing, where the Federal transports lay, were two small gunboats, and what they did during the battle of April 6th makes a separate chapter in the action. In the early morning they were out of sight, though within sound of the continuous firing. How the battle was going, however, was evident. The masses of the blue-clad troops appeared through the trees on the river bank, showing that under the continuous and fierce assaults they were falling back upon the Landing. The *Tyler*, commanded by Lieutenant Gwin, and afterward the *Lexington*, commanded by Lieutenant Shirk, which arrived at four o'clock, strove to keep the Confederate army from the Landing. After the surrender of Prentiss, General Withers set his division in motion to the right toward this point. Chalmers' and Jackson's brigades marched into the ravine of Dill's Branch and into the range of the Federal gunboats and batteries which silenced Gage's battery, the only one Withers had, and played havoc with the Confederate skirmishers. All the rest of the afternoon, until nightfall, the river sailors kept up their continuous bombard-

ment, and in connection with the field batteries on the bank checked General Withers' desperate attempt on the Landing. The dauntless brigade of Chalmers, whose brave Southerners held their ground near the foot of the ravine and maintained the conflict after the

battle was ended elsewhere, was swept by the gunboats' fire. When Buell's army, that had been hurrying up to Grant's assistance, reached the battle-field, Gwin sent a messenger ashore in the evening to General Nelson, who had just arrived, and asked in what manner he could now be of service. It was pitch dark; except for the occasional firing of the pickets the armies were resting after the terrific combat. In reply to Gwin's inquiry, General Nelson requested that the gunboats keep on firing during the night, and that every ten minutes an 8-inch shell should be launched in the direction of the Confederate camp. With great precision Gwin followed out this course. Through the forest the shells shrieked and exploded over the exhausted Confederates, showering branches and limbs upon them where they slept, and tearing great gashes in the earth. The result was that they got little rest, and rest was necessary. Slowly a certain demoralization became evident—results that bore fruit in the action that opened on the morrow. Here we see pictured—in the lower part of the page—the captain's gig and crew near the *Lexington*, ready to row their commander out into the stream.

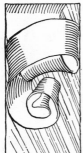
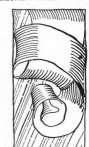

of the evening was made by three Confederate brigades close to the Landing, in the hope of gaining that important point. But by means of a battery of many guns on the bluff of Dill's Branch, aided by the gunboats in the river, the charge was repulsed. Beauregard then gave orders to desist from further attack all along his lines, to suspend operations till morning. When General Bragg heard this he was furious with rage. He had counted on making an immediate grand assault in the darkness, believing that he could capture a large part of the Federal army.

When the messenger informed him of Beauregard's order, he inquired if he had already delivered it to the other commanders. " Yes," was the reply. " If you had not," rejoined the angry Bragg, " I would not obey it. The battle is lost." But Bragg's fears were not shared by his compatriots.

Further mention is due the two little wooden gunboats, *Tyler* and *Lexington,* for their share in the great fight. The *Tyler* had lain all day opposite the mouth of Dill's Branch which flowed through a deep, marshy ravine, into the Tennessee just above the Landing. Her commander, Lieutenant Gwin, was eager for a part in the battle, and when he saw the Confederate right pushing its way toward the Landing, he received permission to open fire. For an hour his guns increased the difficulties of Jackson's and Chalmers' brigades as they made their way to the surrounding of Prentiss. Later on the *Lexington* joined her sister, and the two vessels gave valuable support to the Union cannon at the edge of the ravine and to Hurlbut's troops until the contest ended. All that night, in the downpour of rain, Lieutenant Gwin, at the request of General Nelson, sent shot crashing through the trees in the direction where the Confederates had bivouacked. This completely broke the rest of the exhausted troops, and had a decided effect upon the next day's result.

Southern hopes were high at the close of this first bloody day at Shiloh. Whatever of victory there was at the end of the

FOURTEENTH IOWA VETERANS
AT LIBBY PRISON, RICHMOND, IN 1862, ON THEIR WAY TO FREEDOM

In the battle of Shiloh the Fourteenth Iowa Infantry formed part of that self-constituted forlorn hope which made the victory of April 7, 1862, possible. It held the center at the "Hornet's Nest," fighting the live-long day against fearful odds. Just as the sun was setting, Colonel William T. Shaw, seeing that he was surrounded and further resistance useless, surrendered the regiment. These officers and men were held as prisoners of war until October 12, 1862, when, moving by Richmond, Virginia, and Annapolis, Maryland, they went to Benton Barracks, Missouri, being released on parole, and were declared exchanged on the 19th of November. This photograph was taken while they were held at Richmond, opposite the cook-houses of Libby Prison. The third man from the left in the front row, standing with his hand grasping the lapel of his coat, is George Marion Smith, a descendant of General Marion of Revolutionary fame. It is through the courtesy of his son, N. H. Smith, that this photograph appears here. The Fourteenth Iowa Infantry was organized at Davenport and mustered in November 6, 1861. At Shiloh the men were already veterans of Forts Henry and Donelson. Those who were not captured fought in the battle of Corinth, and after the prisoners were exchanged they took part in the Red River expedition and several minor engagements. They were mustered out November 16, 1864, when the veterans and recruits were consolidated in two companies and assigned to duty in Springfield, Illinois, till August, 1865. These two companies were mustered out on August 8th. The regiment lost during service five officers and fifty-nine enlisted men killed and mortally wounded, and one officer and 138 enlisted men by disease. Iowa sent nine regiments of cavalry, four batteries of light artillery and fifty-one regiments of infantry to the Union armies, a grand total of 76,242 soldiers.

day belonged to the Confederates. They had pressed the Federals back more than a mile and now occupied their ground and tents of the night before. They had captured General Prentiss with some thousands of his men as a result of his brave stand at the " Hornet's Nest."

But their hopes were mingled with grave fears. General Van Dorn with an army of twenty thousand men was hastening from Arkansas to join the Confederate forces at Shiloh; but the roads were bad and he was yet far away. On the other hand, Buell was coming from Nashville to join Grant's army. Should he arrive during the night, the contest of the next day would be unequal and the Confederates would risk losing all that they had gained. Moreover, Beauregard's army, with its long, muddy march from Corinth and its more than twelve hours' continuous fighting, was worn and weary almost to exhaustion.

The Union army was stunned and bleeding, but not disabled, at the close of the first day's battle. Caught unawares, the men had made a noble stand. Though pressed back from their position and obliged to huddle for the night around the Landing, while thousands of their comrades had fallen on the gory field, they had hopes of heavy reenforcements during the night. And, indeed, early in the evening the cry ran along the Union lines that Buell's army had come. The advance guard had arrived late in the afternoon and had assisted Hurlbut in the closing scene on the bluff of Dill's ravine; others continued to pour in during the night. And, furthermore, General Lew Wallace's division, though it had taken a wrong road from Crump's Landing and had not reached the field in time for the fighting of the 6th, now at last had arrived. Buell and Wallace had brought with them twenty-five thousand fresh troops to be hurled on the Confederates on the morning of the 7th. But Van Dorn had not come. The preponderance of numbers now was with the Union army.

Everyone knew that the battle was not over, that the issue

THE MOUNTED POLICE OF THE WEST.

Stalwart horsemen such as these bore the brunt of keeping order in the turbulent regions fought over by the armies in the West. The bugle call, "Boots and Saddles!" might summon them to fight, or to watch the movements of the active Confederates, Van Dorn and Price. It was largely due to their daring and bravery that the Confederate forces were held back from the Mississippi so as not to embarrass the movements of Grant and the gunboats. Of this unattached cavalry of the Army of the Ohio were the men in the upper picture—Company D, Fourth Kentucky Volunteers, enlisted at Louisville, December, 1861.

OFFICERS OF THE FOURTH KENTUCKY CAVALRY.

must be decided on the coming day, and the weary thousands of both sides sank down on the ground in a drenching rain to get a little rest and to gain a little strength for the desperate struggle that was sure to come on the morrow.

Beauregard rested hopes upon a fresh dispatch announcing that Buell was delayed and the dreaded junction of two Federal armies therefore impossible. Meanwhile Grant and Buell were together in Sherman's camp and it was decided that Buell's troops should attack Beauregard next morning. One division of Buell stood to arms all night.

At the break of day on Monday, April 7th, all was astir in both camps on the field of Shiloh, and the dawn was greeted with the roar of cannon. The troops that Grant now advanced into the contest were all, except about ten thousand, the fresh recruits that Wallace and Buell had brought, while the Confederates had not a single company that had not been on the ground the day before. Some military historians believe that Beauregard would have won a signal victory if neither army had been reenforced during the night. But now under the changed conditions the Confederates were at a great disadvantage, and yet they fought for eight long hours with heroic valor.

The deafening roar of the cannon that characterized the beginning of the day's battle was followed by the rattle of musketry, so continuous that no ear could distinguish one shot from another. Nelson's division of Buell's army was the first to engage the Confederates. Nelson commanded the Federal left wing, with Hardee and Breckinridge immediately opposed to him. The Union center was under the command of Generals McCook and Crittenden; the right wing was commanded by McClernand, with Hurlbut next, while Sherman and Lew Wallace occupied the extreme right. The Confederate left wing was commanded by the doughty Bragg and next to him was General Polk.

Shiloh Church was again the storm center and in it

THE FLEET THAT CLEARED THE RIVER

"A spear-thrust in the back" was delivered to the Confederacy by the inland-river fleet that cut it in two. The squadron of Flag-Officer Davis is here lying near Memphis. Thus appeared the Federal gunboats on June 5, 1862, two miles above the city. Fort Pillow had been abandoned the previous day, but the Confederate river-defense flotilla still remained below and the Federals, still smarting from the disaster inflicted on the "Cincinnati," were determined to bring on a decisive engagement and, if possible, clear the river of their antagonists. Meanwhile four new vessels had joined the Federal squadron. These were river steamers which Charles Ellet, Jr., had converted into rams in the short space of six weeks. Their principle was as old as history, but it was now to be tried for the first time in aid of the Federal cause. On these heights above the river the inhabitants of Memphis were crowded on the morning of June 6, 1862, as the Federal squadron moved down-stream against the Confederate gunboats that were drawn up in double line of battle opposite the city. Everyone wanted to see the outcome of the great fight that was impending, for if its result proved adverse to the Confederates, Memphis would fall into Federal hands and another stretch of the Mississippi would be lost to the South. In the engagement at Memphis two of the Ellet rams accompanied the squadron—the "Queen of the West" commanded by Charles Ellet, and the "Monarch" commanded by his younger brother, Major Alfred Ellet. The Confederate flotilla was destroyed, but with the loss of Charles Ellet, from a mortal wound.

MEMPHIS, TENNESSEE ON THE HEIGHTS

LIEUTENANT–COLONEL
ALFRED W. ELLET

ONE OF THE THREE
ELLETS AT MEMPHIS

General Beauregard made his headquarters. Hour after hour the columns in blue and gray surged to and fro, first one then the other gaining the advantage and presently losing it. At times the smoke of burning powder enveloped the whole field and hid both armies from view. The interesting incidents of this day of blood would fill a volume. General Hindman of the Southern side had a novel experience. His horse was struck by a bursting shell and torn to a thousand fragments. The general, thrown ten feet high, fell to the ground, but leaped to his feet unhurt and asked for another horse.

Early in the afternoon, Beauregard became convinced that he was fighting a losing battle and that it would be the part of prudence to withdraw the army before losing all. He thereupon sent the members of his staff to the various corps commanders ordering them to prepare to retreat from the field, at the same time making a show of resuming the offensive. The retreat was so skilfully made, the front firing-line being kept intact, that the Federals did not suspect it for some time. Some hours before nightfall the fighting had ceased. The Federals remained in possession of the field and the Confederates were wading through the mud on the road to Corinth.

It was a dreary march for the bleeding and battered Confederate army. An eye-witness described it in the following language:

"I made a detour from the road on which the army was retreating that I might travel faster and get ahead of the main body. In this ride of twelve miles alongside of the routed army, I saw more of human agony and woe than I trust I will ever again be called upon to witness. The retreating host wound along a narrow and almost impassable road, extending some seven or eight miles in length. Here was a line of wagons loaded with wounded, piled in like bags of grain, groaning and cursing; while the mules plunged on in mud and water belly-deep, the water sometimes coming into the wagons. Next came a straggling regiment of infantry, pressing on past the

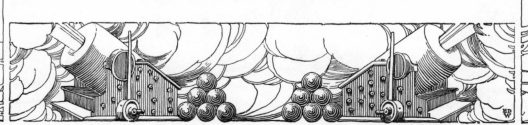

A LOCOMOTIVE THAT

HANGED EIGHT

MEN AS SPIES

In April, 1862, J. J. Andrews, a citizen of Kentucky and a spy in General Buell's employment, proposed seizing a locomotive on the Western and Atlantic Railroad at some point below Chattanooga and running it back to that place, cutting telegraph wires and burning bridges on the way. General O. M.

Mitchel authorized the plan and twenty-two men volunteered to carry it out. On the morning of April 12th, the train they were on stopped at Big Shanty station for breakfast. The bridge-burners (who were in citizens' clothes) detached the locomotive and three box-cars and started at full speed for Chattanooga, but after a run of about a hundred miles their fuel was exhausted and their pursuers were in sight. The whole party was captured. Andrews was condemned as a spy and hanged at Atlanta, July 7th. The others were confined at Chattanooga, Knoxville, and afterward at Atlanta, where seven were executed as spies. Of the fourteen survivors, eight escaped from prison; and of these, six eventually reached the Union lines. Six were removed to Richmond and confined in Castle Thunder until they were exchanged in 1863. The Confederates attempted to destroy the locomotive when they evacuated Atlanta.

wagons; then a stretcher borne on the shoulders of four men, carrying a wounded officer; then soldiers staggering along, with an arm broken and hanging down, or other fearful wounds, which were enough to destroy life. And, to add to the horrors of the scene, the elements of heaven marshaled their forces—a fitting accompaniment of the tempest of human desolation and passion which was raging. A cold, drizzling rain commenced about nightfall, and soon came harder and faster, then turned to pitiless, blinding hail. This storm raged with violence for three hours. I passed long wagon trains filled with wounded and dying soldiers, without even a blanket to shelter them from the driving sleet and hail, which fell in stones as large as partridge eggs, until it lay on the ground two inches deep.

" Some three hundred men died during that awful retreat, and their bodies were thrown out to make room for others who, although wounded, had struggled on through the storm, hoping to find shelter, rest, and medical care."

Four days after the battle, however, Beauregard reported to his government, " this army is more confident of ultimate success than before its encounter with the enemy." Addressing the soldiers, he said: " You have done your duty. . . . Your countrymen are proud of your deeds on the bloody field of Shiloh; confident in the ultimate result of your valor."

The news of these two fearful days at Shiloh was astounding to the American people. Never before on the continent had there been anything approaching it. Bull Run was a skirmish in comparison with this gigantic conflict. The losses on each side exceeded ten thousand men. General Grant tells us that after the second day he saw an open field so covered with dead that it would have been possible to walk across it in any direction stepping on dead bodies, without a foot touching the ground. American valor was tried to the full on both sides at Shiloh, and the record shows that it was equal to the test.

THE BIGGEST GUN OF ALL—THE 20-INCH MONSTER FOR WHICH NO TARGET WOULD SERVE

A photograph of the only 20-inch gun made during the war. It weighed 117,000 pounds. On March 30, 1861, a 15-inch Columbiad was heralded in *Harper's Weekly* as the biggest gun in the world, but three years later this was exceeded. In 1844 Lieutenant (later Brigadier-General) Thomas Jefferson Rodman of the Ordnance Department commenced a series of tests to find a way to obviate the injurious strains set up in the metal, by cooling a large casting from the exterior. He finally developed his theory of casting a gun with the core hollow and then cooling it by a stream of water or cold air through it. So successful was this method that the War Department, in 1860, authorized a 15-inch smooth-bore gun. It proved a great success. General Rodman then projected his 20-inch smooth-bore gun, which was made in 1864 under his direction at Fort Pitt, Pittsburg, Pennsylvania. It was mounted at Fort Hamilton, New York Harbor, very soon afterwards, but on account of the tremendous size and destructive effect of its projectiles it was fired only four times during the war. It was almost impossible to get a target that would withstand the shots and leave anything to show what had happened. These four shots were fired with 50, 75, 100 and 125 pounds of powder. The projectile weighed 1,080 pounds, and the maximum pressure on the bore was 25,000 pounds. In March, 1867, it was again fired four times with 125, 150, 175 and 200 pounds of powder, each time with an elevation of twenty-five degrees, the projectile attaining a maximum range of 8,001 yards. This is no mean record even compared with twentieth century pieces.

THE BIGGEST GUN IN THE WORLD.

We publish on page 205 an accurate drawing of the great Fifteen-inch Gun at Fort Monroe, Virginia; and also a picture, from a recent sketch, showing the experiments which are being made with a view to test it. It is proper that we should say that the small drawing is from the lithograph which is published in MAJOR BARNARD's "Notes on Sea-Coast Defense," published by Mr. D. Van Nostrand. of this city.

This gun was cast at Pittsburgh, Pennsylvania, by Knapp, Rudd, & Co., under the directions of Captain T. J. Rodman, of the Ordnance Corps. Its dimensions are as follows:

Total length	190	inches.
Length of calibre of bore	156	"
Length of ellipsoidal chamber	9	"
Total length of bore	165	"
Maximum exterior diameter	48	"

NEWS OF MARCH 30, 1861

THE "CHEESE BOX" THAT MADE HISTORY
AS IT APPEARED FOUR MONTHS LATER

In this remarkable view of the "Monitor's" turret, taken in July, 1862, is seen as clearly as on the day after the great battle the effect of the Confederate fire upon Ericsson's novel craft. As the two vessels approached each other about half-past eight on that immortal Sunday morning, the men within the turret waited anxiously for the first shot of their antagonist. It soon came from her bow gun and went wide of the mark. The "Virginia" no longer had the broadside of a wooden ship at which to aim. Not until the "Monitor" was alongside the big ironclad at close range came the order "Begin firing" to the men in the "cheese box." Then the gun-ports of the turret were triced back, and it began to revolve for the first time in battle. As soon as the guns were brought to bear, two 11-inch solid shot struck the "Virginia's" armor; almost immediately she replied with her broadside, and Lieutenant Greene and his gunners listened anxiously to the shells bursting against their citadel. They made no more impression than is apparent in the picture. Confident in the protection of their armor, the Federals reloaded with a will and came again and again to close quarters with their adversary, hurling two great projectiles about every eight minutes.

MEN ON THE "MONITOR" WHO FOUGHT WITH WORDEN

Here on the deck of the "Monitor" sit some of the men who held up the hands of Lieutenant Worden in the great fight with the "Virginia." In the picture, taken in July, 1862, only four months afterward, one of the nine famous dents on the turret are visible. It required courage not only to fight in the "Monitor" for the first time but to embark on her at all, for she was a strange and untried invention at which many high authorities shook their heads. But during the battle, amid all the difficulties of breakdowns by the new untried machinery, Lieutenant S. Dana Greene coolly directed his men, who kept up a fire of remarkable accuracy. Twenty of the forty-one 11-inch shot fired from the "Monitor" took effect, more or less, on the iron plates of the "Virginia." The

ADMIRAL J. L. WORDEN

"Monitor" was struck nine times on her turret, twice on the pilot-house, thrice on the deck, and eight times on the side. While Greene was fighting nobly in the turret, Worden with the helmsman in the pilot-house was bravely maneuvering his vessel and seeking to ram his huge antagonist. Twice he almost succeeded and both times Greene's guns were used on the "Virginia" at point-blank range with telling effect. Toward the close of the action Worden was blinded by a shell striking near one of the peepholes in the pilot-house and the command devolved upon Greene. Worden, even in his agony of pain while the doctor was attending his injuries, asked constantly about the progress of the battle; and when told that the "Minnesota" was safe, he said, "Then I can die happy."

DAVID
GLASGOW
FARRAGUT
THE MAN
WHO
DARED AT
NEW
ORLEANS
AND
MOBILE
BAY

"ANY MAN
WHO IS
PREPARED
FOR
DEFEAT
WOULD BE
HALF DE-
FEATED
BEFORE
HE COM-
MENCED "

THE COMMANDER OF THE FEDERAL FLEET AT NEW ORLEANS

"Who is this Farragut?" So the younger generation of Americans must have wondered, at the news of late January, 1862. Farragut was to have a flag in the Gulf and was expected to capture New Orleans. Thus far in the War, he had done nothing but sit on an obscure retiring board in the Navy Department at Washington. But Commander David D. Porter knew him, for it was with Porter's own father in the famous old "Essex" that Farragut as a mere boy had proved worthy to command a fighting ship. And now it was Porter who had recommended him for a task considered gravely dangerous by all, foolhardy by not a few. This was no less than to pass the forts below New Orleans, defeat a powerful and determined Confederate flotilla, capture the city, and then sweep up the Mississippi and split the Confederacy in two. To this Farragut rigidly held himself and the brave men under him, when, in the dark hour before dawn of April 24, 1862, they faced the terrible bombardment of the forts and fought their way through the flames of fire rafts desperately maneuvered by the opposing gunboats. Next day New Orleans was Farragut's. Leaving it to the co-operating army under General B. F. Butler, Farragut pushed on up the river, passed and repassed the fortifications at Vicksburg, but the army needed to drive home the wedge thus firmly entered by the navy was not yet ready. It was another year before the sturdy blows of Farragut were effectually supplemented ashore.

THE MEN WHO DARED—SAILORS ON THE "HARTFORD" AFTER PASSING THE NEW ORLEANS FORTS

On this page of unwritten history McPherson and Oliver, the New Orleans war-time photographers, have caught the crew of the staunch old "Hartford" as they relaxed after their fiery test. In unconscious picturesqueness grouped about the spar-deck, the men are gossiping or telling over again their versions of the great deeds done aboard the flagship. Some have seized the opportunity for a little plain sewing, while all are interested in the new and unfamiliar process of "having their pictures taken." The notable thing about the picture is the number of young faces. Only a few of the old salts whose bearded and weather-beaten faces give evidence of service in the old navy still remain. After the great triumph in Mobile Bay, Farragut said of these men: "I have never seen a crew come up like ours. They are ahead of the old set in small arms, and fully equal to them at the great guns. They arrived here a mere lot of boys and young men, and have now

fattened up and knocked the nine-inch guns about like twenty-four pounders, to the astonishment of everybody. There was but one man who showed fear and he was allowed to resign. This was the most desperate battle I ever fought since the days of the old 'Essex.'" "It was the anxious night of my life," wrote Farragut later. The spar-deck shown below recalls another speech. "Don't flinch from that fire, boys! There is a hotter fire for those who don't do their duty!" So shouted Farragut with his ship fast aground and a huge fire-raft held hard against her wooden side by the little Confederate tug "Mosher." The ship seemed all ablaze and the men, "breathing fire," were driven from their guns. Farragut, calmly pacing the poop-deck, called out his orders, caring nothing for the rain of shot from Fort St. Philip. The men, inspired by such coolness, leaped to their stations again and soon a shot pierced the boiler of the plucky "Mosher" and sank her.

SPAR-DECK OF THE "HARTFORD"

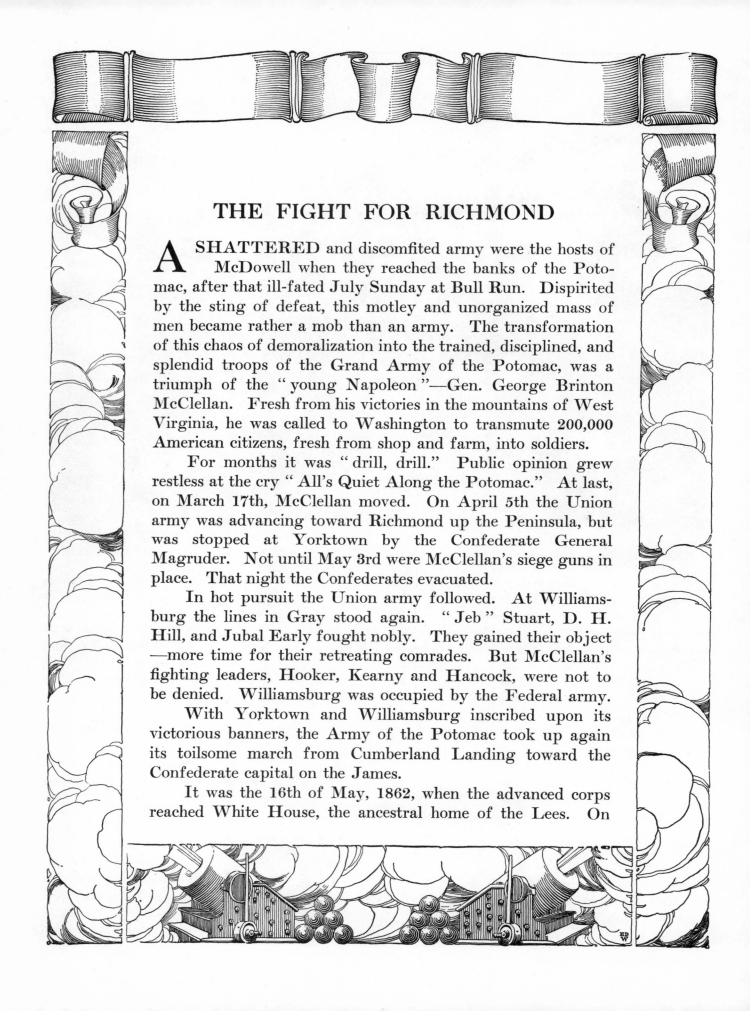

THE FIGHT FOR RICHMOND

A SHATTERED and discomfited army were the hosts of McDowell when they reached the banks of the Potomac, after that ill-fated July Sunday at Bull Run. Dispirited by the sting of defeat, this motley and unorganized mass of men became rather a mob than an army. The transformation of this chaos of demoralization into the trained, disciplined, and splendid troops of the Grand Army of the Potomac, was a triumph of the " young Napoleon "—Gen. George Brinton McClellan. Fresh from his victories in the mountains of West Virginia, he was called to Washington to transmute 200,000 American citizens, fresh from shop and farm, into soldiers.

For months it was " drill, drill." Public opinion grew restless at the cry " All's Quiet Along the Potomac." At last, on March 17th, McClellan moved. On April 5th the Union army was advancing toward Richmond up the Peninsula, but was stopped at Yorktown by the Confederate General Magruder. Not until May 3rd were McClellan's siege guns in place. That night the Confederates evacuated.

In hot pursuit the Union army followed. At Williamsburg the lines in Gray stood again. " Jeb " Stuart, D. H. Hill, and Jubal Early fought nobly. They gained their object —more time for their retreating comrades. But McClellan's fighting leaders, Hooker, Kearny and Hancock, were not to be denied. Williamsburg was occupied by the Federal army.

With Yorktown and Williamsburg inscribed upon its victorious banners, the Army of the Potomac took up again its toilsome march from Cumberland Landing toward the Confederate capital on the James.

It was the 16th of May, 1862, when the advanced corps reached White House, the ancestral home of the Lees. On

"LITTLE MAC" PREPARING FOR THE CAMPAIGN—A ROYAL AIDE

A picture taken in the fall of 1861, when McClellan was at the headquarters of General George W. Morell (who stands at the extreme left), commanding a brigade in Fitz John Porter's Division. Morell was then stationed on the defenses of Washington at Minor's Hill in Virginia, and General McClellan was engaged in transforming the raw recruits in the camps near the national capital into the finished soldiers of the Army of the Potomac. "Little Mac," as they called him, was at this time at the height of his popularity. He appears in the center between two of his favorite aides-de-camp—Lieut.-Cols. A. V. Colburn and N. B. Sweitzer—whom he usually selected, he writes, "when hard riding is required." Farther to the right stand two distinguished visitors—the Prince de Joinville, son of King Louis Phillippe of France, and his nephew, the Count de Paris, who wears the uniform of McClellan's staff, on which he was to serve throughout the Peninsula Campaign.

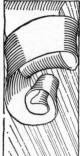
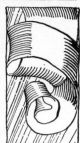

every side were fields of wheat, and, were it not for the presence of one hundred thousand men, there was the promise of a full harvest. It was here that General McClellan took up his headquarters, a distance of twenty-four miles from Richmond.

In the Confederate capital a panic had seized the people. As the retreating army of Johnston sought the environs of Richmond and news of the invading hosts was brought in, fear took possession of the inhabitants and many wild rumors were afloat as to the probable capture of the city. But it was not a fear that Johnston would not fight. The strategic policy of the Southern general had been to delay the advance of the Northern army. Fortunately for him, the rainy weather proved a powerful ally. The time had now come when he should change his position from the defensive to the offensive. The Army of Northern Virginia had been brought to bay, and it now turned to beat off the invaders and save its capital.

On the historic Peninsula lay two of the greatest and most splendid armies that had ever confronted each other on the field of battle. The engagement, now imminent, was to be the first in that series of contests, between the Army of the Potomac and the Army of Northern Virginia, ending three years thereafter, at Appomattox, when the war-worn veterans of gray should lay down their arms, in honor, to the war-worn veterans of blue.

The Union advance was retarded by the condition of the weather and the roads. Between McClellan's position at White House and the waiting Confederate army lay the Chickahominy, an erratic and sluggish stream, that spreads itself out in wooded swamps and flows around many islands, forming a valley from half a mile to a mile wide, bordered by low bluffs. In dry weather it is but a mere brook, but a moderate shower will cause it to rise quickly and to offer formidable opposition to any army seeking its passage. The valley is covered with trees whose tops reach to the level of

RAMPARTS THAT BAFFLED McCLELLAN. (Hasty fortifications of the Confederates at Yorktown.) It was against such fortifications as these, which Magruder had hastily reenforced with sand-bags, that McClellan spent a month preparing his heavy batteries. Magruder had far too few soldiers to man his long line of defenses properly, and his position could have been taken by a single determined attack. This rampart was occupied by the Confederate general, D. H. Hill, who had been the first to enter Yorktown in order to prepare it for siege. He was the last to leave it on the night of May 3, 1862.

WRECKED ORDNANCE. (Gun exploded by the Confederates on General Hill's rampart, Yorktown.) Although the Confederates abandoned 200 pieces of ordnance at Yorktown, they were able to render most of them useless before leaving. Hill succeeded in terrorizing the Federals with grape-shot, and some of this was left behind. After the evacuation the ramparts were overrun by Union trophy seekers. The soldier resting his hands upon his musket is one of the Zouaves whose bright and novel uniforms were so conspicuous early in the war. This spot was directly on the line of the British fortification of 1781.

ANOTHER VOICELESS GUN. (Confederate ramparts southeast of Yorktown.) A 32-pounder Navy gun which had been burst, wrecking its embrasure. The Federal soldier seated on the sand-bags is on guard-duty to prevent camp-followers from looting the vacant fort.

THE MISSING RIFLE. (Extensive sand-bag fortifications of the Confederates at Yorktown.) The shells and carriage were left behind by the Confederates, but the rifled gun to which they belonged was taken along in the retreat. Such pieces as they could not remove they spiked.

GUNS THE UNION LOST AND RECOVERED. (A two-gun Confederate battery in the entrenchments south of Yorktown.) The near gun is a 32-pounder navy; the far one, a 24-pounder siege-piece. More than 3,000 pieces of naval ordnance fell into the hands of the Confederates early in the war, through the ill-advised and hasty abandonment of Norfolk Navy Yard by the Federals. Many of these guns did service at Yorktown and subsequently on the James River against the Union.

THE CONFEDERATE COMMAND OF THE RIVER. (Battery Magruder, Yorktown.) Looking north up the river, four of the five 8-inch Columbiads composing this section of the battery are visible. The grape-shot and spherical shells, which had been gathered in quantities to prevent the Federal fleet from passing up the river, were abandoned on the hasty retreat of the Confederates, the guns being spiked. The vessels in the river are transport ships, with the exception of the frigate just off shore.

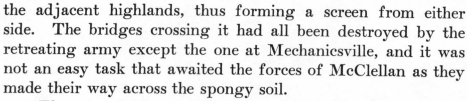

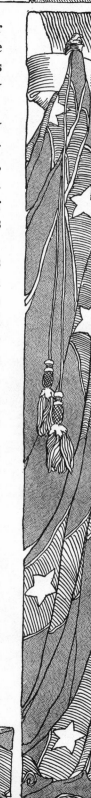

the adjacent highlands, thus forming a screen from either side. The bridges crossing it had all been destroyed by the retreating army except the one at Mechanicsville, and it was not an easy task that awaited the forces of McClellan as they made their way across the spongy soil.

The van of the Union army reached the Chickahominy on May 20th. The bridge was gone but the men under General Naglee forded the little river, reaching the plateau beyond, and made a bold reconnaissance before the Confederate lines. In the meantime, newly constructed bridges were beginning to span the Chickahominy, and the Federal army soon was crossing to the south bank of the river.

General McClellan had been promised reenforcements from the north. General McDowell with forty thousand men had started from Fredericksburg to join him north of the Chickahominy. For this reason, General McClellan had thrown the right wing of his army on the north of the river while his left would rest on the south side of the stream. This position of his army did not escape the eagle eye of the Confederate general, Joseph E. Johnston, who believed the time had now come to give battle, and perhaps destroy the small portion of the Union forces south of the river.

Meanwhile, General "Stonewall" Jackson, in the Shenandoah, was making threatening movements in the direction of Washington, and McDowell's orders to unite with McClellan were recalled.

The roads in and about Richmond radiate from that city like the spokes of a wheel. One of these is the Williamsburg stage-road, crossing the Chickahominy at Bottom's Bridge, only eleven miles from Richmond. It was along this road that the Federal corps of Keyes and Heintzelman had made their way. Their orders were "to go prepared for battle at a moment's notice" and "to bear in mind that the Army of the Potomac has never been checked."

Parallel to this road, and about a mile to the northward,

TWO KEEPERS OF THE GOAL

The North expected General McClellan to possess himself of this citadel of the Confederacy in June, 1862, and it seemed likely the expectation would be realized. In the upper picture we get a near view of the State House at Richmond, part of which was occupied as a Capitol by the Confederate Congress during the war. In this building were stored the records and archives of the Confederate Government, many of which were

THE GOAL—THE CONFEDERATE CAPITOL

lost during the hasty retreat of President Davis and his cabinet at the evacuation of Richmond, April, 1865. Below, we see the city of Richmond from afar, with the Capitol standing out boldly on the hill. McClellan was not destined to reach this coveted goal, and it would not have meant the fall of the Confederacy had he then done so. When Lincoln entered the building in 1865, the Confederacy had been beaten as much by the blockade as by the operations of Grant and Sherman with vastly superior forces.

COPYRIGHT BY PATRIOT PUB. CO.

THE SPIRES OF RICHMOND

Here are the portraits of the two military leaders who were conspicuous in the Confederate attack upon McClellan's camp at Fair Oaks. General D. H. Hill did most of the fierce fighting which drove back the Federals on the first day, and only the timely arrival of Sumner's troops enabled the Federals to hold their ground. Had they failed they would have been driven into the morasses of the Chickahominy, retreat across which would have been difficult as the bridges were partly submerged by the swollen stream. After General Johnston was wounded, General G. W. Smith was in command during the second day's fighting.

GENERAL G. W. SMITH, C. S. A.

GENERAL D. H. HILL, C. S. A.

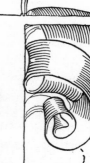

runs the Richmond and York River Railroad. Seven miles from Richmond another highway intersects the one from Williamsburg, known as the Nine Mile road. At the point of this intersection once grew a clump of seven pines, hence the name of "Seven Pines," often given to the battle fought on this spot. A thousand yards beyond the pines were two farmhouses in a grove of oaks. This was Fair Oaks Farm. Where the Nine Mile road crossed the railroad was Fair Oaks Station.

Southeast of Seven Pines was White Oak Swamp. Casey's division of Keyes' corps was stationed at Fair Oaks Farm. A fifth of a mile in front lay his picket line, extending crescent shape, from the swamp to the Chickahominy. Couch's division of the same corps was at Seven Pines, with his right wing extending along the Nine Mile road to Fair Oaks Station. Heintzelman's corps lay to the rear; Kearney's division guarded the railroad at Savage's Station and Hooker's the approaches to the White Oak Swamp. This formed three lines of defense. It was a well-wooded region and at this time was in many places no more than a bog. No sooner had these positions been taken, than trees were cut to form abatis, rifle-pits were hastily dug, and redoubts for placing artillery were constructed. The picket line lay along a dense growth of woods. Through an opening in the trees, the Confederate army could be seen in force on the other side of the clearing.

The plans of the Confederate general were well matured. On Friday, May 30th, he gave orders that his army should be ready to move at daybreak.

That night the "windows of heaven seemed to have been opened" and the "fountains of the deep broken up." The storm fell like a deluge. It was the most violent storm that had swept over that region for a generation. Throughout the night the tempest raged. The thunderbolts rolled without cessation. The sky was white with the electric flashes. The earth was thoroughly drenched. The lowlands became a

THE ADVANCE THAT BECAME A RETREAT

Here, almost within sight of the goal (Richmond), we see McClellan's soldiers preparing the way for the passage of the army and its supplies. The soil along the Chickahominy was so marshy that in order to move the supply trains and artillery from the base at White House and across the river to the army, corduroy approaches to the bridges had to be built. It was well that the men got this early practice in road-building. Thanks to the work kept up, McClellan was able to unite the divided wings of the army almost at will

"REGULARS" NEAR FAIR OAKS—OFFICERS OF McCLELLAN'S HORSE ARTILLERY BRIGADE

These trained soldiers lived up to the promise in their firm-set features. Major Hays and five of his Lieutenants and Captains here—Pennington, Tidball, Hains, Robertson and Barlow had, by '65, become general officers. From left to right (standing) are Edw. Pendleton, A. C. M. Pennington, Henry Benson, H. M. Gibson, J. M. Wilson, J. C. Tidball, W. N. Dennison; (sitting) P. C. Hains, H. C. Gibson, Wm. Hays, J. M. Robertson, J. W. Barlow; (on ground) R. H. Chapin, Robert Clarke, A. C. Vincent.

morass. From mud-soaked beds the soldiers arose the next morning to battle.

Owing to the storm the Confederates did not move so early as intended. However, some of the troops were in readiness by eight o'clock. Hour after hour the forces of Longstreet and Hill awaited the sound of the signal-gun that would tell them General Huger was in his position to march. Still they waited. It was near noon before General Hill, weary of waiting, advanced to the front, preceded by a line of skirmishers, along the Williamsburg road. The Union pickets were lying at the edge of the forest. The soldiers in the pits had been under arms for several hours awaiting the attack. Suddenly there burst through the woods the soldiers of the South. A shower of bullets fell beneath the trees and the Union pickets gave way. On and on came the lines of gray in close columns. In front of the abatis had been planted a battery of four guns. General Naglee with four regiments, the Fifty-sixth and One hundredth New York and Eleventh Maine and One hundred and fourth Pennsylvania, had gone forward, and in the open field met the attacking army. The contest was a stubborn one. Naglee's men charged with their bayonets and pressed the gray lines back again to the edge of the woods. Here they were met by a furious fire of musketry and quickly gave way, seeking the cover of the rifle-pits at Fair Oaks Farm. The Confederate infantrymen came rushing on.

But again they were held in check. In this position, for nearly three hours the Federals waged an unequal combat against three times their number. Then, suddenly a galling fire plowed in on them from the left. It came from Rains' brigade, which had executed a flank movement. At the same time the brigade of Rodes rushed toward them. The Federals saw the hopelessness of the situation. The officers at the batteries tried to spike their guns but were killed in the attempt. Hastily falling back, five guns were left to be turned on them

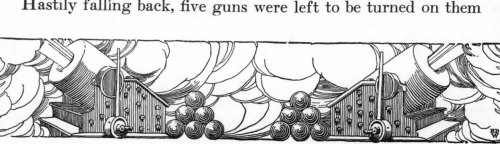

CUSTER AND HIS CLASSMATE—NOW A CONFEDERATE PRISONER

Friends and even relatives who had been enlisted on opposite sides in the great Civil War met each other during its vicissitudes upon the battle-field. Here, caught by the camera, is one of the many instances. On the left sits Lieutenant J. B. Washington, C. S. A., who was an aide to General Johnston at Fair Oaks. Beside him sits Lieutenant George A. Custer, of the Fifth U. S. Cavalry, aide on McClellan's staff, later famous cavalry general and Indian fighter. Both men were West Point graduates and had attended the military academy together. On the morning of May 31, 1862, at Fair Oaks, Lieutenant Washington was captured by some of General Casey's pickets. Later in the day his former classmate ran across him and a dramatic meeting was thus recorded by the camera.

in their retreat. This move was not too soon. In another minute they would have been entirely surrounded and captured. The gray lines pressed on. The next stand would be made at Seven Pines, where Couch was stationed. The forces here had been weakened by sending relief to Casey. The situation of the Federals was growing critical. At the same time General Longstreet sent reenforcements to General Hill. Couch was forced out of his position toward the right in the direction of Fair Oaks Station and was thus separated from the main body of the army, then in action.

The Confederates pushed strongly against the Federal center. Heintzelman came to the rescue. The fight waged was a gallant one. For an hour and a half the lines of blue and gray surged back and forth. The Federals were gradually giving way. The left wing, alone, next to the White Oak Swamp, was holding its own.

At the same time over at Fair Oaks Station whither Couch had been forced, were new developments. He was about to strike the Confederate army on its left flank, but just when the guns were being trained, there burst across the road the troops of General G. W. Smith, who up to this time had been inactive. These men were fresh for the fight, superior in number, and soon overpowered the Northerners. It looked for a time as if the whole Union army south of the Chickahominy was doomed.

Over at Seven Pines the center of McClellan's army was about to be routed. Now it was that General Heintzelman personally collected about eighteen hundred men, the fragments of the broken regiments, and took a decided stand at the edge of the timber. He was determined not to give way. But this alone would not nor did not save the day. To the right of this new line of battle, there was a rise of ground. From here the woods abruptly sloped to the rear. If this elevation were once secured by the Confederates, all would be lost and rout would be inevitable. The quick eye of General

PROFESSOR LOWE IN HIS BALLOON AT A CRITICAL MOMENT

As soon as Professor Lowe's balloon soars above the top of the trees the Confederate batteries will open upon him, and for the next few moments shells and bullets from the shrapnels will be bursting and whistling about his ears. Then he will pass out of the danger-zone to an altitude beyond the reach of the Confederate artillery. After the evacuation of Yorktown, May 4, 1862, Professor Lowe, who had been making daily observations from his balloon, followed McClellan's divisions, which was to meet Longstreet next day at Williamsburg. On reaching the fortifications of the abandoned city, Lowe directed the men who were towing the still inflated balloon in which he was riding to scale the corner of the fort nearest to his old camp, where the last gun had been fired the night before. This fort had devoted a great deal of effort to attempting to damage the too inquisitive balloon, and a short time previously one of the best Confederate guns had burst, owing to over-charging and too great an elevation to reach the high altitude. The balloonist had witnessed the explosion and a number of gunners had been killed and wounded within his sight. His present visit was in order to touch and examine the pieces and bid farewell to what he then looked upon as a departed friend. This is indicated as the same gun on page 371.

Keyes took in the situation. He was stationed on the left; to reach the hill would necessitate taking his men between the battle-lines. The distance was nearly eight hundred yards. Calling on a single regiment to follow he made a dash for the position. The Southern troops, divining his intention, poured a deadly volley into his ranks and likewise attempted to reach this key to the situation. The Federals gained the spot just in time. The new line was formed as a heavy mass of Confederates came upon them. The tremendous Union fire was too much for the assaulting columns, which were checked. They had forced the Federal troops back from their entrenchments a distance of two miles, but they never got farther than these woods. The river fog now came up as the evening fell and the Southern troops spent the night in the captured camps, sleeping on their arms. The Federals fell back toward the river to an entrenched camp.

Meanwhile at Fair Oaks Station the day was saved, too, in the nick of time, for the Federals. On the north side of the Chickahominy were stationed the two divisions of Sedgwick and Richardson, under command of General Sumner. Scarcely had the battle opened when McClellan at his headquarters, six miles away, heard the roar and rattle of artillery. He was sick at the time, but he ordered General Sumner to be in readiness. At this time there were four bridges across the river—two of them were Bottom's Bridge and the railroad bridge. To go by either of these would consume too much time in case of an emergency. General Sumner had himself constructed two more bridges, lying between the others. The heavy flood of the preceding night, which was still rising, had swept one of these partially away. In order to save time, he put his men under arms and marched them to the end of the upper bridge and there waited throughout the greater part of the afternoon for orders to cross. Before them rolled a muddy and swollen stream, above whose flood was built a rude and unstable structure. From the other side

THE PHOTOGRAPH THE BALLOONIST RECOGNIZED FORTY–EIGHT YEARS AFTER

"When I saw the photograph showing my inflation of the balloon *Intrepid* to reconnoiter the battle of Fair Oaks," wrote Professor T. S. C. Lowe in the *American Review of Reviews* for February, 1911, "it surprised me very much indeed. Any one examining the picture will see my hand at the extreme right, resting on the network, where I was measuring the amount of gas already in the balloon, preparatory to completing the inflation from gas in the smaller balloon in order that I might ascent to a greater height. This I did within a space of five minutes, saving a whole hour at the most vital point of the battle." A close examination of this photograph will reveal Professor Lowe's hand resting on the network of the balloon, although his body is not in the photograph. It truly is remarkable that Professor Lowe should have seen and recognized, nearly half a century afterward, this photograph taken at one of the most critical moments of his life.

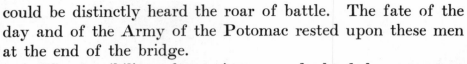

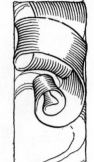

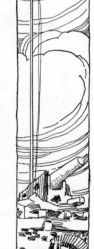

could be distinctly heard the roar of battle. The fate of the day and of the Army of the Potomac rested upon these men at the end of the bridge.

The possibility of crossing was doubted by everyone, including the general himself. The bridge had been built of logs, held together and kept from drifting by the stumps of trees. Over the river proper it was suspended by ropes attached to trees, felled across the stream.

At last the long-expected order to advance came. The men stepped upon the floating bridge. It swayed to and fro as the solid column passed over it. Beneath the men was the angry flood which would engulf all if the bridge should fall. Gradually the weight pressed it down between the solid stumps and it was made secure till the army had crossed. Had the passage been delayed another hour the flood would have rendered it impassable.

Guided by the roar of battle the troops hurried on. The artillery was left behind in the mud of the Chickahominy. The steady, rolling fire of musketry and the boom of cannon told of deadly work in front. It was nearly six o'clock before Sedgwick's column deployed into line in the rear of Fair Oaks Station. They came not too soon. Just now there was a lull in the battle. The Confederates were gathering themselves for a vigorous assault on their opponents' flaming front. Their lines were re-forming. General Joseph E. Johnston himself had immediate command. President Jefferson Davis had come out from his capital to witness the contest. Rapidly the Confederates moved forward. A heavy fusillade poured from their batteries and muskets. Great rents were made in the line of blue. It did not waver. The openings were quickly filled and a scorching fire was sent into the approaching columns. Again and again the charge was repeated only to be repulsed. Then came the order to fix bayonets. Five regiments—Thirty-fourth and Eighty-second New York, Fifteenth and Twentieth Massachusetts and Seventh Michigan

THE SLAUGHTER FIELD AT FAIR OAKS.

Over this ground the fiercest fighting of the two days' battle took place, on May 31, 1862. Some 400 soldiers were buried here, where they fell, and their hastily dug graves appear plainly in the picture. In the redoubt seen just beyond the two houses was the center of the Federal line of battle, equi-distant, about a mile and a half, from both Seven Pines and Fair Oaks. The entrenchments near these farm dwellings were begun on May 28th by Casey's Division, 4th Corps. There was not time to finish them before the Confederate attack opened the battle, and the artillery of Casey's Division was hurriedly placed in position behind the incomplete works.

THE UNFINISHED REDOUBT.

In the smaller picture we see the inside of the redoubt at the left background of the picture above. The scene is just before the battle and picks and shovels were still busy throwing up the embankments to strengthen this center of the Federal defense. Casey's artillery was being hurriedly brought up. In the background General Sickles' Brigade appears drawn up in line of battle. When the Confederates first advanced Casey's artillery did telling work, handsomely repelling the attack early in the afternoon of May 31st. Later in the day Confederate sharpshooters from vantage points in neighboring trees began to pick off the officers and the gunners and the redoubt had to be relinquished. The abandoned guns were turned against the retreating Federals.

THE "REDHOT BATTERY."

On the afternoon of May 31st, at Fair Oaks, the Confederates were driving the Federal soldiers through the woods in disorder when this battery (McCarthy's) together with Miller's battery opened up with so continuous and severe a fire that the Federals were able to make a stand and hold their own for the rest of the day. The guns grew so hot from constant firing that it was only with the greatest care that they could be swabbed and loaded. These earthworks were thrown up for McCarthy's Battery, Company C, 1st Pennsylvania Artillery, near Savage's Station. The soldiers nicknamed it the "Redhot Battery."

—pushed to the front. Into the woods where the Confederates had fallen back the charge was made. Driving the Southern lines back in confusion, these dashing columns saved the day for the Army of the Potomac.

Night was now settling over the wooded field. Here and there flashes of light could be seen among the oaks, indicating a diligent search for the wounded. General Johnston ordered his troops to sleep on the field. A few minutes later he was struck by a rifle-ball and almost immediately a shell hit him, throwing him from his horse, and he was borne off the field. The first day of the battle was over.

The disability of the Southern commander made it possible for the promotion of a new leader upon whom the fortunes of the Army of Northern Virginia would soon rest. This was General Robert E. Lee; although the immediate command for the next day's contest fell upon General G. W. Smith. Early Sunday morning the battle was again in progress. The command of Smith, near Fair Oaks Station, advanced down the railroad, attacking Richardson, whose lines were north of it and were using the embankment as a fortification. Longstreet's men were south of the railroad. The firing was heavy all along this line, the opposing forces being not more than fifty yards from each other. For an hour and a half the musketry fire was intensely heavy. It was, indeed, a continuous roar. The line of gray could not withstand the galling fire and for the first time that day fell back. But the Union line had been broken, too. A brief lull ensued. Both sides were gathering themselves for another onslaught. It was then that there were heard loud shouts from the east of the railroad.

There, coming through the woods, was a large body of Federal troops. They were the men of Hooker. They formed a magnificent body of soldiers and seemed eager for the fray. Turning in on the Williamsburg road they rapidly deployed to the right and the left. In front of them was an open field, with a thick wood on the other side. The Confederates had

AIMING THE GUNS AT FAIR OAKS.

Here we see the beginning of the lull in the fighting of the second day at Fair Oaks, which it has been asserted led to a fatal delay and the ruin of McClellan's Peninsula Campaign. The first day's battle at Fair Oaks, May 31, 1862, was decidedly a Federal reverse which would have developed into a rout had not Sumner, crossing his troops on the perilous Grapevine Bridge, come up in time to rally the retreating men. Here we see some of them within the entrenchments at Fair Oaks Station on the Richmond & York River Railroad. The order will soon come to cease firing at the end of the second day's fighting, the result of which was to drive the Confederates back to Richmond. McClellan did not pursue. The heavy rainstorm on the night of May 30th had made the movement of artillery extremely difficult, and McClellan waited to complete the bridges and build entrenchments before advancing. This delay gave the Confederates time to reorganize their forces and place them under the new commander, Robert E. Lee, who while McClellan lay inactive effected a junction with "Stonewall" Jackson. Then during the Seven Days' Battles Lee steadily drove McClellan from his position, within four or five miles of Richmond, to a new position on the James River. From this secure and advantageous water base McClellan planned a new line of advance upon the Confederate Capital. In the smaller picture we see the interior of the works at Fair Oaks Station, which were named Fort Sumner in honor of the General who brought up his Second Corps and saved the day. The camp of the Second Corps is seen beyond the fortifications to the right.

FORT SUMNER, NEAR FAIR OAKS.

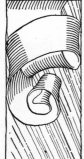

posted themselves in this forest and were waiting for their antagonists. The Federals marched upon the field in double-quick time; their movements became a run, and they began firing as they dashed forward. They were met by a withering fire of field artillery and a wide gap being opened in their ranks. It immediately filled. They reached the edge of the woods and as they entered its leafy shadows the tide of battle rolled in with them. The front line was lost to view in the forest, except for an occasional gleam of arms from among the trees. The din and the clash and roar of battle were heard for miles. Bayonets were brought into use. It was almost a hand-to-hand combat in the heavy forest and tangled slashings. The sound of battle gradually subsided, then ceased except for the intermittent reports of small arms, and the second day's fight was over.

The Confederate forces withdrew toward Richmond. The Federal troops could now occupy without molestation the positions they held the previous morning. The forest paths were strewn with the dead and the dying. Many of the wounded were compelled to lie under the scorching sun for hours before help reached them. Every farmhouse became an improvised hospital where the suffering soldiers lay. Many were placed upon cars and taken across the Chickahominy. The dead horses were burned. The dead soldiers, blue and gray, found sometimes lying within a few feet of each other, were buried on the field of battle. The two giants had met in their first great combat and were even now beginning to gird up their loins for a desperate struggle before the capital of the Confederacy.

"FLYING ARTILLERY" IN THE ATTEMPT ON RICHMOND

THE CANNONEERS WHO KEPT UP WITH THE CAVALRY—IN THIS SWIFTEST BRANCH OF THE SERVICE
EACH MAN RIDES HORSEBACK

Here are drawn up Harry Benson's Battery A, of the Second United States Artillery, and Horatio Gates Gibson's Batteries C and G, combined of the Third United States Artillery, near Fair Oaks, Virginia. They arrived there just too late to take part in the battle of June, 1862. By "horse artillery," or "flying artillery" as it is sometimes called, is meant an organization equipped usually with 10-pounder rifled guns, with all hands mounted. In ordinary light artillery the cannoneers either ride on the gun-carriage or go afoot. In "flying artillery" each cannoneer has a horse. This form is by far the most mobile of all, and is best suited to accompany cavalry on account of its ability to travel rapidly. With the exception of the method of mounting the cannoneers, there was not any difference between the classes of field batteries except as they were divided between "light" and "heavy." In the photograph above no one is riding on the gun-carriages, but all have separate mounts. Battery A of the Second United States Artillery was in Washington in January, 1861, and took part in the expedition for the relief of Fort Pickens, Florida. It went to the Peninsula, fought at Mechanicsville May 23–24, 1862, and took part in the Seven Days' battles before Richmond June 25th to July 1st. Batteries C and G of the Third United States Artillery were at San Francisco, California, till October 1861, when they came East, and also went to the Peninsula and served at Yorktown and in the Seven Days.

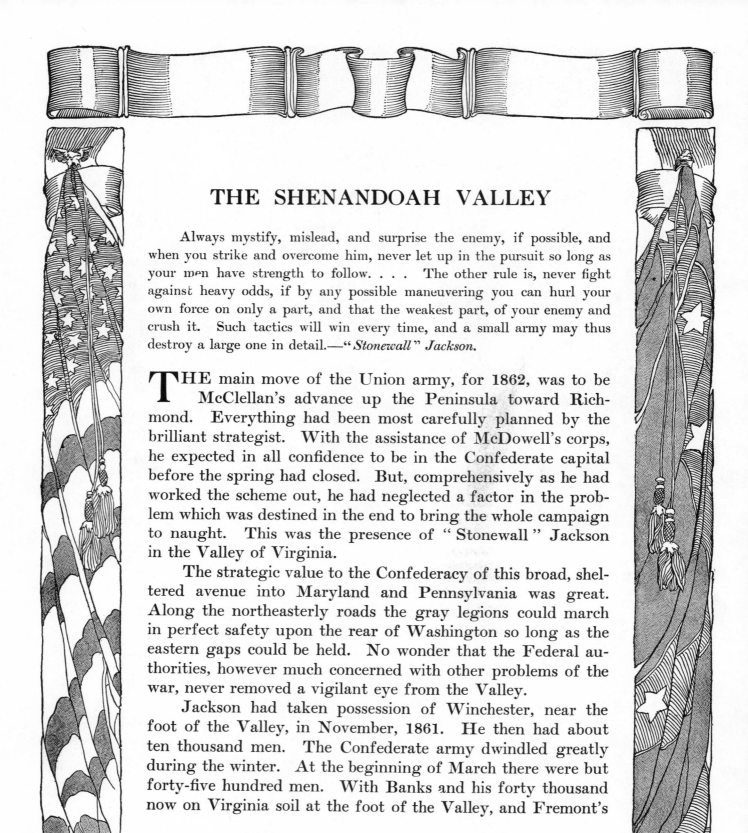

THE SHENANDOAH VALLEY

Always mystify, mislead, and surprise the enemy, if possible, and when you strike and overcome him, never let up in the pursuit so long as your men have strength to follow. . . . The other rule is, never fight against heavy odds, if by any possible maneuvering you can hurl your own force on only a part, and that the weakest part, of your enemy and crush it. Such tactics will win every time, and a small army may thus destroy a large one in detail.—"Stonewall" Jackson.

THE main move of the Union army, for 1862, was to be McClellan's advance up the Peninsula toward Richmond. Everything had been most carefully planned by the brilliant strategist. With the assistance of McDowell's corps, he expected in all confidence to be in the Confederate capital before the spring had closed. But, comprehensively as he had worked the scheme out, he had neglected a factor in the problem which was destined in the end to bring the whole campaign to naught. This was the presence of "Stonewall" Jackson in the Valley of Virginia.

The strategic value to the Confederacy of this broad, sheltered avenue into Maryland and Pennsylvania was great. Along the northeasterly roads the gray legions could march in perfect safety upon the rear of Washington so long as the eastern gaps could be held. No wonder that the Federal authorities, however much concerned with other problems of the war, never removed a vigilant eye from the Valley.

Jackson had taken possession of Winchester, near the foot of the Valley, in November, 1861. He then had about ten thousand men. The Confederate army dwindled greatly during the winter. At the beginning of March there were but forty-five hundred men. With Banks and his forty thousand now on Virginia soil at the foot of the Valley, and Fremont's

"STONEWALL" JACKSON
AT WINCHESTER
1862

It is the great good fortune of American hero-lovers that they can gaze here upon the features of Thomas Jonathan Jackson precisely as that brilliant Lieutenant-General of the Confederate States Army appeared during his masterly "Valley Campaign" of 1862. Few photographers dared to approach this man, whose silence and modesty were as deep as his mastery of warfare. Jackson lived much to himself. Indeed, his plans were rarely known even to his immediate subordinates, and herein lay the secret of those swift and deadly surprises that raised him to first rank among the world's military figures. Jackson's ability and efficiency won the utter confidence of his ragged troops; and their marvelous forced marches, their contempt for privations if under his guidance, put into his hands a living weapon such as no other leader in the mighty conflict had ever wielded.

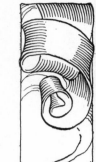

army approaching the head, why should the Federal commander even think about this insignificant fragment of his foe? But the records of war have shown that a small force, guided by a master mind, sometimes accomplishes more in effective results than ten times the number under a less active and able commander.

The presence of Banks compelled Jackson to withdraw to Woodstock, fifty miles south of Winchester. If McClellan ever experienced any anxiety as to affairs in the Valley, it seems to have left him now, for he ordered Banks to Manassas on March 16th to cover Washington, leaving General Shields and his division of seven thousand men to hold the Valley. When Jackson heard of the withdrawal, he resolved that, cut off as he was from taking part in the defense of Richmond, he would do what he could to prevent any aggrandizement of McClellan's forces.

Shields hastened to his station at Winchester, and Jackson, on the 23d of March, massed his troops at Kernstown, about three miles south of the former place. Deceived as to the strength of his adversary, he led his weary men to an attack on Shields' right flank about three o'clock in the afternoon. He carried the ridge where the Federals were posted, but the energy of his troops was spent, and they had to give way to the reserves of the Union army after three hours of stubborn contest. The Federal ranks were diminished by six hundred; the Confederate force by more than seven hundred. Kernstown was a Union victory; yet never in history did victory bring such ultimate disaster upon the victors.

At Washington the alarm was intense over Jackson's audacious attack. Williams' division of Banks' troops was halted on its way to Manassas and sent back to Winchester. Mr. Lincoln transferred Blenker's division, nine thousand strong, to Fremont. These things were done at once, but they were by no means the most momentous consequence of Kernstown. The President began to fear that Jackson's goal was

NANCY HART
THE CONFEDERATE GUIDE AND SPY

The women of the mountain districts of Virginia were as ready to do scout and spy work for the Confederate leaders as were their men-folk. Famous among these fearless girls who knew every inch of the regions in which they lived was Nancy Hart. So valuable was her work as a guide, so cleverly and often had she led Jackson's cavalry upon the Federal outposts in West Virginia, that the Northern Government offered a large reward for her capture. Lieutenant-Colonel Starr of the Ninth West Virginia finally caught her at Summerville in July, 1862. While in a temporary prison, she faced the camera for the first time in her life, displaying more alarm in front of the innocent contrivance than if it had been a body of Federal soldiery. She posed for an itinerant photographer, and her captors placed the hat decorated with a military feather upon her head. Nancy managed to get hold of her guard's musket, shot him dead, and escaped on Colonel Starr's horse to the nearest Confederate detachment. A few days later, July 25th, she led two hundred troopers under Major Bailey to Summerville. They reached the town at four in the morning, completely surprising two companies of the Ninth West Virginia. They fired three houses, captured Colonel Starr, Lieutenant Stivers and other officers, and a large number of the men, and disappeared immediately over the Sutton road. The Federals made no resistance.

Washington. After consulting six of his generals he became
convinced that McClellan had not arranged proper protection
for the city. Therefore, McDowell and his corps of thirty-
seven thousand men were ordered to remain at Manassas.
The Valley grew to greater importance in the Federal eyes.
Banks was made entirely independent of McClellan and the
defense of this region became his sole task. McClellan, to his
great chagrin, saw his force depleted by forty-six thousand
men. There were now four Union generals in the East operating independently one of the other.

General Ewell with eight thousand troops on the upper
Rappahannock and General Johnson with two brigades were
now ordered to cooperate with Jackson. These reenforcements were badly needed. Schenck and Milroy, of Fremont's
corps, began to threaten Johnson. Banks, with twenty thousand, was near Harrisonburg.

The Confederate leader left General Ewell to watch
Banks while he made a dash for Milroy and Schenck. He
fought them at McDowell on May 8th and they fled precipitately to rejoin Fremont. The swift-acting Jackson now darted
at Banks, who had fortified himself at Strasburg. Jackson
stopped long enough to be joined by Ewell. He did not attack
Strasburg, but stole across the Massanutten Mountain unknown to Banks, and made for Front Royal, where a strong
Union detachment was stationed under Colonel Kenly. Early
on the afternoon of May 23d, Ewell rushed from the forest.
Kenly and his men fled before them toward Winchester. A
large number were captured by the cavalry before they had
gotten more than four miles away.

Banks at Strasburg realized that Jackson was approaching from the rear, the thing he had least expected and had
made no provision for. His fortifications protected his front
alone. There was nothing to be done but retreat to Winchester. Even that was prevented by the remarkable speed
of Jackson's men, who could march as much as thirty-five

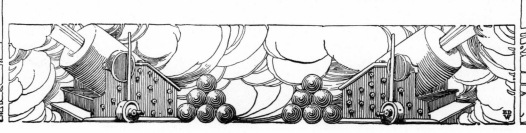

THE GERMAN DIVISION SENT AGAINST JACKSON

Blenker's division, composed of three brigades of German volunteers, was detached from the Army of the Potomac in March, 1862, to assist Frémont in his operations against Jackson. The German troops were but poorly equipped, many of them carrying old-pattern Belgian and Austrian muskets. When they united with Frémont he was obliged to rearm them with Springfield rifles from his own stores. When the combined forces met Jackson and Ewell at Cross Keys, five of Blenker's regiments were sent forward to the first attack. In the picture Brigadier-General Louis Blenker is standing, with his hand on his belt, before the door. At his left is Prince Felix Salm-Salm, a Prussian military officer, who joined the Federal army as a colonel of volunteers. At the right of Blenker is General Stahel, who led the advance of the Federal left at Cross Keys.

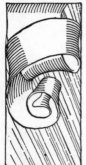

miles a day. On May 24th, the Confederates overtook and struck the receding Union flank near Newtown, inflicting heavy loss and taking many prisoners. Altogether, three thousand of Banks' men fell into Jackson's hands.

This exploit was most opportune for the Southern arms. It caused the final ruin of McClellan's hopes. Banks received one more attack from Ewell's division the next day as he passed through Winchester on his way to the shelter of the Potomac. He crossed at Williamsport late the same evening and wrote the President that his losses, though serious enough, might have been far worse " considering the very great disparity of forces engaged, and the long-matured plans of the enemy, which aimed at nothing less than entire capture of our force." Mr. Lincoln now rescinded his resolution to send McDowell to McClellan. Instead, he transferred twenty thousand of the former's men to Fremont and informed McClellan that he was not, after all, to have the aid of McDowell's forty thousand men.

Fremont was coming from the west; Shields lay in the other direction, but Jackson was not the man to be trapped. He managed to hold Fremont while he marched his main force quickly up the Valley. At Port Republic he drove Carroll's brigade of Shields' division away and took possession of a bridge which Colonel Carroll had neglected to burn. Fremont in pursuit was defeated by Ewell at Cross Keys. Jackson immediately put his force of twelve thousand over the Shenandoah at Port Republic and burned the bridge. Safe from the immediate attack by Fremont, he fell upon Tyler and Carroll, who had not more than three thousand men between them. The Federals made a brave stand, but after many hours' fighting were compelled to retreat. Jackson emerged through Swift Run Gap on the 17th of June, to assist in turning the Union right on the Peninsula, and Banks and Shields, baffled and checkmated at every move, finally withdrew from the Valley.

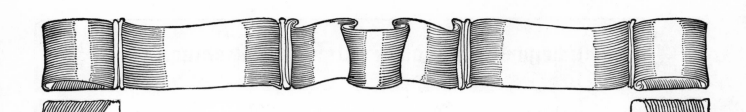

THE SEVEN DAYS' BATTLES

McClellan's one hope, one purpose, was to march his army out of the swamps and escape from the ceaseless Confederate assaults to a point on James River where the resistless fire of the gunboats might protect his men from further attack and give them a chance to rest. To that end, he retreated night and day, standing at bay now and then as the hunted stag does, and fighting desperately for the poor privilege of running away.

And the splendid fighting of his men was a tribute to the skill and genius with which he had created an effective army out of what he had described as "regiments cowering upon the banks of the Potomac, some perfectly raw, others dispirited by recent defeat, others going home." Out of a demoralized and disorganized mass reenforced by utterly untrained civilians, McClellan had within a few months created an army capable of stubbornly contesting every inch of ground even while effecting a retreat the very thought of which might well have disorganized an army. —*George Cary Eggleston, in " The History of the Confederate War."*

GENERAL LEE was determined that the operations in front of Richmond should not degenerate into a siege, and that the Army of Northern Virginia should no longer be on the defensive. To this end, early in the summer of 1862, he proceeded to increase his fighting force so as to make it more nearly equal in number to that of his antagonist. Every man who could be spared from other sections of the South was called to Richmond. Numerous earthworks soon made their appearance along the roads and in the fields about the Confederate capital, giving the city the appearance of a fortified camp. The new commander in an address to the troops said that the army had made its last retreat.

Meanwhile, with the spires of Richmond in view, the Army of the Potomac was acclimating itself to a Virginia summer. The whole face of the country for weeks had been a

veritable bog. Now that the sweltering heat of June was coming on, the malarious swamps were fountains of disease. The polluted waters of the sluggish streams soon began to tell on the health of the men. Malaria and typhoid were prevalent; the hospitals were crowded, and the death rate was appalling.

Such conditions were not inspiring to either general or army. McClellan was still hoping for substantial reenforcements. McDowell, with his forty thousand men, had been promised him, but he was doomed to disappointment from that source. Yet in the existing state of affairs he dared not be inactive. South of the Chickahominy, the army was almost secure from surprise, owing to well-protected rifle-pits flanked by marshy thickets or covered with felled trees. But the Federal forces were still divided by the fickle stream, and this was a constant source of anxiety to the commander. He proceeded to transfer all of his men to the Richmond side of the river, excepting the corps of Franklin and Fitz John Porter. About the middle of June, General McCall with a force of eleven thousand men joined the Federal army north of the Chickahominy, bringing the entire fighting strength to about one hundred and five thousand. So long as there remained the slightest hope of additional soldiers, it was impossible to withdraw all of the army from the York side of the Peninsula, and it remained divided.

That was a brilliant initial stroke of the Confederate general when he sent his famous cavalry leader, J. E. B. Stuart, with about twelve hundred Virginia troopers, to encircle the army of McClellan. Veiling his intentions with the utmost secrecy, Stuart started June 12, 1862, in the direction of Fredericksburg as if to reenforce "Stonewall" Jackson. The first night he bivouacked in the pine woods of Hanover. No fires were kindled, and when the morning dawned, his men swung upon their mounts without the customary bugle-call of "Boots and Saddles." Turning to the east, he surprised and captured a Federal picket; swinging around a corner of the road, he

McDOWELL AND McCLELLAN—TWO UNION LEADERS WHOSE
PLANS "STONEWALL" JACKSON FOILED

In General McClellan's plan for the Peninsula Campaign of 1862, General McDowell, with the First Army Corps of 37,000 men, was assigned a m st important part, that of joining him before Richmond. Lincoln had reluctantly consented to the plan, fearing sufficient protection was not provided for Washington. By the battle of Kernstown, March 23d, in the Valley of Virginia, Jackson, though defeated, so alarmed the Administration that McDowell was ordered to remain at Manassas to protect the capital. The reverse at Kernstown was therefore a real triumph for Jackson, but with his small force he had to keep up the game of holding McDowell, Banks, and Frémont from reënforcing McClellan. If he failed, 80,000 troops might move up to Richmond from the west while McClellan was approaching from the North. But Jackson, on May 23d and 25th, surprised Banks' forces at Front Royal and Winchester, forcing a retreat to the Potomac. At the news of this event McDowell was ordered not to join McClellan in front of Richmond.

suddenly came upon a squadron of Union cavalry. The Confederate yell rent the air and a swift, bold charge by the Southern troopers swept the foe on.

They had not traveled far when they came again to a force drawn up in columns of fours, ready to dispute the passage of the road. This time the Federals were about to make the charge. A squadron of the Confederates moved forward to meet them. Some Union skirmishers in their effort to get to the main body of their troops swept into the advancing Confederates and carried the front ranks of the squadron with them. These isolated Confederates found themselves in an extremely perilous position, being gradually forced into the Federal main body. Before they could extricate themselves, nearly every one in the unfortunate front rank was shot or cut down.

The Southern cavalrymen swept on and presently found themselves nearing the York River Railroad—McClellan's supply line. As they approached Tunstall's Station they charged down upon it, with their characteristic yell, completely surprising a company of Federal infantry stationed there. These at once surrendered. Telegraph wires were cut and a tree felled across the track to obstruct the road. This had hardly been done before the shriek of a locomotive was heard. A train bearing Union troops came thundering along, approaching the station. The engineer, taking in the situation at a glance, put on a full head of steam and made a rush for the obstruction, which was easily brushed aside. As the train went through a cut the Confederates fired upon it, wounding and killing some of the Federal soldiers in the cars.

Riding all through a moonlit night, the raiders reached Sycamore Ford of the Chickahominy at break of day. As usual this erratic stream was overflowing its banks. They started to ford it, but finding that it would be a long and wearisome task, a bridge was hastily improvised at another place where the passage was made with more celerity. Now,

Copyright by *Review of Reviews Co.*

JOHNSTON AND LEE—A PHOTOGRAPH OF 1869.

These men look enough alike to be brothers. They were so in arms, at West Point, in Mexico and throughout the war. General Joseph E. Johnston (on the left), who had led the Confederate forces since Bull Run, was wounded at Fair Oaks. That wound gave Robert E. Lee (on the right) his opportunity to act as leader. After Fair Oaks, Johnston retired from the command of the army defending Richmond. The new commander immediately grasped the possibilities of the situation which confronted him. The promptness and completeness with which he blighted McClellan's high hopes of reaching Richmond showed at one stroke that the Confederacy had found its great general. It was only through much sifting that the North at last picked military leaders that could rival him in the field.

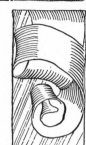

on the south bank of the river, haste was made for the confines of Richmond, where, at dawn of the following day, the troopers dropped from their saddles, a weary but happy body of cavalry.

Lee thus obtained exact and detailed information of the position of McClellan's army, and he laid out his campaign accordingly. Meanwhile his own forces in and about Richmond were steadily increasing. He was planning for an army of nearly one hundred thousand and he now demonstrated his ability as a strategist. Word had been despatched to Jackson in the Shenandoah to bring his troops to fall upon the right wing of McClellan's army. At the same time Lee sent General Whiting north to make a feint of joining Jackson and moving upon Washington. The ruse proved eminently successful. The authorities at Washington were frightened, and McClellan received no more reenforcements. Jackson now began a hide-and-seek game among the mountains, and managed to have rumors spread of his army being in several places at the same time, while skilfully veiling his actual movements.

It was not until the 25th of June that McClellan had definite knowledge of Jackson's whereabouts. He was then located at Ashland, north of the Chickahominy, within striking distance of the Army of the Potomac. McClellan was surprised but he was not unprepared. Seven days before he had arranged for a new base of supplies on the James, which would now prove useful if he were driven south of the Chickahominy.

On the very day he heard of Jackson's arrival at Ashland, McClellan was pushing his men forward to begin his siege of Richmond—that variety of warfare which his engineering soul loved so well. His advance guard was within four miles of the Confederate capital. His strong fortifications were bristling upon every vantage point, and his fond hope was that within a few days, at most, his efficient artillery, for which the Army of the Potomac was famous, would be

THE FLEET THAT FED THE ARMY

THE ABANDONED BASE

White House, Virginia, June 27, 1862.—Up the James and the Pamunkey to White House Landing came the steam and sailing vessels laden with supplies for McClellan's second attempt to reach Richmond. Tons of ammunition and thousands of rations were sent forward from here to the army on the Chickahominy in June, 1862. A short month was enough to cause McClellan to again change his plans, and the army base was moved to the James River. The Richmond and York Railroad was lit up by burning cars along its course to the Chickahominy. Little was left to the Confederates save the charred ruins of the White House itself.

belching forth its sheets of fire and lead into the beleagured city. In front of the Union encampment, near Fair Oaks, was a thick entanglement of scrubby pines, vines, and ragged bushes, full of ponds and marshes. This strip of woodland was less than five hundred yards wide. Beyond it was an open field half a mile in width. The Union soldiers pressed through the thicket to see what was on the other side and met the Confederate pickets among the trees. The advancing column drove them back. Upon emerging into the open, the Federal troops found it filled with rifle-pits, earthworks, and redoubts. At once they were met with a steady and incessant fire, which continued from eight in the morning until five in the afternoon. At times the contest almost reached the magnitude of a battle, and in the end the Union forces occupied the former position of their antagonists. This passage of arms, sometimes called the affair of Oak Grove or the Second Battle of Fair Oaks, was the prelude to the Seven Days' Battles.

The following day, June 26th, had been set by General " Stonewall " Jackson as the date on which he would join Lee, and together they would fall upon the right wing of the Army of the Potomac. The Federals north of the Chickahominy were under the direct command of General Fitz John Porter. Defensive preparations had been made on an extensive scale. Field works, heavily armed with artillery, and rifle-pits, well manned, covered the roads and open fields and were often concealed by timber from the eye of the opposing army. The extreme right of the Union line lay near Mechanicsville on the upper Chickahominy. A tributary of this stream from the north was Beaver Dam Creek, upon whose left bank was a steep bluff, commanding the valley to the west. This naturally strong position, now well defended, was almost impregnable to an attack from the front.

Before sunrise of the appointed day the Confederate forces were at the Chickahominy bridges, awaiting the arrival of Jackson. To reach these some of the regiments had

ELLERSON'S MILL—WHERE HILL ASSAULTED.

Not until after nightfall of June 26, 1862, did the Confederates of General A. P. Hill's division cease their assaults upon this position where General McCall's men were strongly entrenched. Time after time the Confederates charged over the ground we see here at Ellerson's Mill, near Mechanicsville. Till 9 o'clock at night they continued to pour volleys at the position, and then at last withdrew. The victory was of little use to the Federals, for Jackson on the morrow, having executed one of the flanking night marches at which he was an adept, fell upon the Federal rear at Gaines' Mill.

THE WASTE OF WAR

Railroad trains loaded with tons of food and ammunition were run deliberately at full speed off the embankment shown in the left foreground. They plunged headlong into the waters of the Pamunkey. This was the readiest means that McClellan could devise for keeping his immense quantity of stores out of the hands of the Confederates in his hasty change of base from White House to the James after Gaines' Mill. This was the bridge of the Richmond and York River Railroad, and was destroyed June 28, 1862, to render the railroad useless to the Confederates.

marched the greater part of the night. For once Jackson was behind time. The morning hours came and went. Noon passed and Jackson had not arrived. At three o'clock, General A. P. Hill, growing impatient, decided to put his troops in motion. Crossing at Meadow Bridge, he marched his men along the north side of the Chickahominy, and at Mechanicsville was joined by the commands of Longstreet and D. H. Hill. Driving the Union outposts to cover, the Confederates swept across the low approach to Beaver Dam Creek. A murderous fire from the batteries on the cliff poured into their ranks. Gallantly the attacking columns withstood the deluge of leaden hail and drew near the creek. A few of the more aggressive reached the opposite bank but their repulse was severe.

Later in the afternoon relief was sent to Hill, who again attempted to force the Union position at Ellerson's Mill, where the slope of the west bank came close to the borders of the little stream. From across the open fields, in full view of the defenders of the cliff, the Confederates moved down the slope. They were in range of the Federal batteries, but the fire was reserved. Every artilleryman was at his post ready to fire at the word; the soldiers were in the rifle-pits sighting along the glittering barrels of their muskets with fingers on the triggers. As the approaching columns reached the stream they turned with the road that ran parallel to the bank.

From every waiting field-piece the shells came screaming through the air. Volley after volley of musketry was poured into the flanks of the marching Southerners. The hillside was soon covered with the victims of the gallant charge. Twilight fell upon the warring troops and there were no signs of a cessation of the unequal combat. Night fell, and still from the heights the lurid flames burst in a display of glorious pyrotechnics. It was nine o'clock when Hill finally drew back his shattered regiments, to await the coming of the morning. The Forty-fourth Georgia regiment suffered most in the fight;

THE BRIDGE THAT STOOD

The force under General McCall was stationed by McClellan on June 19, 1862, to observe the Meadow and Mechanicsville bridges over the Chickahominy which had only partially been destroyed.   On the afternoon of June 26th, General A. P. Hill crossed at Meadow Bridge, driving the Union skirmish-line back to Beaver Dam Creek.   The divisions of D. H. Hill and Longstreet had been waiting at Mechanicsville Bridge (shown in this photograph) since 8 A.M. for A. P. Hill to open the way for them to cross.   They passed over in time to bear a decisive part in the Confederate attack at Gaines' Mill on the 27th.

DOING DOUBLE DUTY

Here are some of McClellan's staff-officers during the strenuous period of the Seven Days' Battles.   One commonly supposes that a general's staff has little to do but wear gold lace and transmit orders.   But it is their duty to multiply the eyes and ears and thinking power of the leader.   Without them he could not direct the movements of his army.   There were so few regular officers of ripe experience that members of the staff were invariably made regimental commanders, and frequently were compelled to divide their time between leading their troops into action and reporting to and consulting with their superior.

three hundred and thirty-five being the dreadful toll, in dead and wounded, paid for its efforts to break down the Union position. Dropping back to the rear this ill-fated regiment attempted to re-form its broken ranks, but its officers were all among those who had fallen. Both armies now prepared for another day and a renewal of the conflict.

The action at Beaver Dam Creek convinced McClellan that Jackson was really approaching with a large force, and he decided to begin his change of base from the Pamunkey to the James, leaving Porter and the Fifth Corps still on the left bank of the Chickahominy, to prevent Jackson's fresh troops from interrupting this great movement. It was, indeed, a gigantic undertaking, for it involved marching an army of a hundred thousand men, including cavalry and artillery, across the marshy peninsula. A train of five thousand heavily loaded wagons and many siege-guns had to be transported; nearly three thousand cattle on the hoof had to be driven. From White House the supplies could be shipped by the York River Railroad as far as Savage's Station. Thence to the James, a distance of seventeen miles, they had to be carried overland along a road intersected by many others from which a watchful opponent might easily attack. General Casey's troops, guarding the supplies at White House, were transferred by way of the York and the James to Harrison's Landing on the latter river. The transports were loaded with all the material they could carry. The rest was burned, or put in cars. These cars, with locomotives attached, were then run into the river.

On the night of June 26th, McCall's Federal division, at Beaver Dam Creek, was directed to fall back to the bridges across the Chickahominy near Gaines' Mill and there make a stand, for the purpose of holding the Confederate army. During the night the wagon trains and heavy guns were quietly moved across the river. Just before daylight the operation of removing the troops began. The Confederates were

THE RETROGRADE CROSSING.

LOWER BRIDGE ON THE CHICKAHOMINY

Woodbury's Bridge on the Chickahominy. Little did General D. F. Woodbury's engineers suspect, when they built this bridge, early in June, 1862, as a means of communication between the divided wings of McClellan's army on the Chickahominy that it would be of incalculable service during battle. When the right wing, under General Fitz John Porter, was engaged on the field of Gaines' Mill against almost the entire army of Lee, across this bridge the division of General Slocum marched from its position in the trenches in front of Richmond on the south bank of the river to the support of Porter's men. The battle lasted until nightfall and then the Federal troops moved across this bridge and rejoined the main forces of the Federal army. Woodbury's engineers built several bridges across the Chickahominy, but among them all the bridge named for their commander proved to be, perhaps, the most serviceable.

equally alert, for about the same time they opened a heavy fire on the retreating columns. This march of five miles was a continuous skirmish; but the Union forces, ably and skilfully handled, succeeded in reaching their new position on the Chickahominy heights.

The morning of the new day was becoming hot and sultry as the men of the Fifth Corps made ready for action in their new position. The selection of this ground had been well made; it occupied a series of heights fronted on the west by a sickle-shaped stream. The battle-lines followed the course of this creek, in the arc of a circle curving outward in the direction of the approaching army. The land beyond the creek was an open country, through which Powhite Creek meandered sluggishly, and beyond this a wood densely tangled with undergrowth. Around the Union position were also many patches of wooded land affording cover for the troops and screening the reserves from view.

Porter had learned from deserters and others that Jackson's forces, united to those of Longstreet and the two Hills, were advancing with grim determination to annihilate the Army of the Potomac. He had less than eighteen thousand men to oppose the fifty thousand Confederates. To protect the Federals, trees had been felled along a small portion of their front, out of which barriers protected with rails and knapsacks were erected. Porter had considerable artillery, but only a small part of it could be used. It was two o'clock, on June 27th, when General A. P. Hill swung his division into line for the attack. He was unsupported by the other divisions, which had not yet arrived, but his columns moved rapidly toward the Union front. The assault was terrific, but twenty-six guns threw a hail-storm of lead into his ranks. Under the cover of this magnificent execution of artillery, the infantry sent messages of death to the approaching lines of gray.

The Confederate front recoiled from the incessant outpour of grape, canister, and shell. The heavy cloud of battle

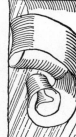

A VAIN RIDE TO SAFETY

During the retreat after Gaines' Mill, McClellan's army was straining every nerve to extricate itself and present a strong front to Lee before he could strike a telling blow at its untenable position. Wagon trains were struggling across the almost impassable White Oak Swamp, while the troops were striving to hold Savage's Station to protect the movement. Thither on flat cars were sent the wounded as we see them in the picture. The rear guard of the Army of the Potomac had hastily provided such field hospital facilities as they could. We see the camp near the railroad with the passing wagon trains in the lower picture. But attention to these wounded men was, perforce, secondary to the necessity of holding the position. Their hopes of relief from their suffering were to be blighted. Lee was about to fall upon the Federal rear guard at Savage's Station. Instead of to a haven of refuge, these men were being railroaded toward the field of carnage, where they must of necessity be left by their retreating companions.

THE STAND AT SAVAGE'S STATION

Here we see part of the encampment to hold which the divisions of Richardson, Sedgwick, Smith, and Franklin fought valiantly when Magruder and the Confederates fell upon them, June 29, 1862. Along the Richmond & York River Railroad, seen in the picture, the Confederates rolled a heavy rifled gun, mounted on car-wheels. They turned its deadly fire steadily upon the defenders. The Federals fought fiercely and managed to hold their ground till nightfall, when hundreds of their bravest soldiers lay on the field and had to be left alone with their wounded comrades who had arrived on the flat cars.

smoke rose lazily through the air, twisting itself among the trees and settling over the forest like a pall. The tremendous momentum of the repulse threw the Confederates into great confusion. Men were separated from their companies and for a time it seemed as if a rout were imminent. The Federals, pushing out from under the protection of their great guns, now became the assailants. The Southerners were being driven back. Many had left the field in disorder. Others threw themselves on the ground to escape the withering fire, while some tenaciously held their places. This lasted for two hours. General Slocum arrived with his division of Franklin's corps, and his arrival increased the ardor of the victorious Federals.

It was then that Lee ordered a general attack upon the entire Union front. Reenforcements were brought to take the place of the shattered regiments. The engagement began with a sharp artillery fire from the Confederate guns. Then the troops moved forward, once more to assault the Union position. In the face of a heavy fire they rushed across the sedgy lowland, pressed up the hillside at fearful sacrifice and pushed against the Union front. It was a death grapple for the mastery of the field. General Lee, sitting on his horse on an eminence where he could observe the progress of the battle, saw, coming down the road, General Hood, of Jackson's corps, who was bringing his brigade into the fight. Riding forward to meet him, Lee directed that he should try to break the line. Hood, disposing his men for the attack, sent them forward, but, reserving the Fourth Texas for his immediate command, he marched it into an open field, halted, and addressed it, giving instructions that no man should fire until ordered and that all should keep together in line.

The forward march was sounded, and the intrepid Hood, leading his men, started for the Union breastworks eight hundred yards away. They moved at a rapid pace across the open, under a continually increasing shower of shot and shell. At every step the ranks grew thinner and thinner. As they

THE TANGLED RETREAT

Through this well-nigh impassable morass of White Oak Swamp, across a single long bridge, McClellan's wagon trains were being hurried the last days of June, 1862. On the morning of the 30th, the rear-guard of the army was hastily tramping after them, and by ten o'clock had safely crossed and destroyed the bridge. They had escaped in the nick of time, for at noon "Stonewall" Jackson opened fire upon Richardson's division and a terrific artillery battle ensued for the possession of this, the single crossing by which it was possible to attack McClellan's rear. The Federal batteries were compelled to retire but Jackson's crossing was prevented on that day by the infantry.

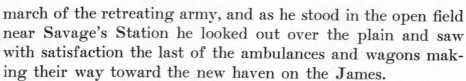

march of the retreating army, and as he stood in the open field near Savage's Station he looked out over the plain and saw with satisfaction the last of the ambulances and wagons making their way toward the new haven on the James.

In the morning of that same day he had already held at bay the forces of Magruder at Allen's Farm. On his way from Fair Oaks, which he left at daylight, he had halted his men at what is known as the "Peach Orchard," and from nine o'clock till eleven had resisted a spirited fire of musketry and artillery. And now as the grim warrior, on this Sunday afternoon in June, turned his eyes toward the Chickahominy he saw a great cloud of dust rising on the horizon. It was raised by the troops of General Magruder who was pressing close behind the Army of the Potomac. The Southern field-guns were placed in position. A contrivance, consisting of a heavy gun mounted on a railroad car and called the "Land Merrimac," was pushed into position and opened fire upon the Union forces. The battle began with a fine play of artillery. For an hour not a musket was fired. The army of blue remained motionless. Then the mass of gray moved across the field and from the Union guns the long tongues of flame darted into the ranks before them. The charge was met with vigor and soon the battle raged over the entire field. Both sides stood their ground till darkness again closed the contest, and nearly eight hundred brave men had fallen in this Sabbath evening's battle. Before midnight Sumner had withdrawn his men and was following after the wagon trains.

The Confederates were pursuing McClellan's army in two columns, Jackson closely following Sumner, while Longstreet was trying to cut off the Union forces by a flank movement. On the last day of June, at high noon, Jackson reached the White Oak Swamp. But the bridge was gone. He attempted to ford the passage, but the Union troops were there to prevent it. While Jackson was trying to force his way across the stream, there came to him the sound of a desperate battle being

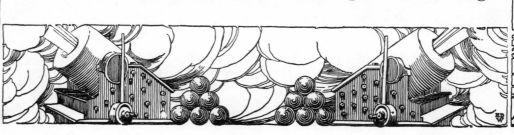

A GRIM CAPTURE

The Second and Sixth Corps of the Federal Army repelled a desperate attack of General Magruder at Savage Station on June 29th. The next day they disappeared, plunging into the depths of White Oak Swamp, leaving only the brave medical officers behind, doing what they could to relieve the sufferings of the men that had to be abandoned. Here we see them at work upon the wounded, who have been gathered from the field. Nothing but the strict arrest of the stern sergeant Death can save these men from capture, and when the Confederates occupied Savage's Station on the morning of June 30th, twenty-five hundred sick and wounded men and their medical attendants became prisoners of war. The Confederate hospital facilities were already taxed to their full capacity in caring for Lee's wounded, and most of these men were confronted on that day with the prospect of lingering for months in the military prisons of the South. The brave soldiers lying helpless here were wounded at Gaines' Mill on June 27th and removed to the great field-hospital established at Savage's Station. The photograph was taken just before Sumner and Franklin withdrew the rear-guard of their columns on the morning of June 30th.

NaN# Seven Days—The Confederate Capital Saved ❖

NaNJune
1862

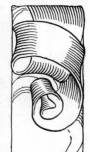

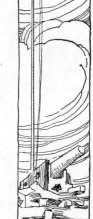

reached the crest of a small ridge, one hundred and fifty yards from the Union line, the batteries in front and on the flank sent a storm of shell and canister plowing into their already depleted files. They quickened their pace as they passed down the slope and across the creek. Not a shot had they fired and amid the sulphurous atmosphere of battle, with the wing of death hovering over all, they fixed bayonets and dashed up the hill into the Federal line. With a shout they plunged through the felled timber and over the breastworks. The Union line had been pierced and was giving way. It was falling back toward the Chickahominy bridges, and the retreat was threatening to develop into a general rout. The twilight was closing in and the day was all but lost to the Army of the Potomac. Now a great shout was heard from the direction of the bridge; and, pushing through the stragglers at the river bank were seen the brigades of French and Meagher, detached from Sumner's corps, coming to the rescue. General Meagher, in his shirt sleeves, was leading his men up the bluff and confronted the Confederate battle line. This put a stop to the pursuit and as night was at hand the Southern soldiers withdrew. The battle of Gaines' Mill, or the Chickahominy, was over.

When Lee came to the banks of the little river the next morning he found his opponent had crossed over and destroyed the bridges. The Army of the Potomac was once more united. During the day the Federal wagon trains were safely passed over White Oak Swamp and then moved on toward the James River. Lee did not at first divine McClellan's intention. He still believed that the Federal general would retreat down the Peninsula, and hesitated therefore to cross the Chickahominy and give up the command of the lower bridges. But now on the 29th the signs of the movement to the James were unmistakable. Early on that morning Longstreet and A. P. Hill were ordered to recross the Chickahominy by the New Bridge and Huger and Magruder were sent in hot pursuit of the Federal forces. It was the brave Sumner who covered the

HEROES OF MALVERN HILL

Brigadier-General J. H. Martindale (seated) and his staff, July 1, 1862. Fitz John Porter's Fifth Corps and Couch's division, Fourth Corps, bore the brunt of battle at Malvern Hill where the troops of McClellan withstood the terrific attacks of Lee's combined and superior forces. Fiery "Prince John" Magruder hurled column after column against the left of the Federal line, but every charge was met and repulsed through the long hot summer afternoon. Martindale's brigade of the Fifth Corps was early called into action, and its commander, by the gallant fighting of his troops, won the brevet of Major-General.

THE NAVY LENDS A HAND

Officers of the *Monitor* at Malvern Hill. Glad indeed were the men of the Army of the Potomac as they emerged from their perilous march across White Oak Swamp to hear the firing of the gunboats on the James. It told them the Confederates had not yet pre-empted the occupation of Malvern Hill, which General Fitz John Porter's Corps was holding. Before the battle opened McClellan went aboard the *Galena* to consult with Commodore John Rodgers about a suitable base on the James. The gunboats of the fleet supported the flanks of the army during the battle and are said to have silenced one of the Confederate batteries.

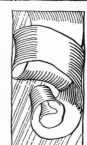
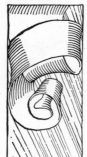

fought not more than two miles away, but he was powerless to give aid.

Longstreet and A. P. Hill had come upon the Federal regiments at Glendale, near the intersection of the Charles City road, guarding the right flank of the retreat. It was Longstreet who, about half-past two, made one of his characteristic onslaughts on that part of the Union army led by General McCall. It was repulsed with heavy loss. Again and again attacks were made. Each brigade seemed to act on its own behalf. They hammered here, there, and everywhere. Repulsed at one place they charged at another. The Eleventh Alabama, rushing out from behind a dense wood, charged across the open field in the face of the Union batteries. The men had to run a distance of six hundred yards. A heavy and destructive fire poured into their lines, but on they came, trailing their guns. The batteries let loose grape and canister, while volley after volley of musketry sent its death-dealing messages among the Southerners. But nothing except death itself could check their impetuous charge. When two hundred yards away they raised the Confederate yell and rushed for Randol's battery.

Pausing for an instant they deliver a volley and attempt to seize the guns. Bayonets are crossed and men engage in a hand-to-hand struggle. The contending masses rush together, asking and giving no quarter and struggling like so many tigers. Darkness is closing on the fearful scene, yet the fighting continues with unabated ferocity. There are the shouts of command, the clash and the fury of the battle, the sulphurous smoke, the flashes of fire streaking through the air, the yells of defiance, the thrust, the parry, the thud of the clubbed musket, the hiss of the bullet, the spouting blood, the death-cry, and beneath all lie the bodies of America's sons, some in blue and some in gray.

While Lee and his army were held in check by the events of June 30th at White Oak Swamp and the other battle at

Again we see the transports and supply schooners at anchor—this time at Harrison's Landing on the James River. In about a month, McClellan had changed the position of his army twice, shifting his base from the Pamunkey to the James. The position he held on Malvern Hill was abandoned after the victory of July 1, 1862, and the army marched to a new base farther down the James, where the heavy losses of men and supplies during the

COPYRIGHT BY PATRIOT PUB CO.

THE SECOND ARMY BASE

Seven Days could be made up without danger and delay. Harrison's Landing was the point selected, and here the army recuperated, wondering what would be the next step. Below we see the historic mansion which did service as General Porter's headquarters, one of McClellan's most efficient commanders. For his services during the Seven Days he was made Major-General of Volunteers. McClellan was his lifelong friend.

WESTOVER HOUSE: HEADQUARTERS OF GENERAL FITZ JOHN PORTER, HARRISON'S LANDING

Glendale or Nelson's Farm, the last of the wagon trains had arrived safely at Malvern Hill. The contest had hardly closed and the smoke had scarcely lifted from the blood-soaked field, when the Union forces were again in motion toward the James. By noon on July 1st the last division reached the position where McClellan decided to turn again upon his assailants. He had not long to wait, for the Confederate columns, led by Longstreet, were close on his trail, and a march of a few miles brought them to the Union outposts. They found the Army of the Potomac admirably situated to give defensive battle. Malvern Hill, a plateau, a mile and a half long and half as broad, with its top almost bare of woods, commanded a view of the country over which the Confederate army must approach. Along the western face of this plateau there are deep ravines falling abruptly in the direction of the James River; on the north and east is a gentle slope to the plain beneath, bordered by a thick forest. Around the summit of the hill, General Mc-Clellan had placed tier after tier of batteries, arranged like an amphitheater. Surmounting these on the crest were massed seven of his heaviest siege-guns. His army surrounded this hill, its left flank being protected by the gunboats on the river.

The morning and early afternoon were occupied with many Confederate attacks, sometimes formidable in their nature, but Lee planned for no general move until he could bring up a force that he considered sufficient to attack the strong Federal position. The Confederate orders were to advance when the signal, a yell, cheer, or shout from the men of Armistead's brigade, was given.

Late in the afternoon General D. H. Hill heard some shouting, followed by a roar of musketry. No other general seems to have heard it, for Hill made his attack alone. It was gallantly done, but no army could have withstood the galling fire of the batteries of the Army of the Potomac as they were massed upon Malvern Hill. All during the evening, brigade after brigade tried to force the Union lines. The gunners

ON DARING DUTY

Lieut.-Colonel Albert V. Colburn, a favorite Aide-de-Camp of General McClellan's.—Here is the bold soldier of the Green Mountain State who bore despatches about the fields of battle during the Seven Days. It was he who was sent galloping across the difficult and dangerous country to make sure that Franklin's division was retreating from White Oak Swamp, and then to carry orders to Sumner to fall back on Malvern Hill. Such were the tasks that constantly fell to the lot of the despatch bearer. Necessarily a man of quick and accurate judgment, perilous chances confronted him in his efforts to keep the movements of widely separated divisions in concert with the plans of the commander. The loss of his life might mean the loss of a battle; the failure to arrive in the nick of time with despatches might mean disaster for the army. Only the coolest headed of the officers could be trusted with this vital work in the field.

stood coolly and manfully by their batteries. The Confederates were not able to make concerted efforts, but the battle waxed hot nevertheless. They were forced to breast one of the most devastating storms of lead and canister to which an assaulting army has ever been subjected. The round shot and grape cut through the branches of the trees and the battle-field was soon in a cloud of smoke. Column after column of Southern soldiers rushed up to the death-dealing cannon, only to be mowed down. The thinned and ragged lines, with a valor born of desperation, rallied again and again to the charge, but to no avail. The batteries on the heights still hurled their missiles of death. The field below was covered with the dead and wounded of the Southland.

The gunboats in the river made the battle scene more awe-inspiring with their thunderous cannonading. Their heavy shells shrieked through the forest, and great limbs were torn from the trees as they hurtled by in their outburst of fury.

Night was falling. The combatants were no longer distinguishable except by the sheets of flame. It was nine o'clock before the guns ceased their fire, and only an occasional shot rang out over the bloody field of Malvern Hill.

The courageous though defeated Confederate, looking up the next day through the drenching rain to where had stood the embrasured wall with its grim batteries and lines of blue, that spoke death to so many of his companions-in-arms, saw only deserted ramparts. The Union army had retreated in the darkness of the night. But this time no foe harassed its march. Unmolested, it sought its new camp at Harrison's Landing, where it remained until August 3d, when, as President Lincoln had been convinced of the impracticability of operating from the James River as a base, orders were issued by General Halleck for the withdrawal of the Army of the Potomac from the Peninsula.

The net military result of the Seven Days was a disappointment to the South. Although thankful that the siege of

AVERELL—THE COLONEL WHO BLUFFED AN ARMY.

Colonel W. W. Averell and Staff.—This intrepid officer of the Third Pennsylvania Cavalry held the Federal position on Malvern Hill on the morning of July 2, 1862, with only a small guard, while McClellan completed the withdrawal of his army to Harrison's Landing. It was his duty to watch the movements of the Confederates and hold them back from any attempt to fall upon the retreating trains and troops. A dense fog in the early morning shut off the forces of A. P. Hill and Longstreet from his view. He had not a single fieldpiece with which to resist attack. When the mist cleared away, he kept up a great activity with his cavalry horses, making the Confederates believe that artillery was being brought up. With apparent reluctance he agreed to a truce of two hours in which the Confederates might bury the dead they left on the hillside the day before. Later, with an increased show of unwillingness, he extended the truce for another two hours. Just before they expired, Frank's Battery arrived to his support, with the news that the Army of the Potomac was safe. Colonel Averell rejoined it without the loss of a man.

[A—22]

Richmond had been raised, the Southern public believed that McClellan should not have been allowed to reach the James River with his army intact.

"That army," Eggleston states, "splendidly organized, superbly equipped, and strengthened rather than weakened in morale, lay securely at rest on the James River, within easy striking distance of Richmond. There was no knowing at what moment McClellan might hurl it again upon Richmond or upon that commanding key to Richmond—the Petersburg position. In the hands of a capable commander McClellan's army would at this time have been a more serious menace than ever to the Confederate capital, for it now had an absolutely secure and unassailable base of operations, while its fighting quality had been improved rather than impaired by its seven days of battling."

General Lee's own official comment on the military problem involved and the difficulties encountered was: "Under ordinary circumstances the Federal army should have been destroyed. Its escape was due to the causes already stated. Prominent among these is the want of correct and timely information. This fact, attributable chiefly to the character of the country, enabled General McClellan skilfully to conceal his retreat and to add much to the obstructions with which nature had beset the way of our pursuing columns; but regret that more was not accomplished gives way to gratitude to the Sovereign Ruler of the Universe for the results achieved."

Whatever the outcome of the Seven Days' Battle another year was to demonstrate beyond question that the wounding of General Johnston at Fair Oaks had left the Confederate army with an even abler commander. On such a field as Chancellorsville was to be shown the brilliancy of Lee as leader, and his skilful maneuvers leading to the invasion of the North. And the succeeding volume will tell, on the other hand, how strong and compact a fighting force had been forged from the raw militia and volunteers of the North.

OFFICERS OF THE THIRD PENNSYLVANIA CAVALRY

AFTER THE SEVEN DAYS

Within a week of the occupation of Harrison's Landing, McClellan's position had become so strong that the Federal commander no longer anticipated an attack by the Confederate forces. General Lee saw that his opponent was flanked on each side by a creek and that approach to his front was commanded by the guns in the entrenchments and those of the Federal navy in the river. Lee therefore deemed it inexpedient to attack, especially as his troops were in poor condition owing to the incessant marching and fighting of the Seven Days. Rest was what both armies needed most, and on July 8th the Confederate forces returned to the vicinity of Richmond. McClellan scoured the country before he was satisfied of the Confederate withdrawal. The Third and Fourth Pennsylvania cavalry made a reconnaisance to Charles City Court House and beyond, and General Averell reported on July 11th that there were no Southern troops south of the lower Chickahominy. His scouting expeditions extended in the direction of Richmond and up the Chickahominy.

CHARLES CITY COURT HOUSE, VIRGINIA, JULY, 1862

THE

FEDERAL

DEFENDER

OF

CORINTH

THE MAN

WHO KEPT

THE

KEY IN THE

WEST

GENERAL W. S. ROSECRANS

The possession of Corinth, Miss., meant the control of the railroads without which the Federal armies could not push down the Mississippi Valley and eastward into Tennessee. Autumn found Rosecrans with about 23,000 men in command at the post where were vast quantities of military stores. On October 3, the indomitable Confederate leaders, Price and Van Dorn, appeared before Corinth, and Rosecrans believing the movement to be a feint sent forward a brigade to an advanced position on a hill. A sharp battle ensued and in a brilliant charge the Confederates at last possessed the hill. Convinced that there was really to be a determined assault on Corinth, Rosecrans disposed his forces during the night. Just before dawn the Confederate cannonade began, the early daylight was passed in skirmishing, while the artillery duel grew hotter. Then a glittering column of Price's men burst from the woods. Grape and canister were poured into them, but on they came, broke through the Federal center and drove back their opponents to the square of the town. Here the Confederates were at last swept back. But ere that Van Dorn's troops had hurled themselves on Battery Robinett to the left of the Federal line, and fought their way over the parapet and into the battery. Their victory was brief. Federal troops well placed in concealment rose up and poured volley after volley into them. They were swept away and Corinth was safe. Rosecrans by a well-planned defense had kept the key to Grant's subsequent control of the West.

GENERAL EARL VAN DORN, C.S.A.

THE CONFEDERATE COMMANDER AT CORINTH

General Earl Van Dorn was born in Mississippi in 1821; he was graduated from West Point in 1842, and was killed in a personal quarrel in 1863. Early in the war General Van Dorn had distinguished himself by capturing the steamer "Star of the West" at Indianola, Texas. He was of a tempestuous nature and had natural fighting qualities. During the month of August he commanded all the Confederate troops in Mississippi except those under General Price, and it was his idea to form a combined movement with the latter's forces and expel the invading Federals from the northern portion of his native State and from eastern Tennessee. The concentration was made and the Confederate army, about 22,000 men, was brought into the disastrous battle of Corinth. Brave were the charges made on the entrenched positions, but without avail.

THE CONFEDERATE SECOND IN COMMAND

General Sterling Price was a civilian who by natural inclination turned to soldiering. He had been made a brigadier-general during the Mexican War, but early allied himself with the cause of the Confederacy. At Pea Ridge, only seven months before the battle of Corinth, he had been wounded. Of the behavior of his men, though they were defeated and turned back on the 4th, he wrote that it was with pride that sisters and daughters of the South could say of the officers and men, "My brother, father, fought at Corinth." And nobly they fought indeed. General Van Dorn, in referring to the end of that bloody battle, wrote these pathetic words: "Exhausted from loss of sleep, wearied from hard marching and fighting, companies and regiments without officers, our troops—let no one censure them—gave way. The day was lost."

GENERAL STERLING PRICE, C.S.A.

BEFORE THE SOD HID THEM

The Gathered Confederate Dead Before Battery Robinett—taken the morning after their desperate attempt to carry the works by assault. No man can look at this awful picture and wish to go to war. These men, a few hours before, were full of life and hope and courage. Without the two last qualities they would not be lying as they are pictured here. In the very foreground, on the left, lies their leader, Colonel Rogers, and almost resting on his shoulder is the body of the gallant Colonel Ross. We are looking from the bottom of the parapet of Battery Robinett. Let an eye-witness tell of what the men saw who looked toward the houses on that bright October day, and then glanced along their musket-barrels and pulled the triggers: "Suddenly we saw a magnificent brigade emerge in our front; they came forward in perfect order, a grand but terrible sight. At their head rode the commander, a man of fine physique, in the prime of life—quiet and cool as though on a drill. The artillery opened, the infantry followed; notwithstanding the slaughter they were closer and closer. Their commander [Colonel Rogers] seemed to bear a charmed life. He jumped his horse across the ditch in front of the guns, and then on foot came on. When he fell, the battle in our front was over."

GENERAL JOHN POPE

THE UNFORTUNATE COMMANDER OF THE ARMY OF VIRGINIA

A SWIFT TURN OF FORTUNE'S WHEEL

Perhaps there is no more pathetic figure in the annals of the War than Pope.   In the West, that fiery furnace where the North's greatest generals were already being molded, he stood out most prominently in the Spring of 1862.   At Washington, the administration was cudgeling its brains for means to meet the popular clamor for an aggressive campaign against Lee after the Peninsula fiasco.   Pope was sent for and arrived in Washington in June.   When the plan to place him at the head of an army whose three corps commanders all out-ranked him, was proposed, he begged to be sent back West.   But he was finally persuaded to undertake a task, the magnitude of which was not yet appreciated at the North.   During a month of preparation he was too easily swayed by the advice and influenced by the plans of civilians, and finally issued a flamboyant address to his army ending with the statement, "My headquarters will be in the saddle."   When this was shown to Lee, he grimly commented, "Perhaps his headquarters will be where his hindquarters ought to be."   There followed the brief campaign, the stunning collision with the solid front of Stonewall Jackson at Cedar Mountain, and the clever strategy that took Pope at a disadvantage on the old battlefield of Bull Run.   Thence his army retreated more badly beaten from a military standpoint than the rout which fled the same field a year before.   A brief summer had marked the rise and fall of Pope. Two years later Sherman bade good-bye to his friend Grant also summoned from the West.   "Remember Pope," was the gist of his warning; "don't stay in Washington; keep in the field."

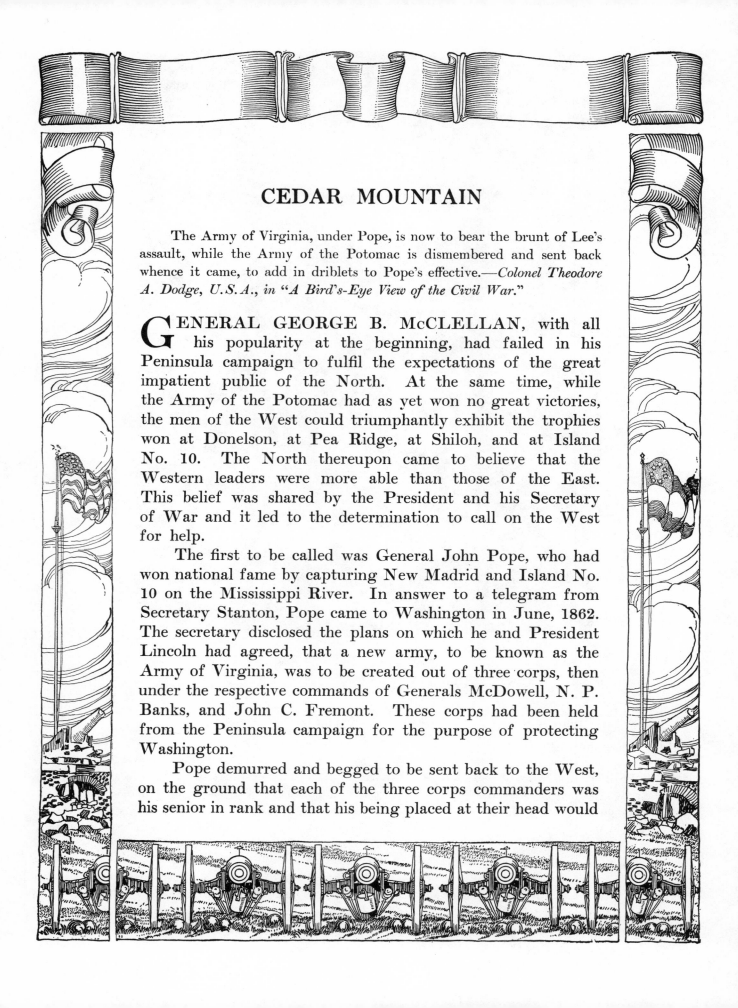

CEDAR MOUNTAIN

The Army of Virginia, under Pope, is now to bear the brunt of Lee's assault, while the Army of the Potomac is dismembered and sent back whence it came, to add in driblets to Pope's effective.—Colonel Theodore A. Dodge, U.S.A., in "A Bird's-Eye View of the Civil War."

GENERAL GEORGE B. McCLELLAN, with all his popularity at the beginning, had failed in his Peninsula campaign to fulfil the expectations of the great impatient public of the North. At the same time, while the Army of the Potomac had as yet won no great victories, the men of the West could triumphantly exhibit the trophies won at Donelson, at Pea Ridge, at Shiloh, and at Island No. 10. The North thereupon came to believe that the Western leaders were more able than those of the East. This belief was shared by the President and his Secretary of War and it led to the determination to call on the West for help.

The first to be called was General John Pope, who had won national fame by capturing New Madrid and Island No. 10 on the Mississippi River. In answer to a telegram from Secretary Stanton, Pope came to Washington in June, 1862. The secretary disclosed the plans on which he and President Lincoln had agreed, that a new army, to be known as the Army of Virginia, was to be created out of three corps, then under the respective commands of Generals McDowell, N. P. Banks, and John C. Fremont. These corps had been held from the Peninsula campaign for the purpose of protecting Washington.

Pope demurred and begged to be sent back to the West, on the ground that each of the three corps commanders was his senior in rank and that his being placed at their head would

A BREATHING SPELL

Federal Encampment at Blackburn's Ford on Bull Run, July 4, 1862. When McClellan went to the Peninsula in March of 1862 he had expected all of McDowell's Corps to be sent him as reënforcement before he made the final advance on Richmond. But the brilliant exploits of Jackson in the Shenandoah required the retention of all the troops in the vicinity of Washington. A new army, in fact, was created to make the campaign which Lincoln had originally wanted McClellan to carry out. The command was given to General John Pope, whose capture of Island No. 10 in the Mississippi had brought him into national importance. The corps of Banks, Frémont, and McDowell were consolidated to form this new army, called the "Army of Virginia." General Frémont refused to serve under his junior, and his force was given to Franz Sigel, who had won fame in 1861 in Missouri. This picture was taken about two weeks after the reorganization was completed. The soldiers are those of McDowell's Corps. They are on the old battlefield of Bull Run, enjoying the leisure of camp life, for no definite plans for the campaign have yet been formed.

WHERE JACKSON STRUCK

Cedar Mountain, Viewed from Pope's Headquarters. On the side of this mountain Jackson established the right of his battle line, when he discovered at noon of August 9th that he was in contact with a large part of Pope's army. He had started from Gordonsville, Pope's objective, to seize Culpeper Court House, but the combat took place in the valley here pictured, some five miles southwest of Culpeper, and by nightfall the fields and slopes were strewn with more than three thousand dead and wounded.

doubtless create a feeling against him. But his protests were of no avail and he assumed command of the Army of Virginia on the 26th of June. McDowell and Banks made no protest; but Fremont refused to serve under one whom he considered his junior, and resigned his position. His corps was assigned to General Franz Sigel.

The new commander, General Pope, on the 14th of July, issued an address to his army that was hardly in keeping with his modesty in desiring at first to decline the honor that was offered him. " I have come to you from the West," he proclaimed, " where we have always seen the backs of our enemies —from an army whose business it has been to seek the adversary and to beat him when found. . . . Meantime I desire you to dismiss from your minds certain phrases which I am sorry to find much in vogue among you. I hear constantly of . . . lines of retreat and bases of supplies. Let us discard such ideas. . . . Let us look before us and not behind."

The immediate object of General Pope was to make the capital secure, to make advances toward Richmond, and, if possible, to draw a portion of Lee's army away from McClellan. His first objective was Gordonsville. From this town, not far from the base of the Blue Ridge Mountains, there was a railroad connecting it with Richmond—a convenient means of furnishing men and supplies to the Confederate army. Pope decided to occupy the town and destroy the railroad. To this end he ordered Banks to Culpeper and thence to send all his cavalry to Gordonsville, capture the town and tear up ten or fifteen miles of the railroad in the direction of Richmond. But, as if a prelude to the series of defeats which General Pope was to suffer in the next six weeks, he failed in this initial movement. The sagacious Lee had divined his intention and had sent General " Stonewall " Jackson with his and General Ewell's divisions on July 13th, to occupy Gordonsville. Ewell arrived in advance of Jackson and held the town for the Confederates.

IN THE LINE OF FIRE

Where the Confederate General Winder was killed at Cedar Mountain. It was while directing the movements of four advance batteries that General Winder was struck by a shell, expiring in a few hours. Jackson reported: "It is difficult within the proper reserve of an official report to do justice to the merits of this accomplished officer. Urged by the medical director to take no part in the movements of the day because of the enfeebled state of his health, his ardent patriotism and military pride could bear no such restraint. Richly endowed with those qualities of mind and person which fit an officer for command and which attract the admiration and excite the enthusiasm of troops, he was rapidly rising to the front rank of his profession."

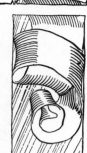

In the campaign we are describing Jackson was the most active and conspicuous figure on the Confederate side. He rested at Gordonsville for two weeks, recuperating his health and that of the army, which had been much impaired in the malarial district of the Peninsula. The fresh mountain air blowing down from the Blue Ridge soon brought back their wonted vigor. On July 27th A. P. Hill was ordered to join him, and the Confederate leader now had about twenty-five thousand men.

The movement on Gordonsville was exactly in accordance with Jackson's own ideas which he had urged upon Lee. Although believing McClellan to be in an impregnable position on the Peninsula, it was not less evident to him that the Union general would be unable to move further until his army had been reorganized and reenforced. This was the moment, he argued, to strike in another direction and carry the conflict into the Federal territory. An army of at least sixty thousand should march into Maryland and appear before the National Capital. President Davis could not be won over to the plan while McClellan was still in a position to be reenforced by sea, but Lee, seeing that McClellan remained inactive, had determined, by sending Jackson westward, to repeat the successful tactics of the previous spring in the Shenandoah valley. Such a move might result in the recall of McClellan.

And so it happened. No sooner had Halleck assumed command of all the Northern armies than the matter of McClellan's withdrawal was agitated and on August 3d the head of the Army of the Potomac, to his bitter disappointment, was ordered to join Pope on the Rappahannock. Halleck was much concerned as to how Lee would act during the Federal evacuation of the Peninsula, uncertain whether the Confederates would attempt to crush Pope before McClellan could reenforce him, or whether McClellan would be attacked as soon as he was out of his strong entrenchments at Harrison's Landing.

THE LEADER OF THE CHARGE

The Hero of the Federal Attack. General Samuel W. Crawford, here seen with his staff, at Cedar Mountain led a charge on the left flank of the Confederate forces that came near being disastrous for Jackson. At about six o'clock the brigade was in line. General Williams reported: "At this time this brigade occupied the interior line of a strip of woods. A field, varying from 250 to 500 yards in width, lay between it and the next strip of woods. In moving across this field the three right regiments and the six companies of the Third Wisconsin were received by a terrific fire of musketry. The Third Wisconsin especially fell under a partial flank fire under which Lieut.-Colonel Crane fell and the regiment was obliged to give way. Of the three remaining regiments which continued the charge (Twenty-eighth New York, Forty-sixth Pennsylvania, and Fifth Connecticut) every field-officer and every adjutant was killed or disabled. In the Twenty-eighth New York every company officer was killed or wounded; in the Forty-sixth Pennsylvania all but five; in the Fifth Connecticut all but eight." It was one of the most heroic combats of the war.

COL. ALFRED N. DUFFIÉ

A Leader of Cavalry. Colonel Alfred N. Duffié was in command of the First Rhode Island Cavalry, in the Cavalry Brigade of the Second Division of McDowell's (Third) Corps in Pope's Army of Virginia. The cavalry had been used pretty well during Pope's advance. On the 8th of August, the day before the battle of Cedar Mountain, the cavalry had proceeded south to the house of Dr. Slaughter. That night Duffié was on picket in advance of General Crawford's troops, which had come up during the day and pitched camp. The whole division came to his support on the next day. When the infantry fell back to the protection of the batteries, the cavalry was ordered to charge the advancing Confederates. "Officers and men behaved admirably, and I cannot speak too highly of the good conduct of all of the brigade," reported General Bayard. After the battle the cavalry covered the retreat of the artillery and ambulances. On August 18th, when the retreat behind the Rappahannoc was ordered, the cavalry again checked the Confederate advance. During the entire campaign the regiment of Colonel Duffié did yeoman's service.

The latter of the two possibilities seemed the more probable, and Pope was therefore ordered to push his whole army toward Gordonsville, in the hope that Lee, compelled to strengthen Jackson, would be too weak to fall upon the retiring Army of the Potomac.

The Union army now occupied the great triangle formed roughly by the Rappahannock and the Rapidan rivers and the range of the Blue Ridge Mountains, with Culpeper Court House as the rallying point. Pope soon found that the capturing of New Madrid and Island No. 10 was easy in comparison with measuring swords with the Confederate generals in the East.

On August 6th Pope began his general advance upon Gordonsville. Banks already had a brigade at Culpeper Court House, and this was nearest to Jackson. The small settlement was the meeting place of four roads by means of which Pope's army of forty-seven thousand men would be united. Jackson, informed of the advance, immediately set his three divisions in motion for Culpeper, hoping to crush Banks, hold the town, and prevent the uniting of the Army of Virginia. His progress was slow. The remainder of Banks's corps reached Culpeper on the 8th. On the morning of the 9th Jackson finally got his troops over the Rapidan and the Robertson rivers. Two miles beyond the latter stream there rose from the plain the slope of Slaughter Mountain, whose ominous name is more often changed into Cedar. This "mountain" is an isolated foothill of the Blue Ridge, some twenty miles from the parent range, and a little north of the Rapidan. From its summit could be seen vast stretches of quiet farmlands which had borne their annual harvests since the days of the Cavaliers. Its gentle slopes were covered with forests, which merged at length into waving grain fields and pasture lands, dotted here and there with rural homes. It was here on the slope of Cedar Mountain that one of the most severe little battles of the war took place.

THE FIRST CLASH

Battlefield of Cedar Mountain, August 9, 1862. Here the Confederate army in its second advance on Washington first felt out the strength massed against it. After Lee's brilliant tactics had turned McClellan's Peninsula Campaign into a fiasco, the Confederate Government resolved to again take the offensive. Plans were formed for a general invasion of the North, the objective points ranging from Cincinnati eastward to the Federal capital and Philadelphia. Immediately after Washington got wind of this, Lincoln (on August 4th) issued a call for three hundred thousand men; and all haste was made to rush the forces of McClellan from the Peninsula and of Cox from West Virginia to the aid of the recently consolidated army under Pope. On August 9, 1862, the vanguards of "Stonewall" Jackson's army and of Pope's intercepting forces met at Cedar Mountain. Banks, with the Second Corps of the Federal army, about eight thousand strong, attacked Jackson's forces of some sixteen thousand. The charge was so furious that Jackson's left flank

was broken and rolled up, the rear of the center fired upon, and the whole line thereby thrown into confusion. Banks, however, received no reenforcements, while Jackson received strong support. The Federal troops were driven back across the ground which they had swept clear earlier in the afternoon.

The Battle of Cedar Mountain, August 9, 1862. The lower picture was taken the day after the battle that had raged for a brief two hours on the previous evening. After an artillery fire that filled half the afternoon, the advanced Federal cavalry was pressed back on the infantry supporting the batteries. Banks underestimated the strength of the Confederates. Instead of sending to Pope for reenforcements, he ordered a charge on the approaching troops. The Confederates, still feeling their way, were unprepared for this movement and were thrown into confusion. But at the moment when the Federal charge was about to end in success, three brigades of A. P. Hill in reserve were called up. They forced the Federals to retrace their steps to the point where the fighting began. Here the Federal retreat, in turn, was halted by General Pope with reenforcements. The Confederates moving up their batteries, a short-range artillery fight was kept up until midnight. At daylight it was found that Ewell and Jackson had fallen back two miles farther up the mountain. Pope advanced to the former Confederate ground and rested, after burying the dead. The following morning the Confederates had disappeared. The loss to both armies was almost three thousand in killed, wounded and missing. The battle had accomplished nothing.

On the banks of Cedar Run, seven miles south of Culpeper and but one or two north of the mountain, Banks's cavalry were waiting to oppose Jackson's advance. Learning of this the latter halted and waited for an attack. He placed Ewell's batteries on the slope about two hundred feet above the valley and sent General Winder to take a strong position on the left. So admirably was Jackson's army stationed that it would have required a much larger force, approaching it from the plains, to dislodge it. And yet, General Banks made an attempt with an army scarcely one-third as large as that of Jackson.

General Pope had made glowing promises of certain success and he well knew that the whole North was eagerly watching and waiting for him to fulfil them. He must strike somewhere and do it soon—and here was his chance at Cedar Mountain. He sent Banks with nearly eight thousand men against this brilliant Southern commander with an army three times as large, holding a strong position on a mountain side.

Banks with his infantry left Culpeper Court House on the morning of August 9th and reached the Confederate stronghold in the afternoon. He approached the mountain through open fields in full range of the Confederate cannon, which presently opened with the roar of thunder. All heedless of danger the brave men ran up the slope as if to take the foe by storm, when suddenly they met a brigade of Ewell's division face to face and a brief, deadly encounter took place. In a few minutes the Confederate right flank began to waver and would no doubt have been routed but for the timely aid of another brigade and still another that rushed down the hill and opened fire on the Federal lines which extended along the eastern bank of Cedar Run.

Meanwhile the Union batteries had been wheeled into position and their deep roar answered that of the foe on the hill. For two or three hours the battle continued with the utmost fury. The ground was strewn with dead and dying

SURVIVORS OF THE FIGHTING TENTH

When Crawford's troops were driven back by A. P. Hill, he halted on the edge of a wheatfield, where he was reenforced by the Tenth Maine. For nearly half an hour it held its own, losing out of its 461 officers and men 173 in killed and wounded. A few days after the battle some survivors had a picture taken on the exact spot where they had so courageously fought. The remains of the cavalry horses can be seen in the trampled field of wheat. From left to right these men are: Lieutenant Littlefield, Lieutenant Whitney, Lieut.-Colonel Fillebrown, Captain Knowlton, and First-Sergeant Jordan, of Company C.

THE HOUSE WELL NAMED

Slaughter's house, overlooking the scene of carnage of Cedar Mountain, stood on the northern slope in the rear of the position taken by the Confederate troops under General Ewell. The brigades of Trimble and Hayes were drawn up near this house, at some distance from the brigade of Early. After the battle the whole of Jackson's army was drawn up on the slopes near it.

and human blood was poured out like water. But the odds were too great and at length, as the shades of evening were settling over the gory field, Banks began to withdraw the remnant of his troops. But he left two thousand of his brave lads—one fourth of his whole army—dead or dying along the hillside, while the Confederate losses were in excess of thirteen hundred.

The dead and wounded of both armies lay mingled in masses over the whole battle-field. While the fighting continued, neither side could send aid or relief to the maimed soldiers, who suffered terribly from thirst and lack of attention as the sultry day gave place to a close, oppressive night.

General Pope had remained at Culpeper, but, hearing the continuous cannonading and knowing that a sharp engagement was going on, hastened to the battle-field in the afternoon with a fresh body of troops under General Ricketts, arriving just before dark. He instantly ordered Banks to withdraw his right wing so as to make room for Ricketts; but the Confederates, victorious as they had been, refused to continue the contest against the reenforcements and withdrew to the woods up the mountain side. Heavy shelling was kept up by the hard-worked artillerymen of both armies until nearly midnight, while the Federal troops rested on their arms in line of battle. For two days the armies faced each other across the valley. Then both quietly withdrew. Pope's first battle as leader of an Eastern army had resulted in neither victory nor defeat.

———

CONFEDERATES CAPTURED AT CEDAR MOUNTAIN, IN CULPEPER COURT HOUSE, AUGUST, 1862

The Confederate prisoners on the balcony seem to be taking their situation very placidly. They have evidently been doing some family laundry, and have hung the results out to dry. The sentries lounging beneath the colonnade below, and the two languid individuals leaning up against the porch and tree, add to the peacefulness of the scene. At the battle of Cedar Mountain, August 9, 1861, the above with other Confederates were captured and temporarily confined in this county town of Culpeper. Like several other Virginia towns, it does not boast a name of its own, but is universally known as Culpeper Court House. A settlement had grown up in the neighborhood of the courthouse, and the scene was enlivened during the sessions of court by visitors from miles around.

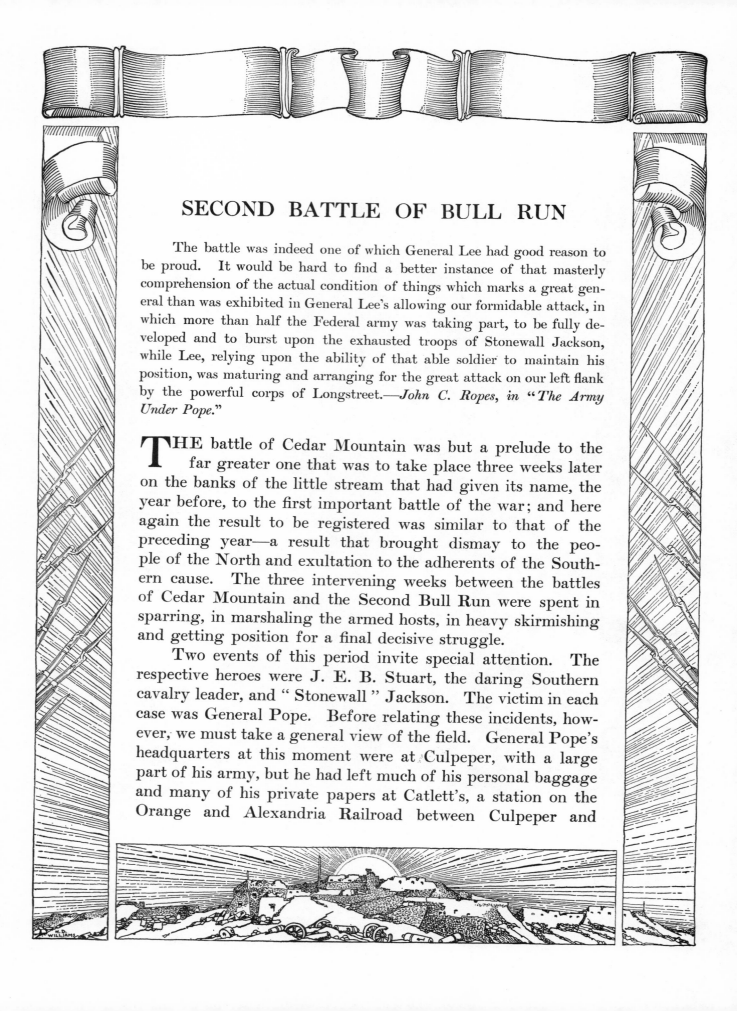

SECOND BATTLE OF BULL RUN

The battle was indeed one of which General Lee had good reason to be proud. It would be hard to find a better instance of that masterly comprehension of the actual condition of things which marks a great general than was exhibited in General Lee's allowing our formidable attack, in which more than half the Federal army was taking part, to be fully developed and to burst upon the exhausted troops of Stonewall Jackson, while Lee, relying upon the ability of that able soldier to maintain his position, was maturing and arranging for the great attack on our left flank by the powerful corps of Longstreet.—*John C. Ropes, in "The Army Under Pope."*

THE battle of Cedar Mountain was but a prelude to the far greater one that was to take place three weeks later on the banks of the little stream that had given its name, the year before, to the first important battle of the war; and here again the result to be registered was similar to that of the preceding year—a result that brought dismay to the people of the North and exultation to the adherents of the Southern cause. The three intervening weeks between the battles of Cedar Mountain and the Second Bull Run were spent in sparring, in marshaling the armed hosts, in heavy skirmishing and getting position for a final decisive struggle.

Two events of this period invite special attention. The respective heroes were J. E. B. Stuart, the daring Southern cavalry leader, and " Stonewall " Jackson. The victim in each case was General Pope. Before relating these incidents, however, we must take a general view of the field. General Pope's headquarters at this moment were at Culpeper, with a large part of his army, but he had left much of his personal baggage and many of his private papers at Catlett's, a station on the Orange and Alexandria Railroad between Culpeper and

THE UNHEEDED WARNING

Here we see Catlett's Station, on the Orange & Alexandria Railroad, which Stuart's cavalry seized in a night sortie on August 22, 1862. The damage done was not severe. Stuart was unable to burn the loaded wagon-trains surrounding the station and had to content himself with capturing horses, which he mounted with wounded Federal soldiers; he escaped at four the next morning, driven off by the approach of a superior force. Pope, at the time, was in possession of the fords of the Rappahannock, trying to check the Confederate advance toward the Shenandoah.

CATLETT'S STATION

At Manassas Junction, as it appeared in the upper picture on August 26, 1862, is one of the great neglected strategic points in the theater of the war. Twenty-five miles from Alexandria and thirty miles in a direct line from Washington, it was almost within long cannon-shot from any point in both the luckless battles of Bull Run. It was on the railway route connecting with Richmond, and at the junction of the railway running across the entrance to the Shenandoah Valley and beyond the Blue Ridge, through Manassas Gap. The Confederates knew its value, and after the first battle of Bull Run built the fortifications which we see in the upper picture, to the left beyond the supply-cars on the railroad. Pope, after the battle of Cedar Mountain, should have covered it, extending his lines so as to protect it from Jackson's incursion through Thoroughfare Gap; instead he held the main force of his army opposing that of Lee.

Stuart's raid, however, so alarmed General Halleck that he immediately telegraphed Pope from Washington: "By no means expose your railroad communication with Alexandria. It is of the utmost importance in sending your supplies and reinforcements." Pope did not fall back upon his railroad communication, however, until after Jackson had seized Manassas Junction.

Manassas Junction, while his vast store of army supplies was at the latter place.

Pope's great source of uncertainty lay in the fact that he did not know whether Lee would move against him or would follow McClellan in the latter's retreat from the Peninsula; nor did he know when the reenforcements promised from McClellan's army would reach him. Meanwhile Lee had decided to let McClellan depart in peace and to advance against Pope, with the whole Confederate army. To this end Longstreet was ordered to the scene and with his corps he reached Gordonsville on August 13th.

A few days later the two Confederate generals, Lee and Longstreet, ascended to the top of Clark's Mountain, from which, through powerful field-glasses, they obtained a good view of Culpeper, about twelve miles away. They saw that Pope's position was weak and determined to attack him without delay. Lee ordered his army to cross the Rapidan. He also sent a courier to gallop across the country with an important dispatch to General Stuart, disclosing his plans. It was now that General Pope met fortune; he captured the courier and learned of Lee's plans. Pope knew that he was not in position to meet Lee's army at Culpeper, and he withdrew from that place and took up a strong position behind the Rappahannock. Lee had strained every nerve to get at his antagonist before the latter left Culpeper and before he could be reenforced by McClellan's army. But sudden rains changed the Rappahannock from a placid stream into a rushing torrent. The Confederates were delayed and meantime the reenforcements from the Peninsula began to reach Pope's army. General Reno with a part of Burnside's corps was on the ground by August 14th. One week later came Generals Kearny and Reynolds —both splendid leaders, both destined to give their lives for their country within a year—to join the Army of Virginia with some thousands of additional fighters from the Army of the Potomac.

WHERE THE THUNDERBOLT FELL

The havoc wrought by the Confederate attack of August 26th on the Federal supply depot at Manassas Junction is here graphically preserved. When Jackson arrived at sunset of that day at Bristoe's Station, on the Orange & Alexandria Railroad, he knew that his daring movement would be reported to Pope's forces by the trains that escaped both north and south. To save themselves, the troops that had already marched twenty-five miles had to make still further exertions. Trimble volunteered to move on Manassas Junction; and, under command of Stuart, a small force moved northward through the woods. At midnight it arrived within half a mile of the Junction. The Federal force greeted it with artillery fire, but when the Confederates charged at the sound of the bugle the gunners abandoned the batteries to the assaulters. Some three hundred of the small Federal garrison were captured, with the immense stores that filled the warehouses to overflowing. The next morning Hill's and Taliaferro's divisions arrived to hold the position. The half-starved troops were now in possession of all that was needed to make them an effective force. Jackson was now in position to control the movements of the Federal army under Pope.

Lee was completely thwarted in his purpose of attacking Pope before his reenforcements arrived. But he was not idle. He sent the dauntless cavalry leader, J. E. B. Stuart, to make a raid around the Union army. Stuart did this effectively, and this was the first of the two notable events of these weeks of sparring. Crossing the Rappahannock at Waterloo Bridge with fifteen hundred mounted men as bold and dauntless as himself, Stuart dashed up the country, riding all day and all night. After the coming of night on the evening of the 22d, in the midst of a torrential rainstorm, while the darkness was so intense that every man was guided by the tread of his brother horsemen, Stuart pounced upon the Federals near Catlett's Station, overpowered the astonished guard, captured nearly two hundred prisoners, scattering the remainder of the troops stationed there far and wide in the darkness, and seized Pope's despatch-book with his plans and private papers. Stuart took also several hundred fine horses and burned a large number of wagons laden with supplies. Among his trophies was a fine uniform cloak and hat which were the personal property of General Pope. These were exchanged on the following day for General Stuart's plumed hat which a few days before had been left behind by that officer when surprised by Federal troops.

Stuart's bold raid proved a serious misfortune for the Union army. But Lee had far greater things in store. His next move was to send Jackson to Pope's rear with a large part of the Confederate army. Stealthily Jackson led his army westward, shielded by the woods, the thickets, and the low hills of the Blue Ridge. It was a quiet rural community through which he passed. The great majority of the simple country folk had never seen an army, though it is true that for many days the far-away boom of cannon had reached their ears from the valley of the Rapidan. Now here was a real army at their very doors. Nor was it a hostile army, for their sympathies were Southern. With baskets and armfuls of

GUARDING THE "O. & A." NEAR UNION MILLS

Jackson's raid around Pope's army on Bristoe and Manassas stations in August, 1862, taught the Federal generals that both railroad and base of supplies must be guarded. Pope's army was out of subsistence and forage, and the single-track railroad was inadequate.

DÉBRIS FROM JACKSON'S RAID ON THE ORANGE AND ALEXANDRIA RAILROAD

This scrap-heap at Alexandria was composed of the remains of cars and engines destroyed by Jackson at Bristoe and Manassas stations. The Confederate leader marched fifty miles in thirty-six hours through Thoroughfare Gap, which Pope had neglected to guard.

bread and pies and cakes they cheered as best they could the tattered and hungry men on the march.

General Lee in the meantime had kept Longstreet in front of Pope's army on the Rappahannock to make daily demonstrations and feints and thus to divert Pope's attention from Jackson's movements and lead him to believe that he was to be attacked in front. The trick was eminently successful. "Stonewall" Jackson suddenly, on August 26th, emerged from the Bull Run Mountains by way of the Thoroughfare Gap and marshaled his clans on the plains of Manassas, but a few miles from the site of the famous battle of the year before.

Pope had taken alarm. He was astonished to find Jackson in his rear, and he had to decide instantly between two courses—to abandon his communications with Fredericksburg on the one hand, or with Alexandria and Washington on the other. He decided to keep in touch with Washington at all hazards. Breaking his camp on the Rappahannock, he hastened with all speed to lead his forces toward Manassas Junction, where he had stored vast quantities of provisions and munitions of war. But he was too late to save them. Jackson had been joined by Stuart and his cavalry. On the evening of the 26th they were still some miles from Manassas and Trimble was sent ahead to make sure the capture before Pope's army could arrive. Through the darkness rode these same hardy men who had a few nights before made their bold raid on Catlett's Station. Before midnight they reached Manassas. They met little opposition. The guard was overpowered. The spoils of this capture were great, including three hundred prisoners, one hundred and seventy-five horses, ten locomotives, seven long trains of provisions, and vast stores and munitions of war.

Next morning the weary and hungry foot soldiers of Jackson's army came upon the scene and whatever else they did they feasted as only hungry men can. An eye-witness wrote, "To see a starving man eating lobster-salad and

A MILITARY TRAIN UPSET BY CONFEDERATES

This is part of the result of General Pope's too rapid advance to head off Lee's army south of the Rappahannock River. Although overtaking the advance of the Confederates at Cedar Mountain, Pope had arrived too late to close the river passes against them. Meanwhile he had left the Orange & Alexandria Railroad uncovered, and Jackson pushed a large force under General Ewell forward across the Bull Run Mountains. On the night of August 26, 1863, Ewell's forces captured Manassas Junction, while four miles above the Confederate cavalry fell upon an empty railroad train returning from the transfer of Federal troops. The train was destroyed. Here we see how well the work was done.

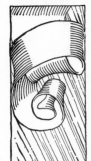

drinking Rhine wine, barefooted and in tatters, was curious; the whole thing was incredible."

The amazement at the North when the news of the capture of Manassas became known cannot be described. But the newspapers belittled it, declaring that it was merely a bold raid and that for any large force to get between Pope's army and Washington before Pope became aware of the attempt was simply impossible.

Jackson had done an astonishing thing. But his position was precarious, nevertheless. Pope was moving toward him with a far larger army, recently augmented by Heintzelman's corps from the Army of the Potomac, while Fitz John Porter with an additional force was not far off. It is true that Longstreet was hastening to the aid of Jackson, but he had to come by the same route which had brought Jackson— through Thoroughfare Gap—and Pope thought he saw a great opportunity. If he could only detain Longstreet at the gap, why should he not crush Jackson with his superior numbers? To this end he sent orders to Porter, to McDowell, and to Kearny and others whose forces were scattered about the country, to concentrate during the night of the 27th and move upon Jackson. McDowell sent Ricketts with a small force—too small—to prevent Longstreet from passing through Thoroughfare Gap, and hastened to join the main army against Jackson. But that able commander was not to be caught in a trap. He moved from Manassas Junction by three roads toward the old battle-field of Bull Run and by noon on the 28th the whole corps was once more united between Centreville and Sudley Spring. Late in the day he encountered King's division of McDowell's corps near the village of Groveton, and a sharp fight was opened and kept up till an hour after dark. The Confederates were left in possession of the field.

The following day, August 29th, was the first of the two days' battle, leaving out of account the fight of the evening

THE TRAIN "STONEWALL" JACKSON AND STUART STOPPED AT BRISTOE

By a move of unparalleled boldness, "Stonewall" Jackson, with twenty thousand men, captured the immense Union supplies at Manassas Junction, August 26, 1862. His was a perilous position. Washington lay one day's march to the north; Warrenton, Pope's headquarters, but twelve miles distant to the southwest; and along the Rappahannock, between "Stonewall" Jackson and Lee, stood the tents of another host which outnumbered the whole Confederate army. "Stonewall" Jackson had seized Bristoe Station in order to break down the railway bridge over Broad Run, and to proceed at his leisure with the destruction of the stores. A train returning empty from Warrenton Junction to Alexandria darted through the station under heavy fire. The line was promptly torn up. Two trains which followed in the same direction as the first went crashing down a high embankment. The report received at Alexandria from the train which escaped ran as fol-

lows: "No. 6 train, engine Secretary, was fired into at Bristoe by a party of cavalry some five hundred strong. They had piled ties on the track, but the engine threw them off. Secretary is completely riddled by bullets." It was a full day before the Federals realized that "Stonewall" Jackson was really there with a large force. Here, in abundance, was all that had been absent for some time; besides commissary stores of all sorts, there were two trains loaded with new clothing, to say nothing of sutler's stores, replete with "extras" not enumerated in the regulations, and also the camp of a cavalry regiment which had vacated in favor of Jackson's men. It was an interesting sight to see the hungry, travel-worn men attacking this profusion and rewarding themselves for all their fatigues and deprivations of the preceding few days, and their enjoyment of it and of the day's rest allowed them. There was a great deal of difficulty for a time in finding what each man needed most, but this was overcome through a crude barter of belongings as the day wore on.

before and the desultory fighting of the preceding ten days. General Pope was still hopeful of crushing Jackson before the arrival of Longstreet, and on the morning of the 29th he ordered a general advance across Bull Run. As the noon hour approached a wild shout that arose from Jackson's men told too well of the arrival of Longstreet. Far away on the hills near Gainesville could be seen the marching columns of Longstreet, who had passed through the gap in safety and who was now rushing to the support of Jackson. The Confederate army was at last to be reunited. Jackson was greatly relieved. Pope had lost his opportunity of fighting the army of his opponent in sections.

The field was almost the same that the opposing forces had occupied a year and a month before when the first great battle of the war was fought. And many of them were the same men. Some who had engaged in that first conflict had gone home and had refused to reenlist; others had found soldiers' graves since then—but still others on both sides were here again, no longer the raw recruits that they were before, but, with their year of hard experience in the field, they were trained soldiers, equal to any in the world.

The two armies faced each other in a line nearly five miles long. There was heavy fighting here and there along the line from the early morning hours, but no general engagement until late in the afternoon. The Union right pressed hard against the Confederate left and by ten o'clock had forced it back more than a mile. But the Confederates, presently reenforced in that quarter, hurled heavy masses of infantry against the Union right and regained much that it had lost. Late in the afternoon fresh regiments under Kearny and Hooker charged the Confederate left, which was swept back and rolled in upon the center. But presently the Southern General Hood, with his famous Texan brigade, rushed forward in a wild, irresistible dash, pressed Kearny back, captured one gun, several flags and a hundred prisoners. Night then closed over

A START TOO LONG DELAYED

Where the troops of General McClellan, waiting near the round-house at Alexandria, were hurried forward to the scene of action where Pope was struggling with Jackson and Ewell. Pope had counted upon the assistance of these reënforcements in making the forward movement by which he expected to hold Lee back. The old bogey of leaving the National Capital defenseless set up a vacillation in General Halleck's mind and the troops were held overlong at Alexandria. Had they been promptly forwarded, "Stonewall" Jackson's blow at Manassas Junction could not have been struck. At the news of that disaster the troops were hurriedly despatched down the railroad toward Manassas. But Pope was already in retreat in three columns toward that point, McDowell had failed to intercept the Confederate reënforcements coming through Thoroughfare Gap, and the situation had become critical. General Taylor, with his brigade of New Jersey troops, was the first of McClellan's forces to be moved forward to the aid of Pope. At Union Mills, Colonel Scammon, commanding the First Brigade, driven back from Manassas Junction, was further pressed by the Confederates on the morning of August 27th. Later in the day General Taylor's brigade arrived by the Fairfax road and, crossing the railroad bridge, met the Confederates drawn up and waiting near Manassas Station. A severe artillery fire greeted the Federals as they emerged from the woods. As General Taylor had no artillery, he was obliged either to retire or charge. He chose the latter. When the Confederate cavalry threatened to surround his small force, however, Taylor fell back in good order across the bridge, where two Ohio regiments assisted in holding the Confederates in check. At this point, General Taylor, who had been wounded in the retreat, was borne past in a litter. Though suffering much, he appealed to the officers to prevent another Bull Run. The brigade retired in good order to Fairfax Court House, where General Taylor died of his wounds a short time afterward.

BRIGADIER–GENERAL
GEORGE W. TAYLOR

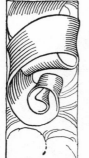

the scene and the two armies rested on their arms until the morning.

The first day's battle is sometimes called the battle of Groveton, but usually it is considered as the first half of the second battle of Bull Run. It was a formidable conflict in itself. The Union loss was at least forty-five hundred men, the Confederate was somewhat larger. Over the gory field lay multitudes of men, the blue and the gray commingled, who would dream of battlefields no more. The living men lay down among the dead in order to snatch a little rest and strength that they might renew the strife in the morning.

It is a strange fact that Lee and Pope each believed that the other would withdraw his army during the night, and each was surprised in the morning to find his opponent still on the ground, ready, waiting, defiant. It was quite certain that on this day, August 30th, there would be a decisive action and that one of the two armies would be victor and the other defeated. The two opposing commanders had called in their outlying battalions and the armies now faced each other in almost full force, the Confederates with over fifty thousand men and the Union forces exceeding their opponents by probably fifteen thousand men. The Confederate left wing was commanded by Jackson, and the right by Longstreet. The extreme left of the Union army was under Fitz John Porter, who, owing to a misunderstanding of orders, had not reached the field the day before. The center was commanded by Heintzelman and the right by Reno.

In the early hours of the morning the hills echoed with the firing of artillery, with which the day was opened. Porter made an infantry attack in the forenoon, but was met by the enemy in vastly superior numbers and was soon pressed back in great confusion. As the hours passed one fearful attack followed another, each side in turn pressing forward and again receding. In the afternoon a large part of

AN UNREALIZED OPPORTUNITY

Here might have been won a Federal victory that would have precluded defeat at Second Bull Run. The corps of General Heintzelman, consisting of the divisions of Hooker and Kearny, was the next detachment of McClellan's forces to arrive to the aid of Pope. On the 28th of August, Heintzelman had pushed forward to Centreville, entering it soon after "Stonewall" Jackson's rear-guard had retired. Instead of pursuing, Heintzelman drew up his forces east of Cub Run, which we see in the picture. Jackson's forces, now in a precarious position, fell back toward Thoroughfare Gap to form a junction with Longstreet's Corps, which Lee had sent forward. The battle was commenced on the west somewhat feebly by Generals McDowell and Sigel. By night-fall the Confederate left had been driven back fully a mile.

MAJOR-GENERAL SAMUEL P. HEINTZELMAN AND STAFF

the Union army made a desperate onslaught on the Confederate left under Jackson. Here for some time the slaughter of men was fearful. It was nearing sunset. Jackson saw that his lines were wavering. He called for reenforcements which did not come and it seemed as if the Federals were about to win a signal victory. But this was not to be. Far away on a little hill at the Confederate right Longstreet placed four batteries in such a position that he could enfilade the Federal columns. Quickly he trained his cannon on the Federal lines that were hammering away at Jackson, and opened fire. Ghastly gaps were soon cut in the Federal ranks and they fell back. But they re-formed and came again and still again, each time only to be mercilessly cut down by Longstreet's artillery. At length Longstreet's whole line rushed forward, and with the coming of darkness, the whole Union front began to waver.

General Lee, seeing this, ordered the Confederates in all parts of the field to advance. With wild, triumphant yells they did so. It was now dark and there was little more fighting; but Lee captured several thousand prisoners. Pope retreated across Bull Run with the remnant of his army and by morning was ensconced behind the field-works at Centreville.

There was no mistaking the fact that General Pope had lost the battle and the campaign. He decided to lead his army back to the entrenchments of Washington. After spending a day behind the embankments at Centreville, the retreat was begun. Lee's troops with Jackson in the advance pursued and struck a portion of the retreating army at Chantilly.

It was late in the afternoon of September 1st. The rain, accompanied by vivid lightning and terrific crashes of thunder, was falling in torrents as Stuart's horsemen, sent in advance, were driven back by the Federal infantry. Jackson now pushed two of A. P. Hill's brigades forward to ascertain the condition of the Union army. General Reno was protecting Pope's right flank, and he lost no time in proceeding against Hill. The latter was promptly checked, and both forces took

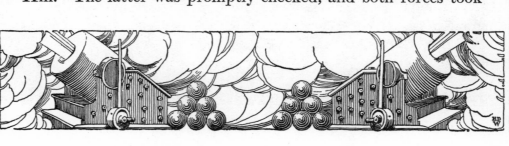

THE TWICE–WON FIELD

MAJOR–GENERAL R. S.
EWELL

MAJOR–GENERAL JAMES
LONGSTREET

Sleeping on their arms on the night of August 29th, the Federal veterans were as confident of having won a victory as were the raw troops in the beginning of the first battle of Bull Run. But the next day's fighting was to tell the tale. General Ewell had been wounded in the knee by a minie ball in the severe fight at Groveton and was unable to lead his command; but for the impetuosity of this commander was substituted that of Longstreet, nicknamed "the War-Horse," whose arrival in the midst of the previous day's engagement had cost the Federals dear. On the morning of the second day Longstreet's batteries opened the engagement. When the general advance came, as the sun shone on the parallel lines of glittering bayonets, it was Longstreet's men bringing their muskets to "the ready" who first opened fire with a long flash of flame. It was they who pressed most eagerly forward and, in the face of the Federal batteries, fell upon the troops of General McDowell at the left and drove them irresistibly back. Although the right Federal wing, in command of General Heintzelman, had not given an inch, it was this turning of the left by Longstreet which put the whole Federal army in retreat, driving them across Bull Run. The Confederates were left in possession of the field, where lay thousands of Federal dead and wounded, and Lee was free to advance his victorious troops into the North unmolested.

THE BATTLE-FIELD OF SECOND BULL RUN (MANASSAS), AUGUST 29–30, 1862

position for battle. One side and then the other fell back in turn as lines were re-formed and urged forward. Night fell and the tempest's fury increased. The ammunition of both armies was so wet that much of it could not be used. Try as they would the Confederates were unable to break the Union line and the two armies finally withdrew. The Confederates suffered a loss of five hundred men in their unsuccessful attempt to demoralize Pope in his retreat, and the Federals more than a thousand, including Generals Stevens and Kearny.

General Kearny might have been saved but for his reckless bravery. He was rounding up the retreat of his men in the darkness of the night when he chanced to come within the Confederate lines. Called on to surrender, he lay flat on his horse's back, sank his spurs into its sides, and attempted to escape. Half a dozen muskets were leveled and fired at the fleeing general. Within thirty yards he rolled from his horse's back dead.

The consternation in Washington and throughout the North when Pope's defeated army reached Arlington Heights can better be imagined than described. General Pope, who bore the brunt of public indignation, begged to be relieved of the command. The President complied with his wishes and the disorganized remnants of the Army of Virginia and the Army of the Potomac were handed to the " Little Napoleon " of Peninsula fame, George B. McClellan.

The South was overjoyed with its victory—twice it had unfurled its banner in triumph on the battlefield at Manassas by the remarkable strategy of its generals and the courage of its warriors on the firing-line. Twice it had stood literally on the road that led to the capital of the Republic, only by some strange destiny of war to fail to enter its precincts on the wave of victory.

THE FIGHTING FORTY-FIRST

"C" Company of the Forty-first New York after the Second Battle of Bull Run, August 30, 1862. When the troops of Generals Milroy and Schurz were hard pressed by overpowering numbers and exhausted by fatigue, this New York regiment, being ordered forward, quickly advanced with a cheer along the Warrenton Turnpike and deployed about a mile west of the field of the conflict of July 21, 1861. The fighting men replied with answering shouts, for with the regiment that came up at the double quick galloped a battery of artillery. The charging Confederates were held and this position was assailed time and again. It became the center of the sanguinary combat of the day, and it was here that the "Bull-Dogs" earned their name. Among the first to respond to Lincoln's call, they enlisted in June, '61, and when their first service was over they stepped forward to a man, specifying no term of service but putting their names on the Honor Roll of "For the War."

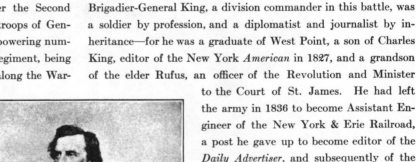

BRIG.-GEN. RUFUS KING

Brigadier-General King, a division commander in this battle, was a soldier by profession, and a diplomatist and journalist by inheritance—for he was a graduate of West Point, a son of Charles King, editor of the New York *American* in 1827, and a grandson of the elder Rufus, an officer of the Revolution and Minister to the Court of St. James. He had left the army in 1836 to become Assistant Engineer of the New York & Erie Railroad, a post he gave up to become editor of the *Daily Advertiser*, and subsequently of the Milwaukee *Sentinel*. At the outbreak of the war Lincoln had appointed him Minister to Rome, but he asked permission to delay his departure, and was made a Brigadier-General of Volunteers. Later he resigned as Minister, and was assigned to McDowell's corps. At the battle of Manassas, in which the Forty-first New York earned honor, he proved an able leader. In 1867 he was again appointed as Minister of the United States to Italy.

THE GENERAL–IN–CHIEF IN 1862

Major-General Henry Wager Halleck; born 1814; West Point 1839; died 1872. Sherman credits Halleck with having first discovered that Forts Henry and Donelson, where the Tennessee and the Cumberland Rivers so closely approach each other, were the keypoints to the defensive line of the Confederates in the West. Succeeding Fremont in November, 1861, Halleck, importuned by both Grant and Foote, authorized the joint expedition into Tennessee, and after its successful outcome he telegraphed to Washington: "Make Buell, Grant, and Pope major-generals of volunteers and give me command in the West. I ask this in return for Donelson and Henry." He was chosen to be General-in-Chief of the Federal Armies at the crisis created by the failure of McClellan's Peninsula Campaign. Halleck held this position from July 11, 1862, until Grant, who had succeeded him in the West, finally superseded him at Washington.

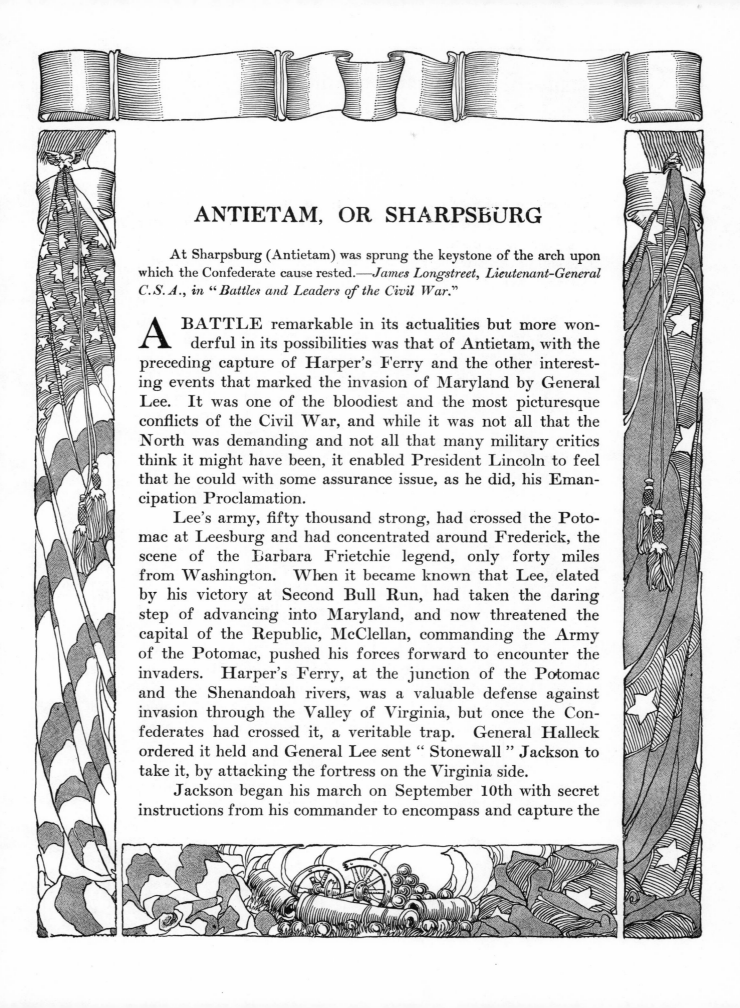

ANTIETAM, OR SHARPSBURG

At Sharpsburg (Antietam) was sprung the keystone of the arch upon which the Confederate cause rested.—*James Longstreet, Lieutenant-General C.S.A., in "Battles and Leaders of the Civil War."*

A BATTLE remarkable in its actualities but more wonderful in its possibilities was that of Antietam, with the preceding capture of Harper's Ferry and the other interesting events that marked the invasion of Maryland by General Lee. It was one of the bloodiest and the most picturesque conflicts of the Civil War, and while it was not all that the North was demanding and not all that many military critics think it might have been, it enabled President Lincoln to feel that he could with some assurance issue, as he did, his Emancipation Proclamation.

Lee's army, fifty thousand strong, had crossed the Potomac at Leesburg and had concentrated around Frederick, the scene of the Barbara Frietchie legend, only forty miles from Washington. When it became known that Lee, elated by his victory at Second Bull Run, had taken the daring step of advancing into Maryland, and now threatened the capital of the Republic, McClellan, commanding the Army of the Potomac, pushed his forces forward to encounter the invaders. Harper's Ferry, at the junction of the Potomac and the Shenandoah rivers, was a valuable defense against invasion through the Valley of Virginia, but once the Confederates had crossed it, a veritable trap. General Halleck ordered it held and General Lee sent "Stonewall" Jackson to take it, by attacking the fortress on the Virginia side.

Jackson began his march on September 10th with secret instructions from his commander to encompass and capture the

Federal garrison and the vast store of war material at this place, made famous a few years before by old John Brown. To conceal his purpose from the inhabitants he inquired along the route about the roads leading into Pennsylvania. It was from his march through Frederick that the Barbara Frietchie story took its rise. But there is every reason to believe that General Jackson never saw the good old lady, that the story is a myth, and that Mr. Whittier, who has given us the popular poem under the title of her name, was misinformed. However, Colonel H. K. Douglas, who was a member of Jackson's staff, relates, in "Battles and Leaders of the Civil War," an interesting incident where his commander on entering Middletown was greeted by two young girls waving a Union flag. The general bowed to the young women, raised his hat, and remarked to some of his officers, "We evidently have no friends in this town." Colonel Douglas concludes, "This is about the way he would have treated Barbara Frietchie."

On the day after Jackson left Frederick he crossed the Potomac by means of a ford near Williamsport and on the 13th he reached Bolivar Heights. Harper's Ferry lies in a deep basin formed by Maryland Heights on the north bank of the Potomac, Loudon Heights on the south bank, and Bolivar Heights on the west. The Shenandoah River breaks through the pass between Loudon and Bolivar Heights and the village lies between the two at the apex formed by the junction of the two rivers.

As Jackson approached the place by way of Bolivar Heights, Walker occupied Loudon Heights and McLaws invested Maryland Heights. All were unopposed except McLaws, who encountered Colonel Ford with a force to dispute his ascent. Ford, however, after some resistance, spiked his guns and retired to the Ferry, where Colonel Miles had remained with the greater portion of the Federal troops. Had Miles led his entire force to Maryland Heights he could no doubt have held his ground until McClellan came to his relief.

JEFFERSON DAVIS

ACCORDING TO HIS WIDOW THE ONLY WAR-TIME PHOTOGRAPH OF THE PRESIDENT OF THE CONFEDERACY

Thus appeared Jefferson Davis, who on the eve of Antietam was facing one of the gravest crises of his career. Eighteen months previously, on February 9, 1861, he had been unanimously elected president of the Confederate States of America. He was then opposed to war. He maintained that the secession of the Southern states should be regarded as a purely peaceful move. But events had swiftly drawn him and his government into the most stupendous civil conflict of modern times. Now, in September, 1862, he was awaiting the decision of fate. The Southern forces had advanced northward triumphantly. Elated by success, they were at this moment invading the territory of the enemy under the leadership of Lee, whose victories had everywhere inspired not only confidence but enthusiasm and devotion. Should he overthrow the Northern armies, the Confederacy would be recognized abroad and its independence probably established at home. Should he be defeated, no one could foretell the result. Antietam was lost. From this time the fortunes of the Confederacy waned.

But General Halleck had ordered him to hold Harper's Ferry to the last, and Miles interpreted this order to mean that he must hold the town itself. He therefore failed to occupy the heights around it in sufficient strength and thus permitted himself to be caught in a trap.

During the day of the 14th the Confederate artillery was dragged up the mountain sides, and in the afternoon a heavy fire was opened on the doomed Federal garrison. On that day McClellan received word from Miles that the latter could hold out for two days longer and the commanding general sent word: "Hold out to the last extremity. If it is possible, reoccupy the Maryland Heights with your entire force. If you can do that I will certainly be able to relieve you. . . . Hold out to the last." McClellan was approaching slowly and felt confident he could relieve the place.

On the morning of the 15th the roar of Confederate artillery again resounded from hill to hill. From Loudon to Maryland Heights the firing had begun and a little later the battle-flags of A. P. Hill rose on Bolivar Heights. Scarcely two hours had the firing continued when Colonel Miles raised the white flag at Harper's Ferry and its garrison of 12,500, with vast military stores, passed into the hands of the Confederates. Colonel Miles was struck by a stray fragment of a Confederate shell which gave him a mortal wound. The force of General Franklin, preparing to move to the garrison's relief, on the morning of the 15th noted that firing at the Ferry had ceased and suspected that the garrison had surrendered, as it had.

The Confederate Colonel Douglas, whose account of the surrender is both absorbing and authoritative, thus describes the surrender in "Battles and Leaders of the Civil War":

"Under instructions from General Jackson, I rode up the pike and into the enemy's lines to ascertain the purpose of the white flag. Near the top of the hill I met General White and staff and told him my mission. He replied that Colonel Miles had been mortally wounded, that he was in command and

LEE LOCKS THE GATES

Sharpsburg, Maryland, September 17, 1862. There were long minutes on that sunny day in the early fall of 1862 when Robert E. Lee, at his headquarters west of Sharpsburg, must have been in almost entire ignorance of how the battle went. Outnumbered he knew his troops were; outfought he knew they never would be. Longstreet, Hood, D. H. Hill, Evans, and D. R. Jones had turned back more than one charge in the morning; but, as the day wore on, Lee perceived that the center must be held. Sharpsburg was the key. He had deceived McClellan as to his numerical strength and he must continue to do so. Lee had practically no reserves at all. At one time General Longstreet reported from the center to General Chilton, Lee's Chief of Staff, that Cooke's North Carolina regiment— still keeping its colors at the front—had not a cartridge left. None but veteran troops could hold a line like this, supported by only two guns of Miller's battery of the Washington Artillery. Of this crisis in the battle General Longstreet wrote afterward: "We were already badly whipped and were holding our ground by sheer force of desperation." Actually in line that day on the Confederate side were only 37,000 men, and opposed to them were numbers that could be footed up to 50,000 more. At what time in the day General Lee must have perceived that the invasion of Maryland must come to an end cannot be told. He had lost 20,000 of his tired, footsore army by straggling on the march, according to the report of Longstreet, who adds: "Nearly one-fourth of the troops who went into the battle were killed or wounded." At dark Lee's rearward movement had begun.

desired to have an interview with General Jackson. . . . I conducted them to General Jackson, whom I found sitting on his horse where I had left him. . . . The contrast in appearances there presented was striking. General White, riding a handsome black horse, was carefully dressed and had on untarnished gloves, boots, and sword. His staff were equally comely in costume. On the other hand, General Jackson was the dingiest, worst-dressed and worst-mounted general that a warrior who cared for good looks and style would wish to surrender to.

"General Jackson . . . rode up to Bolivar and down into Harper's Ferry. The curiosity in the Union army to see him was so great that the soldiers lined the sides of the road. . . . One man had an echo of response all about him when he said aloud: 'Boys, he's not much for looks, but if we'd had him we wouldn't have been caught in this trap.'"

McClellan had failed to reach Harper's Ferry in time to relieve it because he was detained at South Mountain by a considerable portion of Lee's army under D. H. Hill and Longstreet. McClellan had come into possession of Lee's general order, outlining the campaign. Discovering by this order that Lee had sent Jackson to attack Harper's Ferry he made every effort to relieve it.

The affair at Harper's Ferry, as that at South Mountain, was but a prelude to the tremendous battle that was to follow two days later on the banks of the little stream called Antietam Creek, in Maryland. When it was known that Lee had led his army across the Potomac the people were filled with consternation—the people, not only of the immediate vicinity, but of Harrisburg, of Baltimore, of Philadelphia. Their fear was intensified by the memory of the Second Bull Run of a few weeks earlier, and by the fact that at this very time General Bragg was marching northward across Kentucky with a great army, menacing Louisville and Cincinnati.

As one year before, the hopes of the North had centered in George B. McClellan, so it was now with the people of the

A REGIMENT THAT FOUGHT AT SOUTH MOUNTAIN—THE THIRTY-FIFTH NEW YORK

Here sits Colonel T. G. Morehead, who commanded the 106th Pennsylvania, of the Second Corps. At 7.20 A.M. the order came to advance, and with a cheer the Second Corps—men who for over two years had never lost a gun nor struck a color—pressed forward. But again they were halted. It was almost an hour later when Sedgwick's division, with Sumner at the head, crossed the Antietam. Arriving nearly opposite the Dunker church, it swept out over the cornfields. On it went, by Greene's right, through the West Woods; here it met the awful counter-stroke of Early's reënforced division and, stubbornly resisting, was hurled back with frightful loss.

COLONEL T. G. MOREHEAD
A HERO OF SEDGWICK'S CHARGE

Early in the morning of September 17, 1862, Knap's battery (shown below) got into the thick of the action of Antietam. General Mansfield had posted it opposite the north end of the West Woods, close to the Confederate line. The guns opened fire at seven o'clock. Practically unsupported, the battery was twice charged upon during the morning; but quickly substituting canister for shot and shell, the men held their ground and stemmed the Confederate advance. Near this spot General Mansfield was mortally wounded while deploying his troops. About noon a section of Knap's battery was detached to the assistance of General Greene, in the East Woods.

KNAP'S BATTERY, JUST AFTER THE BLOODY WORK AT ANTIETAM

East. They were ready to forget his failure to capture Richmond in the early summer and to contrast his partial successes on the Peninsula with the drastic defeat of his successor at the Second Bull Run.

When McClellan, therefore, passed through Maryland to the scene of the coming battle, many of the people received him with joy and enthusiasm. At Frederick City, he tells us in his "Own Story," he was "nearly overwhelmed and pulled to pieces," and the people invited him into their houses and gave him every demonstration of confidence.

The first encounter, a double one, took place on September 14th, at two passes of South Mountain, a continuation of the Blue Ridge, north of the Potomac. General Franklin, who had been sent to relieve Harper's Ferry, met a Confederate force at Crampton's Gap and defeated it in a sharp battle of three hours' duration. Meanwhile, the First and Ninth Army Corps, under Burnside, encountered a stronger force at Turner's Gap seven miles farther up. The battle here continued many hours, till late in the night, and the Union troops were victorious. General Reno was killed. Lee's loss was nearly twenty-seven hundred, of whom eight hundred were prisoners. The Federals lost twenty-one hundred men and they failed to save Harper's Ferry.

Lee now placed Longstreet and D. H. Hill in a strong position near Keedysville, but learning that McClellan was advancing rapidly, the Confederate leader decided to retire to Sharpsburg, where he could be more easily joined by Jackson.

September 16th was a day of intense anxiety and unrest in the valley of the Antietam. The people who had lived in the farmhouses that dotted the golden autumn landscape in this hitherto quiet community had now abandoned their homes and given place to the armed forces. It was a day of marshaling and maneuvering of the gathering thousands, preparatory to the mighty conflict that was clearly seen to be inevitable. Lee had taken a strong position on the west bank of Antietam

THE FIRST TO FALL

This photograph was taken back of the rail fence on the Hagerstown pike, where "Stonewall" Jackson's men attempted to rally in the face of Hooker's ferocious charge that opened the bloodiest day of the Civil War—September 17, 1862. Hooker, advancing to seize high ground nearly three-quarters of a mile distant, had not gone far before the glint of the rising sun disclosed the bayonet-points of a large Confederate force standing in a cornfield in his immediate front. This was a part of Jackson's Corps which had arrived during the morning of the 16th from the capture of Harper's Ferry and had been posted in this position to surprise Hooker in his advance. The outcome was a terrible surprise to the Confederates. All of Hooker's batteries hurried into action and opened with canister on the cornfield. The Confederates stood bravely up against this fire, and as Hooker's men advanced they made a determined resistance. Back and still farther back were Jackson's men driven across the open field, every stalk of corn in which was cut down by the battle as closely as a knife could have done it. On the ground the slain lay in rows precisely as they had stood in ranks. From the cornfield into a small patch of woods (the West Woods) the Confederates were driven, leaving the sad result of the surprise behind them. As the edge of the woods was approached by Hooker's men the resistance became stronger and more stubborn. Nearly all the units of two of Jackson's divisions were now in action, and cavalry and artillery were aiding them. "The two lines," says General Palfrey, "almost tore each other to pieces." General Starke and Colonel Douglas on the Confederate side were killed. More than half of Lawton's and Hays' brigades were either killed or wounded. On the Federal side General Ricketts lost a third of his division. The energy of both forces was entirely spent and reënforcements were necessary before the battle could be continued. Many of Jackson's men wore trousers and caps of Federal blue, as did most of the troops which had been engaged with Jackson in the affair at Harper's Ferry. A. P. Hill's men, arriving from Harper's Ferry that same afternoon, were dressed in new Federal uniforms—a part of their booty—and at first were mistaken for Federals by the friends who were anxiously awaiting them.

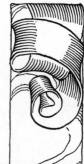

Creek a few miles from where it flows into the Potomac. He made a display of force, exposing his men to the fire of the Federal artillery, his object being to await the coming of Jackson's command from Harper's Ferry. It is true that Jackson himself had arrived, but his men were weary with marching and, moreover, a large portion of his troops under A. P. Hill and McLaws had not yet reached the field.

McClellan spent the day arranging his corps and giving directions for planting batteries. With a few companions he rode along the whole front, frequently drawing the fire of the Confederate batteries and thus revealing their location. The right wing of his army, the corps of Generals Hooker, Mansfield, and Sumner, lay to the north, near the village of Keedysville. General Porter with two divisions of the Fifth Corps occupied the center and Burnside was on the left of the Union lines. Back of McClellan's lines was a ridge on which was a signal station commanding a view of the entire field. Late on the afternoon of the 16th, Hooker crossing the Antietam, advanced against Hood's division on the Confederate left. For several hours there was heavy skirmishing, which closed with the coming of darkness.

The two great armies now lay facing each other in a grand double line three miles in length. At one point (the Union right and the Confederate left) they were so near together that the pickets could hear each other's tread. It required no prophet to foretell what would happen on the morrow.

Beautiful and clear the morning broke over the Maryland hills on the fateful 17th of September, 1862. The sunlight had not yet crowned the hilltops when artillery fire announced the opening of the battle. Hooker's infantry soon entered into the action and encountered the Confederates in an open field, from which the latter were presently pressed back across the Hagerstown pike to a line of woods where they made a determined stand. Hooker then called on General Mansfield to come to his aid, and the latter quickly did so, for he had led

THE THRICE–FOUGHT GROUND

The field beyond the leveled fence is covered with both Federal and Confederate dead. Over this open space swept Sedgwick's division of Sumner's Second Corps, after passing through the East and entering the West Woods. This is near where the Confederate General Ewell's division, reënforced by McLaws and Walker, fell upon Sedgwick's left flank and rear. Nearly two thousand Federal soldiers were struck down, the division losing during the day more than forty per cent. of its entire number. One regiment lost sixty per cent.—the highest regimental loss sustained. Later the right of the Confederate line crossed the turnpike at the Dunker church (about half a mile to the left of the picture) and made two assaults upon Greene, but they were repulsed with great slaughter. General D. R. Jones, of Jackson's division, had been wounded. The brave Starke who succeeded him was killed; and Lawton, who followed Starke, had fallen wounded.

RUIN OF MUMMA'S HOUSE, ANTIETAM

A flaming mansion was the guidon for the extreme left of Greene's division when (early in the morning) he had moved forward along the ridge leading to the East Woods. This dwelling belonged to a planter by the name of Mumma. It stood in the very center of the Federal advance, and also at the extreme left of D. H. Hill's line. The house had been fired by the Confederates, who feared that its thick walls might become a vantage-point for the Federal infantry. It burned throughout the battle, the flames subsiding only in the afternoon. Before it, just across the road, a battery of the First Rhode Island Light Artillery had placed its guns. Twice were they charged, but each time they were repulsed. From Mumma's house it was less than half a mile across the open field to the Dunker church. The fence-rails in the upper picture were those of the field enclosing Mumma's land, and the heroic dead pictured lying there were in full sight from the burning mansion.

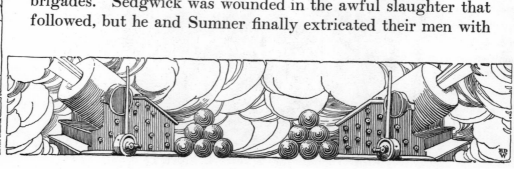

his corps across the Antietam after dark the night before. Mansfield, however, a gallant and honored veteran, fell mortally wounded while deploying his troops, and General Alpheus S. Williams, at the head of his first division, succeeded to the command.

There was a wood west of the Sharpsburg and Hagerstown turnpike which, with its outcropping ledges of rock, formed an excellent retreat for the Confederates and from this they pushed their columns into the open fields, chiefly of corn, to meet the Union attacks. For about two hours the battle raged at this point, the lines swaying to and fro, with fearful slaughter on both sides. At length, General Greene, who commanded a division of the fallen Mansfield's corps, gained possession of part of the coveted forest, near a little white church, known as the Dunker's Chapel. This was on high ground and was the key to the Confederate left wing. But Greene's troops were exposed to a galling fire from D. H. Hill's division and he called for reenforcements.

General Sumner then sent Sedgwick's division across the stream and accompanied the troops to the aid of their hard-pressed comrades. And the experience of this body of the gallant Second Corps during the next hour was probably the most thrilling episode of the whole day's battle. Sedgwick's troops advanced straight toward the conflict. They found Hooker wounded and his and Williams' troops quite exhausted. A sharp artillery fire was turned on Sedgwick before he reached the woods west of the Hagerstown pike, but once in the shelter of the thick trees he passed in safety to the western edge. Here the division found itself in an ambush. Heavy Confederate reenforcements—ten brigades, in fact—Walker's men, and McLaws', having arrived from Harper's Ferry—were hastening up, and they not only blocked the front, but worked around to the rear of Sedgwick's isolated brigades. Sedgwick was wounded in the awful slaughter that followed, but he and Sumner finally extricated their men with

THE HARVEST OF "BLOODY LANE"

Here, at "Bloody Lane" in the sunken road, was delivered the most telling blow of which the Federals could boast in the day's fighting at Antietam, September 17, 1862. In the lower picture we see the officers whose work first began to turn the tide of battle into a decisive advantage which the Army of the Potomac had every reason to expect would be gained by its superior numbers. On the Federal right Jackson, with a bare four thousand men, had taken the fight out of Hooker's eighteen thousand in the morning, giving ground at last to Sumner's fresh troops. On the Federal left, Burnside (at the lower bridge) failed to advance against Longstreet's Corps, two-thirds of which had been detached for service elsewhere. It was at the center that the forces of French and Richardson, skilfully fought by their leaders, broke through the Confederate lines and, sweeping beyond the sunken road, seized the very citadel of the center. Meagher's Irish Brigade had fought its way to a crest from which a plunging fire could be poured upon the Confederates in the sunken road. Meagher's ammunition was exhausted, and Caldwell threw his force into the position and continued the terrible combat. When the Confederates executed their flanking movement to the left, Colonel D. R. Cross, of the Fifth New Hampshire, seized a position which exposed Hill's men to an enfilading fire. (In the picture General Caldwell is seen standing to the left of the tree, and Colonel Cross leans on his sword at the extreme right. Between them stands Lieut.-Colonel George W. Scott, of the Sixty-first New York Infantry, while at the left before the tent stands Captain George W. Bulloch, A.C.S. General Caldwell's hand rests on the shoulder of Captain George H. Caldwell; to his left is seated Lieutenant C. A. Alvord.)

BRIGADIER-GENERAL CALDWELL AND STAFF

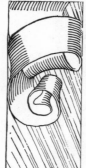

a loss of two thousand, over three hundred left dead on the ghastly field. Franklin now sent forward some fresh troops and after obstinately fighting, the Federals finally held a cornfield and most of the coveted wood over which the conflict had raged till the ground was saturated with blood.

Before the close of this bloody conflict on the Union right another, almost if not quite as deadly, was in progress near the center. General French, soon joined by General Richardson, both of Sumner's corps, crossed the stream and made a desperate assault against the Southerners of D. H. Hill's division, stationed to the south of where the battle had previously raged—French on a line of heights strongly held by the Confederates, Richardson in the direction of a sunken road, since known as " Bloody Lane." The fighting here was of a most desperate character and continued nearly four hours. French captured a few flags, several hundred prisoners, and gained some ground, but he failed to carry the heights. Richardson was mortally wounded while leading a charge and was succeeded by General Hancock; but his men finally captured Bloody Lane with the three hundred living men who had remained to defend it. The final Federal charge at this point was made by Colonel Barlow, who displayed the utmost bravery and self-possession in the thickest of the fight, where he won a brigadier-generalship. He was wounded, and later carried off the field. The Confederates had fought desperately to hold their position in Bloody Lane, and when it was captured it was filled with dead bodies. It was now about one o'clock and the infantry firing ceased for the day on the Union right, and center.

Let us now look on the other part of the field. Burnside held the Federal left wing against Lee's right, and he remained inactive for some hours after the battle had begun at the other end of the line. In front of Burnside was a triple-arched stone bridge across the Antietam, since known as " Burnside's Bridge." Opposite this bridge, on the slope which extends to a

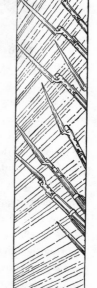

SHERRICK'S HOUSE

In three distinct localities the battle waxed fierce from dawn to dusk on that terrible day at Antietam, September 17, 1862. First at the Federal right around the Dunker church; then at the sunken road, where the centers of both armies spent themselves in sanguinary struggle; lastly, late in the day, the struggle was renewed and ceased on the Sharpsburg road. When Burnside finally got his troops in motion, Sturgis' division of the Ninth Corps was first to cross the creek; his men advanced through an open ravine under a withering fire till they gained the opposite crest and held it until reënforced by Wilcox. To their right ran the Sharpsburg road, and an advance was begun in the direction of the Sherrick house.

The fighting along the Sharpsburg road might have resulted in a Confederate disaster had it not been for the timely arrival of the troops of General A. P. Hill. His six brigades of Confederate veterans had been the last to leave Harper's Ferry, remaining behind Jackson's main body in order to attend to the details of the surrender. Just as the Federal Ninth Corps was in the height of its advance, a cloud of dust on Harper's Ferry road cheered the Confederates to redoubled effort. Out of the dust the brigades of Hill debouched upon the field. Their fighting blood seemed to have but mounted more strongly during their march of eighteen miles. Without waiting for orders, Hill threw his men into the fight and the progress of the

GENERAL A. P. HILL, C. S. A.

Ninth Corps was stopped. Lee had counted on the arrival of Hill in time to prevent any successful attempt upon the Confederate right held by Longstreet's Corps, two-thirds of which had been detached in the thick of the fighting of the morning, when Lee's left and center suffered so severely. Burnside's delay at the bridge could not have been more fortunate for Lee if he had fixed its duration himself. Had the Confederate left been attacked at the time appointed, the outcome of Antietam could scarcely have been other than a decisive victory for the Federals. Even at the time when Burnside's tardy advance began, it must have prevailed against the weakened and wearied Confederates had not the fresh troops of A. P. Hill averted the disaster.

AFTER THE ADVANCE

In the advance along the Sharpsburg road near the Sherrick house the 79th New York "Highlanders" deployed as skirmishers. From orchards and cornfields and from behind fences and haystacks the Confederate sharpshooters opened upon them, but they swept on, driving in a part of Jones' division and capturing a battery just before A. P. Hill's troops arrived. With these reënforcements the Confederates drove back the brave Highlanders from the suburbs of Sharpsburg, which they had reached. Stubborn Scotch blood would permit only a reluctant retreat. Sharp fighting occurred around the Sherrick house with results seen in the lower picture. Night closed the battle, both sides exhausted.

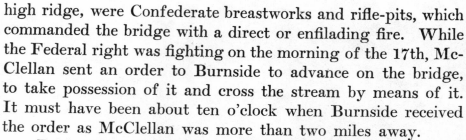

high ridge, were Confederate breastworks and rifle-pits, which commanded the bridge with a direct or enfilading fire. While the Federal right was fighting on the morning of the 17th, McClellan sent an order to Burnside to advance on the bridge, to take possession of it and cross the stream by means of it. It must have been about ten o'clock when Burnside received the order as McClellan was more than two miles away.

Burnside's chief officer at this moment was General Jacob D. Cox (afterward Governor of Ohio), who had succeeded General Reno, killed at South Mountain. On Cox fell the task of capturing the stone bridge. The defense of the bridge was in the hands of General Robert Toombs, a former United States senator and a member of Jefferson Davis' Cabinet. Perhaps the most notable single event in the life of General Toombs was his holding of the Burnside Bridge at Antietam for three hours against the assaults of the Federal troops. The Confederates had been weakened at this point by the sending of Walker to the support of Jackson, where, as we have noticed, he took part in the deadly assault upon Sedgwick's division. Toombs, therefore, with his one brigade had a heavy task before him in defending the bridge with his small force, notwithstanding his advantage of position.

McClellan sent several urgent orders to advance at all hazards. Burnside forwarded these to Cox, and in the fear that the latter would be unable to carry the bridge by a direct front attack, he sent Rodman with a division to cross the creek by a ford some distance below. This was accomplished after much difficulty. Meanwhile, in rapid succession, one assault after another was made upon the bridge and, about one o'clock, it was carried, at the cost of five hundred men. The Confederates fell back. A lull in the fighting along the whole line of battle now ensued.

Burnside, however, received another order from McClellan to push on up the heights and to the village of Sharpsburg. The great importance of this move, if successful, was

THE SEVENTEENTH NEW YORK ARTILLERY DRILLING BEFORE THE CAPITAL

In the background rises the dome of the Capitol which this regiment remained to defend until it was ordered to Petersburg, in 1864. It appears in parade formation. The battery commander leads it, mounted. The battery consists of six pieces, divided into three platoons of two guns each. In front of each platoon is the platoon commander, mounted. Each piece, with its limber and caisson, forms a section; the chief of section is mounted, to the right and a little to the rear of each piece. The cannoneers are mounted on the limbers and caissons in the rear. To the left waves the notched guidon used by both the cavalry and light artillery.

A LIGHT BATTERY AT FORT WHIPPLE, DEFENSES OF WASHINGTON

This photograph shows the flat nature of the open country about Washington. There were no natural fortifications around the city. Artificial works were necessary throughout. Fort Whipple lay to the south of Fort Corcoran, one of the three earliest forts constructed. It was built later, during one of the recurrent panics at the rumor that the Confederates were about to descend upon Washington. This battery of six guns, the one on the right hand, pointing directly out of the picture, looks quite formidable. One can imagine the burst of fire from the underbrush which surrounds it, should it open upon the foe. At present it is simply drilling.

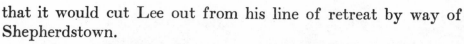

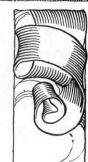

that it would cut Lee out from his line of retreat by way of Shepherdstown.

After replenishing the ammunition and adding some fresh troops, Cox advanced at three o'clock with the utmost gallantry toward Sharpsburg. The Confederates disputed the ground with great bravery. But Cox swept all before him and was at the edge of the village when he was suddenly confronted by lines in blue uniforms who instantly opened fire. The Federals were astonished to see the blue-clad battalions before them. They must be Union soldiers; but how did they get there? The matter was soon explained. They were A. P. Hill's division of Lee's army which had just arrived from Harper's Ferry, and they had dressed themselves in the uniforms that they had taken from the Federal stores.

Hill had come just in time to save Lee's headquarters from capture. He checked Cox's advance, threw a portion of the troops into great confusion, and steadily pressed them back toward the Antietam. In this, the end of the battle, General Rodman fell mortally wounded. Cox retired in good order and Sharpsburg remained in the hands of the Confederates.

Thus, with the approach of nightfall, closed the memorable battle of Antietam. For fourteen long hours more than one hundred thousand men, with five hundred pieces of artillery, had engaged in titanic combat. As the pall of battle smoke rose and cleared away, the scene presented was one to make the stoutest heart shudder. There lay upon the ground, scattered for three miles over the valleys and the hills or in the improvised hospitals, more than twenty thousand men. Horace Greeley was probably right in pronouncing this the bloodiest day in American history.

Although tactically it was a drawn battle, Antietam was decisively in favor of the North inasmuch as it ended the first Confederate attempt at a Northern invasion. General Lee realized that his ulterior plans had been thwarted by this engagement and after a consultation with his corps commanders

"STAND TO HORSE!"—AN AMERICAN VOLUNTEER CAVALRYMAN, OCTOBER, 1862

"He's not a regular—but he's 'smart.'" This tribute to the soldierly bearing of the trooper above was bestowed, forty-nine years after the taking of the picture, by an officer of the U. S. cavalry, himself a Civil War veteran. The recipient of such high praise is seen as he "stood to horse" a month after the battle of Antietam. The war was only in its second year, but his drill is quite according to army regulations— hand to bridle, six inches from the bit. His steady glance as he peers from beneath his hat into the sun- light tells its own story. Days and nights in the saddle without food or sleep, sometimes riding along the 60-mile picket-line in front of the Army of the Potomac, sometimes faced by sudden encounters with the Southern raiders, have all taught him the needed confidence in himself, his horse, and his equipment.

he determined to withdraw from Maryland. On the night of the 18th the retreat began and early the next morning the Confederate army had all safely recrossed the Potomac.

The great mistake of the Maryland campaign from the standpoint of the Confederate forces, thought General Longstreet, was the division of Lee's army, and he believed that if Lee had kept his forces together he would not have been forced to abandon the campaign. At Antietam, he had less than forty thousand men, who were in poor condition for battle while McClellan had about eighty-seven thousand, most of whom were fresh and strong, though not more than sixty thousand were in action.

The moral effect of the battle of Antietam was incalculably great. It aroused the confidence of the Northern people. It emboldened President Lincoln to issue five days after its close the proclamation freeing the slaves in the seceded states. He had written the proclamation long before, but it had lain inactive in his desk at Washington. All through the struggles of the summer of 1862 he had looked forward to the time when he could announce his decision to the people. But he could not do it then. With the doubtful success of Federal arms, to make such a bold step would have been a mockery and would have defeated the very end he sought.

The South had now struck its first desperate blow at the gateways to the North. By daring, almost unparalleled in warfare, it had swung its courageous army into a strategical position where with the stroke of fortune it might have hammered down the defenses of the National capital on the south and then sweep on a march of invasion into the North. The Northern soldiers had parried the blow. They had saved themselves from disaster and had held back the tide of the Confederacy as it beat against the Mason and Dixon line, forcing it back into the State of Virginia where the two mighty fighting bodies were soon to meet again in a desperate struggle for the right-of-way at Fredericksburg.

THE MEDIATOR

President Lincoln's Visit to the Camps at Antietam, October 8, 1862. Yearning for the speedy termination of the war, Lincoln came to view the Army of the Potomac, as he had done at Harrison's Landing. Puzzled to understand how Lee could have circumvented a superior force on the Peninsula, he was now anxious to learn why a crushing blow had not been struck. Lincoln (after Gettysburg) expressed the same thought: "Our army held the war in the hollow of their hand and they would not close it!" On Lincoln's right stands Allan Pinkerton, the famous detective and organizer of the Secret Service of the army. At the President's left is General John A. McClernand, soon to be entrusted by Lincoln with reorganizing military operations in the West.

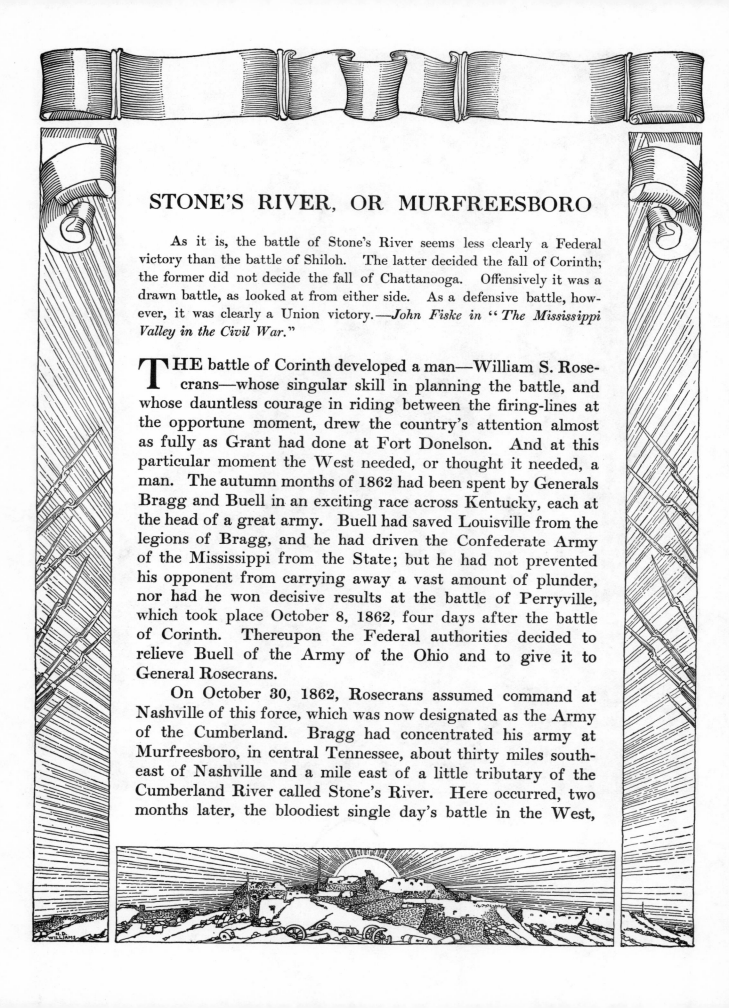

STONE'S RIVER, OR MURFREESBORO

As it is, the battle of Stone's River seems less clearly a Federal victory than the battle of Shiloh. The latter decided the fall of Corinth; the former did not decide the fall of Chattanooga. Offensively it was a drawn battle, as looked at from either side. As a defensive battle, however, it was clearly a Union victory.—*John Fiske in " The Mississippi Valley in the Civil War."*

THE battle of Corinth developed a man—William S. Rosecrans—whose singular skill in planning the battle, and whose dauntless courage in riding between the firing-lines at the opportune moment, drew the country's attention almost as fully as Grant had done at Fort Donelson. And at this particular moment the West needed, or thought it needed, a man. The autumn months of 1862 had been spent by Generals Bragg and Buell in an exciting race across Kentucky, each at the head of a great army. Buell had saved Louisville from the legions of Bragg, and he had driven the Confederate Army of the Mississippi from the State; but he had not prevented his opponent from carrying away a vast amount of plunder, nor had he won decisive results at the battle of Perryville, which took place October 8, 1862, four days after the battle of Corinth. Thereupon the Federal authorities decided to relieve Buell of the Army of the Ohio and to give it to General Rosecrans.

On October 30, 1862, Rosecrans assumed command at Nashville of this force, which was now designated as the Army of the Cumberland. Bragg had concentrated his army at Murfreesboro, in central Tennessee, about thirty miles southeast of Nashville and a mile east of a little tributary of the Cumberland River called Stone's River. Here occurred, two months later, the bloodiest single day's battle in the West,

MEN WHO LEARNED WAR WITH SHERMAN

The Twenty-first Michigan Infantry. In the Murfreesboro campaign, the regiment, detached from its old command, fought in the division of Brigadier-General "Phil" Sheridan, a leader who became scarcely less renowned in the West than Sherman and gave a good account of himself and his men at Stone's River. Most of the faces in the picture are those of boys, yet severe military service has already given them the unmistakable carriage of the soldier. The terrible field of Chickamauga lay before them, but a few months in the future; and after that, rejoining their beloved "Old Tecumseh," they were to march with him to the sea and witness some of the closing scenes in the struggle.

a conflict imminent as soon as the news came (on December 26th) that the Federals were advancing from Nashville.

General Bragg did not lose a moment in marshaling his army into well-drawn battle-lines. His army was in two corps with a cavalry division under General Wheeler, Forrest and Morgan being on detached service. The left wing, under General Hardee, and the center, under Polk, were sent across Stone's River, the right wing, a division under John C. Breckinridge, remaining on the eastern side of the stream to guard the town. The line was three miles in length, and on December 30th the Federal host that had come from Nashville stood opposite, in a parallel line. It was also in three sections. The left wing, opposite Breckinridge, was commanded by Thomas L. Crittenden, whose brother was a commander in the Confederacy. They were sons of the famous United States senator from Kentucky, John J. Crittenden. The Federal center, opposite Polk, was commanded by George H. Thomas, and the right wing, opposing the Confederate left, was led by Alexander McD. McCook, one of the well-known "Fighting Mc-Cook" brothers. The effective Federal force was about forty-three thousand men; the Confederate army numbered about thirty-eight thousand. That night they bivouacked within musket range of each other and the camp-fires of each were clearly seen by the other as they shone through the cedar groves that interposed. Thus lay the two great armies, ready to spring upon each other in deadly combat with the coming of the morning.

Rosecrans had permitted McCook to thin out his lines over too much space, while on that very part of the field Bragg had concentrated his forces for the heaviest attack. The plans of battle made by the two opposing commanders were strikingly similar. Rosecrans' plan was to throw his left wing, under Crittenden, across the river upon the Confederate right under Breckinridge, to crush it in one impetuous dash, and to swing around through Murfreesboro to the Franklin road and

FIGHTERS IN THE WEST

This picture of Company C of the Twenty-first Michigan shows impressively the type of men that the rough campaigning west of the Alleghanies had molded into veterans. These were Sherman's men, and under the watchful eye and in the inspiring presence of that general thousands of stalwart lads from the sparsely settled States were becoming the very bone and sinew of the Federal fighting force. The men of Sherman, like their leader, were forging steadily to the front. They had become proficient in the fighting which knows no fear, in many hard-won combats in the early part of the war. Greater and more magnificent conflicts awaited those who did not find a hero's grave.

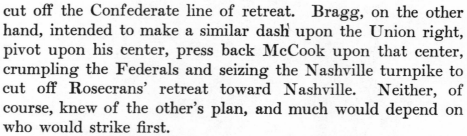

cut off the Confederate line of retreat. Bragg, on the other hand, intended to make a similar dash upon the Union right, pivot upon his center, press back McCook upon that center, crumpling the Federals and seizing the Nashville turnpike to cut off Rosecrans' retreat toward Nashville. Neither, of course, knew of the other's plan, and much would depend on who would strike first.

At the early light of the last day of the year the Confederate left wing moved upon the Union right in a magnificent battle-line, three-quarters of a mile in length and two columns deep. At the same time the Confederate artillery opened with their cannon. McCook was astonished at so fierce and sudden a charge. The gallant Patrick Cleburne, one of the ablest commanders in the Southern armies, led his division, which had been brought from the Confederate right, in the charge. The Federal lines were ill prepared for this sudden onslaught, and before McCook could arrange them several batteries were overpowered and eleven of the heavy guns were in the hands of the Confederates.

Slowly the Union troops fell back, firing as they went; but they had no power to check the impetuous, overwhelming charge of the onrushing foe. McCook's two right divisions, under Johnson and Jeff. C. Davis, were driven back, but his third division, which was commanded by a young officer who had attracted unusual attention at the battle of Perryville— Philip H. Sheridan—held its ground. At the first Confederate advance, Sill's brigade of Sheridan's division drove the troops in front of it back into their entrenchments, and in the charge the brave Sill lost his life.

While the battle raged with tremendous fury on the Union right, Rosecrans was three miles away, throwing his left across the river. Hearing the terrific roar of battle at the other end of the line, Rosecrans hastened to begin his attack on Breckinridge hoping to draw a portion of the Confederate force away from McCook. But as the hours of the forenoon

A CAMP MEETING WITH A PURPOSE

There was something of extreme interest taking place when this photograph was taken at Corinth. With arms stacked, the soldiers are gathered about an improvised stand sheltered with canvas, listening to a speech upon a burning question of the hour—the employment of colored troops in the field. A question upon which there were many different and most decided opinions prevailing in the North, and but one nearly universal opinion holding south of Mason and Dixon's line. General Thomas, at the moment this photograph was taken, was addressing the assembled troops on this subject. Some prominent Southerners, among them General Patrick Cleburne, favored the enrollment of Negroes in the Confederate army.

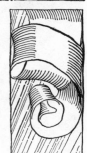
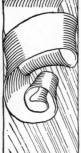

passed he was dismayed as he noted that the sound of battle was coming nearer, and he rightly divined that his right wing was receding before the dashing soldiers of the South. He ordered McCook to dispute every inch of the ground; but McCook's command was soon torn to pieces and disorganized, except the division of Sheridan.

The latter stood firm against the overwhelming numbers, a stand that attracted the attention of the country and brought him military fame. He checked the onrushing Confederates at the point of the bayonet; he formed a new line under fire. In his first position Sheridan held his ground for two hours. The Confederate attack had also fallen heavily on Negley, who was stationed on Sheridan's left, and on Palmer, both of Thomas' center. Rousseau commanding the reserves, and Van Cleve of Crittenden's forces were ordered to the support of the Union center and right. Here, for two hours longer the battle raged with unabated fury, and the slaughter of brave men on both sides was appalling. Three times the whole Confederate left and center were thrown against the Union divisions, but failed to break the lines. At length when their cartridge boxes were empty Sheridan's men could do nothing but retire for more ammunition, and they did this in good order to a rolling plain near the Nashville road. But Rousseau of Thomas' center was there to check the Confederate advance.

It was now past noon, and still the battle roar resounded unceasingly through the woods and hills about Murfreesboro. Though both hosts had struggled and suffered since early morning, they still held to their guns, pouring withering volleys into each other's ranks. The Federal right and center had been forced back at right angles to the position they had held when day dawned; and the Confederate left was swung around at right angles to its position of the morning. The Federal left rested on Stone's River, while Bragg's right was on the same stream and close to the line in blue. Meantime, Rosecrans had massed his artillery on a little hill over-

LEADERS OF A GALLANT STAND AT STONE'S RIVER

General William P. Carlin and Staff. Early in the war Carlin made a name for himself as colonel of the Thirty-eighth Illinois Infantry, which was stationed at Pilot Knob, Missouri, and was kept constantly alert by the raids of Price and Jeff Thompson. Carlin rose rapidly to be the commander of a brigade, and joined the forces in Tennessee in 1862. He distinguished himself at Perryville and in the advance to Murfreesboro. At Stone's River his brigade, almost surrounded, repulsed an overwhelming force of Confederates. This picture was taken a year after that battle, while the brigade was in winter quarters at Ringgold, Georgia. The band-stand was built by the General's old regiment.

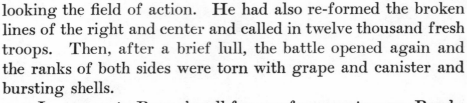

looking the field of action. He had also re-formed the broken lines of the right and center and called in twelve thousand fresh troops. Then, after a brief lull, the battle opened again and the ranks of both sides were torn with grape and canister and bursting shells.

In answer to Bragg's call for reenforcements came Breckinridge with all but one brigade of his division, a host of about seven thousand fresh troops. The new Confederate attack began slowly, but increased its speed at every step. Suddenly, a thundering volley burst from the line in blue, and the front ranks of the attacking column disappeared. Again, a volley tore through the ranks in gray, and the assault was abandoned.

The battle had raged for nearly eleven hours, when night enveloped the scene, and the firing abated slowly and died away. It had been a bloody day—this first day's fight at Stone's River—and except at Antietam it had not thus far been surpassed in the war. The advantage was clearly with the Confederates. They had pressed back the Federals for two miles, had routed their right wing and captured many prisoners and twenty-eight heavy guns. But Rosecrans determined to hold his ground and try again.

The next day was New Year's and but for a stray fusillade, here and there, both armies remained inactive, except that each quietly prepared to renew the contest on the morrow. The renewal of the battle on January 2nd was fully expected on both sides, but there was little fighting till four in the afternoon. Rosecrans had sent General Van Cleve's division on January 1st across the river to seize an elevation from which he could shell the town of Murfreesboro. Bragg now sent Breckinridge to dislodge the division, and he did so with splendid effect. But Breckinridge's men came into such a position as to be exposed to the raking fire of fifty-two pieces of Federal artillery on the west side of the river. Returning the deadly and constant fire as best they could, they stood the storm of shot and shell for half an hour when they retreated to a place

AN UNCEASING WORK OF WAR

In the picture the contraband laborers often pressed into service by Federals are repairing the "stringer" track near Murfreesboro after the battle of Stone's River. The long lines of single-track road, often involving a change from broad-gauge to narrow-gauge, were entirely inadequate for the movement of troops in that great area. In these isolated regions the railroads often became the supreme objective of both sides. When disinclined to offer battle, each struck in wild raids against the other's line of communication. Sections of track were tipped over embankments; rails were torn up, heated red-hot in bonfires, and twisted so that they could never be used again. The wrecking of a railroad might postpone a maneuver for months, or might terminate a campaign suddenly in defeat. Each side in retreat burned its bridges and destroyed the railroad behind it. Again advancing, each had to pause for the weary work of repair.

of safety, leaving seventeen hundred of their number dead or wounded on the field. That night the two armies again lay within musket shot of each other. The next day brought no further conflict and during that night General Bragg moved away to winter quarters at Shelbyville, on the Elk River.

Murfreesboro, or Stone's River, was one of the great battles of the war. The losses were about thirteen thousand to the Federals and over ten thousand to the Confederates. Both sides claimed victory—the South because of Bragg's signal success on the first day; the North because of Breckinridge's fearful repulse at the final onset and of Bragg's retreating in the night and refusing to fight again. A portion of the Confederate army occupied Shelbyville, Tennessee, and the larger part entrenched at Tullahoma, eighteen miles to the southeast.

Six months after the battle of Stone's River, the Federal army suddenly awoke from its somnolent condition—a winter and spring spent in raids and unimportant skirmishes—and became very busy preparing for a long and hasty march. Rosecrans' plan of campaign was brilliant and proved most effective. He realized that Tullahoma was the barrier to Chattanooga, and determined to drive the Confederates from it.

On June 23, 1863, the advance began. The cavalry, under General Stanley, had received orders to advance upon Shelbyville on the 24th, and during that night to build immense and numerous camp-fires before the Confederate stronghold at Shelbyville, to create the impression that Rosecrans' entire army was massing at that point. But the wily leader of the Federals had other plans, and when Stanley, supported by General Granger, had built his fires, the larger force was closing in upon Tullahoma.

The stratagem dawned upon Bragg too late to check Rosecrans' plans. Stanley and Granger made a brilliant capture of Shelbyville, and Bragg retired to Tullahoma; but finding here that every disposition had been made to fall upon his rear, he continued his southward retreat toward Chattanooga.

[Part VI]

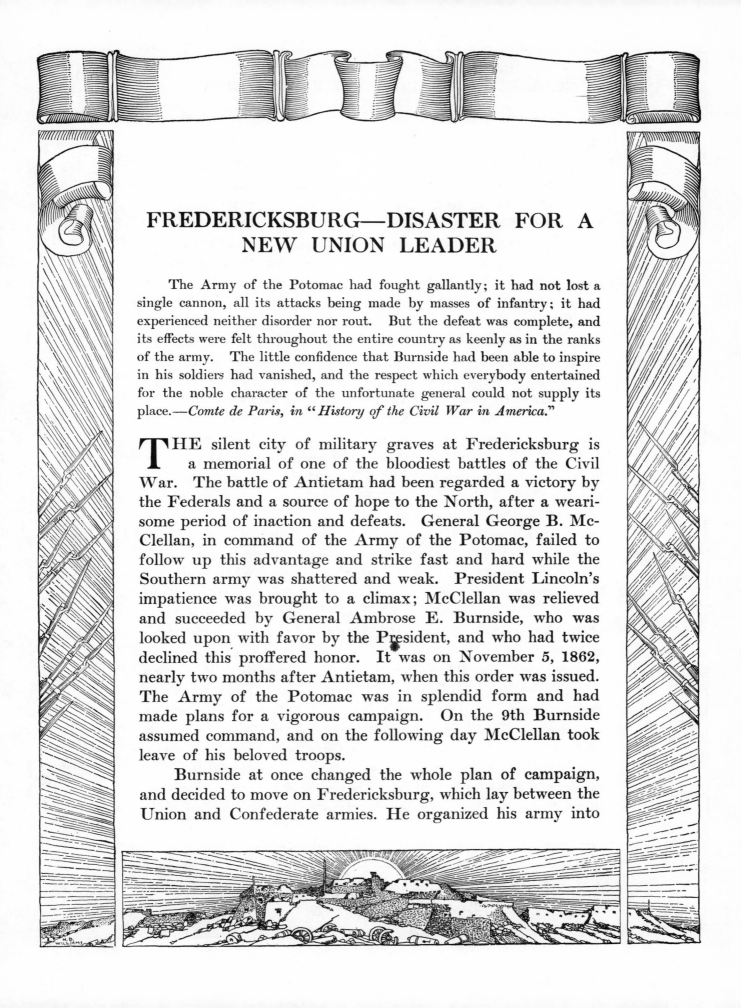

FREDERICKSBURG—DISASTER FOR A NEW UNION LEADER

The Army of the Potomac had fought gallantly; it had not lost a single cannon, all its attacks being made by masses of infantry; it had experienced neither disorder nor rout. But the defeat was complete, and its effects were felt throughout the entire country as keenly as in the ranks of the army. The little confidence that Burnside had been able to inspire in his soldiers had vanished, and the respect which everybody entertained for the noble character of the unfortunate general could not supply its place.—*Comte de Paris, in "History of the Civil War in America."*

THE silent city of military graves at Fredericksburg is a memorial of one of the bloodiest battles of the Civil War. The battle of Antietam had been regarded a victory by the Federals and a source of hope to the North, after a wearisome period of inaction and defeats. General George B. McClellan, in command of the Army of the Potomac, failed to follow up this advantage and strike fast and hard while the Southern army was shattered and weak. President Lincoln's impatience was brought to a climax; McClellan was relieved and succeeded by General Ambrose E. Burnside, who was looked upon with favor by the President, and who had twice declined this proffered honor. It was on November 5, 1862, nearly two months after Antietam, when this order was issued. The Army of the Potomac was in splendid form and had made plans for a vigorous campaign. On the 9th Burnside assumed command, and on the following day McClellan took leave of his beloved troops.

Burnside at once changed the whole plan of campaign, and decided to move on Fredericksburg, which lay between the Union and Confederate armies. He organized his army into

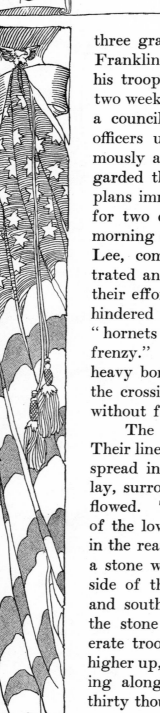

three grand divisions, under Generals Sumner, Hooker, and Franklin, commanding the right, center, and left, and moved his troops from Warrenton to Falmouth. A delay of some two weeks was due to the failure of arrival of the pontoons. In a council of war held on the night of December 10th the officers under Burnside expressed themselves almost unanimously as opposed to the plan of battle, but Burnside disregarded their views and determined to carry out his original plans immediately. After some delay and desultory fighting for two days, the crossing of the army was effected by the morning of December 13th. By this time General Robert E. Lee, commanding the Confederates, had his army concentrated and entrenched on the hills surrounding the town. In their efforts to place their bridges the Federals were seriously hindered by the firing of the Confederate sharpshooters—"hornets that were stinging the Army of the Potomac into a frenzy." The Confederate fire continued until silenced by a heavy bombardment of the city from the Federal guns, when the crossing of the army into Fredericksburg was completed without further interference.

The forces of Lee were in battle array about the town. Their line stretched for five miles along the range of hills which spread in crescent shape around the lowland where the city lay, surrounding it on all sides save the east, where the river flowed. The strongest Confederate position was on the slopes of the lowest hill of the range, Marye's Heights, which rose in the rear of the town. Along the foot of this hill there was a stone wall, about four feet in height, bounding the eastern side of the Telegraph road, which at this point runs north and south, being depressed a few feet below the surface of the stone wall, thus forming a breastwork for the Confederate troops. Behind it a strong force was concealed, while higher up, in several ranks, the main army was massed, stretching along the line of hills. The right wing, consisting of thirty thousand troops on an elevation near Hamilton's Cross-

THE SECOND LEADER AGAINST RICHMOND

Major-General Ambrose Everett Burnside was a West Point graduate, inventor of a breech-loading rifle, commander of a brigade in the first battle of Bull Run, captor of Roanoke Island and Newberne (North Carolina), and commander of the Federal left at Antietam. He was appointed to the command of the Army of the Potomac and succeeded General George B. McClellan on November 8, 1862. He was a brave soldier, but was an impatient leader and inclined to be somewhat reckless. He pressed rapidly his advance against Lee and massed his entire army along Stafford Heights, on the east bank of the Rappahannock, opposite Fredericksburg. According to General W. B. Franklin (who commanded the left grand division of the army), the notion that a serious battle was necessary to Federal control of the town "was not entertained by any one." General Sumner (who led the advance of Burnside's army) held this opinion but he had not received orders to cross the river. Crossing was delayed nearly a month and this delay resulted in the Federal disaster on December 13th. This put an abrupt end to active operations by Burnside against Lee. This picture was taken at Warrenton, November 24th, on the eve of the departure of the army for its march to Fredericksburg.

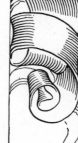

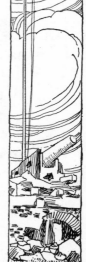

ing of the Fredericksburg and Potomac Railroad, was commanded by "Stonewall" Jackson. The left, on Marye's Heights and Marye's Hill, was commanded by the redoubtable Longstreet. The Southern forces numbered about seventy-eight thousand.

Into the little city below and the adjoining valleys, the Federal troops had been marching for two days. Franklin's Left Grand Division of forty thousand was strengthened by two divisions from Hooker's Center Grand Division, and was ordered to make the first attack on the Confederate right under Jackson. Sumner's Right Grand Division, also reenforced from Hooker's forces, was formed for assault against the Confederate's strongest point at Marye's Hill.

All this magnificent and portentous battle formation had been effected under cover of a dense fog, and when it lifted on that fateful Saturday there was revealed a scene of truly military grandeur. Concealed by the somber curtain of nature the Southern hosts had fixed their batteries and entrenched themselves most advantageously upon the hills, and the Union legions, massed in menacing strength below, now lay within easy cannon-shot of their foe. The Union army totaled one hundred and thirteen thousand men. After skirmishing and gathering of strength, it was at length ready for the final spring and the death-grapple.

When the sun's rays broke through the fog during the forenoon of December 13th, Franklin's Grand Division was revealed in full strength in front of the Confederate right, marching and countermarching in preparation for the coming conflict. Officers in new, bright uniforms, thousands of bayonets gleaming in the sunshine, champing steeds, rattling gun-carriages whisking artillery into proper range of the foe, infantry, cavalry, batteries, with officers and men, formed a scene of magnificent grandeur which excited the admiration even of the Confederates. This maneuver has been called the grandest military scene of the war.

THE DETAINED GUNS

Fredericksburg, February, 1863. In the foreground, looking from what is approximately the same position as the opening picture, are three guns of Tyler's Connecticut battery. It was from all along this ridge that the town had suffered its bombardment in December of the previous year. Again the armies were separated by the Rappahannock River. There was a new commander at the head of the Army of the Potomac—General Hooker. The plundered and deserted town now held by the Confederates was to be made the objective of another attack. The heights beyond were once more to be assaulted; bridges were to be rebuilt. But all to no purpose. This ground of much contention was deserted some time before Lee advanced to his invasion of Pennsylvania. Very slowly the inhabitants of Fredericksburg

had returned to their ruined homes. The town was a vast Federal cemetery, the dead being buried in gardens and backyards, for during its occupancy almost every dwelling had been turned into a temporary hospital. After the close of the war these bodies were gathered and a National Cemetery was established on Willis' Hill, on Marye's Heights, the point successfully defended by Lee's veterans.

Heavy pontoon-boats, each on its separate wagon, were sometimes as necessary as food or ammunition. At every important crossing of the many rivers that had to be passed in the Peninsula Campaign the bridges had been destroyed. There were few places where these streams were fordable. Pontoons, therefore, made a most important adjunct to the Army of the Potomac.

PONTOON–BOATS IN TRANSIT

Yet with all this brave show, we have seen that Burnside's subordinate officers were unanimous in their belief in the rashness of the undertaking. Enthusiasm was sadly lacking. The English military writer, Colonel Henderson, has explained why this was so:

And yet that vast array, so formidable of aspect, lacked that moral force without which physical power, even in its most terrible form, is but an idle show. Not only were the strength of the Confederate position, the want of energy of preliminary movements, the insecurity of their own situation, but too apparent to the intelligence of the regimental officers and men, but they mistrusted their commander. Northern writers have recorded that the Army of the Potomac never went down to battle with less alacrity than on this day at Fredericksburg.

The first advance began at 8:30 in the morning, while the fog was still dense, upon Jackson's right. Reynolds ordered Meade with a division, supported by two other divisions under Doubleday and Gibbon, to attack Jackson at his weakest point, the extreme right of the Confederate lines, and endeavor to seize one of the opposing heights. The advance was made in three lines of battle, which were guarded in front and on each flank by artillery which swept the field in front as the army advanced. The Confederates were placed to have an enfilading sweep from both flanks along the entire front line of march. When Reynolds' divisions had approached within range, Jackson's small arms on the left poured in a deadly fire, mowing down the brave men in the Union lines in swaths, leaving broad gaps where men had stood.

This fire was repeated again and again, as the Federals pressed on, only to be repulsed. Once only was the Confederate line broken, when Meade carried the crest, capturing flags and prisoners. The ground lost by the Confederates was soon recovered, and the Federals were forced to retire. Some of the charges made by the Federals during this engagement were heroic in the extreme, only equaled by the opposition met

THE FLAMING HEIGHTS

This photograph from the Fredericksburg river-bank recalls a terrible scene. On those memorable days of December 11 and 12, 1862, from these very trenches shown in the foreground, the ragged gray riflemen saw on that hillside across the river the blue of the uniforms of the massed Federal troops. The lines of tents made great white spaces, but the ground could hardly be seen for the host of men who were waiting, alas! to die by thousands on this coveted shore. From these hills, too, burst an incessant flaming and roaring cannon fire. Siege-guns and field artillery poured shot and shell into the town of Fredericksburg. Every house became a target, though deserted except for a few hardy and venturesome riflemen. There was scarcely a dwelling that escaped. Ruined and battered and bloody, Fredericksburg three times was a Federal hospital, and its backyards became little cemeteries.

A TARGET AT FREDERICKSBURG FOR THE FEDERAL GUNS

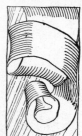
from the foe. In one advance, knapsacks were unslung and bayonets fixed; a brigade marched across a plowed field, and passed through broken lines of other brigades, which were retiring to the rear in confusion from the leaden storm.

The fire became incessant and destructive; many fell, killed or wounded; the front line slackened its pace, and without orders commenced firing. A halt seemed imminent, and a halt in the face of the terrific fire to which the men were exposed meant death; but, urged on by regimental commanders in person, the charge was renewed, when with a shout they leaped the ditches, charged across the railroad, and upon the foe, killing many with the bayonet and capturing several hundred prisoners. But this was only a temporary gain. In every instance the Federals were shattered and driven back. Men were lying dead in heaps, the wounded and dying were groaning in agony. Soldiers were fleeing; officers were galloping to and fro urging their lines forward, and begging their superior officers for assistance and reenforcement.

A dispatch to Burnside from Franklin, dated 2:45, was as follows: " My left has been very badly handled; what hope is there of getting reenforcements across the river? " Another dispatch, dated 3:45, read: " Our troops have gained no ground in the last half hour."

In their retreat the fire was almost as destructive as during the assault. Most of the wounded were brought from the field after this engagement, but the dead were left where they fell. It was during this engagement that General George D. Bayard was mortally wounded by a shot which had severed the sword belt of Captain Gibson, leaving him uninjured. The knapsack of a soldier who was in a stooping posture was struck by a ball, and a deck of cards was sent flying twenty feet in the air. Those witnessing the ludicrous scene called to him, " Oh, deal me a hand! " thus indicating the spirit of levity among soldiers even amid such surroundings. Another soldier sitting on the ground suddenly leaped high above the

THE BRIDGES THAT A BAND OF MUSIC THREATENED

At Franklin Crossing, on the Rappahannock, occurred an incident that proves how little things may change the whole trend of the best-laid plans. The left Union wing under the command of General Franklin, composed of the First Army Corps under General Reynolds, and the Sixth under General W. F. Smith, was crossing to engage in the battle of Fredericksburg. For two days they poured across these yielding planks between the swaying boats to the farther shore. Now, in the crossing of bridges, moving bodies of men must break step or even well-built structures might be threatened. The colonel of one of the regiments in General Devens' division that led the van ordered his field music to strike up just as the head of the column swept on to the flimsy planking; before the regiment was half-way across, unconsciously the men had fallen into step and the whole fabric was swaying to the cadenced feet. Vibrating like a great fiddle-string, the bridge would have sunk and parted, but a keen eye had seen the danger. "Stop that music!" was the order, and a staff officer spurred his horse through the men, shouting at top voice. The lone charge was made through the marching column: some jumped into the pontoons to avoid the hoofs; a few went overboard; but the head of the column was reached at last, and the music stopped. A greater blunder than this, however, took place on the plains beyond. Owing to a misunderstanding of orders, 37,000 troops were never brought into action; 17,000 men on their front bore the brunt of a long day's fighting.

heads of his comrades as a shell struck the spot, scooping a wheelbarrowful of earth, but the man was untouched.

Entirely independent of the action in which the Left Grand Division under Franklin was engaged against the right wing of the Confederate line, Sumner's Right Grand Division was engaged in a terrific assault upon the works on Marye's Heights, the stronghold of the Confederate forces. Their position was almost impregnable, consisting of earthworks, wood, and stone barricades running along the sunken road near the foot of Marye's Hill. The Federals were not aware of the sunken road, nor of the force of twenty-five hundred under General Cobb concealed behind the stone wall, this wall not being new work as a part of the entrenchments, but of earlier construction. When the advance up the road was made they were harassed by shot and shell and rifle-balls at every step, but the men came dashing into line undismayed by the terrific fire which poured down upon them.

The Irish Brigade, the second of Hancock's division, under General Meagher, made a wonderful charge. When they returned from the assault but two hundred and fifty out of twelve hundred men reported under arms from the field, and all these were needed to care for their wounded comrades. The One Hundred and Sixteenth Pennsylvania regiment was new on the field of battle, but did fearless and heroic service. The approach was completely commanded by the Confederate guns. Repeatedly the advance was repulsed by well-directed fire from the batteries.

Once again Sumner's gallant men charged across a railroad cut, running down one side and up the other, and still again attempted to escape in the same manner, but each time they were forced to retire precipitately by a murderous fire from the Confederate batteries. Not only was the Confederate fire disastrous upon the approach and the successive repulses by the foe, but it also inflicted great damage upon the masses of the Federal army in front of Marye's Hill.

OFFICERS OF THE FAMOUS "IRISH BRIGADE"

"The Irish Brigade" (consisting of the Twenty-eighth Massachusetts, Sixty-third, Sixty-ninth and Eighty-eighth New York and the One Hundred and Sixteenth Pennsylvania) was commanded by General Thomas F. Meagher and advanced in Hancock's Division to the first assault at Marye's Heights, on December 13, 1862. In this charge the Irish soldiers moved steadily up the ridge until within a few yards of a sunken road, from which unexpected fire mowed them down. Of the 1,315 men which Meagher led into battle, 545 fell in that charge. The officer standing is Colonel Patrick Kelly, of the Eighty-eighth New York, who was one of the valiant heroes of this charge, and succeeded to the command of the Irish Brigade after General Meagher. He was killed at Petersburg. The officer seated is Captain Clooney, of the same regiment, who was killed at Antietam. Sitting next to him is Father Dillon, Chaplain of the Sixty-third New York, and to the right Father Corby, Chaplain of the Eighty-eighth New York; the latter gave absolution to Caldwell's Division, of Hancock's Corps, under a very heavy fire at Gettysburg. By the side of Colonel Kelly stands a visiting priest. The identification of this group has been furnished by Captain W. L. D. O'Grady, of the Eighty-eighth New York.

The Confederates' effective and successful work on Marye's Hill in this battle was not alone due to the natural strength of their position, but also to the skill and generalship of the leaders, and to the gallantry, courage, and well-directed aim of their cannoneers and infantry.

Six times the heroic Union troops dashed against the invulnerable position, each time to be repulsed with terrific loss. General Couch, who had command of the Second Corps, viewing the scene of battle from the steeple of the court-house with General Howard, says: "The whole plain was covered with men, prostrate and dropping, the live men running here and there, and in front closing upon each other, and the wounded coming back. I had never before seen fighting like that, nothing approaching it in terrible uproar and destruction."

General Howard reports that Couch exclaimed: "Oh, great God! see how our men, our poor fellows, are falling!" At half-past one Couch signaled Burnside: "I am losing. Send two rifle batteries."

The point and method of attack made by Sumner was anticipated by the Confederates, careful preparation having been made to meet it. The fire from the Confederate batteries harassed the Union lines, and as they advanced steadily, heroically, without hurrah or battle-cry, the ranks were cut to pieces by canister and shell and musket-balls. Heavy artillery fire was poured into the Union ranks from front, right, and left with frightful results. Quickly filling up the decimated ranks they approached the stone wall masking the death-trap where General Cobb lay with a strong force awaiting the approach. Torrents of lead poured into the bodies of the defenseless men, slaying, crushing, destroying the proud army of a few hours before. As though in pity, a cloud of smoke momentarily shut out the wretched scene but brought no balm to the helpless victims of this awful carnage. The ground was so thickly strewn with dead bodies as seriously to impede the movements of a renewed attack. These repeated assaults in such good

THE SUMMIT OF SLAUGHTER

Marye's House marked the center of the Confederate position on the Heights, before which the Federals fell three deep in one of the bravest and bloodiest assaults of the war. The eastern boundary of the Marye estate was a retaining wall, along which ran a sunken road; on the other side of this was a stone wall, shoulder high, forming a perfect infantry parapet. Here two brigades of Confederates were posted and on the crest above them were the supporting batteries, while the slope between was honeycombed with the rifle-pits of the sharpshooters, one of which is seen in the picture. Six times did the Federals, raked by the deadly fire of the Washington Artillery, advance to within a hundred yards of the sunken road, only to be driven back by the rapid volleys of the Confederate infantry concealed there. Less than three of every five men in Hancock's division came back from their charge on these death-dealing heights. The complete repulse of the day and the terrific slaughter were the barren results of an heroic effort to obey orders.

order caused some apprehension on the part of General Lee, who said to Longstreet after the third attack, " General, they are massing very heavily and will break your line, I am afraid." But the great general's fears proved groundless.

General Cobb was borne from the field mortally wounded, and Kershaw took his place in the desperate struggle. The storm of shot and shell which met the assaults was terrific. Men fell almost in battalions; the dead and wounded lay in heaps. Late in the day the dead bodies, which had become frozen from the extreme cold, were stood up in front of the soldiers as a protection against the awful fire to shield the living, and at night were set up as dummy sentinels.

The steadiness of the Union troops, and the silent, determined heroism of the rank and file in these repeated, but hopeless, assaults upon the Confederate works, were marvelous, and amazed even their officers. The real greatness in a battle is the fearless courage, the brave and heroic conduct, of the men under withering fire. It was the enlisted men who were the glory of the army. It was they, the rank and file, who stood in the front, closed the gaps, and were mowed down in swaths like grass by cannon and musket-balls.

After the sixth disastrous attempt to carry the works of the Confederate left it was night; the Federal army was repulsed and had retired; hope was abandoned, and it was seen that the day was lost to the Union side. Then the shattered Army of the Potomac sought to gather the stragglers and care for the wounded. Fredericksburg, the beautiful Virginia town, was a pitiable scene in contrast to its appearance a few days before. Ancestral homes were turned into barracks and hospitals. The charming drives and stately groves, the wonted pleasure grounds of Colonial dames and Southern cavaliers, were not filled with grand carriages and gay parties, but with war horses, soldiers, and military accouterments. Aside from desultory firing by squads and skirmishers at intervals there was no renewal of the conflict.

THE FATEFUL CROSSING

From this, the Lacy House, which Sumner had made his headquarters, he directed the advance of his right grand division of the Army of the Potomac on December 11, 1862. Little did he dream that his men of the Second Corps were to bear the brunt of the fighting and the most crushing blow of the defeat on the 13th. Soon after three o'clock on the morning of the 11th the columns moved out with alacrity to the river bank and before daybreak, hidden at first by the fog, the pontoniers began building the bridges. Confederate sharpshooters drove off the working party from the bridge below the Lacy House and also from the middle bridge farther down. As the mist cleared, volunteers ferried themselves over in the boats and drove off the riflemen. At last, at daybreak of the 12th, the town of Fredericksburg was occupied, but the whole of another foggy day was consumed in getting the army concentrated on the western shore. Nineteen batteries (one hundred and four guns) accompanied Sumner's troops, but all save seven of these were ordered back or left in the streets of Fredericksburg. Late on the morning of the 13th the confused and belated orders began to arrive from Burnside's headquarters across the river; one was for Sumner to assault the Confederate batteries on Marye's Heights. At nightfall Sumner's men retired into Fredericksburg, leaving 4,800 dead or wounded on the field. "Oh, those men, those men over there! I cannot get them out of my mind!" wailed Burnside in an agony of failure. Yet he was planning almost in the same breath to lead in person his old command, the Ninth Corps, in another futile charge in the morning. On the night of the 14th, better judgment prevailed and the order came to retire across the Rappahannock.

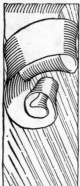
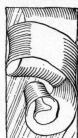

The bloody carnage was over, the plan of Burnside had ended in failure, and thousands of patriotic and brave men, blindly obedient to their country's command, were the toll exacted from the Union army. Burnside, wild with anguish at what he had done, walking the floor of his tent, exclaimed, "Oh, those men—those men over there," pointing to the battlefield, "I am thinking of them all the time." In his report of the battle to Washington, Burnside gave reasons for the issue, and in a manly way took the responsibility upon himself, and most highly commended his officers and men. He said, "For the failure in the attack I am responsible, as the extreme gallantry, courage, and endurance shown by them [officers and men] were never excelled."

President Lincoln's verdict in regard to this battle is adverse to the almost unanimous opinion of the historians. In his reply, December 22d, to General Burnside's report of the battle, he says, "Although you were not successful, the attempt was not an error, nor the failure other than an accident." Burnside, at his own request, was relieved of the command of the Army of the Potomac, however, on January 25, 1863, and was succeeded by General Hooker. The Union loss in killed, wounded, and missing was 12,653, and the Confederates lost 5,377.

After the battle the wounded lay on the field in their agony exposed to the freezing cold for forty-eight hours before arrangements were effected to care for them. Many were burned to death by the long, dead grass becoming ignited by cannon fire. The scene witnessed by the army of those screaming, agonizing, dying comrades was dreadful and heartrending. Burnside's plan had been to renew the battle, but the overwhelming opinion of the other officers prevailed. The order was withdrawn and the defeated Union army slipped away under the cover of darkness on December 15th, and encamped in safety across the river. The battle of Fredericksburg had passed into history.

NEW LEADERS AND NEW PLANS

General Joseph Hooker and his Staff. These were the men whose work it was, during the winter after Fredericksburg, to restore the *esprit de corps* of the Army of the Potomac. The tireless energy and magnetic personality of Hooker soon won officers from their disaffection and put an end to desertions—which had been going on at the rate of two hundred per day before he took command. By spring everything seemed propitious for an aggressive campaign, the plans for which were brilliantly drawn and at first vigorously carried out, giving truth to Lincoln's expressed belief that Hooker was "a trained and skilful soldier." In that remarkable letter of admonition to Hooker upon assuming command, Lincoln added: "But beware of rashness, beware of rashness; with energy and with sleepless vigilance go forward and give us victories." By some strange fate it was not rashness but quite the contrary which compassed the failure of "Fighting Joe" Hooker at Chancellorsville. His first forward advance was executed with his usual bold initiative. Before Lee could fully divine his purpose, Hooker with thirty-six thousand men was across his left flank in a favorable position, with the main body of his army at hand ready to give battle. Then came Hooker's inexplicable order to fall back upon Chancellorsville. That very night, consulting in the abandoned Federal position, Lee and Jackson formed the plan which drove Hooker back across the Rappahannock in ignominious defeat.

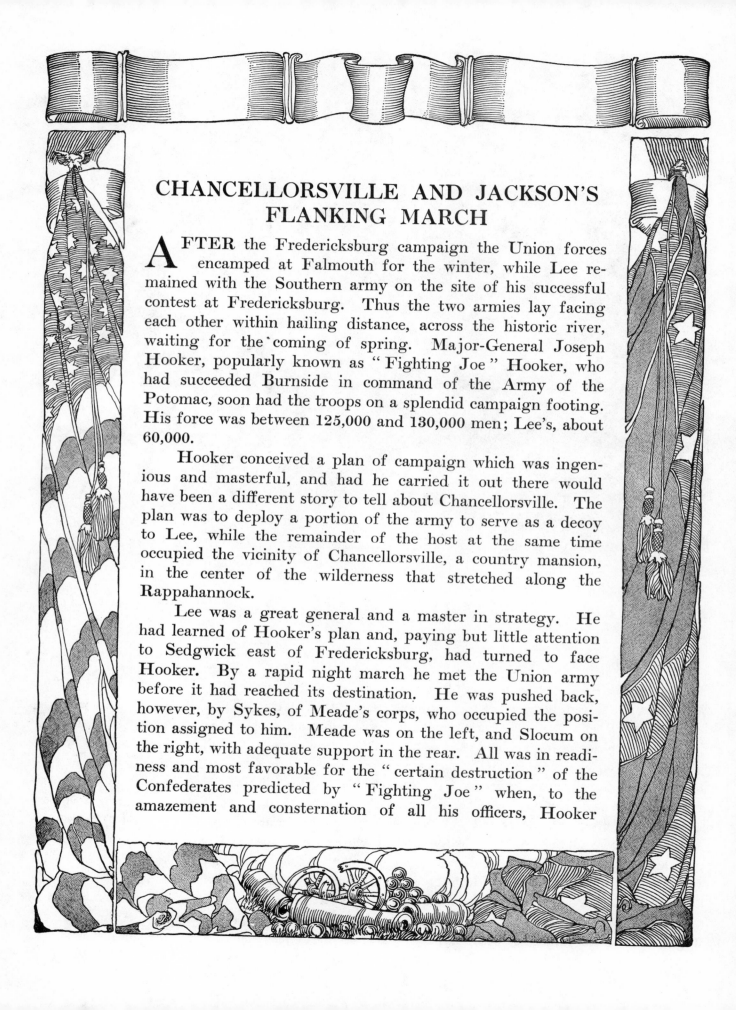

CHANCELLORSVILLE AND JACKSON'S FLANKING MARCH

AFTER the Fredericksburg campaign the Union forces encamped at Falmouth for the winter, while Lee remained with the Southern army on the site of his successful contest at Fredericksburg. Thus the two armies lay facing each other within hailing distance, across the historic river, waiting for the coming of spring. Major-General Joseph Hooker, popularly known as "Fighting Joe" Hooker, who had succeeded Burnside in command of the Army of the Potomac, soon had the troops on a splendid campaign footing. His force was between 125,000 and 130,000 men; Lee's, about 60,000.

Hooker conceived a plan of campaign which was ingenious and masterful, and had he carried it out there would have been a different story to tell about Chancellorsville. The plan was to deploy a portion of the army to serve as a decoy to Lee, while the remainder of the host at the same time occupied the vicinity of Chancellorsville, a country mansion, in the center of the wilderness that stretched along the Rappahannock.

Lee was a great general and a master in strategy. He had learned of Hooker's plan and, paying but little attention to Sedgwick east of Fredericksburg, had turned to face Hooker. By a rapid night march he met the Union army before it had reached its destination. He was pushed back, however, by Sykes, of Meade's corps, who occupied the position assigned to him. Meade was on the left, and Slocum on the right, with adequate support in the rear. All was in readiness and most favorable for the "certain destruction" of the Confederates predicted by "Fighting Joe" when, to the amazement and consternation of all his officers, Hooker

A MAN OF WHOM MUCH WAS EXPECTED

General Joseph Hooker.   A daring and experienced veteran of the Mexican War, Hooker had risen in the Civil War from brigade commander to be the commander of a grand division of the Army of the Potomac, and had never been found wanting.   His advancement
to the head of the Army of the Potomac, on January 26, 1863, was a tragic episode in his own career and in that of the Federal arms.
Gloom hung heavy over the North after Fredericksburg.   Upon Hooker fell the difficult task of redeeming the unfulfilled political
pledges for a speedy lifting of that gloom.   It was his fortune only to deepen it.

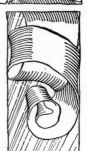
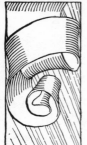

ordered the whole army to retire to the position it had occupied the day before, leaving the advantage to his opponents.

Lee quickly moved his army into the position thus relinquished, and began feeling the Federal lines with skirmishers and some cannonading during the evening of May 1st. By the next morning the two armies were in line of battle.

The danger in which the Confederate army now found itself was extreme. One large Federal army was on its front, while another was at its rear, below Fredericksburg. But Lee threw the hopes of success into one great and decisive blow at Hooker's host. Dividing an army in the face of the foe is extremely dangerous and contrary to all accepted theories of military strategy; but there comes a time when such a course proves the salvation of the legions in peril. Such was the case at Chancellorsville on May 2, 1863.

At 7 A.M. the cannonading began its death-song and was soon followed by infantry demonstrations, but without serious results. The action was continued. Early in the afternoon, Hooker by a ruse was beguiled into the belief that Lee's army was in full retreat. What Hooker had seen and believed to be a retreat was the marching of Jackson's forces, about twenty-six thousand strong, from the battlefield. What he did not see, however, was that, after a few miles, Jackson turned abruptly and made for the right flank of the Federal host, the Eleventh Corps, under Howard. It was after half-past five when Jackson broke from the woods into which he had marched in a paralyzing charge upon the unprepared troops of Howard.

The approach of this Confederate force was first intimated to the Federals by the bending of shrubbery, the stampede of rabbits and squirrels, and the flocks of birds in wild flight, as before a storm. Then appeared a few skirmishers, then a musket volley, and then the storm broke in all its fury —the war scream, the rattling musketry, the incessant roar of cannon. The Confederates fought heroically. The knowledge

"STONEWALL" JACKSON—TWO WEEKS BEFORE HIS MORTAL WOUND

The austere, determined features of the victor of Chancellorsville, just as they appeared two weeks before the tragic shot that cost the Confederacy its greatest Lieutenant-General—and, in the opinion of sound historians, its chief hope for independence. Only once had a war photograph of Jackson been taken up to April, 1863, when, just before the movement toward Chancellorsville, he was persuaded to enter a photographer's tent at Hamilton's Crossing, some three miles below Fredericksburg, and to sit for his last portrait. At a glance one can feel the self-expression and power in this stern worshiper of the God of Battles; one can understand the eulogy written by the British military historian, Henderson: "The fame of 'Stonewall' Jackson is no longer the exclusive property of Virginia and the South; it has become the birthright of every man privileged to call himself an American."

that "Old Jack" was on the field was inspiration enough for them. The charge was so precipitous, so unexpected and terrific that it was impossible for the Federals to hold their lines and stand against the impact of that awful onslaught which carried everything before it. The regiments in Jackson's path, resisting his advance, were cut to pieces and swept along as by a tidal wave, rolled up like a scroll, multitudes of men, horses, mules, and cattle being piled in an inextricable mass. Characteristic of Jackson's brilliant and unexpected movements, it was like an electric flash, knocking the Eleventh Corps into impotence, as Jackson expected it would. This crowning and final stroke of Jackson's military genius was not impromptu, but the result of his own carefully worked-out plan, which had been approved by Lee.

General Hooker was spending the late afternoon hours in his headquarters at the Chancellor house. To the eastward there was considerable firing, where his men were carrying out the plan of striking Lee in flank. Jackson was retreating, of that he was sure, and Sickles, with Pleasanton's cavalry and other reenforcements, was in pursuit. Everything seemed to be going well. About half-past six the sounds of battle grew suddenly louder and seemed to come from another direction. A staff-officer went to the front of the house and turned his field-glass toward the west.

"My God, here they come!"

At the startled cry Hooker sprang upon his horse and dashed down the road. He encountered portions of the Eleventh Corps pouring out of the forest—a badly mixed crowd of men, wagons, and ambulances. They brought the news that the right wing was overwhelmed. Hurriedly Hooker sought his old command, Berry's division of the Third Corps, stationed in support of the Eleventh. "Forward, with the bayonet!" he commanded.

An officer who witnessed the scene says the division advanced with a firm and steady step, cleaving the multitude

WHERE "STONEWALL" JACKSON FELL

In this tangled nook Lee's right-hand man was shot through a terrible mistake of his own soldiers. It was the second of May, 1863. After his brilliant flank march, the evening attack on the rear of Hooker's army had just been driven home. About half-past eight, Jackson had ridden beyond his lines to reconnoiter for the final advance. A single rifle-shot rang out in the darkness. The outposts of the two armies were engaged. Jackson turned toward his own line, where the Eighteenth North Carolina was stationed. The regiment, keenly on the alert and startled by the group of strange horsemen riding through the gloom, fired a volley that brought several men and horses to the earth. Jackson was struck once in the right hand and twice in the left arm, a little below the shoulder. His horse dashed among the trees; but with his bleeding right hand Jackson succeeded in seizing the reins and turning the frantic animal back into the road. Only with difficulty was the general taken to the rear so that his wounds might be dressed. To his attendants he said, "Tell them simply that you have a wounded Confederate officer." To one who asked if he was seriously hurt, he replied: "Don't bother yourself about me. Win the battle first and attend to the wounded afterward." He was taken to Guiney's Station. At first it was hoped that he would recover, but pneumonia set in and his strength gradually ebbed. On Sunday evening, May 10th, he uttered the words which inspired the young poet, Sidney Lanier, to write his elegy, beautiful in its serene resignation.

of disbanded Federals as the bow of a vessel cleaves the waves of the sea. It struck the advance of the Confederates obliquely and checked it, with the aid of the Twelfth Corps artillery.

A dramatic, though tragic, feature of the rout was the charge of the Eighth Pennsylvania cavalry, under Major Keenan, in the face of almost certain death, to save the artillery of the Third Corps from capture. The guns rested upon low ground and within reach of the Confederates. The Federals had an equal opportunity to seize the artillery, but required a few minutes to prepare themselves for action. The Confederate advance must be checked for these few moments, and for this purpose Keenan gallantly led his five hundred cavalrymen into the woods, while his comrades brought the guns to bear upon the columns in gray. He gained the necessary time, but lost his life at the head of his regiment, together with Captain Arrowsmith and Adjutant Haddock, who fell by his side.

The light of day had faded from the gruesome scene. The mighty turmoil was silenced as darkness gathered, but the day's carnage was not ended. No camp-fires were lighted in the woods or on the plain. The two hostile forces were concealed in the darkness, watching through the shadows, waiting for—they knew not what. Finally at midnight the order " Forward " was repeated in subdued tones along the lines of Sickles' corps. Out over the open and into the deep, dark thicket the men in blue pursued their stealthy advance upon the Confederate position. Then the tragedies of the night were like that of the day, and the moon shed her peaceful rays down upon those shadowy figures as they struggled forward through the woods, in the ravines, over the hillocks. The Federals, at heavy loss, gained the position, and the engagement assumed the importance of a victory.

It was on this day that death robbed the South of one of her most beloved warriors. After darkness had

THE STONE WALL AT FREDERICKSBURG

Behind the deadly stone wall of Marye's Heights after Sedgwick's men had swept across it in the gallant charge of May 3, 1863.   This was one of the strongest natural positions stormed during the war.   In front of this wall the previous year, nearly 6,000 of Burnside's men had fallen, and it was not carried.   Again in the Chancellorsville campaign Sedgwick's Sixth Corps was ordered to assault it.   It was defended the second time with the same death-dealing stubbornness but with less than a fourth of the former numbers—9,000 Confederates against 20,000 Federals.   At eleven o'clock in the morning the line of battle, under Colonel Hiram Burnham, moved out over the awful field of the year before, supported to right and left by flanking columns.   Up to within twenty-five yards of the wall they pressed, when again the flame of musketry fire belched forth, laying low in six minutes 36.5 per cent. of the Fifth Wisconsin and the Sixth Maine.   The assailants wavered and rallied, and then with one impulse both columns and line of battle hurled themselves upon the wall in a fierce hand-to-hand combat.   A soldier of the Seventh Massachusetts happened to peer through a crack in a board fence and saw that it covered the flank of the double line of Confederates in the road.   Up and over the fence poured the Federals and drove the Confederates from the heights.

overspread the land, Jackson, accompanied by members of his staff, undertook a reconnaissance of the Federal lines. He was planning a night attack. He came upon a line of Union infantry lying on its arms and was forced to turn back along the plank road, on both sides of which he had stationed his own men with orders to fire upon any body of men approaching from the direction of the Federal battle-lines. The little cavalcade of Confederate officers galloped along the highway, directly toward the ambuscade, and apparently forgetful of the strict orders left with the skirmishers. A sudden flash of flame lighted the scene for an instant, and within that space of time the Confederacy was deprived of one of its greatest captains—Jackson was severely wounded, and by his own men and through his own orders. When the news spread through Jackson's corps and through the Confederate army the grief of the Southern soldiers was heartbreaking to witness. The sorrow spread even into the ranks of the Federal army, which, while opposed to the wounded general on many hard-fought battle-grounds, had learned to respect and admire " Stonewall " Jackson.

The loss of Jackson to the South was incalculable. Lee had pronounced him the right arm of the whole army. Next to Lee, Jackson was considered the ablest general in the Confederate army. His shrewdness of judgment, his skill in strategy, his lightning-like strokes, marked him as a unique and brilliant leader. Devoutly religious, gentle and noble in character, the nation that was not to be disunited lost a great citizen, as the Confederate army lost a great captain, when a few days later General Jackson died.

That night orders passed from the Federal headquarters to Sedgwick, below Fredericksburg, eleven miles away. Between him and Hooker stood the Confederate army, flushed with its victories of the day. Immediately in his front was Fredericksburg, with a strong guard of Southern warriors. Beyond loomed Marye's Heights, the battle-ground on which

THE WORK OF ONE SHELL

Part of the Havoc Wrought on Marye's Heights by the Assault of Sedgwick on May 3, 1863.   No sooner had they seized the stone wall than the victorious Federals swarmed up and over the ridge above, driving the Confederates from the rifle-pits, capturing the guns of the famous Washington Artillery which had so long guarded the Heights, and inflicting slaughter upon the assaulting columns.   If Sedgwick had had cavalry he could have crushed the divided forces of Early and cleared the way for a rapid advance to attack Lee's rear.   In the picture we see Confederate caisson wagons and horses destroyed by a lucky shot from the Second Massachusetts' siege-gun battery planted across the river at Falmouth to support Sedgwick's assault.   Surveying the scene stands General Herman Haupt, Chief of the Bureau of Military Railways, the man leaning against the stump.   By him is W. W. Wright, Superintendent of the Military Railroad.   The photograph was taken on May 3d, after the battle.   The Federals held Marye's Heights until driven off by fresh forces which Lee had detached from his main army at Chancellorsville and sent against Sedgwick on the afternoon of the 4th.

Burnside had in the preceding winter left so many of his brave men in the vain endeavor to drive the Confederate defenders from the crest.

The courageous Sedgwick, notwithstanding the formidable obstacles that lay on the road to Chancellorsville, responded immediately to Hooker's order. He was already on the south side of the river, but he was farther away than Hooker supposed. Shortly after midnight he began a march that was fraught with peril and death. Strong resistance was offered the advancing blue columns as they came to the threshold of Fredericksburg, but they swept on and over the defenders, and at dawn were at the base of the heights. On the crest waved the standards of the Confederate Washington Artillery. At the foot of the slope was the stone wall before which the Federals had fought and died but a few months before, in the battle of Fredericksburg. Reenforcements were arriving in the Confederate trenches constantly. The crest and slopes bristled with cannon and muskets. The pathways around the heights were barricaded. The route to the front seemed blocked; still, the cry for help from Hooker was resounding in the ears of Sedgwick

Gathering his troops, he attacked directly upon the stone wall and on up the hillside, in the face of a terrific storm of artillery and musketry. The first assault failed; a flank movement met with no better success; and the morning was nearly gone when the Confederates finally gave way at the point of the bayonet before the irresistible onset of men in blue. The way to Chancellorsville was open; but the cost to the Federals was appalling. Hundreds of the soldiers in blue lay wrapped in death upon the bloody slopes of Marye's Heights.

It was the middle of the afternoon, and not at daybreak, as Hooker had directed, when Sedgwick appeared in the rear of Lee's legions. A strong force of Confederates under Early prevented his further advance toward a juncture with Hooker's army at Chancellorsville. Since five o'clock in the

THE DEMOLISHED HEADQUARTERS

From this mansion, Hooker's headquarters during the battle of Chancellorsville, he rode away after the injury he received there on May 3d, never to return. The general, dazed after Jackson's swoop upon the right, was besides in deep anxiety as to Sedgwick. The latter's forty thousand men had not yet come up. Hooker was unwilling to suffer further loss without the certainty of his coöperation. So he decided to withdraw his army. The movement was the signal for increased artillery fire from the Confederate batteries, marking the doom of the old Chancellor house. Its end was accompanied by some heart-rending scenes. Major Bigelow thus describes them: "Missiles pierced the walls or struck in the brickwork; shells exploded in the upper rooms, setting the building on fire; the chimneys were demolished and their fragments rained down upon the wounded about the building. All this time the women and children (including some slaves) of the Chancellor family, nineteen persons in all, were in the cellar. The wounded were removed from in and around the building, men of both armies nobly assisting one another in the work."

morning the battle had been raging at the latter place, and Jackson's men, now commanded by Stuart, though being mowed down in great numbers, vigorously pressed the attack of the day while crying out to one another "Remember Jackson," as they thought of their wounded leader.

While this engagement was at its height General Hooker, leaning against a pillar of the Chancellor house, was felled to the ground, and for a moment it was thought he was killed. The pillar had been shattered by a cannon-ball. Hooker soon revived under the doctor's care and with great force of will he mounted his horse and showed himself to his anxious troops. He then withdrew his army to a stronger position, well guarded with artillery. The Confederates did not attempt to assail it. The third day's struggle at Chancellorsville was finished by noon, except in Lee's rear, where Sedgwick fought all day, without success, to reach the main body of Hooker's army. The Federals suffered very serious losses during this day's contest. Even then it was believed that the advantage rested with the larger Army of the Potomac and that the Federals had an opportunity to win. Thirty-seven thousand Union troops, the First, and three-quarters of the Fifth Corps, had been entirely out of the fight on that day. Five thousand men of the Eleventh Corps, who were eager to retrieve their misfortune, were also inactive.

When night came, and the shades of darkness hid the sights of suffering on the battlefield, the Federal army was resting in a huge curve, the left wing on the Rappahannock and the right on the Rapidan. In this way the fords across the rivers which led to safety were in control of the Army of the Potomac. Lee moved his corps close to the bivouacs of the army in blue. But, behind the Confederate battle-line, there was a new factor in the struggle in the person of Sedgwick, with the remnants of his gallant corps, which had numbered nearly twenty-two thousand when they started for the front, but now were depleted by their terrific charge upon Marye's Heights

RED MEN WHO SUFFERED IN SILENCE

In modern warfare the American Indian seems somehow to be entirely out of place. We think of him with the tomahawk and scalping-knife and have difficulty in conceiving him in the ranks, drilling, doing police duty, and so on. Yet more than three thousand Indians were enlisted in the Federal army. The Confederates enlisted many more in Missouri, Arkansas, and Texas. In the Federal army the red men were used as advance sharpshooters and rendered meritorious service. This photograph shows some of the wounded Indian sharpshooters on Marye's Heights after the second battle of Fredericksburg. A hospital orderly is attending to the wants of the one on the left-hand page, and the wounds of the others have been dressed. In the entry of John L. Marye's handsome mansion close by lay a group of four Indian sharpshooters, each with the loss of a limb—of an arm at the shoulder, of a leg at the knee, or with an amputation at the thigh. They neither spoke nor moaned, but suffered and died, mute in their agony. During the campaign of 1864, from the Wilderness to Appomattox, Captain Ely S. Parker, a gigantic Indian, became one of Grant's favorite aids. Before the close of the war he had been promoted to the rank of colonel, and it was he who drafted in a beautiful handwriting the terms of Lee's surrender. He stood over six feet in height and was a conspicuous figure on Grant's staff. The Southwestern Indians engaged in some of the earliest battles under General Albert Pike, a Northerner by birth, but a Southern sympathizer.

and the subsequent hard and desperate struggle with Early in the afternoon.

Lee was between two fires—Hooker in front and Sedgwick in the rear, both of whose forces were too strong to be attacked simultaneously. Again the daring leader of the Confederate legions did the unexpected, and divided his army in the presence of the foe, though he was without the aid of his great lieutenant, "Stonewall" Jackson.

During the night Lee made his preparations, and when dawn appeared in the eastern skies the movement began. Sedgwick, weak and battered by his contact with Early on the preceding afternoon, resisted bravely, but to no avail, and the Confederates closed in upon him on three sides, leaving the way to Banks's Ford on the Rappahannock open to escape. Slowly the Federals retreated and, as night descended, rested upon the river bank. After dark the return to the northern side was begun by Sedgwick's men, and the Chancellorsville campaign was practically ended.

The long, deep trenches full of Federal and Confederate dead told the awful story of Chancellorsville. If we gaze into these trenches, which by human impulse we are led to do, after the roar and din of the carnage is still, the scene greeting the eye will never be forgotten. Side by side, the heroes in torn and bloody uniforms, their only shrouds, were gently laid.

The Union loss in killed and wounded was a little over seventeen thousand, and it cost the South thirteen thousand men to gain this victory on the banks of the Rappahannock. The loss to both armies in officers was very heavy.

The two armies were weary and more than decimated. It appeared that both were glad at the prospect of a cessation of hostilities. On the night of May 5th, in a severe storm, Hooker conveyed his corps safely across the river and settled the men again in their cantonments of the preceding winter at Falmouth. The Confederates returned to their old encampment at Fredericksburg.

[Part VII]

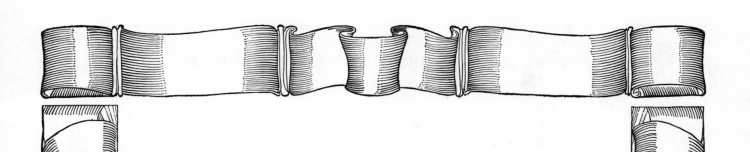

VICKSBURG AND PORT HUDSON

On the banks of this, the greatest river in the world, the most decisive and far-reaching battle of the war was fought. Here at Vicksburg over one hundred thousand gallant soldiers and a powerful fleet of gunboats and ironclads in terrible earnestness for forty days and nights fought to decide whether the new Confederate States should be cut in twain; whether the great river should flow free to the Gulf, or should have its commerce hindered. We all know the result—the Union army under General Grant, and the Union navy under Admiral Porter were victorious. The Confederate army, under General Pemberton, numbering thirty thousand men, was captured and General Grant's army set free for operating in other fields. It was a staggering blow from which the Confederacy never rallied.—*Lieutenant-General Stephen D. Lee, C.S.A., at the dedication of the Massachusetts Volunteers' statue at the Vicksburg National Military Park, Vicksburg, Mississippi, November 14, 1903.*

THE Mississippi River, in its lower course, winds like a mighty serpent from side to side along a vast alluvial bottom, which in places is more than forty miles in width. On the eastern bank, these great coils here and there sweep up to the bluffs of the highlands of Tennessee and Mississippi. On these cliffs are situated Memphis, Port Hudson, Grand Gulf, and Vicksburg. The most important of these from a military point of view was Vicksburg, often called the "Gibraltar of the West." Situated two hundred feet above the current, on a great bend of the river, its cannon could command the waterway for miles in either direction, while the obstacles in the way of a land approach were almost equally insurmountable.

The Union arms had captured New Orleans, in the spring of 1862, and Memphis in June of that year; but the Confederates still held Vicksburg and Port Hudson and the two hundred and fifty miles of river that lies between them. The military

object of the Federal armies in the West was to gain control of the entire course of the great Mississippi that it might "roll unvexed to the sea," to use Lincoln's terse expression, and that the rich States of the Southwest, from which the Confederacy drew large supplies and thousands of men for her armies, might be cut off from the rest of the South. If Vicksburg were captured, Port Hudson must fall. The problem, therefore, was how to get control of Vicksburg.

On the promotion of Halleck to the command of all the armies of the North, with headquarters at Washington, Grant was left in superior command in the West and the great task before him was the capture of the "Gibraltar of the West." Vicksburg might have been occupied by the Northern armies at any time during the first half of the year 1862, but in June of that year General Bragg sent Van Dorn with a force of fifteen thousand to occupy and fortify the heights. Van Dorn was a man of prodigious energy. In a short time he had hundreds of men at work planting batteries, digging rifle-pits above the water front and in the rear of the town, mounting heavy guns and building bomb-proof magazines in tiers along the hillsides. All through the summer, the work progressed under the direction of Engineer S. H. Lockett, and by the coming of winter the city was a veritable Gibraltar.

From the uncompleted batteries on the Vicksburg bluffs, the citizens and the garrison soldiers viewed the advance division of Farragut's fleet, under Commander Lee, in the river, on May 18, 1862. Fifteen hundred infantry were on board, under command of General Thomas Williams, and with them was a battery of artillery. Williams reconnoitered the works, and finding them too strong for his small force he returned to occupy Baton Rouge. The authorities at Washington now sent Farragut peremptory orders to clear the Mississippi and accordingly about the middle of June, a flotilla of steamers and seventeen mortar schooners, under Commander D. D. Porter, departed from New Orleans and steamed up the river.

BEFORE VICKSBURG

AFTER VICKSBURG

The close-set mouth, squared shoulders and lowering brow in this photograph of Grant, taken in December, 1862, tell the story of the intensity of his purpose while he was advancing upon Vicksburg—only to be foiled by Van Dorn's raid on his line of communications at Holly Springs. His grim expression and determined jaw betokened no respite for the Confederates, however. Six months later he marched into the coveted stronghold. This photograph was taken by James Mullen at Oxford, Mississippi, in December, 1862, just before Van Dorn's raid balked the general's plans.

This photograph was taken in the fall of 1863, after the capture of the Confederacy's Gibraltar had raised Grant to secure and everlasting fame. His attitude is relaxed and his eyebrows no longer mark a straight line across the grim visage. The right brow is slightly arched with an almost jovial expression. But the jaw is no less vigorous and determined, and the steadfast eyes seem to be peering into that future which holds more victories. He still has Chattanooga and his great campaigns in the East to fight and the final magnificent struggle in the trenches at Petersburg.

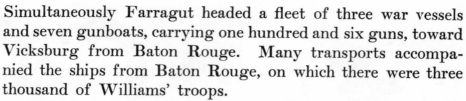

Simultaneously Farragut headed a fleet of three war vessels and seven gunboats, carrying one hundred and six guns, toward Vicksburg from Baton Rouge. Many transports accompanied the ships from Baton Rouge, on which there were three thousand of Williams' troops.

The last days of June witnessed the arrival of the combined naval forces of Farragut and Porter below the Confederate stronghold. Williams immediately disembarked his men on the Louisiana shore, opposite Vicksburg, and they were burdened with implements required in digging trenches and building levees.

The mighty Mississippi, at this point and in those days, swept in a majestic bend and formed a peninsula of the western, or Louisiana shore. Vicksburg was situated on the eastern, or Mississippi shore, below the top of the bend. Its batteries of cannon commanded the river approach for miles in either direction. Federal engineers quickly recognized the strategic position of the citadel on the bluff; and also as quickly saw a method by which the passage up and down the river could be made comparatively safe for their vessels, and at the same time place Vicksburg " high and dry " by cutting a channel for the Mississippi through the neck of land that now held it in its sinuous course.

While Farragut stormed the Confederate batteries at Vicksburg, Williams began the tremendous task of diverting the mighty current across the peninsula. Farragut's bombardment by his entire fleet failed to silence Vicksburg's cannon-guards, although the defenders likewise failed to stop the progress of the fleet. The Federal naval commander then determined to dash past the fortifications, trusting to the speed of his vessels and the stoutness of their armor to survive the tremendous cannonade that would fall upon his flotilla. Early in the morning of June 28th the thrilling race against death began, and after two hours of terrific bombardment aided by the mortar boats stationed on both banks, Farragut's fleet with

WHERE GRANT'S CAMPAIGN WAS HALTED

The Courthouse at Oxford, Mississippi. The second attempt to capture Vicksburg originated with Grant. Since he had sprung into fame at Fort Donelson early in 1862, he had done little to strengthen his reputation; but to all urgings of his removal Lincoln replied: "I can't spare this man; he fights." He proposed to push southward through Mississippi to seize Jackson, the capital. If this could be accomplished, Vicksburg (fifty miles to the west) would become untenable. At Washington his plan was overruled to the extent of dividing his forces. Sherman, with a separate expedition, was to move from Memphis down the Mississippi directly against Vicksburg. It was Grant's hope that by marching on he could unite with Sherman in an assault upon this key to the Mississippi. Pushing forward from Grand Junction, sixty miles, Grant reached Oxford December 5, 1862, but his supplies were still drawn from Columbus, Kentucky, over a single-track road to Holly Springs, and thence by wagon over roads which were rapidly becoming impassable. Delay ensued in which Van Dorn destroyed Federal stores at Holly Springs worth $1,500,000. This put an end to Grant's advance. In the picture we see an Illinois regiment guarding some of the 1200 Confederate prisoners taken during the advance and here confined in the Courthouse.

the exception of three vessels passed through the raging inferno to the waters above Vicksburg, with a loss of fifteen killed and thirty wounded. On the 1st of July Flag-Officer Davis with his river gunboats arrived from Memphis and joined Farragut.

Williams and his men, including one thousand negroes, labored like Titans to complete their canal, but a sudden rise of the river swept away the barriers with a terrific roar, and the days of herculean labor went for naught. Again Williams' attempt to subdue the stronghold was abandoned, and he returned with his men when Farragut did, on July 24th, to Baton Rouge to meet death there on August 5th when General Breckinridge made a desperate but unsuccessful attempt to drive the Union forces from the Louisiana capital.

Farragut urged upon General Halleck the importance of occupying the city on the bluff with a portion of his army; but that general gave no heed; and while even then it was too late to secure the prize without a contest, it would have been easy in comparison to that which it required a year later.

In the mean time, the river steamers took an important part in the preliminary operations against the city. Davis remained at Memphis with his fleet for about three weeks after the occupation of that city on the 6th of June, meanwhile sending four gunboats and a transport up the White River, with the Forty-sixth Indiana regiment, under Colonel Fitch. The object of the expedition, undertaken at Halleck's command, was to destroy Confederate batteries and to open communication with General Curtis, who was approaching from the west. It failed in the latter purpose but did some effective work with the Southern batteries along the way.

The one extraordinary incident of the expedition was the disabling of the *Mound City,* one of the ironclad gunboats, and the great loss of life that it occasioned. When near St. Charles the troops under Fitch were landed, and the *Mound City* moving up the river, was fired on by concealed batteries

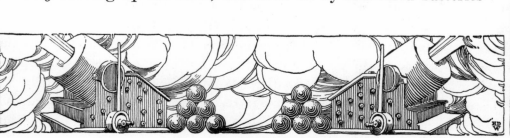

WHERE VICKSBURG'S FATE WAS SEALED

The Battle-field of Champion's Hill. Here on May 16, 1863, Grant crowned his daring maneuver against Vicksburg from the south with complete success. Once across the river below Grand Gulf, after an easy victory at Port Gibson, he was joined by Sherman. The army struck out across the strange country south of the Big Black River and soon had driven Pemberton's southern outposts across that stream. Grant was now on solid ground; he had successfully turned the flank of the Confederates and he grasped the opportunity to strike a telling blow. Pressing forward to Raymond and Jackson, he captured both, and swept westward to meet the astounded Pemberton, still vacillating between attempting a junction with Johnston or attacking Grant in the rear. But Grant, moving with wonderful precision, prevented either movement. On May 16th a battle ensued which was most decisive around Champion's Hill. Pemberton was routed and put to flight, and on the next day the Federals seized the crossings of the Big Black River. Spiking their guns at Haynes' Bluff, the Confederates retired into Vicksburg, never to come out again except as prisoners. In eighteen days from the time he crossed the Mississippi, Grant had gained the advantage for which the Federals had striven for more than a year at Vicksburg.

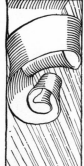

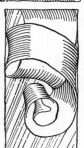

under the direction of Lieutenant Dunnington. A 32-pound shot struck the vessel, crashed through the side and passed through the steam-drum. The steam filled the vessel in an instant. Many of the men were so quickly enveloped in the scalding vapor that they had no chance to escape. Others leaped overboard, some being drowned and some rescued through the efforts of the *Conestoga* which was lying near. While straining every nerve to save their lives, the men had to endure a shower of bullets from Confederate sharpshooters on the river banks. Of the one hundred and seventy-five officers and men of the *Mound City* only twenty-five escaped death or injury in that fearful catastrophe. Meanwhile, Colonel Fitch with his land forces rushed upon the Confederate batteries and captured them. The unfortunate vessel was at length repaired and returned to service.

For some time it had been known in Federal military and naval circles that a powerful ironclad similar to the famous *Monitor* of Eastern waters was being rushed to completion up the Yazoo. The new vessel was the *Arkansas*. On July 15th, she steamed through the Union fleet, bravely exchanging broadsides, and lodged safely under the guns of Vicksburg. That evening the Federal boats in turn ran past the doughty *Arkansas,* but failed to destroy her.

The month of July had not been favorable to the Federal hopes. Farragut had returned to New Orleans. General Williams had gone with him as far as Baton Rouge. Davis now went with his fleet back to Helena. Halleck was succeeded by Grant. Vicksburg entered upon a period of quiet.

But this condition was temporary. The city's experience of blood and fire had only begun. During the summer and autumn of 1862, the one thought uppermost in the mind of General Grant was how to gain possession of the stronghold. He was already becoming known for his bull-dog tenacity. In the autumn, two important changes took place, but one day apart. On October 14th, General John C. Pemberton

THE BRIDGE THE CONFEDERATES BURNED AT BIG BLACK RIVER

THE FIRST FEDERAL CROSSING—SHERMAN'S PONTOONS

The pursuit of Pemberton's army brought McClernand's Corps to the defenses of the Big Black River Bridge early on May 17, 1863. McPherson was close behind. McClernand's division carried the defenses and Bowen and Vaughn's men fled with precipitate haste over the dreary swamp to the river and crossed over and burned the railroad and other bridges just in time to prevent McClernand from following. The necessary delay was aggravating to Grant's forces. The rest of the day and night was consumed in building bridges. Sherman had the only pontoon-train with the army and his bridge was the first ready at Bridgeport, early in the evening.

succeeded Van Dorn in command of the defenses of Vicksburg, and on the next day David D. Porter succeeded Davis as commander of the Federal fleet on the upper Mississippi.

So arduous was the task of taking Vicksburg that the wits of General Grant, and those of his chief adviser, General W. T. Sherman, were put to the test in the last degree to accomplish the end. Grant knew that the capture of this fortified city was of great importance to the Federal cause, and that it would ever be looked upon as one of the chief acts in the drama of the Civil War.

The first plan attempted was to divide the army, Sherman taking part of it from Memphis and down the Mississippi on transports, while Grant should move southward along the line of the Mississippi Central Railroad to cooperate with Sherman, his movements to be governed by the efforts of the scattered Confederate forces in Mississippi to block him. But the whole plan was destined to failure, through the energies of General Van Dorn and others of the Confederate army near Grant's line of communication.

The authorities at Washington preferred the river move upon Vicksburg, as the navy could keep the line of communication open. The stronghold now stood within a strong line of defense extending from Haynes' Bluff on the Yazoo to Grand Gulf on the Mississippi, thirty miles below Vicksburg. To prepare for Sherman's attack across the swamps of the Yazoo, Admiral Porter made several expeditions up that tortuous stream to silence batteries and remove torpedoes. In one of these he lost one of the Eads ironclads, the *Cairo*, blown up by a torpedo, and in another the brave Commander Gwin, one of the heroes of Shiloh, was mortally wounded.

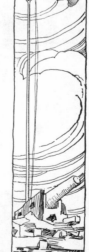

Sherman, with an army of thirty-two thousand men, left Memphis on December 20th, and landed a few days later some miles north of Vicksburg on the banks of the Yazoo. On the 29th he made a daring attack in three columns on the Confederate lines of defense at Chickasaw Bayou and suffered a

Vicksburg, taken under fire.

THE GATE TO THE MISSISSIPPI

The handwriting is that of Surgeon Bixby, of the Union hospital ship "Red Rover." In his album he pasted this unique photograph from the western shore of the river where the Federal guns and mortars threw a thousand shells into Vicksburg during the siege. The prominent building is the courthouse, the chief landmark during the investment. Here at Vicksburg the Confederates were making their last brave stand for the possession of the Mississippi River, that great artery of traffic. If it were wrested from them the main source of their supplies would be cut off. Pemberton, a brave and capable officer and a Pennsylvanian by birth, worked unremittingly for the cause he had espoused. Warned by the early attacks of General Williams and Admiral Farragut, he had left no stone unturned to render Vicksburg strongly defended. It had proved impregnable to attack on the north and east, and the powerful batteries planted on the river-front could not be silenced by the fleet nor by the guns of the Federals on the opposite shore. But Grant's masterful maneuver of cutting loose from his base and advancing from the south had at last out-generaled both Pemberton and Johnston. Nevertheless, Pemberton stoutly held his defenses. His high river-battery is photographed below, as it frowned upon the Federals opposite.

decisive repulse. His loss was nearly two thousand men; the Confederate loss was scarcely two hundred.

Two hundred feet above the bayou, beyond where the Federals were approaching, towered the Chickasaw Bluffs, to which Pemberton hastened troops from Vicksburg as soon as he learned Sherman's object. At the base of the bluff, and stretching away to the north and west were swamps and forests intersected by deep sloughs, overhung with dense tangles of vines and cane-brakes. Federal valor vied with Confederate pluck in this fight among the marshes and fever-infested jungle-land.

One of Sherman's storming parties, under General G. W. Morgan, came upon a broad and deep enlargement of the bayou, McNutt Lake, which interposed between it and the Confederates in the rifle-pits on the slopes and crest of the bluff. In the darkness of the night of December 28th, the Federal pontoniers labored to construct a passage-way across the lake. When morning dawned the weary pontoniers were chagrined to discover their well-built structure spanning a slough leading in another direction than toward the base of the bluff. The bridge was quickly taken up, and the Federals recommenced their labors, this time in daylight and within sight and range of the Southern regiments on the hill. The men in blue worked desperately to complete the span before driven away by the foe's cannon; but the fire increased with every minute, and the Federals finally withdrew.

Another storming party attempted to assail the Confederates from across a sandbar of the bayou, but was halted at the sight and prospect of overcoming a fifteen-foot bank on the farther side. The crumbling bank was surmounted with a levee three feet high; the steep sides of the barrier had crumbled away, leaving an overhanging shelf, two feet wide. Two companies of the Sixth Missouri regiment volunteered to cross the two hundred yards of exposed passage, and to cut a roadway through the rotten bank to allow their comrades a free

THE WELL–DEFENDED CITADEL

Behind these fortifications Pemberton, driven from the Big Black River, gathered his twenty-one thousand troops to make the last stand for the saving of the Mississippi to the Confederacy.   In the upper picture we see Fort Castle, one of the strongest defenses of the Confederacy.   It had full sweep of the river; here "Whistling Dick" (one of the most powerful guns in possession of the South) did deadly work.   In the lower picture we see the fortifications to the east of the town, before which Grant's army was now entrenching.   When Vicksburg had first been threatened in 1862, the Confederate fortifications had been laid out and work begun on them in haste with but five hundred spades, many of the soldiers delving with their bayonets.   The sites were so well chosen and the work so well done that they had withstood attacks for a year.   They were to hold out still longer.   By May 18th the Federals had completely invested Vicksburg, and Grant and Sherman rode out to Haynes' Bluff to view the open river to the north, down which abundant supplies were now coming for the army.   Sherman, who had not believed that the plan could succeed, frankly acknowledged his mistake.   But the Mississippi was not yet theirs.   Sherman, assaulting the fortifications of Vicksburg, the next day, was repulsed.   A second attack, on the 22d, failed and on the 25th Grant settled down to starve Pemberton out.

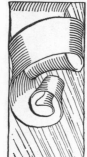
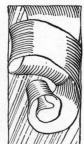

path to the bluff beyond. To add to the peril of the crossing, the sandbar was strewn with tangles of undergrowth and fallen trees, and the Confederate shells and bullets were raining upon the ground. Still, the gallant troops began their dash. From the very start, a line of wounded and dead Missourians marked the passage of the volunteers. The survivors reached the bank and desperately sought to dig the roadway. From the shrubbery on the bank suddenly appeared Confederate sharpshooters who poured their fire into the laboring soldiers; the flame of the discharging muskets burned the clothing of the Federals because the hostile forces were so close. Human endurance could not stand before this carnage, and the brave Missourians fled from the inferno. Sherman now found the northern pathway to Vicksburg impassable, and withdrew his men to the broad Mississippi.

Earlier in the same month had occurred two other events which, with the defeat of Chickasaw, go to make up the triple disaster to the Federals. On the 11th, General Nathan Forrest, one of the most brilliant cavalry leaders on either side, began one of those destructive raids which characterize the Civil War. With twenty-five hundred horsemen, Forrest dashed unopposed through the country north of Grant's army, tore up sixty miles of railroad and destroyed all telegraph lines.

Meantime, on December 20th, the day on which Sherman left Memphis, General Van Dorn pounced upon Holly Springs, in Mississippi, like an eagle on its prey, capturing the guard of fifteen hundred men and burning the great store of supplies, worth $1,500,000, which Grant had left there. Through the raids of Forrest and Van Dorn, Grant was left without supplies and for eleven days without communication with the outside world. He marched northward to Grand Junction, in Tennessee, a distance of eighty miles, living off the country. It was not until January 8, 1863, that he heard, through Washington, of the defeat of Sherman in his assault on Chickasaw Bluffs.

THE WORK OF THE BESIEGERS

Battery Sherman, on the Jackson Road, before Vicksburg. Settling down to a siege did not mean idleness for Grant's army. Fortifications had to be opposed to the formidable one of the Confederates and a constant bombardment kept up to silence their guns, one by one. It was to be a drawn-out duel in which Pemberton, hoping for the long-delayed relief from Johnston, held out bravely against starvation and even mutiny. For twelve miles the Federal lines stretched around Vicksburg, investing it to the river bank, north and south. More than eighty-nine battery positions were constructed by the Federals. Battery Sherman was exceptionally well built—not merely revetted with rails or cotton-bales and floored with rough timber, as lack of proper material often made necessary. Gradually the lines were drawn closer and closer as the Federals moved up their guns to silence the works that they had failed to take in May. At the time of the surrender Grant had more than 220 guns in position, mostly of heavy caliber. By the 1st of July besieged and besiegers faced each other at a distance of half-pistol shot. Starving and ravaged by disease, the Confederates had repelled repeated attacks which depleted their forces, while Grant, re-enforced to three times their number, was showered with supplies and ammunition that he might bring about the long-delayed victory which the North had been eagerly awaiting since Chancellorsville.

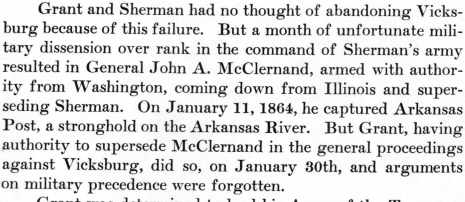

Grant and Sherman had no thought of abandoning Vicksburg because of this failure. But a month of unfortunate military dissension over rank in the command of Sherman's army resulted in General John A. McClernand, armed with authority from Washington, coming down from Illinois and superseding Sherman. On January 11, 1864, he captured Arkansas Post, a stronghold on the Arkansas River. But Grant, having authority to supersede McClernand in the general proceedings against Vicksburg, did so, on January 30th, and arguments on military precedence were forgotten.

Grant was determined to lead his Army of the Tennessee below Vicksburg and approach the city from the south, without breaking with his base of supplies up the river. Two projects, both of which were destined to fail, were under way during the winter and spring months of 1863. One of these was to open a way for the river craft through Lake Providence, west of the Mississippi, through various bayous and rivers into the Red River, a detour of four hundred miles.

Another plan was to cut a channel through the peninsula of the great bend of the Mississippi, opposite Vicksburg. For six weeks, thousands of men worked like marmots digging this ditch; but, meantime, the river was rising and, on March 8th, it broke over the embankment and the men had to run for their lives. Many horses were drowned and a great number of implements submerged. The "Father of Waters" had put a decisive veto on the project and it had to be given up. Still another plan that failed was to cut through the Yazoo Pass and approach from the north by way of the Coldwater, the Tallahatchie, and the Yazoo rivers.

Failure with Grant only increased his grim determination. He *would* take Vicksburg. His next plan was destined to bring success. It was to transfer his army by land down the west bank of the Mississippi to a point below the city and approach it from the south and west. This necessitated the running of the batteries by Porter's fleet—an extremely

INVESTING BY INCHES

Logan's Division undermining the most formidable redoubt in the defenses of Vicksburg. The position was immediately in front of this honeycombed slope on the Jackson road. Upon these troops fell most of the labor of sapping and mining, which finally resulted in the wrecking of the fort so gallantly defended by the veterans of the Third Louisiana. As the Federal lines crept up, the men working night and day were forced to live in burrows. They became proficient in such gopher work as the picture shows. Up to the "White House" (Shirley's) the troops could be marched in comparative safety, but a short distance beyond they were exposed to the Confederate sharpshooters, who had only rifles and muskets to depend on; their artillery had long since been silenced. Near this house was constructed "Coonskin's" Tower; it was built of railway iron and cross-ties under the direction of Second Lieutenant Henry C. Foster, of Company B, Twenty-third Indiana. A backwoodsman and dead-shot, he was particularly active in paying the Confederate sharpshooters in their own coin. He habitually wore a cap of raccoon fur, which gave him his nickname and christened the tower, from which the interior of the Confederate works could be seen.

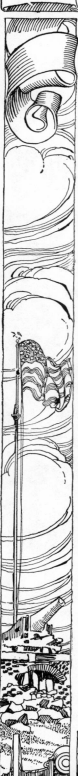

perilous enterprise. The army was divided into four corps, commanded respectively by Sherman, McClernand, McPherson, and Hurlbut. The latter was stationed at Memphis. On March 29th, the movement of McClernand from Milliken's Bend to a point opposite Grand Gulf was begun. He was soon followed by McPherson and a few weeks later by Sherman. It required a month for the army, with its heavy artillery, to journey through the swamps and bogs of Louisiana.

While this march was in progress, something far more exciting was taking place on the river. Porter ran the batteries of Vicksburg with his fleet. After days of preparation the fleet of vessels, protected by cotton bales and hay about the vital parts of the boats, with heavy logs slung near the water-line—seven gunboats, the ram *General Price,* three transports, and various barges were ready for the dangerous journey on the night of April 16th. Silently in the darkness, they left their station near the mouth of the Yazoo, at a quarter past nine. For an hour and a half all was silence and expectancy. The bluffs on the east loomed black against the night sky. Suddenly, the flash of musketry fire pierced the darkness.

In a few minutes every battery overlooking the river was a center of spurting flame. A storm of shot and shell was rained upon the passing vessels. Not one escaped being struck many times. The water of the river was lashed into foam by the shots and shell from the batteries. The gunboats answered with their cannon. The air was filled with flying missiles. Several houses on the Louisiana shore burst into flame and the whole river from shore to shore was lighted with vivid distinctness. A little later, a giant flame leaped from the bosom of the river. A vessel had caught fire. It was the transport *Henry Clay.* It burned to the water's edge, nearly all its crew escaping to other vessels. Grant described the scene as " magnificent, but terrible "; Sherman pronounced it " truly sublime."

By three in the morning, the fleet was below the city and ready to cooperate with the army. One vessel had been

THE FIRST MONUMENT AT THE MEETING PLACE

Independence Day, 1863, was a memorable anniversary of the nation's birth; it brought to the anxious North the momentous news that Meade had won at Gettysburg and that Vicksburg had fallen in the West. The marble shaft in the picture was erected to mark the spot where Grant and Pemberton met on July 3d to confer about the surrender. Under a tree, within a few hundred feet of the Confederate lines, Grant greeted his adversary as an old acquaintance. They had fought in the same division for a time in the Mexican War. Each spoke but two sentences as to the surrender, for Grant lived up to the nickname he gained at Donelson, and Pemberton's pride was hurt. The former comrades walked and talked awhile on other things, and then returned to their lines. Next day the final terms were arranged by correspondence, and the Confederates marched out with colors flying; they stacked their arms and, laying their colors upon them, marched back into the city to be paroled. Those who signed the papers not to fight until exchanged numbered 29,391. The tree where the commanders met was soon carried away, root and branch, by relic-hunters. Subsequently the monument which replaced it was chipped gradually into bits, and in 1866 a 64-pounder cannon took its place as a permanent memorial.

VICKSBURG IN POSSESSION OF THE FEDERALS

destroyed, several others were crippled; thirteen men had been wounded, but Grant had the assistance he needed. About a week later, six more transports performed the same feat and ran the batteries; each had two barges laden with forage and rations in tow.

Grant's next move was to transfer the army across the river and to secure a base of supplies. There, on the bluff, was Grand Gulf, a tempting spot. But the Confederate guns showed menacingly over the brow of the hill. After a fruitless bombardment by the fleet on April 29th, it was decided that a more practical place to cross the river must be sought below.

Meanwhile, Sherman was ordered by his chief to advance upon the formidable Haynes' Bluff, on the Yazoo River, some miles above the scene of his repulse in the preceding December. The message had said, "Make a demonstration on Haynes' Bluff, and make all the *show* possible." Sherman's transports, and three of Porter's gunboats, were closely followed by the Confederate soldiers who had been stationed at the series of defenses on the range of hills, and when they arrived at Snyder's Mill, just below Haynes' Bluff, on April 30th, General Hébert and several Louisiana regiments were awaiting them. On that day and the next the Confederates fiercely engaged the Union fleet and troops, and on May 2d Sherman withdrew his forces to the western bank of the Mississippi and hastened to Grant. The feint had been most successful. The Confederates had been prevented from sending reenforcements to Grand Gulf, and Grant's crossing was greatly facilitated.

The fleet passed the batteries of Grand Gulf and stopped at Bruinsburg, six miles below. A landing was soon made, the army taken across on April 30th, and a march to Port Gibson, twelve miles inland, was begun. General Bowen, Confederate commander at Grand Gulf, came out and offered battle. He was greatly outnumbered, but his troops fought gallantly throughout most of the day, May 1st, before yielding

A VIGILANT PATROLLER—THE "SILVER LAKE"

In the picture the "Silver Lake" is lying off Vicksburg after its fall. While Admiral Porter was busy attacking Vicksburg with the Mississippi squadron, Lieutenant-Commander Le Roy Fitch, with a few small gunboats, was actively patrolling the Tennessee and Cumberland Rivers. It was soon seen that the hold upon Tennessee and Kentucky gained by the Federals by the fall of Forts Henry and Donelson would be lost without adequate assistance from the navy, and Admiral Porter was authorized to purchase small light-draft river steamers and add them to Fitch's flotilla as rapidly as they could be converted into gunboats. One of the first to be completed was the "Silver Lake." The little stern-wheel steamer first distinguished herself on February 3, 1863, at Dover, Tennessee, where she (with Fitch's flotilla) assisted in routing 4,500 Confederates, who were attacking the Federals at that place. The little vessel continued to render yeoman's service with the other gunboats, ably assisted by General A. W. Ellet's marine brigade.

the field. Port Gibson was then occupied by the Union army, and Grand Gulf, no longer tenable, was abandoned by the Confederates.

Grant now prepared for a campaign into the interior of Mississippi. His first intention was to cooperate with General Banks in the capture of Port Hudson, after which they would move together upon Vicksburg. But hearing that Banks would not arrive for ten days, Grant decided that he would proceed to the task before him without delay. His army at that time numbered about forty-three thousand. That under Pemberton probably forty thousand, while there were fifteen thousand Confederate troops at Jackson, Mississippi, soon to be commanded by General Joseph E. Johnston, who was hastening to that capital.

The Federal leader now determined on the bold plan of making a dash into the interior of Mississippi, beating Johnston and turning on Pemberton before their forces could be joined. This campaign is pronounced the most brilliant in the Civil War. It was truly Napoleonic in conception and execution. Grant knew that his base of supplies at Grand Gulf would be cut off by Pemberton as soon as he moved away from it. He decided, therefore, against the advice of his generals, to abandon his base altogether.

A more daring undertaking could scarcely be imagined. With a few days' rations in their haversacks the troops were to make a dash that would possibly take several weeks into the heart of a hostile country. This was certainly defying fate. When General Halleck heard of Grant's daring scheme he wired the latter from Washington, ordering him to move his army down the river and cooperate with Banks. Fortunately, this order was received too late to interfere with Grant's plans.

As soon as Sherman's divisions joined the main army the march was begun, on May 7th. An advance of this character must be made with the greatest celerity and Grant's army showed amazing speed. McPherson, who commanded the right

THE CONFEDERACY CUT IN TWAIN

The Levee at Vicksburg, February, 1864.   For seven months the Federals had been in possession of the city, and the Mississippi—
now open through its entire course—cut off the struggling Confederacy in the East from the South and Southwest, the storehouses of
their resources and their main dependence in continuing the struggle.   But even such a blow as this, coming on top of Gettysburg,
did not force the brave people of the South to give up the struggle.   In the picture the only remaining warlike signs are the tents
on the opposite shore.   But on both sides of the river the Confederates were still desperately striving to reunite their territory.   In
the East another year and more of the hardest kind of fighting was ahead; another severing in twain of the South was inevitable before
peace could come, and before the muskets could be used to shoot the crows, and before their horses could plough the neglected fields.

wing, proceeded toward Jackson by way of Raymond and at the latter place encountered five thousand Confederates, on May 12th, who blocked his way and were prepared for fight. The battle of Raymond lasted two hours. McPherson was completely successful and the Confederates hastened to join their comrades in Jackson.

McPherson lost no time. He moved on toward Jackson, and as the last of his command left Raymond the advance of Sherman's corps reached it. That night, May 13th, Grant ordered McPherson and Sherman to march upon Jackson next morning by different roads, while McClernand was held in the rear near enough to reenforce either in case of need. The rain fell in torrents that night and, as Grant reported, in places the water was a foot deep in the road. But nothing could daunt his determined army. At eleven o'clock in the morning of the 14th, a concerted attack was made on the capital of Mississippi. A few hours' brisk fighting concluded this act of the drama, and the Stars and Stripes were unfurled on the State capitol. Among the spoils were seventeen heavy guns. That night, Grant slept in the house which Johnston had occupied the night before.

Meantime, Johnston had ordered Pemberton to detain Grant by attacking him in the rear. But Pemberton considered it more advisable to move toward Grand Gulf to separate Grant from his base of supplies, not knowing that Grant had abandoned his base. And now, with Johnston's army scattered, Grant left Sherman to burn bridges and military factories, and to tear up the railroads about Jackson while he turned fiercely on Pemberton. McPherson's corps took the lead. Grant called on McClernand to follow without delay. Then, hearing that Pemberton was marching toward him, he called on Sherman to hasten from Jackson. At Champion's Hill (Baker's Creek) Pemberton stood in the way, with eighteen thousand men.

The battle was soon in progress—the heaviest of the

WITHIN THE PARAPET AT PORT HUDSON IN THE SUMMER OF 1863

These fortifications withstood every attack of Banks' powerful army from May 24 to July 9, 1863. Like Vicksburg, Port Hudson could be reduced only by a weary siege. These pictures, taken within the fortifications, show in the distance the ground over which the investing army approached to the two unsuccessful grand assaults they made upon the Confederate defenders. The strength of the works is apparent. A continuous line of parapet, equally strong, had been thrown up for the defense of Port Hudson, surrounding the town for a distance of three miles and more, each end terminating on the river-bank. Four powerful forts were located at the salients, and the line throughout was defended by thirty pieces of field artillery. Brigadier-General Beall, who commanded the post in 1862, constructed these works. Major-General Frank Gardner succeeded him in command at the close of the year.

THE WELL–DEFENDED WORKS

CONFEDERATE FORTIFICATIONS BEFORE PORT HUDSON

Gardner was behind these defenses with a garrison of about seven thousand when Banks approached Port Hudson for the second time on May 24th. Gardner was under orders to evacuate the place and join his force to that of Johnston at Jackson, Mississippi, but the courier who brought the order arrived at the very hour when Banks began to bottle up the Confederates. On the morning of May 25th Banks drove in the Confederate skirmishers and outposts and, with an army of thirty thousand, invested the fortifications from the eastward. At 10 A.M., after an artillery duel of more than four hours, the Federals advanced to the assault of the works. Fighting in a dense forest of magnolias, amid thick undergrowth and among ravines choked with felled timber, the progress of the troops was too slow for a telling attack. The battle has been described as "a gigantic bushwhack." The Federals at the center reached the ditch in front of the Confederate works but were driven off. At nightfall the attempt was abandoned. It had cost Banks nearly two thousand men.

campaign. It continued for seven or eight hours. The Confederates were defeated with a loss of nearly all their artillery and about half their force, including four thousand men who were cut off from the main army and failed to rejoin it. On the banks of the Big Black River, a few miles westward, the Confederates made another stand, and here the fifth battle of the investment of Vicksburg took place. It was short, sharp, decisive. The Confederates suffered heavy losses and the remainder hastened to the defenses of Vicksburg. They had set fire to the bridge across the Big Black, and Grant's army was detained for a day—until the Confederates were safely lodged in the city.

The Federal army now invested Vicksburg, occupying the surrounding hills. It was May 18th when the remarkable campaign to reach Vicksburg came to an end. In eighteen days, the army had marched one hundred and eighty miles through a hostile country, fought and won five battles, captured a State capital, had taken twenty-seven heavy cannon and sixty field-pieces, and had slain or wounded six thousand men and captured as many more. As Grant and Sherman rode out on the hill north of the city, the latter broke into enthusiastic admiration of his chief, declaring that up to that moment he had felt no assurance of success, and pronouncing the campaign one of the greatest in history.

The great problem of investing Vicksburg was solved at last. Around the doomed city gleamed the thousands of bayonets of the Union army. The inhabitants and the army that had fled to it as a city of refuge were penned in. But the Confederacy was not to yield without a stubborn resistance. On May 19th, an advance was made on the works and the besieging lines drew nearer and tightened their coils. Three days later, on May 22nd, Grant ordered a grand assault by his whole army. The troops, flushed with their victories of the past three weeks, were eager for the attack. All the corps commanders set their watches by Grant's in order to begin

THE GUN THAT FOOLED THE FEDERALS

A "Quaker gun" that was mounted by the Confederates in the fortifications on the bluff at the river-front before Port Hudson. This gun was hewn out of a pine log and mounted on a carriage, and a black ring was painted around the end facing the river. Throughout the siege it was mistaken by the Federals for a piece of real ordnance. To such devices as this the beleaguered garrison was compelled constantly to resort in order to impress the superior forces investing Port Hudson with the idea that the position they sought to capture was formidably defended. The ruse was effective. Port Hudson was not again attacked from the river after the passing of Farragut's two ships.

WITHIN "THE CITADEL"

This bastion fort, near the left of the Confederate line of defenses at Port Hudson, was the strongest of their works, and here Weitzel and Grover's divisions of the Federals followed up the attack (begun at daylight of June 14th) that Banks had ordered all along the line in his second effort to capture the position. The only result was simply to advance the Federal lines from fifty to two hundred yards nearer. In front of the "citadel" an advance position was gained from which a mine was subsequently run to within a few yards of the fort.

the assault at all points at the same moment—ten o'clock in the morning. At the appointed time, the cannon from the encircling lines burst forth in a deafening roar. Then came the answering thunders from the mortar-boats on the Louisiana shore and from the gunboats anchored beneath the bluff. The gunboats' fire was answered from within the bastions protecting the city. The opening of the heavy guns on the land side was followed by the sharper crackle of musketry—thousands of shots, indistinguishable in a continuous roll.

The men in the Federal lines leaped from their hiding places and ran to the parapets in the face of a murderous fire from the defenders of the city, only to be mowed down by hundreds. Others came, crawling over the bodies of their fallen comrades—now and then they planted their colors on the battlements of the besieged city, to be cut down by the galling Confederate fire. Thus it continued hour after hour, until the coming of darkness. The assault had failed. The Union loss was about three thousand brave men; the Confederate loss was probably not much over five hundred.

Grant had made a fearful sacrifice; he was paying a high price but he had a reason for so doing—Johnston with a reenforcing army was threatening him in the rear; by taking Vicksburg at this time he could have turned on Johnston, and could have saved the Government sending any more Federal troops; and, to use his own words, it was needed because the men "would not have worked in the trenches with the same zeal, believing it unnecessary, as they did after their failure, to carry the enemy's works."

On the north side of the city overlooking the river, were the powerful batteries on Fort Hill, a deadly menace to the Federal troops, and Grant and Sherman believed that if enfiladed by the gunboats this position could be carried. At their request Admiral Porter sent the *Cincinnati* on May 27th to engage the Confederate guns, while four vessels below the town did the same to the lower defenses. In half an hour five

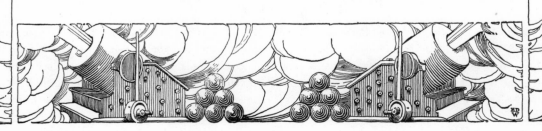

THE FIRST INDIANA HEAVY ARTILLERY AT BATON ROUGE

PHOTOGRAPHS THAT FURNISHED VALUABLE SECRET–SERVICE INFORMATION TO THE
CONFEDERATES

The clearest and most trustworthy evidence of an opponent's strength is of course an actual photograph. Such evidence, in spite of the early stage of the art and the difficulty of "running in" chemical supplies on "orders to trade," was supplied the Confederate leaders in the Southwest by Lytle, the Baton Rouge photographer—really a member of the Confederate secret service. Here are photographs of the First Indiana Heavy Artillery (formerly the Twenty-first Indiana Infantry), showing its strength and position on the arsenal grounds at Baton Rouge. As the Twenty-first Indiana, the regiment had been at Baton Rouge during the first Federal occupation, and after the fall of Port Hudson it returned there for garrison duty. Little did its officers suspect that the quiet man photographing the batteries at drill was about to convey the "information" beyond their lines to their opponents.

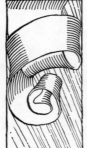

of the *Cincinnati's* guns were disabled; and she was in a sinking condition. She was run toward the shore and sank in three fathoms of water.

The army now settled down to a wearisome siege. For six weeks, they encircled the city with trenches, approaching nearer and nearer to the defending walls; they exploded mines; they shot at every head that appeared above the parapets. One by one the defending batteries were silenced. The sappers slowly worked their way toward the Confederate ramparts. Miners were busy on both sides burrowing beneath the fortifications. At three o'clock on the afternoon of June 25th a redoubt in the Confederate works was blown into the air, breaking into millions of fragments and disclosing guns, men, and timber. With the mine explosion, the Federal soldiers before the redoubt began to dash into the opening, only to meet with a withering fire from an interior parapet which the Confederates had constructed in anticipation of this event. The carnage was appalling to behold; and when the soldiers of the Union finally retired they had learned a costly lesson which withheld them from attack when another mine was exploded on July 1st.

Meantime, let us take a view of the river below and the life of the people within the doomed city. Far down the river, two hundred and fifty miles from Vicksburg, was Port Hudson. The place was fortified and held by a Confederate force under General Gardner. Like Vicksburg, it was besieged by a Federal army, under Nathaniel P. Banks, of Cedar Mountain fame. On May 27th, he made a desperate attack on the works and was powerfully aided by Farragut with his fleet in the river. But aside from dismounting a few guns and weakening the foe at a still heavier cost to their own ranks, the Federals were unsuccessful. Again, on June 10th, and still again on the 14th, Banks made fruitless attempts to carry Port Hudson by storm. He then, like Grant at Vicksburg, settled down to a siege. The defenders of Port Hudson proved their courage by enduring every hardship.

"MY

EXECUTIVE

OFFICER,

MR. DEWEY"

THE

FUTURE ADMIRAL

AS CIVIL WAR

LIEUTENANT

In the fight with the batteries at Port Hudson, March 14, 1863, Farragut, in the "Hartford" lashed to the "Albatross," got by, but the fine old consort of the "Hartford," the "Mississippi," went down—her gunners fighting to the last. Farragut, in anguish, could see her enveloped in flames lighting up the river. She had grounded under the very guns of a battery, and not until actually driven off by the flames did her men leave her. When the "Mississippi" grounded, the shock threw her lieutenant-commander into the river, and in confusion he swam toward the shore; then, turning about, he swam back to his ship. Captain Smith thus writes in his report: "I consider that I should be neglecting a most important duty should I omit to mention the coolness of my executive officer, Mr. Dewey, and the steady, fearless, and gallant manner in which the officers and men of the 'Mississippi' defended her, and the orderly and quiet manner in which she was abandoned after being thirty-five minutes aground under the fire of the enemy's batteries. There was no confusion in embarking the crew, and the only noise was from the enemy's cannon." Lieutenant-Commander George Dewey, here mentioned at the age of 26, was to exemplify in Manila Bay on May 1, 1898, the lessons he was learning from Farragut.

At Vicksburg, during the whole six weeks of the siege, the men in the trenches worked steadily, advancing the coils about the city. Grant received reenforcement and before the end of the siege his army numbered over seventy thousand. Day and night, the roar of artillery continued. From the mortars across the river and from Porter's fleet the shrieking shells rose in grand parabolic curves, bursting in midair or in the streets of the city, spreading havoc in all directions. The people of the city burrowed into the ground for safety. Many whole families lived in these dismal abodes, their walls of clay being shaken by the roaring battles that raged above the ground. In one of these dens, sixty-five people found a home. The food supply ran low, and day by day it became scarcer. At last, by the end of June, there was nothing to eat except mule meat and a kind of bread made of beans and corn meal.

It was ten o'clock in the morning of July 3d. White flags were seen above the parapet. The firing ceased. A strange quietness rested over the scene of the long bombardment. On the afternoon of that day, the one, too, on which was heard the last shot on the battlefield of Gettysburg, Grant and Pemberton stood beneath an oak tree, in front of McPherson's corps, and opened negotiations for the capitulation. On the following morning, the Nation's birthday, about thirty thousand soldiers laid down their arms as prisoners of war and were released on parole. The losses from May 1st to the surrender were about ten thousand on each side.

Three days later, at Port Hudson, a tremendous cheer arose from the besieging army. The Confederates within the defenses were at a loss to know the cause. Then some one shouted the news, "Vicksburg has surrendered!"

The end had come. Port Hudson could not hope to stand alone; the greater fortress had fallen. Two days later, July 9th, the gallant garrison, worn and weary with the long siege, surrendered to General Banks. The whole course of the mighty Mississippi was now under the Stars and Stripes.

[Part VIII]

WHILE LINCOLN SPOKE AT GETTYSBURG, NOVEMBER 19, 1863 — DURING THE FAMOUS ADDRESS IN DEDICATION OF THE CEMETERY

The most important American address is brief: "Fourscore and seven years ago our fathers brought forth on this continent a new nation, conceived in liberty, and dedicated to the proposition that all men are created equal. Now we are engaged in a great civil war, testing whether that nation, or any nation so conceived and so dedicated, can long endure. We are met on a great battlefield of that war. We have come to dedicate a portion of that field as a final resting-place for those who here gave their lives that that nation might live. It is altogether fitting and proper that we should do this. But in a larger sense, we cannot dedicate, we cannot consecrate, we cannot hallow this ground. The brave men, living and dead, who struggled here, have consecrated it far above our poor power to add or detract. The world will little note, nor long remember, what we say here, but it can never forget what they did here. It is for us, the living, rather, to be dedicated here to the unfinished work which they who fought here have thus far so nobly advanced. It is rather for us to be here dedicated to the great task remaining before us;—that from these honored dead, we take increased devotion to that cause for which they gave the last full measure of devotion;—that we here highly resolve that these dead shall not have died in vain, that this nation, under God, shall have a new birth of freedom, and that government of the people, by the people, for the people, shall not perish from the earth."

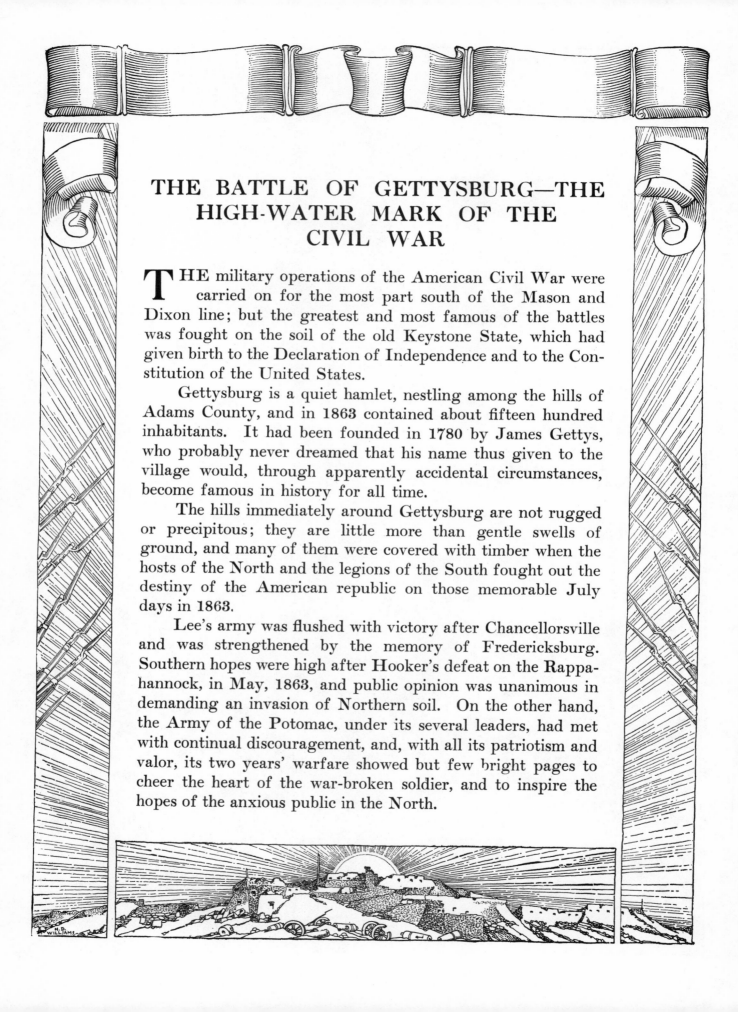

THE BATTLE OF GETTYSBURG—THE HIGH-WATER MARK OF THE CIVIL WAR

THE military operations of the American Civil War were carried on for the most part south of the Mason and Dixon line; but the greatest and most famous of the battles was fought on the soil of the old Keystone State, which had given birth to the Declaration of Independence and to the Constitution of the United States.

Gettysburg is a quiet hamlet, nestling among the hills of Adams County, and in 1863 contained about fifteen hundred inhabitants. It had been founded in 1780 by James Gettys, who probably never dreamed that his name thus given to the village would, through apparently accidental circumstances, become famous in history for all time.

The hills immediately around Gettysburg are not rugged or precipitous; they are little more than gentle swells of ground, and many of them were covered with timber when the hosts of the North and the legions of the South fought out the destiny of the American republic on those memorable July days in 1863.

Lee's army was flushed with victory after Chancellorsville and was strengthened by the memory of Fredericksburg. Southern hopes were high after Hooker's defeat on the Rappahannock, in May, 1863, and public opinion was unanimous in demanding an invasion of Northern soil. On the other hand, the Army of the Potomac, under its several leaders, had met with continual discouragement, and, with all its patriotism and valor, its two years' warfare showed but few bright pages to cheer the heart of the war-broken soldier, and to inspire the hopes of the anxious public in the North.

THE CRISIS BRINGS FORTH THE MAN

Major-General George Gordon Meade and Staff. Not men, but a man is what counts in war, said Napoleon; and Lee had proved it true in many a bitter lesson administered to the Army of the Potomac. At the end of June, 1863, for the third time in ten months, that army had a new commander. Promptness and caution were equally imperative in that hour. Meade's fitness for the post was as yet undemonstrated; he had been advanced from the command of the Fifth Corps three days before the army was to engage in its greatest battle. Lee must be turned back from Harrisburg and Philadelphia and kept from striking at Baltimore and Washington, and the somewhat scattered Army of the Potomac must be concentrated. In the very first flush of his advancement, Meade exemplified the qualities of sound generalship that placed his name high on the list of Federal commanders.

Leaving General Stuart with ten thousand cavalry and a part of Hill's corps to prevent Hooker from pursuing, Lee crossed the Potomac early in June, 1863, concentrated his army at Hagerstown, Maryland, and prepared for a campaign in Pennsylvania, with Harrisburg as the objective. His army was organized in three corps, under the respective commands of Longstreet, Ewell, and A. P. Hill. Lee had divided his army so as to approach Harrisburg by different routes and to assess the towns along the way for large sums of money. Late in June, he was startled by the intelligence that Stuart had failed to detain Hooker, and that the Federals had crossed the Potomac and were in hot pursuit.

Lee was quick to see that his plans must be changed. He knew that to continue his march he must keep his army together to watch his pursuing antagonist, and that such a course in this hostile country would mean starvation, while the willing hands of the surrounding populace would minister to the wants of his foe. Again, if he should scatter his forces that they might secure the necessary supplies, the parts would be attacked singly and destroyed. Lee saw, therefore, that he must abandon his invasion of the North or turn upon his pursuing foe and disable him in order to continue his march. But that foe was a giant of strength and courage, more than equal to his own; and the coming together of two such forces in a mighty death-struggle meant that a great battle must be fought, a greater battle than this Western world had hitherto known.

The Army of the Potomac had again changed leaders, and George Gordon Meade was now its commander. Hooker, after a dispute with Halleck, resigned his leadership, and Meade, the strongest of the corps commanders, was appointed in his place, succeeding him on June 28th. The two great armies—Union and Confederate—were scattered over portions of Maryland and southern Pennsylvania. Both were marching northward, along almost parallel lines. The Confederates

ROBERT E. LEE IN 1863

It was with the gravest misgivings that Lee began his invasion of the North in 1863. He was too wise a general not to realize that a crushing defeat was possible. Yet, with Vicksburg already doomed, the effort to win a decisive victory in the East was imperative in its importance. Magnificent was the courage and fortitude of Lee's maneuvering during that long march which was to end in failure. Hitherto he had made every one of his veterans count for two of their antagonists, but at Gettysburg the odds had fallen heavily against him. Jackson, his resourceful ally, was no more. Longstreet advised strongly against giving battle, but Lee unwaveringly made the tragic effort which sacrificed more than a third of his splendid army.

were gradually pressing toward the east, while the Federals were marching along a line eastward of that followed by the Confederates. The new commander of the Army of the Potomac was keeping his forces interposed between the legions of Lee and the Federal capital, and watching for an opportunity to force the Confederates to battle where the Federals would have the advantage of position. It was plain that they must soon come together in a gigantic contest; but just where the shock of battle would take place was yet unknown. Meade had ordered a general movement toward Harrisburg, and General Buford was sent with four thousand cavalry to intercept the Confederate advance guard.

On the night of June 30th Buford encamped on a low hill, a mile west of Gettysburg, and here on the following morning the famous battle had its beginning.

On the morning of July 1st the two armies were still scattered, the extremes being forty miles apart. But General Reynolds, with two corps of the Union army, was but a few miles away, and was hastening to Gettysburg, while Longstreet and Hill were approaching from the west. Buford opened the battle against Heth's division of Hill's corps. Reynolds soon joined Buford, and three hours before noon the battle was in progress on Seminary Ridge. Reynolds rode out to his fighting-lines on the ridge, and while placing his troops, a little after ten o'clock in the morning, he received a sharpshooter's bullet in the brain. The gallant Federal leader fell dead. John F. Reynolds, who had been promoted for gallantry at Buena Vista in the Mexican War, was one of the bravest and ablest generals of the Union army. No casualty of the war brought more widespread mourning to the North than the death of Reynolds.

But even this calamity could not stay the fury of the battle. By one o'clock both sides had been greatly reenforced, and the battle-line extended north of the town from Seminary Ridge to the bank of Rock Creek. Here for hours the roar

HANCOCK, "THE SUPERB"

Every man in this picture was wounded at Gettysburg. Seated, is Winfield Scott Hancock; the boy-general, Francis C. Barlow (who was struck almost mortally), leans against the tree. The other two are General John Gibbon and General David B. Birney. About four o'clock on the afternoon of July 1st a foam-flecked charger dashed up Cemetery Hill bearing General Hancock. He had galloped thirteen miles to take command. Apprised of the loss of Reynolds, his main dependence, Meade knew that only a man of vigor and judgment could save the situation. He chose wisely, for Hancock was one of the best all-round soldiers that the Army of the Potomac had developed. It was he who re-formed the shattered corps and chose the position to be held for the decisive struggle.

of the battle was unceasing. About the middle of the afternoon a breeze lifted the smoke that had enveloped the whole battle-line in darkness, and revealed the fact that the Federals were being pressed back toward Gettysburg. General Carl Schurz, who after Reynolds' death directed the extreme right near Rock Creek, leaving nearly half of his men dead or wounded on the field, retreated toward Cemetery Hill, and in passing through the town the Confederates pursued and captured a large number of the remainder. The left wing, now unable to hold its position owing to the retreat of the right, was also forced back, and it, too, took refuge on Cemetery Hill, which had been selected by General O. O. Howard; and the first day's fight was over. It was several hours before night, and had the Southerners known of the disorganized condition of the Union troops, they might have pursued and captured a large part of the army. Meade, who was still some miles from the field, hearing of the death of Reynolds, had sent Hancock to take general command until he himself should arrive.

Hancock had ridden at full speed and arrived on the field between three and four o'clock in the afternoon. His presence soon brought order out of chaos. His superb bearing, his air of confidence, his promise of heavy reenforcements during the night, all tended to inspire confidence and to renew hope in the ranks of the discouraged army. Had this day ended the affair at Gettysburg, the usual story of the defeat of the Army of the Potomac would have gone forth to the world. Only the advance portions of both armies had been engaged; and yet the battle had been a formidable one. The Union loss was severe. A great commander had fallen, and the rank and file had suffered the fearful loss of ten thousand men.

Meade reached the scene late in the night, and chose to make this field, on which the advance of both armies had accidentally met, the place of a general engagement. Lee had come to the same decision, and both called on their outlying

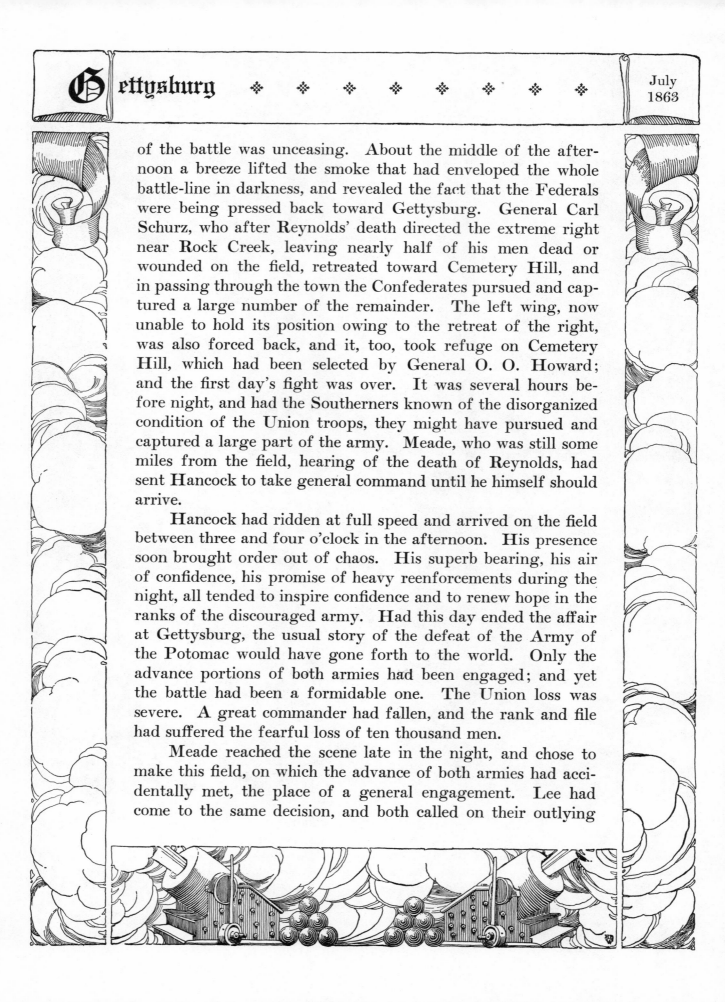

MUTE PLEADERS IN THE CAUSE OF PEACE

There was little time that could be employed by either side in caring for those who fell upon the fields of the almost uninterrupted fighting at Gettysburg. On the morning of the 4th, when Lee began to abandon his position on Seminary Ridge, opposite the Federal right, both sides sent forth ambulance and burial details to remove the wounded and bury the dead in the torrential rain then falling. Under cover of the hazy atmosphere, Lee was get-

MEN OF THE IRON BRIGADE

ting his whole army in motion to retreat. Many an unfinished shallow grave, like the one above, had to be left by the Confederates. In this lower picture some men of the Twenty-fourth Michigan infantry are lying dead on the field of battle. This regiment—one of the units of the Iron Brigade—left seven distinct rows of dead as it fell back from battle-line to battle-line, on the first day. Three-fourths of its members were struck down.

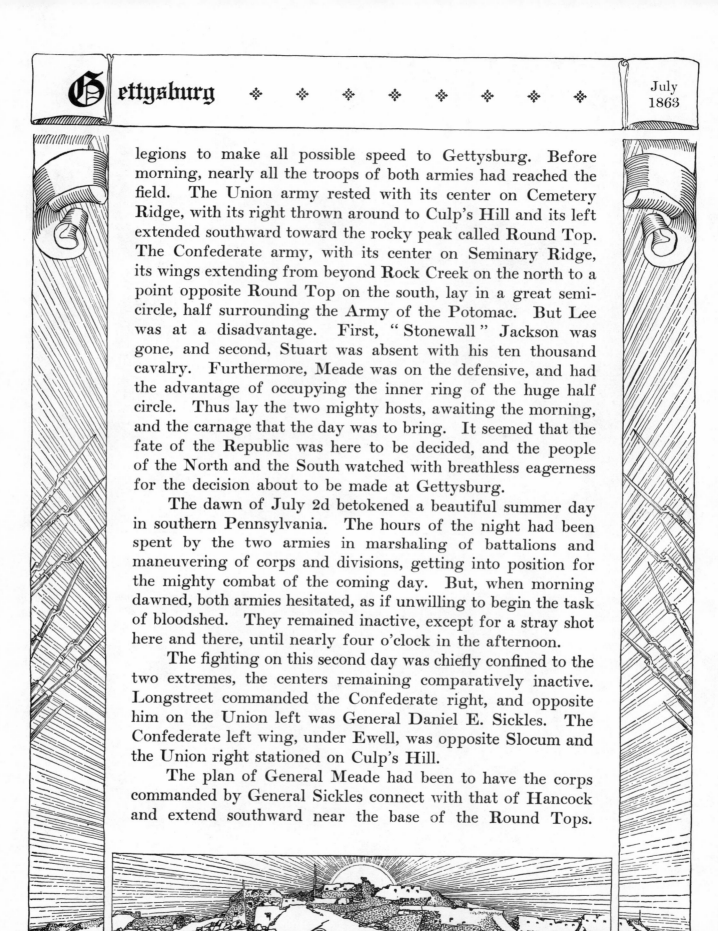

legions to make all possible speed to Gettysburg. Before morning, nearly all the troops of both armies had reached the field. The Union army rested with its center on Cemetery Ridge, with its right thrown around to Culp's Hill and its left extended southward toward the rocky peak called Round Top. The Confederate army, with its center on Seminary Ridge, its wings extending from beyond Rock Creek on the north to a point opposite Round Top on the south, lay in a great semicircle, half surrounding the Army of the Potomac. But Lee was at a disadvantage. First, "Stonewall" Jackson was gone, and second, Stuart was absent with his ten thousand cavalry. Furthermore, Meade was on the defensive, and had the advantage of occupying the inner ring of the huge half circle. Thus lay the two mighty hosts, awaiting the morning, and the carnage that the day was to bring. It seemed that the fate of the Republic was here to be decided, and the people of the North and the South watched with breathless eagerness for the decision about to be made at Gettysburg.

The dawn of July 2d betokened a beautiful summer day in southern Pennsylvania. The hours of the night had been spent by the two armies in marshaling of battalions and maneuvering of corps and divisions, getting into position for the mighty combat of the coming day. But, when morning dawned, both armies hesitated, as if unwilling to begin the task of bloodshed. They remained inactive, except for a stray shot here and there, until nearly four o'clock in the afternoon.

The fighting on this second day was chiefly confined to the two extremes, the centers remaining comparatively inactive. Longstreet commanded the Confederate right, and opposite him on the Union left was General Daniel E. Sickles. The Confederate left wing, under Ewell, was opposite Slocum and the Union right stationed on Culp's Hill.

The plan of General Meade had been to have the corps commanded by General Sickles connect with that of Hancock and extend southward near the base of the Round Tops.

THE FIRST DAY'S TOLL

The lives laid down by the blue-clad soldiers in the first day's fighting made possible the ultimate victory at Gettysburg. The stubborn resistance of Buford's cavalry and of the First and Eleventh Corps checked the Confederate advance for an entire day. The delay was priceless; it enabled Meade to concentrate his army upon the heights to the south of Gettysburg, a position which proved impregnable. To a Pennsylvanian, General John F. Reynolds, falls the credit of the determined stand that was made that day. Commanding the advance of the army, he promptly went to Buford's support, bringing up his infantry and artillery to hold back the Confederates.

McPHERSON'S WOODS

At the edge of these woods General Reynolds was killed by a Confederate sharpshooter in the first vigorous contest of the day. The woods lay between the two roads upon which the Confederates were advancing from the west, and General Doubleday (in command of the First Corps) was ordered to take the position so that the columns of the foe could be enfiladed by the infantry, while contending with the artillery posted on both roads. The Iron Brigade under General Meredith was ordered to hold the ground at all hazards. As they charged, the troops shouted: "If we can't hold it, where will you find the men who can?" On they swept, capturing General Archer and many of his Confederate brigade that had entered the woods from the other side. As Archer passed to the rear, Doubleday, who had been his classmate at West Point, greeted him with "Good morning! I'm glad to see you!"

Sickles found this ground low and disadvantageous as a fighting-place. In his front he saw the high ground along the ridge on the side of which the peach orchard was situated, and advanced his men to this position, placing them along the Emmitsburg road, and back toward the Trostle farm and the wheat-field, thus forming an angle at the peach orchard. The left flank of Hancock's line now rested far behind the right flank of Sickles' forces. The Third Corps was alone in its position in advance of the Federal line. The Confederate troops later marched along Sickles' front so that Longstreet's corps overlapped the left wing of the Union army. The Northerners grimly watched the bristling cannon and the files of men that faced them across the valley, as they waited for the battle to commence.

The boom of cannon from Longstreet's batteries announced the beginning of the second day's battle. Lee had ordered Longstreet to attack Sickles in full force. The fire was quickly answered by the Union troops, and before long the fight extended from the peach orchard through the wheat-field and along the whole line to the base of Little Round Top. The musketry commenced with stray volleys here and there— then more and faster, until there was one continuous roar, and no ear could distinguish one shot from another. Longstreet swept forward in a magnificent line of battle, a mile and a half long. He pressed back the Union infantry, and was seriously threatening the artillery.

At the extreme left, close to the Trostle house, Captain John Bigelow commanded the Ninth Battery, Massachusetts Light Artillery. He was ordered to hold his position at all hazards until reenforced. With double charges of grape and canister, again and again he tore great gaps in the advancing line, but it re-formed and pressed onward until the men in gray reached the muzzles of the Federal guns. Again Bigelow fired, but the heroic band had at last to give way to the increased numbers of the attack, which finally resulted in a hand-

FEDERAL DEAD AT GETTYSBURG, JULY 1, 1863

All the way from McPherson's Woods back to Cemetery Hill lay the Federal soldiers, who had contested every foot of that retreat until nightfall. The Confederates were massing so rapidly from the west and north that there was scant time to bring off the wounded and none for attention to the dead. There on the field lay the shoes so much needed by the Confederates, and the grim task of gathering them began. The dead were stripped of arms, ammunition, caps, and accoutrements as well—in fact, of everything that would be of the slightest use in enabling Lee's poorly equipped army to continue the internecine strife. It was one of war's awful expedients.

SEMINARY RIDGE, BEYOND GETTYSBURG

Along this road the Federals retreated toward Cemetery Hill in the late afternoon of July 1st. The success of McPherson's Woods was but temporary, for the Confederates under Hill were coming up in overpowering numbers, and now Ewell's forces appeared from the north. The First Corps, under Doubleday, "broken and defeated but not dismayed," fell back, pausing now and again to fire a volley at the pursuing Confederates. It finally joined the Eleventh Corps, which had also been driven back to Cemetery Hill. Lee was on the field in time to watch the retreat of the Federals, and advised Ewell to follow them up, but Ewell (who had lost 3,000 men) decided upon discretion. Night fell with the beaten Federals, reënforced by the Twelfth Corps and part of the Third, facing nearly the whole of Lee's army.

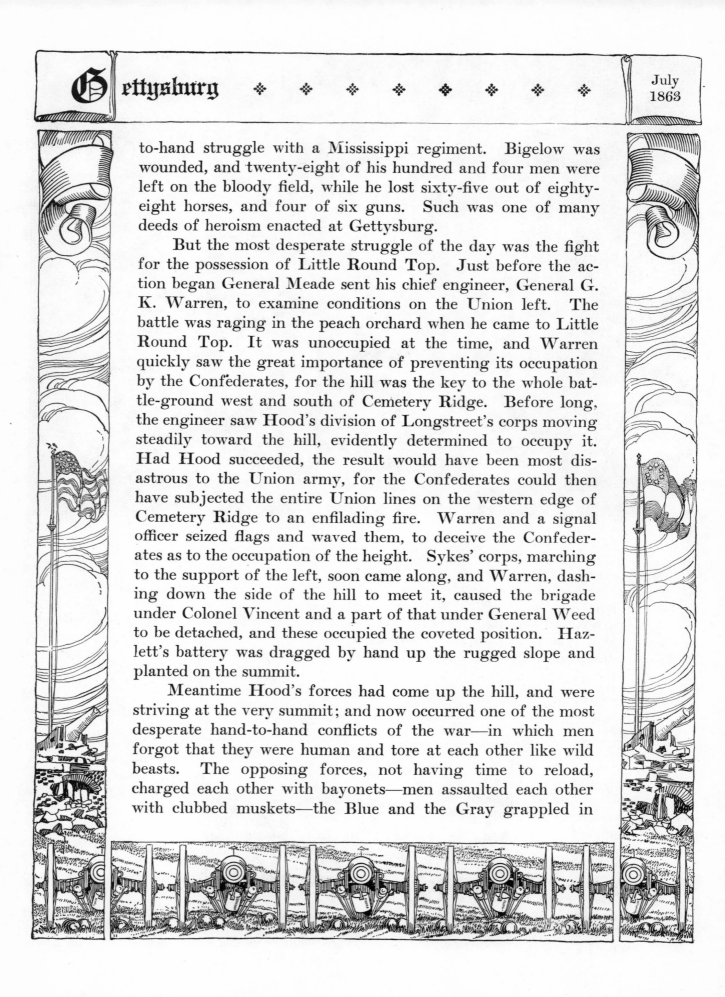

to-hand struggle with a Mississippi regiment. Bigelow was wounded, and twenty-eight of his hundred and four men were left on the bloody field, while he lost sixty-five out of eighty-eight horses, and four of six guns. Such was one of many deeds of heroism enacted at Gettysburg.

But the most desperate struggle of the day was the fight for the possession of Little Round Top. Just before the action began General Meade sent his chief engineer, General G. K. Warren, to examine conditions on the Union left. The battle was raging in the peach orchard when he came to Little Round Top. It was unoccupied at the time, and Warren quickly saw the great importance of preventing its occupation by the Confederates, for the hill was the key to the whole battle-ground west and south of Cemetery Ridge. Before long, the engineer saw Hood's division of Longstreet's corps moving steadily toward the hill, evidently determined to occupy it. Had Hood succeeded, the result would have been most disastrous to the Union army, for the Confederates could then have subjected the entire Union lines on the western edge of Cemetery Ridge to an enfilading fire. Warren and a signal officer seized flags and waved them, to deceive the Confederates as to the occupation of the height. Sykes' corps, marching to the support of the left, soon came along, and Warren, dashing down the side of the hill to meet it, caused the brigade under Colonel Vincent and a part of that under General Weed to be detached, and these occupied the coveted position. Hazlett's battery was dragged by hand up the rugged slope and planted on the summit.

Meantime Hood's forces had come up the hill, and were striving at the very summit; and now occurred one of the most desperate hand-to-hand conflicts of the war—in which men forgot that they were human and tore at each other like wild beasts. The opposing forces, not having time to reload, charged each other with bayonets—men assaulted each other with clubbed muskets—the Blue and the Gray grappled in

IN THE DEVIL'S DEN

Upon this wide, steep hill, about five hundred yards due west of Little Round Top and one hundred feet lower, was a chasm named by the country folk "the Devil's Den." When the position fell into the hands of the Confederates at the end of the second day's fighting, it became the stronghold of their sharpshooters, and well did it fulfill its name. It was a most dangerous post to occupy, since the Federal batteries on the Round Top were constantly shelling it in an effort to dislodge the hardy riflemen, many of whom met the fate of the one in the picture. Their deadly work continued, however, and many a gallant officer of the Federals was picked off during the fighting on the afternoon of the second day. General Vincent was one of the first victims; General Weed fell likewise; and as Lieutenant Hazlett bent over him to catch his last words, a bullet through the head prostrated that officer lifeless on the body of his chief.

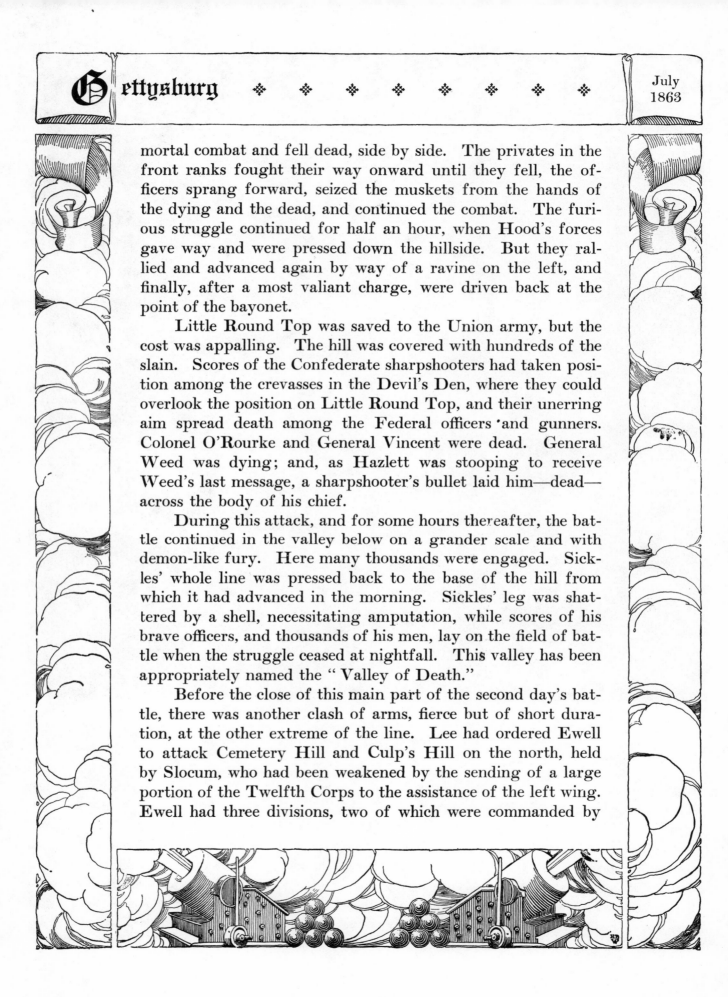

mortal combat and fell dead, side by side. The privates in the front ranks fought their way onward until they fell, the officers sprang forward, seized the muskets from the hands of the dying and the dead, and continued the combat. The furious struggle continued for half an hour, when Hood's forces gave way and were pressed down the hillside. But they rallied and advanced again by way of a ravine on the left, and finally, after a most valiant charge, were driven back at the point of the bayonet.

Little Round Top was saved to the Union army, but the cost was appalling. The hill was covered with hundreds of the slain. Scores of the Confederate sharpshooters had taken position among the crevasses in the Devil's Den, where they could overlook the position on Little Round Top, and their unerring aim spread death among the Federal officers and gunners. Colonel O'Rourke and General Vincent were dead. General Weed was dying; and, as Hazlett was stooping to receive Weed's last message, a sharpshooter's bullet laid him—dead—across the body of his chief.

During this attack, and for some hours thereafter, the battle continued in the valley below on a grander scale and with demon-like fury. Here many thousands were engaged. Sickles' whole line was pressed back to the base of the hill from which it had advanced in the morning. Sickles' leg was shattered by a shell, necessitating amputation, while scores of his brave officers, and thousands of his men, lay on the field of battle when the struggle ceased at nightfall. This valley has been appropriately named the " Valley of Death."

Before the close of this main part of the second day's battle, there was another clash of arms, fierce but of short duration, at the other extreme of the line. Lee had ordered Ewell to attack Cemetery Hill and Culp's Hill on the north, held by Slocum, who had been weakened by the sending of a large portion of the Twelfth Corps to the assistance of the left wing. Ewell had three divisions, two of which were commanded by

THE UNGUARDED LINK

Little Round Top, the key to the Federal left at Gettysburg, which they all but lost on the second day —was the scene of hand-to-hand fighting rarely equaled since long-range weapons were invented. Twice the Confederates in fierce conflict fought their way near to this summit, but were repulsed. Had they gained it, they could have planted artillery which would have enfiladed the left of Meade's line, and Gettysburg might have been turned into an overwhelming defeat. Beginning at the right, the Federal line stretched in the form of a fish-hook, with the barb resting on Culp's Hill, the center at the bend in the hook on Cemetery Hill, and the left (consisting of General Sickles' Third Corps) forming the shank to the southward as far as Round Top. On his own responsibility Sickles had advanced a portion of his line, leaving Little Round Top unprotected. Upon this advanced line of Sickles, at the Peach Orchard on the Emmitsburg road, the Confederates fell in an effort to turn what they supposed to be Meade's left flank. Only the promptness of General Warren, who discovered the gap and remedied it in time, saved the key.

Generals Early and Johnson. It was nearly sunset when he sent Early to attack Cemetery Hill. Early was repulsed after an hour's bloody and desperate hand-to-hand fight, in which muskets and bayonets, rammers, clubs, and stones were used. Johnson's attack on Culp's Hill was more successful. After a severe struggle of two or three hours General Greene, who alone of the Twelfth Corps remained on the right, succeeded, after reenforcement, in driving the right of Johnson's division away from its entrenchments, but the left had no difficulty in taking possession of the abandoned works of Geary and Ruger, now gone to Round Top and Rock Creek to assist the left wing.

Thus closed the second day's battle at Gettysburg. The harvest of death had been frightful. The Union loss during the two days had exceeded twenty thousand men; the Confederate loss was nearly equal. The Confederate army had gained an apparent advantage in penetrating the Union breastworks on Culp's Hill. But the Union lines, except on Culp's Hill, were unbroken. On the night of July 2d, Lee and his generals held a council of war and decided to make a grand final assault on Meade's center the following day. Against this decision Longstreet protested in vain. His counsel was that Lee withdraw to the mountains, compel Meade to follow, and then turn and attack him. But Lee was encouraged by the arrival of Pickett's division and of Stuart's cavalry, and Longstreet's objections were overruled. Meade and his corps commanders had met and made a like decision—that there should be a fight to the death at Gettysburg.

That night a brilliant July moon shed its luster upon the ghastly field on which thousands of men lay, unable to rise. Many of them no longer needed help. Their last battle was over, and their spirits had fled to the great Beyond. But there were great numbers, torn and gashed with shot and shell, who were still alive and calling for water or for the kindly touch of a helping hand. Nor did they call wholly in vain. Here and

THE HEIGHT OF THE BATTLE-TIDE

Near this gate to the local cemetery of Gettysburg there stood during the battle this sign: "All persons found using firearms in these grounds will be prosecuted with the utmost rigor of the law." Many a soldier must have smiled grimly at these words, for this gateway became the key of the Federal line, the very center of the cruelest use of firearms yet seen on this continent. On the first day Reynolds saw the value of Cemetery Hill in case of a retreat. Howard posted his reserves here, and Hancock greatly strengthened the position. One hundred and fifty Confederate guns were turned against it that last afternoon. In five minutes every man of the Federals had been forced to cover; for an hour and a half the shells fell fast, dealing death and laying waste the summer verdure in the little graveyard. Up to the very guns of the Federals on Cemetery Hill, Pickett led his devoted troops. At night of the 3d it was one vast slaughter-field. On this eminence, where thousands were buried, was dedicated the soldiers' National Cemetery.

there in the moonlight little rescuing parties were seeking out whom they might succor. They carried many to the improvised hospitals, where the surgeons worked unceasingly and heroically, and many lives were saved.

All through the night the Confederates were massing artillery along the crest of Seminary Ridge. The sound horses were carefully fed and watered, while those killed or disabled were replaced by others. The ammunition was replenished and the guns were placed in favorable positions and made ready for their work of destruction.

On the other side, the Federals were diligently laboring in the moonlight, and ere the coming of the day they had planted batteries on the brow of the hill above the town as far as Little Round Top. The coming of the morning revealed the two parallel lines of cannon, a mile apart, which signified only too well the story of what the day would bring forth.

The people of Gettysburg, which lay almost between the armies, were awakened on that fateful morning—July 3, 1863 —by the roar of artillery from Culp's Hill, around the bend toward Rock Creek. This knoll in the woods had, as we have seen, been taken by Johnson's men the night before. When Geary and Ruger returned and found their entrenchments occupied by the Confederates they determined to recapture them in the morning, and began firing their guns at daybreak. Seven hours of fierce bombardment and daring charges were required to regain them. Every rod of space was disputed at the cost of many a brave man's life. At eleven o'clock this portion of the Twelfth Corps was again in its old position.

But the most desperate onset of the three days' battle was yet to come—Pickett's charge on Cemetery Ridge—preceded by the heaviest cannonading ever heard on the American continent.

With the exception of the contest at Culp's Hill and a cavalry fight east of Rock Creek, the forenoon of July 3d

The Now-or-never Charge of Pickett's Men. When the Confederate artillery opened at one o'clock on the afternoon of July 3d, Meade and his staff were driven from their headquarters on Cemetery Ridge. Nothing could live exposed on that hillside, swept by cannon that were being worked as fast as human hands could work them. It was the beginning of Lee's last effort to wrest victory from the odds that were against him. Longstreet, on the morning of the 3d, had earnestly advised against renewing the battle against the Gettysburg heights. But Lee saw that in this moment the fate of the South hung in the balance; that if the Army of Northern Virginia did not win, it would never again become the aggressor. Pickett's division, as yet not engaged, was the force Lee designated for the assault; every man was a Virginian, forming a veritable Tenth Legion in valor. Auxiliary divisions swelled the charging column to 15,000. In the middle of the afternoon the Federal guns ceased firing. The time for the charge had come. Twice Pickett

PICKETT—THE MARSHALL NEY OF GETTYSBURG

asked of Longstreet if he should go forward. Longstreet merely bowed in answer. "Sir, I shall lead my division forward," said Pickett at last, and the heavy-hearted Longstreet bowed his head. As the splendid column swept out of the woods and across the plain the Federal guns reopened with redoubled fury. For a mile Pickett and his men kept on, facing a deadly greeting of round shot, canister, and the bullets of Hancock's resolute infantry. It was magnificent—but every one of Pickett's brigade commanders went down and their men fell by scores and hundreds around them. A hundred led by Armistead, waving his cap on his sword-point, actually broke through and captured a battery, Armistead falling beside a gun. It was but for a moment. Longstreet had been right when he said: "There never was a body of fifteen thousand men who could make that attack successfully." Before the converging Federals the thinned ranks of Confederates drifted wearily back toward Seminary Ridge. Victory for the South was not to be.

MEADE'S HEADQUARTERS ON CEMETERY RIDGE

passed with only an occasional exchange of shots at irregular
intervals. At noon there was a lull, almost a deep silence, over
the whole field. It was the ominous calm that precedes the
storm. At one o'clock signal guns were fired on Seminary
Ridge, and a few moments later there was a terrific outburst
from one hundred and fifty Confederate guns, and the whole
crest of the ridge, for two miles, was a line of flame. The scene
was majestic beyond description. The scores of batteries were
soon enveloped in smoke, through which the flashes of burning
powder were incessant.

The long line of Federal guns withheld their fire for some
minutes, when they burst forth, answering the thunder of
those on the opposite hill. An eye-witness declares that the
whole sky seemed filled with screaming shells, whose sharp ex-
plosions, as they burst in mid-air, with the hurtling of the fragments, formed a running accompaniment to the deep, tremendous roar of the guns.

Many of the Confederate shots went wild, passing over
the Union army and plowing up the earth on the other side of
Cemetery Ridge. But others were better aimed and burst
among the Federal batteries, in one of which twenty-seven out
of thirty-six horses were killed in ten minutes. The Confederate fire seemed to be concentrated upon one point between
Cemetery Ridge and Little Round Top, near a clump of
scrub oaks. Here the batteries were demolished and men and
horses were slain by scores. The spot has been called " Bloody
Angle."

The Federal fire proved equally accurate and the destruction on Seminary Ridge was appalling. For nearly two hours
the hills shook with the tremendous cannonading, when it gradually slackened and ceased. The Union army now prepared
for the more deadly charge of infantry which it felt was sure
to follow.

They had not long to wait. As the cannon smoke drifted
away from between the lines fifteen thousand of Longstreet's

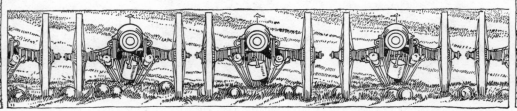

The prelude to Pickett's magnificent charge was a sudden deluge of shells from 150 long-range Confederate guns trained upon Cemetery Ridge. General Meade and his staff were instantly driven from their headquarters (already illustrated) and within five minutes the concentrated artillery fire had swept every unsheltered position on Cemetery Ridge clear of men. In the woods, a mile and a half distant, Pickett and his men watched the effect of the bombardment, expecting the order to "Go Forward" up the slope (shown in the picture). The Federals had instantly opened with their eighty available guns, and for three hours the most terrific artillery duel of the war was kept up. Then the Federal fire slackened, as though the batteries were silenced. The Confederates' artillery ammunition also was now low. "For God's sake, come on!" was the word to Pickett. And at Longstreet's reluctant nod the commander led his 14,000 Virginians across the plain in their tragic charge up Cemetery Ridge.

WHERE PICKETT CHARGED

In that historic charge was Armistead, who achieved a momentary victory and met a hero's death. On across the Emmitsburg road came Pickett's dauntless brigades, coolly closing up the fearful chasms torn in their ranks by the canister. Up to the fence held by Hays' brigade dashed the first gray line, only to be swept into confusion by a cruel enfilading fire. Then the brigades of Armistead and Garnett moved forward, driving Hays' brigade back through the batteries on the crest. Despite the death-dealing bolts on all sides, Pickett determined to capture the guns; and, at the order, Armistead, leaping the fence and waving his cap on his sword-point, rushed forward, followed by about a hundred of his men. Up to the very crest they fought the Federals back, and Armistead, shouting, "Give them the cold steel, boys!" seized one of the guns. For a moment the Confederate flag waved triumphantly over the Federal battery. For a brief interval the fight raged fiercely at close quarters. Armistead was shot down beside the gun he had taken, and his men were driven back. Pickett, as he looked around the top of the ridge he had gained, could see his men fighting all about with clubbed muskets and even flag-staffs against the troops that were rushing in upon them from all sides. Flesh and blood could not hold the heights against such terrible odds, and with a heart full of anguish Pickett ordered a retreat. The despairing Longstreet, watching from Seminary Ridge, saw through the smoke the shattered remnants drift sullenly down the slope and knew that Pickett's glorious but costly charge was ended.

GENERAL L. A. ARMISTEAD, C.S.A.

corps emerged in grand columns from the wooded crest of Seminary Ridge under the command of General Pickett on the right and General Pettigrew on the left. Longstreet had planned the attack with a view to passing around Round Top, and gaining it by flank and reverse attack, but Lee, when he came upon the scene a few moments after the final orders had been given, directed the advance to be made straight toward the Federal main position on Cemetery Ridge.

The charge was one of the most daring in warfare. The distance to the Federal lines was a mile. For half the distance the troops marched gayly, with flying banners and glittering bayonets. Then came the burst of Federal cannon, and the Confederate ranks were torn with exploding shells. Pettigrew's columns began to waver, but the lines re-formed and marched on. When they came within musket-range, Hancock's infantry opened a terrific fire, but the valiant band only quickened its pace and returned the fire with volley after volley. Pettigrew's troops succumbed to the storm. For now the lines in blue were fast converging. Federal troops from all parts of the line now rushed to the aid of those in front of Pickett. The batteries which had been sending shell and solid shot changed their ammunition, and double charges of grape and canister were hurled into the column as it bravely pressed into the sea of flame. The Confederates came close to the Federal lines and paused to close their ranks. Each moment the fury of the storm from the Federal guns increased.

"Forward," again rang the command along the line of the Confederate front, and the Southerners dashed on. The first line of the Federals was driven back. A stone wall behind them gave protection to the next Federal force. Pickett's men rushed upon it. Riflemen rose from behind and hurled a death-dealing volley into the Confederate ranks. A defiant cheer answered the volley, and the Southerners placed their battle-flags on the ramparts. General Armistead grasped the flag from the hand of a falling bearer, and leaped upon the

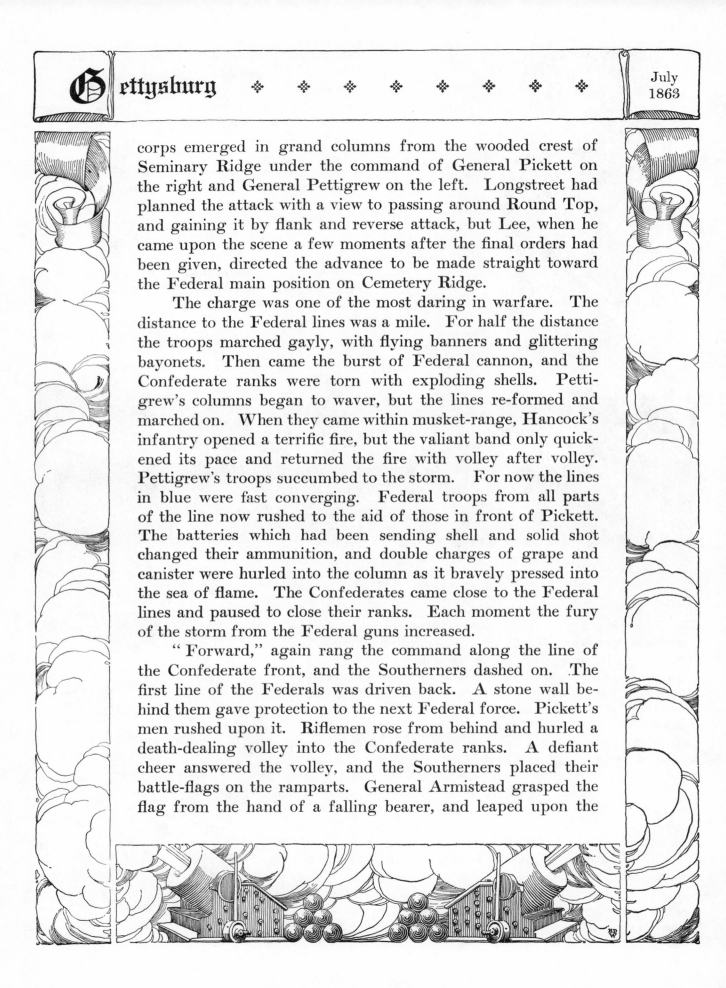

THE MAN WHO HELD THE CENTER

Headquarters of Brigadier-General Alexander S. Webb. It devolved upon the man pictured here (booted and in full uniform, before his headquarters tent to the left of the picture) to meet the shock of Pickett's great charge. With four Pennsylvania regiments (the Sixty-Ninth, Seventy-First, Seventy-Second, and One Hundred and Sixth) of Hancock's Second Corps, Webb was equal to the emergency. Stirred to great deeds by the example of a patriotic ancestry, he felt that upon his holding his position depended the out-come of the day. His front had been the focus of the Confederate artillery fire. Batteries to right and left of his line were practically silenced. Young Lieutenant Cushing, mortally wounded, fired the last serviceable gun and fell dead as Pickett's men came on. Cowan's First New York Battery on the left of Cushing's used canister on the assailants at less than ten yards. Webb at the head of the Seventy-Second Pennsylvania fought back the on-rush, posting a line of slightly wounded in his rear. Webb himself fell wounded but his command checked the assault till Hall's brilliant charge turned the tide at this point.

wall, waving it in triumph. Almost instantly he fell among the Federal troops, mortally wounded. General Garnett, leading his brigade, fell dead close to the Federal line. General Kemper sank, wounded, into the arms of one of his men.

Pickett had entered a death-trap. Troops from all directions rushed upon him. Clubbed muskets and barrel-staves now became weapons of warfare. The Confederates began surrendering in masses and Pickett ordered a retreat. Yet the energy of the indomitable Confederates was not spent. Several supporting brigades moved forward, and only succumbed when they encountered two regiments of Stannard's Vermont brigade, and the fire of fresh batteries.

As the remnant of the gallant division returned to the works on Seminary Ridge General Lee rode out to meet them. His demeanor was calm. His features gave no evidence of his disappointment. With hat in hand he greeted the men sympathetically. "It was all my fault," he said. "Now help me to save that which remains."

The battle of Gettysburg was over. The cost in men was frightful. The losses of the two armies reached fifty thousand, about half on either side. More than seven thousand men had fallen dead on the field of battle.

The tide could rise no higher; from this point the ebb must begin. Not only here, but in the West the Southern cause took a downward turn; for at this very hour of Pickett's charge, Grant and Pemberton, a thousand miles away, stood under an oak tree on the heights above the Mississippi and arranged for the surrender of Vicksburg.

Lee could do nothing but lead his army back to Virginia. The Federals pursued but feebly. The Union victory was not a very decisive one, but, supported as it was by the fall of Vicksburg, the moral effect on the nation and on the world was great. The period of uncertainty was ended. It required but little prophetic vision to foresee that the Republic would survive the dreadful shock of arms.

MAJOR–GENERAL GEORGE ARMSTRONG CUSTER WITH GENERAL PLEASONTON

The *beau sabreur* of the Federal service is pictured here in his favorite velvet suit, with General Alfred Pleason-ton, who commanded the cavalry at Gettysburg. This photograph was taken at Warrenton, Va., three months after that battle. At the time this picture was taken, Custer was a brigadier-general in command of the second brigade of the third division of General Pleasonton's cavalry. General Custer's impetuosity finally cost him his own life and the lives of his entire command at the hands of the Sioux Indians June 25, 1876. Custer was born in 1839 and graduated at West Point in 1861. As captain of volunteers he served with McClellan on the Peninsula. In June, 1863, he was made brigadier-general of volunteers and as the head of a brigade of cavalry distinguished himself at Gettysburg. Later he served with Sheridan in the Shenandoah, won honor at Cedar Creek, and was brevetted major-general of volunteers on October 19, 1864. Under Sheridan he participated in the battles of Five Forks, Dinwiddie Court House, and other important cavalry engagements of Grant's last campaign.

SUMTER

Searching all history for a parallel, it is impossible to find any defenses of a beleaguered city that stood so severe a bombardment as did this bravely defended and never conquered fortress of Sumter, in Charleston Harbor. It is estimated that about eighty thousand projectiles were discharged from the fleet and the marsh batteries, and yet Charleston, with its battered water-front, was not abandoned until all other Confederate positions along the Atlantic Coast were in Federal hands and Sherman's triumphant army was sweeping in from the West and South. The picture shows Sumter from the Confederate Fort Johnson. The powerful batteries in the foreground played havoc with the Federal fleet whenever it came down the main ship-channel to engage the forts. Protected by almost impassable swamps, morasses, and a network of creeks to the eastward, Fort Johnson held an almost impregnable position; and from its protection by Cummings' Point, on which was Battery Gregg, the Federal fleet could not approach nearer than two miles. Could it have been taken by land assault or reduced by gun-fire, Charleston would have fallen.

These views show the result of the bombardment from August 17 to 23, 1863. The object was to force the surrender of the fort and thus effect an entrance into Charleston. The report of Colonel John W. Turner, Federal chief of artillery runs: "The fire from the breaching batteries upon Sumter was incessant, and kept up continuously from daylight till dark, until the evening of the 23d. . . . The fire upon the gorge had, by the morning of the 23d, succeeded in destroying every gun upon the parapet of it. The para-

pet and ramparts of the gorge were completely demolished for nearly the entire length of the face, and in places everything was swept off down to the arches, the *débris* forming an accessible ramp to the top of the ruins. Nothing further being gained by a longer fire upon this face, all the guns were directed this day upon the southeasterly flank, and continued an incessant fire throughout the day. The demolition of the fort at the close of the day's firing was complete, so far as its offensive powers were considered." So fared Sumter.

WHERE SHOT AND SHELL STRUCK SUMTER

SOME OF THE 450 SHOT A DAY

THE LIGHTHOUSE ABOVE THE DÉBRIS

THE PARROTT IN BATTERY STRONG

This 300-pounder rifle was directed against Fort Sumter and Battery Wagner.   The length of bore of the gun before it burst was 136 inches.   It weighed 26,000 pounds.   It fired a projectile weighing 250 pounds, with a maximum charge of powder of 25 pounds. The gun was fractured at the twenty-seventh round by a shell bursting in the muzzle, blowing off about 20 inches of the barrel. After the bursting the gun was "chipped" back beyond the termination of the fracture and afterwards fired 371 rounds with as good results as before the injury.   At the end of that time the muzzle began to crack again, rendering the gun entirely useless.

TWO PARROTTS IN BATTERY STEVENS

Battery Stevens lay just east of Battery Strong.   It was begun July 27, 1863.   Most of the work was done at night, for the fire from the adjacent Confederate forts rendered work in daylight dangerous.   By August 17th, most of the guns were in position, and two days later the whole series of batteries "on the left," as they were designated, were pounding away at Fort Sumter.

IN CHARLESTON AFTER THE BOMBARDMENT

So long as the Confederate flag flew over the ramparts of Sumter, Charleston remained the one stronghold of the South that was firmly held. That flag was never struck. It was lowered for an evacuation, not a surrender. The story of Charleston's determined resistance did not end in triumph for the South, but it did leave behind it a sunset glory, in which the valor and dash of the Federal attack is paralleled by the heroism and self-sacrifice of the Confederate defense, in spite of wreck and ruin.

The lower picture was taken after the war, when relic-hunters had removed the shells, and a beacon light had been erected where once stood the parapet. On September 8, 1863, at the very position in these photographs, the garrison repelled a bold assault with musketry fire alone, causing the Federals severe loss. The flag of the Confederacy floated triumphantly over the position during the whole of the long struggle. Every effort of the Federals to reduce the crumbling ruins into submission was unavailing. It stood the continual bombardment of ironclads until it was nothing but a mass of brickdust, but still the gallant garrison held it.

SCENE OF THE NIGHT ATTACK ON SUMTER, SEPTEMBER 8, 1863

It is strange that despite the awful destruction the loss of lives within the fort was few. For weeks the bombardment, assisted by the guns of the fleet, tore great chasms in the parapet. Fort Sumter never fell, but was abandoned only on the approach of Sherman's army. It had withstood continuous efforts against it for 587 days. From April, 1863, to September of the same year, the fortress was garrisoned by the First South Carolina Artillery, enlisted as regulars. Afterward the garrison was made up of detachments of infantry from Georgia, North Carolina, and South Carolina. Artillerists also served turns of duty during this period.

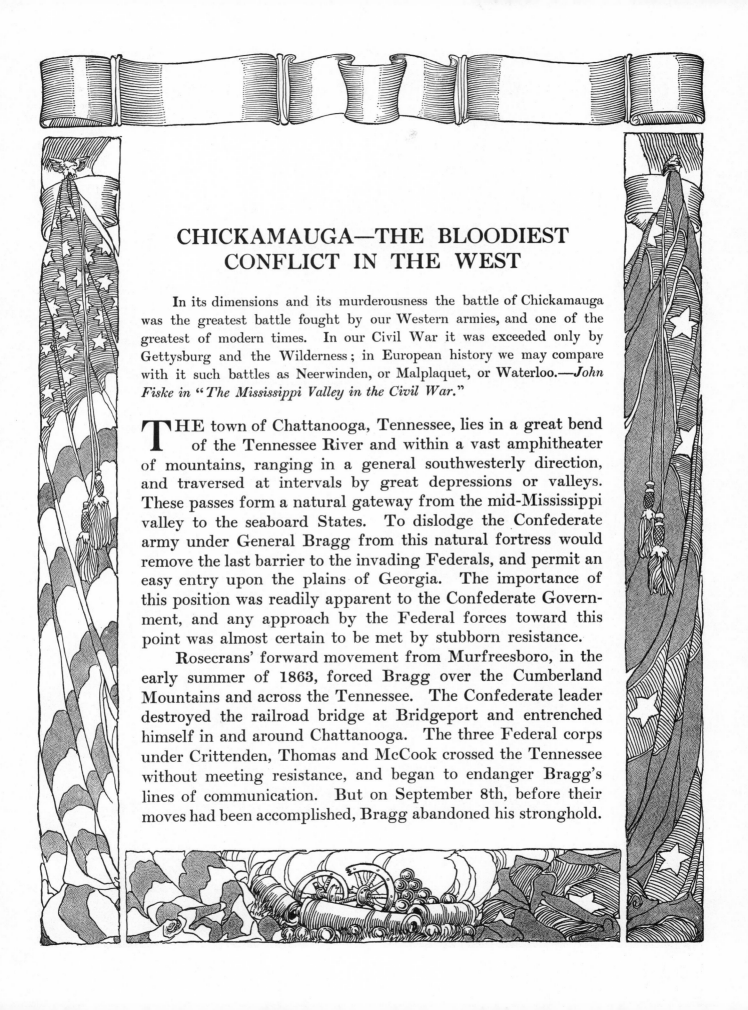

CHICKAMAUGA—THE BLOODIEST CONFLICT IN THE WEST

In its dimensions and its murderousness the battle of Chickamauga was the greatest battle fought by our Western armies, and one of the greatest of modern times. In our Civil War it was exceeded only by Gettysburg and the Wilderness; in European history we may compare with it such battles as Neerwinden, or Malplaquet, or Waterloo.—*John Fiske in "The Mississippi Valley in the Civil War."*

THE town of Chattanooga, Tennessee, lies in a great bend of the Tennessee River and within a vast amphitheater of mountains, ranging in a general southwesterly direction, and traversed at intervals by great depressions or valleys. These passes form a natural gateway from the mid-Mississippi valley to the seaboard States. To dislodge the Confederate army under General Bragg from this natural fortress would remove the last barrier to the invading Federals, and permit an easy entry upon the plains of Georgia. The importance of this position was readily apparent to the Confederate Government, and any approach by the Federal forces toward this point was almost certain to be met by stubborn resistance.

Rosecrans' forward movement from Murfreesboro, in the early summer of 1863, forced Bragg over the Cumberland Mountains and across the Tennessee. The Confederate leader destroyed the railroad bridge at Bridgeport and entrenched himself in and around Chattanooga. The three Federal corps under Crittenden, Thomas and McCook crossed the Tennessee without meeting resistance, and began to endanger Bragg's lines of communication. But on September 8th, before their moves had been accomplished, Bragg abandoned his stronghold.

Crittenden the next day marched around the north end of Lookout and entered the town, while Hazen and Wagner crossed over from the opposite bank of the Tennessee.

Rosecrans believed that Bragg was in full retreat toward Rome, Georgia, and Crittenden, leaving one brigade in Chattanooga, was ordered to pursue. Bragg encouraged his adversary in the belief that he was avoiding an engagement and sent spies as deserters into the Federal ranks to narrate the details of his flight. Meanwhile, he was concentrating at Lafayette, about twenty-five miles south of Chattanooga. Hither General S. B. Buckner, entirely too weak to cope with Burnside's heavy column approaching from Kentucky, brought his troops from Knoxville. Breckinridge and two brigades arrived from Mississippi, while twelve thousand of Lee's veterans, under Lee's most trusted and illustrious lieutenant, Longstreet, were hastening from Virginia to add their numbers to Bragg's Army of Tennessee.

The three corps of the Union army, as we have seen, were now separated over a wide extent of territory by intervening ridges, so intent was Rosecrans on intercepting the vanished Bragg. But the latter, by no means vanished, and with his face toward Chattanooga, considered the position of his antagonist and discovered his own army almost opposite the Federal center. Crittenden was advancing toward Ringgold, and the remoteness of Thomas' corps on his right precluded any immediate union of the Federal forces.

Bragg was quick to grasp the opportunity made by Rosecrans' division of the army in the face of his opponent. He at once perceived the possibilities of a master-stroke; to crush Thomas' advanced divisions with an overwhelming force.

The attempt failed, owing to a delay in the attack, which permitted the endangered Baird and Negley to fall back. Bragg then resolved to throw himself upon Crittenden, who had divided his corps. Polk was ordered to advance upon that portion of it at Lee and Gordon's Mills, but when Bragg came

THE CONFEDERATE LEADER AT CHICKAMAUGA

Major-General Braxton Bragg, C.S.A.   Born, 1815; West Point, 1837; Died, 1876.   Bragg's name before 1861 was perhaps better known in military annals than that of any other Southern leader because of his brilliant record in the Mexican War.   In the Civil War he distinguished himself first at Shiloh and by meritorious services thereafter.   But his delays rendered him scarcely a match for Rosecrans, to say nothing of Grant and Sherman.   Flanked out of two strong positions, he missed the opportunity presented by Rosecrans' widely separated forces and failed to crush the Army of the Cumberland in detail, as it advanced to the battle of Chickamauga.   The error cost the Confederates the loss of Tennessee, eventually.

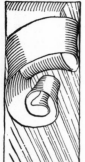

to the front September 13th, expecting to witness the annihilation of the Twenty-first Corps, he found to his bitter disappointment that the bishop-general had made no move and that Crittenden had reunited his divisions and was safe on the west bank of the Chickamauga. Thus his splendid chances of breaking up the Army of the Cumberland were ruined.

When Bragg's position became known to Rosecrans, great was his haste to effect the concentration of his army. Couriers dashed toward Alpine with orders for McCook to join Thomas with the utmost celerity. The former started at once, shortly after midnight on the 13th, in response to Thomas's urgent call. It was a real race of life and death, attended by the greatest hardships. Ignorant of the roads, McCook submitted his troops to a most exhausting march, twice up and down the mountain, fifty-seven miles of the most arduous toil, often dragging artillery up by hand and letting it down steep declines by means of ropes. But he closed up with Thomas on the 17th, and the Army of the Cumberland was saved from its desperate peril.

Crittenden's corps now took position at Lee and Gordon's Mills on the left bank of Chickamauga Creek, and the Federal troops were all within supporting distance. In the Indian tongue Chickamauga means " The River of Death," a name strangely prophetic of that gigantic conflict soon to be waged by these hostile forces throughout this beautiful and heretofore peaceful valley.

The Confederate army, its corps under Generals Polk, D. H. Hill, and Buckner, was stationed on the east side of the stream, its right wing below Lee and Gordon's Mills, and the left extending up the creek toward Lafayette. On the Federal side Thomas was moved to the left, with Crittenden in the center and McCook on the right. Their strength has been estimated at fifty-five to sixty-nine thousand men. On the 18th, Longstreet's troops were arriving from Virginia, and by the morning of the 19th the greater part of the Confederate army

COPYRIGHT, 1911, REVIEW OF REVIEWS CO.

THOMAS—THE "ROCK OF CHICKAMAUGA" WHO BECAME THE "SLEDGE OF NASHVILLE"

Major-General George Henry Thomas, Virginia-born soldier loyal to the Union; commended for gallantry in the Seminole War, and for service in Mexico; won the battle of Mill Spring, January 19, 1862; commanded the right wing of the Army of the Tennessee against Corinth and at Perryville, and the center at Stone's River. Only his stability averted overwhelming defeat for the Federals at Chickamauga. At Lookout Mountain and Missionary Ridge he was a host in himself. After Sherman had taken Atlanta he sent Thomas back to Tennessee to grapple with Hood. How he crushed Hood by his sledge-hammer blows is told in the story of "Nashville." Thomas, sitting down in Nashville, bearing the brunt of Grant's impatience, and ignoring completely the proddings from Washington to advance before he was ready, while he waited grimly for the psychological moment to strike the oncoming Confederate host under Hood, is one of the really big dramatic figures of the entire war. It has been well said of Thomas that every promotion he received was a reward of merit; and that during his long and varied career as a soldier no crisis ever arose too great for his ability.

had crossed the Chickamauga. The two mighty armies were now face to face, and none could doubt that the impending struggle would be attended by frightful loss to both sides.

It was Bragg's intention to send Polk, commanding the right wing, in a flanking movement against the Federal left under Thomas, and thus intervene between it and Chattanooga. The first encounter, at 10 o'clock in the morning of the 19th, resulted in a Confederate repulse, but fresh divisions were constantly pushed forward under the deadly fire of the Federal artillery. The Federals were gradually forced back by the incessant charge of the Confederates; but assailed and assailant fought with such great courage and determination that any decided advantage was withheld from either. Meanwhile, the Federal right was hard pressed by Hood, commanding Longstreet's corps, and a desperate battle ensued along the entire line. It seemed, however, more like a struggle between separate divisions than the clash of two great armies. When night descended the Federals had been forced back from the creek, but the result had been indecisive.

Disaster to the Union army had been averted by the use of powerful artillery when the infantry seemed unable to withstand the onslaught. Rosecrans had assumed the defensive, and his troops had so far receded as to enable the Confederates to form their lines on all the territory fought over on that day. During the night preparations were made in both camps for a renewal of the battle on the following morning, which was Sunday. A fresh disposition of the troops was made by both leaders. Near midnight General Longstreet arrived on the field, and was at once placed in command of the Confederate left, Polk retaining the right. Not all of Longstreet's troops arrived in time for the battle, but Bragg's force has been estimated at fifty-one to seventy-one thousand strong.

Thomas was given command of the Union left, with McCook at his right, while Crittenden's forces occupied the center, but to the rear of both Thomas and McCook. Thomas had

BEFORE CHICKAMAUGA—IN THE RUSH OF EVENTS

Rarely does the camera afford such a perfectly contemporaneous record of the march of events so momentous. This photograph shows the hotel at Stevenson, Alabama, during the Union advance that ended in Chickamauga. Sentinels are parading the street in front of the hotel, several horses are tied to the hotel posts, and the officers evidently have gone into the hotel headquarters. General Alexander McDowell McCook, commanding the old Twentieth Army Corps, took possession of the hotel as temporary headquarters on the movement of the Army of the Cumberland from Tullahoma. On August 29, 1863, between Stevenson and Caperton's Ferry, on the Tennessee River, McCook gathered his boats and pontoons, hidden under the dense foliage of overhanging trees, and when ready for his crossing suddenly launched them into and across the river. Thence the troops marched over Sand Mountain and at length into Lookout Valley. During the movements the army was in extreme peril, for McCook was at one time three days' march from Thomas, so that Bragg might have annihilated the divisions in detail. Finally the scattered corps were concentrated along Chickamauga Creek, where the bloody struggle of September 19th and 20th was so bravely fought.

spent the night in throwing up breastworks on the brow of Snodgrass Hill, as it was anticipated that the Confederates would concentrate their attack upon his position.

Hostilities began with a general movement of the Confederate right wing in an attempt to flank the Union left. General Bragg had ordered Polk to begin the attack at daybreak, but it was nearly ten o'clock in the morning before Breckinridge's division, supported by General Cleburne, advanced upon Thomas' entrenchments. Fighting desperately, the Confederates did not falter under the heavy fire of the Federals, and it seemed as if the latter must be driven from their position. Rosecrans, in response to urgent requests for reenforcements, despatched troops again and again to the aid of Thomas, and the assault was finally repulsed. Cleburne's division was driven back with heavy loss, and Breckinridge, unable to retain any advantage, was forced to defend his right, which was being seriously menaced. The battle at this point had been desperately waged, both sides exhibiting marked courage and determination. As on the previous day, the Confederates had been the aggressors, but the Federal troops had resisted all attempts to invade their breastworks.

However, the fortunes of battle were soon to incline to the side of the Southern army. Bragg sent Stewart's division forward, and it pressed Reynolds' and Brannan's men back to their entrenchments. Rosecrans sent Wood word to close up on Reynolds. Through some misunderstanding in giving or interpreting this order, General Wood withdrew his division from its position on the right of Brannan. By this movement a large opening was left almost in the center of the battle-line. Johnson's, Hindman's, and Kershaw's divisions rushed into the gap and fell upon the Union right and center with an impetus that was irresistible. The Confederate general, Bushrod Johnson, has given us an unforgetable picture of the thrilling event: " The resolute and impetuous charge, the rush of our heavy columns sweeping out from the shadow and gloom of the forest

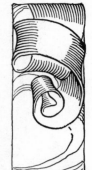

ON THE WAY TO CHICKAMAUGA

This solitary observer, if he was standing here September 20, 1863, shortly before this was photographed, certainly gazed at the base of the hill to the left. For through the pass called Rossville Gap a column in blue was streaming—Steedman's Division of the Reserve Corps, rushing to aid Thomas, so sore pressed at Chickamauga. Those slopes by Chickamauga Creek witnessed the deadliest battle in the West and the highest in percentage of killed and wounded of the entire war. It was fought as a result of Rosecrans' attempt to maneuver Bragg out of Chattanooga. The Federal army crossed the Tennessee River west of the city, passed through the mountain-ranges, and came upon Bragg's line of communications. Finding his position untenable, the Southern leader moved southward and fell upon the united forces of Rosecrans along Chickamauga Creek. The vital point in the Federal line was the left, held by Thomas. Should that give way, the army would be cut off from Chattanooga, with no base to fall back on. The heavy fighting of September 19th showed that Bragg realized the situation. Brigades and regiments were shattered. For a time, the Union army was driven back. But at nightfall Thomas had regained the lost ground. He re-formed during the night in order to protect the road leading into Chattanooga. Since the second day was foggy till the middle of the forenoon, the fighting was not renewed till late. About noon a break was made in the right of the Federal 'attle-line, into which the eager Longstreet promptly hurled his men. Colonel Dodge writes: "Everything seems lost. The entire right of the army, with Rosecrans and his staff, is driven from the field in utter rout. But, unknown even to the commanding general, Thomas, the Rock of Chickamauga, stands there at bay, surrounded, facing two to one. Heedless of the wreck of one-half the army, he knows not how to yield."

into the open fields flooded with sunlight, the glitter of arms, the onward dash of artillery and mounted men, the retreat of the foe, the shouts of the hosts of our army, the dust, the smoke, the noise of fire-arms—of whistling balls, and grape-shot, and of bursting shell—made up a battle-scene of unsurpassed grandeur. Here, General Hood gave me the last order I received from him on the field, 'Go ahead and keep ahead of everything.'" A moment later, and Hood fell, severely wounded, with a minie ball in his thigh.

Wood's right brigade was shattered even before it had cleared the opening. Sheridan's entire division, and part of Davis' and Van Cleve's, were driven from the field. Longstreet now gave a fine exhibition of his military genius. The orders of battle were to separate the two wings of the opposing army. But with the right wing of his opponents in hopeless ruin, he wheeled to the right and compelled the further withdrawal of Federal troops in order to escape being surrounded. The brave soldier-poet, William H. Lytle, fell at the head of his brigade as he strove to re-form his line. McCook and Crittenden were unable, in spite of several gallant efforts, to rally their troops and keep back the onrushing heroes of Stone's River and Bull Run. The broken mass fled in confusion toward Chattanooga, carrying with it McCook, Crittenden, and Rosecrans. The latter telegraphed to Washington that his army had been beaten. In this famous charge the Confederates took several thousand prisoners and forty pieces of artillery.

Flushed with victory, the Confederates now concentrated their attack upon Thomas, who thus far, on Horseshoe Ridge and its spurs, had repelled all attempts to dislodge him. The Confederates, with victory within their grasp, and led by the indomitable Longstreet, swarmed up the slopes in great numbers, but they were hurled back with fearful slaughter. Thomas was looking anxiously for Sheridan, whom, as he knew, Rosecrans had ordered with two brigades to his support.

THE TOO-ADVANCED POSITION

Crawfish Spring, to the South of the Chickamauga Battle-field. Rosecrans, in concentrating his troops on the 18th of September, was still possessed of the idea that Bragg was covering his retreat upon his railroad connections at Dalton. Instead, the Confederate commander had massed his forces on the other side of Chickamauga and was only awaiting the arrival of Longstreet to assume the aggressive. On the morning of the 19th, McCook's right wing at Crawfish Spring was strongly threatened by the Confederates, while the real attack was made against the left in an effort to turn it and cut Rosecrans off from a retreat upon Chattanooga. All day long, brigade after brigade was marched from the right of the Federal line in order to extend the left under Thomas and withstand this flanking movement. Even after nightfall, Thomas, trying to re-form his lines and carry them still farther to the left for the work of the morrow, brought on a sharp conflict in the darkness. The Confederates had been held back, but at heavy cost. That night, at the Widow Glenn's house, Rosecrans consulted his generals. The exhausted Thomas, when roused from sleep for his opinion, invariably answered, "I would strengthen the left." There seemed as yet to be no crisis at hand, and the council closed with a song by the debonair McCook.

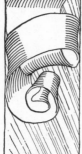

But in Longstreet's rout of the right wing Sheridan, with the rest, had been carried on toward Chattanooga, and he found himself completely cut off from Thomas, as the Confederates were moving parallel to him. Yet the indomitable Sheridan, in spite of his terrible experience of the morning, did not give up the attempt. Foiled in his efforts to get through McFarland's Gap, he moved quickly on Rossville and came down the Lafayette road toward Thomas' left flank.

Meanwhile, advised by the incessant roar of musketry, General Gordon Granger, in command of the reserve corps near Rossville, advanced rapidly with his fresh troops. Acting with promptness and alacrity under orders, Granger sent Steedman to Thomas' right.

Directly across the line of Thomas' right was a ridge, on which Longstreet stationed Hindman with a large command, ready for an attack on Thomas' flank—a further and terrible menace to the nearly exhausted general, but it was not all. In the ridge was a small gap, and through this Kershaw was pouring his division, intent on getting to Thomas' rear. Rosecrans thus describes the help afforded to Thomas: " Steedman, taking a regimental color, led the column. Swift was the charge and terrible the conflict, but the enemy was broken."

The fighting grew fiercer, and at intervals was almost hand to hand. The casualties among the officers, who frequently led their troops in person, were mounting higher and higher as the moments passed. All the afternoon the assaults continued, but the Union forces stood their ground. Ammunition ran dangerously low, but Steedman had brought a small supply, and when this was distributed each man had about ten rounds. Finally, as the sun was setting in the west, the Confederate troops advanced in a mighty concourse. The combined forces of Kershaw, Law, Preston, and Hindman once more rushed forward, gained possession of their lost ridge at several points, but were unable to drive their attack home. In many places the Union lines stood firm and both sides

WHERE THE LINES WERE SWEPT BACK

Lee & Gordon's mill, seen in the picture, marked the extreme right of the Federal line on the second day at Chickamauga. From it, northward, were posted the commands of McCook and Crittenden, depleted by the detachments of troops the day before to strengthen the left. All might have gone well if the main attack of the Confederates had continued to the left, as Rosecrans expected. But hidden in the woods, almost within a stone's throw of the Federal right on that misty morning, was the entire corps of Longstreet, drawn up in columns of brigades at half distance—"a masterpiece of tactics," giving space for each column to swing right or left. Seizing a momentous opportunity which would have lasted but thirty minutes at the most, Longstreet hurled them through a gap which, owing to a misunderstanding, had been left open, and the entire Federal right was swept from the field.

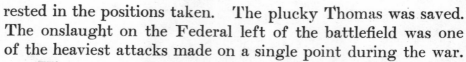

rested in the positions taken. The plucky Thomas was saved. The onslaught on the Federal left of the battlefield was one of the heaviest attacks made on a single point during the war.

History records no grander spectacle than Thomas' stand at Chickamauga. He was ever afterwards known as "The Rock of Chickamauga." Under the cover of darkness, Thomas, having received word from Rosecrans to withdraw, retired his army in good order to Rossville, and on the following day rejoined Rosecrans in Chattanooga. The battle of Chickamauga, considering the forces engaged, was one of the most destructive of the Civil War. The Union army lost approximately sixteen thousand men, and while the loss to the Confederate army is not definitely known, it was probably nearly eighteen thousand. The personal daring and tenacious courage displayed in the ranks of both armies have never been excelled on any battlefield. The Confederate generals, Helm, Deshler, and Preston Smith were killed; Adams, Hood, Brown, Gregg, Clayton, Hindman, and McNair were wounded. The Federal side lost Lytle. The battle is generally considered a Confederate victory, and yet, aside from the terrible loss of human life, no distinct advantage accrued to either side. The Federal army retained possession of Chattanooga, but the Confederates had for the time checked the Army of the Cumberland from a further occupation of Southern soil.

It is a singular coincidence that the generals-in-chief of both armies exercised but little supervision over the movements of their respective troops. The brunt of the battle fell, for the most part, upon the commanders of the wings. To the subordinate generals on each side were awarded the highest honors. Longstreet, because of his eventful charge, which swept the right wing of the Union army from the field, was proclaimed the victor of Chickamauga; and to General Thomas, who by his firmness and courage withstood the combined attack of the Confederate forces when disaster threatened on every side, is due the brightest laurels from the adherents of the North.

THE HOUSE WHENCE HELP CAME

Here, at his headquarters, holding the Federal line of retreat at Rossville Gap (the Confederate objective in the battle), General Gordon Granger heard with increasing anxiety the sounds of the conflict, three miles away, growing more and more ominous.   Finally, in disobedience of orders, he set in motion his three brigades to the relief of Thomas, pushing forward two of them under Steedman.   These arrived upon the field early in the afternoon, the most critical period of the battle, as Longstreet charged afresh on Thomas' right and rear.   Seizing a battle-flag, Steedman (at the order of General Granger) led his command in a counter-charge which saved the Army of the Cumberland.   This old house at Rossville was built by John Ross, a chief of the Cherokee Indians, and he lived in it till 1832, giving his name to the hamlet.   Half-breed descend-ants of the Cherokees who had intermarried with both whites and Negroes were numerous in the vicinity of Chickamauga, and many of them fought with their white neighbors on the Confederate side.

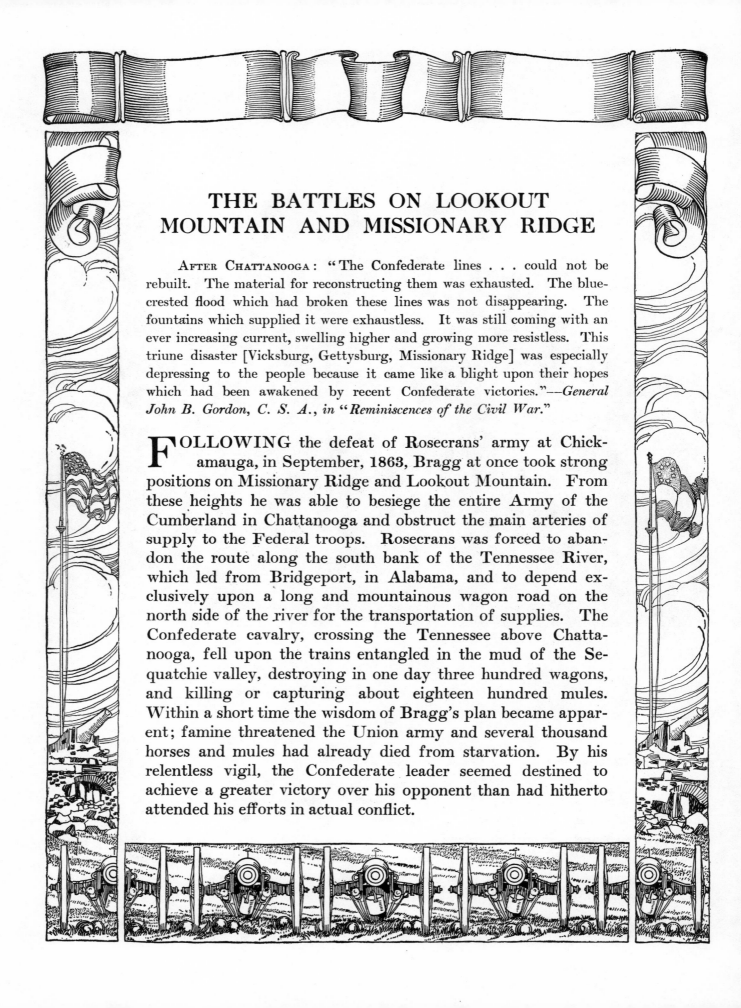

THE BATTLES ON LOOKOUT MOUNTAIN AND MISSIONARY RIDGE

AFTER CHATTANOOGA: "The Confederate lines . . . could not be rebuilt. The material for reconstructing them was exhausted. The blue-crested flood which had broken these lines was not disappearing. The fountains which supplied it were exhaustless. It was still coming with an ever increasing current, swelling higher and growing more resistless. This triune disaster [Vicksburg, Gettysburg, Missionary Ridge] was especially depressing to the people because it came like a blight upon their hopes which had been awakened by recent Confederate victories."—*General John B. Gordon, C. S. A., in "Reminiscences of the Civil War."*

FOLLOWING the defeat of Rosecrans' army at Chickamauga, in September, 1863, Bragg at once took strong positions on Missionary Ridge and Lookout Mountain. From these heights he was able to besiege the entire Army of the Cumberland in Chattanooga and obstruct the main arteries of supply to the Federal troops. Rosecrans was forced to abandon the route along the south bank of the Tennessee River, which led from Bridgeport, in Alabama, and to depend exclusively upon a long and mountainous wagon road on the north side of the river for the transportation of supplies. The Confederate cavalry, crossing the Tennessee above Chattanooga, fell upon the trains entangled in the mud of the Sequatchie valley, destroying in one day three hundred wagons, and killing or capturing about eighteen hundred mules. Within a short time the wisdom of Bragg's plan became apparent; famine threatened the Union army and several thousand horses and mules had already died from starvation. By his relentless vigil, the Confederate leader seemed destined to achieve a greater victory over his opponent than had hitherto attended his efforts in actual conflict.

THE BESIEGED

At this point, where Citico Creek joins the Tennessee, the left of the Eleventh Corps of the Army of the Cumberland rested on the river bank, the limit of the Federal line of defense, east of Chattanooga.   Here, on high ground overlooking the stream, was posted Battery McAloon to keep the Confederates back from the river, so that timber and firewood could be rafted down to the besieged army.   In the chill of autumn, with scanty rations, the soldiers had a hard time keeping warm, as all fuel within the lines had been consumed.   The Army of the Cumberland was almost conquered by hardship.   Grant feared that the soldiers "could not be got out of their trenches to assume the offensive."   But it was these very men who achieved the most signal victory in the battle of Chattanooga.

Meanwhile, a complete reorganization of the Federal forces in the West was effected. Under the title of the Military Division of the Mississippi, the Departments of the Ohio, the Cumberland, and the Tennessee were united with Grant as general commanding, and Rosecrans was replaced by Thomas at the head of the Army of the Cumberland.

A hurried concentration of the Federal forces was now ordered by General Halleck. Hooker with fifteen thousand men of the Army of the Potomac came rapidly by rail to Bridgeport. Sherman, with a portion of his army, about twenty thousand strong, was summoned from Vicksburg and at once embarked in steamers for Memphis. General Grant decided to assume personal charge of the Federal forces; but before he reached his new command, Thomas, ably assisted by his chief engineer, General W. F. Smith, had begun to act on a plan which Rosecrans had conceived, and which proved in the end to be a brilliant conception. This was to seize a low range of hills known as Raccoon Mountain on the peninsula made by a bend of the river, on its south side and west of Chattanooga, and establish a wagon road to Kelly's Ferry, a point farther down the river to which supplies could be brought by boat from Bridgeport, and at the same time communication effected with Hooker.

A direct line was not only secured to Bridgeport, but Hooker advanced with a portion of his troops into Lookout Valley and after a short but decisive skirmish drove the Confederates across Lookout Creek, leaving his forces in possession of the hills he had gained. The route was now opened between Bridgeport and Brown's Ferry; abundant supplies were at once available and the Army of the Cumberland relieved of its perilous position.

Unlike the condition which had prevailed at Chickamauga, reenforcements from all sides were hastening to the aid of Thomas' army; Hooker was already on the ground; Sherman was advancing rapidly from Memphis, and he arrived in

OPENING "THE CRACKER LINE"

The U. S. S. *Chattanooga* was the first steamboat built by the Federals on the upper Tennessee River.   Had the gunboats on the Ohio been able to come up the Tennessee River nearly three hundred miles, to the assistance of Rosecrans, Bragg could never have bottled him up in Chattanooga.   But between Florence and Decatur, Alabama, Muscle Shoals lay in the stream, making the river impassable.   While Bragg's pickets invested the railroad and river, supplies could not be brought up from Bridgeport; and besides, with the exception of one small steamboat (the *Dunbar*), the Federals had no boats on the river.   General W. F. Smith, Chief Engineer of the Army of the Cumberland, had established a saw-mill with an old engine at Bridgeport for the purpose of getting out lumber from logs rafted down the river, with which to construct pontoons. Here Captain Arthur Edwards, Assistant Quartermaster, had been endeavoring since the siege began to build a steamboat consisting of a flat-bottom scow, with engine, boiler, and stern-wheel mounted upon it. On October 24th, after many difficulties and discouragements had been overcome, the vessel was launched successfully and christened the *Chattanooga*.   On the 29th she made her trial trip.   That very night, Hooker, in the battle of Wauhatchie, definitely established control of the new twelve-mile "Cracker Line" from Kelley's Ferry, which Grant had ordered for the relief of the starving army.   The next day the little *Chattanooga*, with steam up, was ready to start from Bridgeport with a heavy load of the much-needed supplies, and her arrival was anxiously awaited at Kelley's Ferry, where the wagon-trains were all ready to rush forward the rations and forage to Chattanooga.   The mechanics were still at work upon the little vessel's unfinished pilot-house and boiler-deck while she and the two barges she was to tow were being loaded, and at 4 A.M. on November 30th she set out to make the 45-mile journey against unfavorable head-winds.

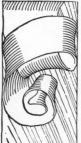

person on November 15th, while Burnside's forces at Knoxville offered protection to the left flank of the Federal army.

The disposition of the Confederate troops at this time was a formidable one; the left flank rested on the northern end of Lookout Mountain and the line extended a distance of twelve miles across Chattanooga Valley to Missionary Ridge. This position was further strengthened by entrenchments throughout the lowlands. Despite the danger which threatened his army from the converging Union forces, General Bragg determined to attack Burnside and despatched Longstreet with twenty thousand of his best troops to Knoxville. His army materially weakened, the Confederate general continued to hold the same extended position, although his combined force was smaller than had opposed Rosecrans alone at Chickamauga.

On the 23d of November, after a long and fatiguing march over roads almost impassable by reason of continuous rains, Sherman crossed the Tennessee by the pontoon bridge at Brown's Ferry, recrossed it above Chattanooga, and was assigned a position to the left of the main army near the mouth of Chickamauga Creek. Grant had now some eighty thousand men, of whom sixty thousand were on the scene of the coming battle, and, though fearful lest Burnside should be dislodged from his position at Knoxville, he would not be diverted from his purpose of sweeping the Confederates from the front of Chattanooga. It had been Grant's plan to attack on the 24th, but information reached him that Bragg was preparing a retreat. He, therefore, on the 23d, ordered Thomas to advance upon Bragg's center.

Preparations for the movement were made in full view of the Confederates; from the appearance of the troops, clad in their best uniforms, the advance line of the Southern army was content to watch this display, in the belief that the maneuvering army was parading in review. Suddenly, the peaceful pageant turned into a furious charge, before which the

THE WELCOME NEWCOMER

The home-made little steamboat *Chattanooga* was beset with difficulties and dangers on her memorable voyage of November 30th. She made but slow progress against the wind and the rapid current of the tortuous Tennessee. Fearful of breaking a steam pipe or starting a leak, she crawled along all day, and then was enveloped in one of the darkest of nights, out of which a blinding rain stung the faces of her anxious crew. Assistant Quartermaster William G. Le Duc, in command of the expedition, helped the pilot to feel his way through the darkness. At last the camp-fires of the Federals became guiding beacons from the shore and soon the *Chattanooga* tied up safely at Kelley's Ferry. The "Cracker Line" was at last opened—in the nick of time, for there were but four boxes of hard bread left in the commissary at Chattanooga, where four cakes of hard bread and one-quarter of a pound of pork were being issued as a three-days' ration.

Confederate pickets, taken by surprise, retreated from the first line of earthworks, and Thomas, with little loss to either side, captured Orchard Knob, between Chattanooga and Missionary Ridge. From this point, which was almost a mile in advance of the position occupied during the morning, Grant directed the movements of his army on the following day.

The Federal position was of less extent than that occupied by the Confederates. Sherman was in command of the left wing, while Thomas held the center, and "Fighting Joe" Hooker, with the Union right in Lookout Valley, threatened Lookout Mountain. The plan of battle was for Sherman to engage the Confederate right and sever communications between Bragg and Longstreet; Hooker was to carry out an assault on the Southern left flank, and at the same time maintain connection with Bridgeport. With both wings assailed by a superior force, it was believed that Bragg must reenforce these positions and permit Thomas, with overwhelming numbers, to concentrate upon the center.

On the 24th, two distinct movements were in progress. Sherman met with but little opposition in his initial attack upon the Confederate right and promptly seized and occupied the north end of Missionary Ridge. The Confederates, late in the afternoon, fought desperately to regain the hill but were finally repulsed, and Sherman fortified the position he had gained. In the mean time, Hooker, early in the day, had begun his operations against Lookout Mountain. Standing like a lone sentinel above the surrounding valleys, its steep, rocky, and deeply furrowed slopes, rising into a high, palisaded crest, frowned defiance upon the advancing troops, while a well-constructed line of defenses completed the imposing barrier.

Hooker had in addition to his own troops a division of Sherman's army (Osterhaus') which, owing to damage to the pontoon bridge at Brown's Ferry, had been prevented from joining its own leader. As ordered by Hooker, General Geary took his division up the valley to Wauhatchie, crossed the creek

WHERE AN ARMY GAVE ITS OWN ORDERS

At Missionary Ridge (seen in the distance in the lower picture) the Army of the Cumberland removed forever from Grant's mind any doubt of its fighting qualities.   Grant, anxious to develop Bragg's strength, ordered Thomas, on November 23d, to demonstrate against the forces on his front.   Moving out as if on parade, the troops under Gordon Granger drove back the Confederates and captured Orchard Knob (or Indian Hill) a day before it had been planned to do so.   Still another surprise awaited Grant on the 25th, when from this eminence he watched the magnificent spectacle of the battle of Chattanooga.   Thomas' men again pressed forward in what was ordered as a demonstration against Missionary Ridge.   Up and over it they drove the Confederates from one entrenchment after another, capturing the guns parked in the lower picture.   "By whose orders are those troops going up the hill?"   "Old Pap" Thomas, who knew his men better than did Grant, replied that it was probably by their own orders.   It was the most signal victory of the day.

THE CAPTURED CONFEDERATE GUNS

and marched down the east bank, sweeping the Confederate outposts before him. The remainder of the command got across by bridges lower down. Gaining the slopes of the mountain the Federal troops rushed on in their advance. From the high palisaded summit, invisible in the low-hanging clouds, the guns of General Stevenson's brigades poured an iron deluge upon them. But on they went, climbing over ledges and boulders, up hill and down, while the soldiers of the South with musket and cannon tried in vain to check them. Position after position was abandoned to the onrushing Federals, and by noon Geary's advanced troops had rounded the north slope of the mountain and passed from the sight of General Hooker, who was watching the contest from a vantage point to the west. Grant and Thomas from the headquarters on Orchard Knob were likewise eager witnesses of the struggle, although the haze was so dense that they caught a glimpse only now and then as the clouds would rise.

Reenforcements came to the Confederates and they availed nothing. Geary's troops had been ordered to halt when they reached the foot of the palisades, but fired by success they pressed impetuously forward. From its higher position at the base of the cliff Cobham's brigade showered volley after volley upon the Confederate main line of defense, while that of Ireland gradually rolled up the flank. The Federal batteries on Moccasin Point across the river were doing what they could to clear the mountain. The Southerners made a last stand in their walls and pits around the Craven house, but were finally driven in force over rocks and precipices into Chattanooga Valley.

Such was the "battle in the clouds," a wonderful spectacle denied the remainder of Hooker's troops holding Lookout Valley. That general says, "From the moment we had rounded the peak of the mountain it was only from the roar of battle and the occasional glimpses our comrades in the valley could catch of our lines and standards that they knew of the

THE MEN WHO COMPLETED THE VICTORY

General Hooker and Staff at Lookout Mountain. Hooker's forces of about 9,700 men had been sent from the East to reënforce Rose-crans, but until the arrival of Grant they were simply so many more mouths to feed in the besieged city. In the battle of Wauhatchie, on the night of October 20th, they drove back the Confederates and established the new line of communication. On November 24th they, too, had a surprise in store for Grant. Their part in the triple conflict was also ordered merely as a "demonstration," but they astounded the eyes and ears of their comrades with the spectacular fight by which they made their way up Lookout Mountain. The next day, pushing on to Rossville, the daring Hooker attacked one of Bragg's divisions and forced it into precipitate retreat.

HOOKER'S CAMP AT THE BASE OF LOOKOUT MOUNTAIN

strife or its progress, and when from these evidences our true condition was revealed to them their painful anxiety yielded to transports of joy which only soldiers can feel in the earliest moments of dawning victory."

By two in the afternoon the clouds had settled completely into the valley and the ensuing darkness put an end to further operations. Hooker established and strengthened a new position and waited for reenforcements, which General Carlin brought from Chattanooga at five o'clock. Until after midnight an irregular fire was kept up, but the Confederates could not break the new line. Before dawn General Stevenson abandoned the summit, leaving behind twenty thousand rations and the camp equipage of his three brigades. Hooker, anticipating this move, sent several detachments to scale the palisades. A party of six men from the Eighth Kentucky regiment, by means of ladders, was the first to reach the summit, and the waving Stars and Stripes greeted the rising sun of November 25th on Lookout Mountain, amid the wild and prolonged cheers of "Fighting Joe's" valiant troops.

The fighting of Sherman and Hooker on the 24th secured to Grant's army a distinct advantage in position. From the north end of Lookout Mountain across Chattanooga Valley to the north end of Missionary Ridge the Union forces maintained an unbroken front.

The morning of the 25th dawned cold, and an impenetrable mist which lay deep in the valleys was soon driven away. From Orchard Knob, a point almost in the center of the united Federal host, General Grant watched the preparations for the battle. At sunrise, Sherman's command was in motion. In his front, an open space intervened between his position and a ridge held by the Confederates, while just beyond rose a much higher hill. Toward the first ridge the attacking column, under General Corse, advanced rapidly and in full view of the foe. For a time it seemed as if the Confederates must recede before the terrific onslaught, but the advance was abruptly

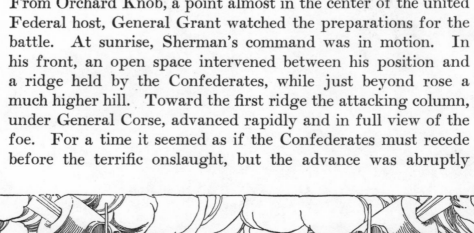

THE BATTLE–FIELD ABOVE THE CLOUDS

Entrenchments on Lookout Mountain.   Up such rugged heights as these, heavily timbered and full of chasms, Hooker's men fought their way on the afternoon of November 24th.   Bridging Lookout Creek, the troops crossed, hidden by the friendly mist, and began ascending the mountain-sides, driving the Confederates from one line of rifle-pits and then from another.   The heavy musketry fire and the boom of the Confederate battery on the top of the mountain apprised the waiting Federals before Chattanooga that the battle had begun.   Now and again the fitful lifting of the mist disclosed to Grant and Thomas, watching from Orchard Knob, the men of Hooker fighting upon the heights.   Then all would be curtained once more.   At two o'clock in the afternoon the mist became so heavy that Hooker and his men could not see what they were doing, and paused to entrench.   By four o'clock, however, he had pushed on to the summit and reported to Grant that his position was impregnable.   Direct communication was then established and reënforcements sent,

checked after a very close and stubborn struggle, when within a short distance of the entrenchment.

Unmindful of the numbers which opposed him, General Hardee not only succeeded in repulsing the attack, but, assuming the offensive, drove back the forces under General John E. Smith, who had sought to turn his left, and captured several hundred prisoners. The Federals, quickly re-forming their lines, renewed the assault and for several hours the fighting was desperate on both sides. A general advance of the Northern forces had been withheld, awaiting the arrival of Hooker who, under orders from Grant, was sweeping down Chickamauga Valley, and was to operate against the Confederate left and rear, in the expectation that Bragg would further weaken his line by massing at those points. But Hooker's army had been delayed several hours by repairs to the bridge crossing Chattanooga Creek. Although Sherman had failed in his attempt to turn the Confederate right he had forced Bragg to draw heavily upon his center for reenforcements. Grant, satisfied that Hooker was not far off, ordered the signal—six guns fired in rapid succession from the battery on Orchard Knob—for a general advance of Thomas' army upon the Confederate center.

It was now three o'clock in the afternoon. The four division commanders of the Army of the Cumberland, Sheridan, Wood, Baird, and Johnson, gave the word to advance. Between Orchard Knob and the base of Missionary Ridge, a mile away, is a broad valley covered for the most part with heavy timber. This had to be crossed before the entrenchments at the foot of the hill could be assaulted. Scarcely were the Cumberland troops in motion when fifty pieces of artillery on the crest of Missionary Ridge opened a terrific fire upon them. But the onward rush of the Federals was not checked in the slightest degree. The line of entrenchments at the base was carried with little opposition. Most of Breckinridge's men abandoned the ditches as the Federal skirmishers approached

THE PEAK OF VICTORY—THE MORNING AFTER THE BATTLE

Pulpit Rock, the Summit of Lookout Mountain. Before dawn of November 25th, Hooker, anticipating the withdrawal of the Confederates, sent detachments to seize the very summit of the mountain, here 2,400 feet high. Six volunteers from the Eighth Kentucky Regiment scaled the palisades by means of the ladders seen in this picture, and made their way to the top. The rest of the regiment quickly followed; then came the Ninety-sixth Illinois. The rays of the rising sun disclosed the Stars and Stripes floating in triumph from the lofty peak "amid the wild and prolonged cheers of the men whose dauntless valor had borne them to that point."

and sought refuge up the hill, breaking and throwing into confusion other troops as they passed through.

At the foot of Missionary Ridge Thomas' army had reached its goal. Its orders carried it no further. But, as General Wood has related, " the enthusiasm and impetuosity of the troops were such that those who first reached the entrenchments at the base of the ridge bounded over them and pressed on up the ascent. . . . Moreover the entrenchments were no protection against the artillery on the ridge. To remain would be destruction—to return would be both expensive in life, and disgraceful. Officers and men, all seemed impressed with this truth. . . . Without waiting for an order the vast mass pressed forward in the race for glory, each man anxious to be the first on the summit. . . . Artillery and musketry could not check the impetuous assault. The troops did not halt to fire. To have done so would have been ruinous. Little was left to the commanders of the troops than to cheer on the foremost—to encourage the weaker of limb and to sustain the very few who seemed to be faint-hearted."

Midway up the slope was a small line of rifle-pits, but these proved of no use in stemming the Federal tide. In the immediate front, however, Major Weaver of the Sixtieth North Carolina rallied a sufficient number of the demoralized Confederates to send a well-directed and effective fire upon the advancing troops. At this point the first line of oncoming Federals was vigorously repulsed, and thrown back to the vacated Confederate trenches. General Bragg, noticing this, rode along the ridge to spread his good news among the troops, but he had not gone far when word was brought that the right flank was broken and that the Federal standard had been seen on the summit. A second and a third flag appeared in quick succession. Bragg sent General Bate to drive the foe back, but the disaster was so great that the latter was unable to repair it. Even the artillery had abandoned the infantry. The Confederate flank had gone, and within an hour of the start from

THE FLANKING PASS

The Gap in Missionary Ridge at Rossville: Through this Georgia mountain-pass runs the road to Ringgold. Rosecrans took advantage of it when he turned Bragg's flank before the battle of Chickamauga; and on November 25, 1863, Thomas ordered Hooker to advance from Lookout Mountain to this point and strike the Confederates on their left flank, while in their front he (Thomas) stood ready to attack. The movement was entirely successful, and in a brilliant battle, begun by Hooker, Bragg's army was swept from Missionary Ridge and pursued in retreat to Georgia.

THE SKIRMISH LINE

Multiply the number of these men by ten, strike out the tents, and we see vividly how the advancing line of Thomas' Army of the Cumberland appeared to the Confederates as they swept up the slope at Missionary Ridge to win the brilliant victory of November 25th. This view of drilling Federal troops in Chattanooga preserves the exact appearance of the line of battle only a couple of months before the picture was taken. The skirmishers, thrown out in advance of the line, are "firing" from such positions as the character of the ground makes most effective. The main line is waiting for the order to charge.

Orchard Knob the crest of Missionary Ridge was occupied by Federal troops. Sheridan did not stop here. He went down the eastern slope, driving all in front of him toward Chickamauga Creek. On a more easterly ridge he rested until midnight, when he advanced to the creek and took many prisoners and stores.

While the Army of the Cumberland accomplished these things, Hooker was advancing his divisions at charging pace from the south. Cruft was on the crest, Osterhaus in the eastern valley, and Geary in the western—all within easy supporting distance. Before Cruft's onrush the left wing of Bragg's army was scattered in all directions from the ridge. Many ran down the eastern slope into Osterhaus' column and the very few who chose a way of flight to the west, were captured by Geary. The bulk of them, however, fell back from trench to trench upon the crest until finally, as the sun was sinking, they found themselves surrounded by Johnson's division of the Army of the Cumberland. Such was the fate of Stewart's division; only a small portion of it got away.

On the Confederate right Hardee held his own against Sherman, but with the left and center routed and in rapid flight Bragg realized the day was lost. He could do nothing but cover Breckinridge's retreat as best he might and order Hardee to retire across Chickamauga Creek.

Thus ended the battle of Chattanooga. Bragg's army had been wholly defeated, and, after being pursued for some days, it found a resting place at Dalton among the mountains of Georgia. The Federal victory was the result of a campaign carefully planned by Generals Halleck and Grant and ably carried out by the efforts of the subordinate generals.

The losses in killed and wounded sustained by Grant were over fifty-eight hundred and those of Bragg about sixty-six hundred, four thousand being prisoners. But the advantage of the great position had been forever wrested from the Southern army.

[Part X]

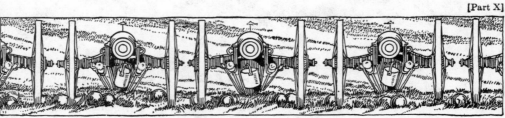

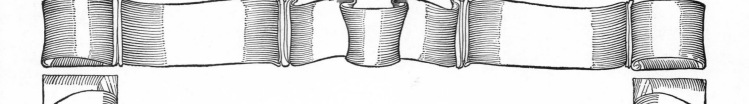

THE BATTLE IN THE WILDERNESS

The volunteers who composed the armies of the Potomac and Northern Virginia were real soldiers now, inured to war, and desperate in their determination to do its work without faltering or failure. This fact—this change in the temper and *morale* of the men on either side—had greatly simplified the tasks set for Grant and Lee to solve. They knew their men. They knew that those men would stand against anything, endure slaughter without flinching, hardship without complaining, and make desperate endeavor without shrinking. The two armies had become what they had not been earlier in the contest, *perfect instruments of war*, that could be relied upon as confidently as the machinist relies upon his engine scheduled to make so many revolutions per minute at a given rate of horse-power, and with the precision of science itself.—*George Cary Eggleston, in "The History of the Confederate War."*

A FTER the battle of Gettysburg, Lee started for the Potomac, which he crossed with some difficulty, but with little interruption from the Federals, above Harper's Ferry, on July 14, 1863. The thwarted invader of Pennsylvania wished to get to the plains of Virginia as quickly as possible, but the Shenandoah was found to be impassable. Meade, in the mean time, had crossed the Potomac east of the Blue Ridge and seized the principal outlets from the lower part of the Valley. Lee, therefore, was compelled to continue his retreat up the Shenandoah until Longstreet, sent in advance with part of his command, had so blocked the Federal pursuit that most of the Confederate army was able to emerge through Chester Gap and move to Culpeper Court House. Ewell marched through Thornton's Gap and by the 4th of August practically the whole Army of Northern Virginia was south of the Rapidan, prepared to dispute the crossing of that river. But Meade, continuing his flank pursuit, halted at

LEE'S MEN

The faces of the veterans in this photograph of 1864 reflect more forcibly than volumes of historical essays, the privations and the courage of the ragged veterans in gray who faced Grant, with Lee as their leader. They did not know that their struggle had already become unavailing; that no amount of perseverance and devotion could make headway against the resources, determination, and discipline of the Northern armies, now that they had become concentrated and wielded by a master of men like Grant. But Grant was as yet little more than a name to the armies of the East. His successes had been won on Western fields—Donelson, Vicksburg, Chattanooga. It was not yet known that the Army of the Potomac under the new general-in-chief was to prove irresistible. So these faces reflect perfect confidence.

CONFEDERATE SOLDIERS IN VIRGINIA, 1864

Though prisoners when this picture was taken—a remnant of Grant's heavy captures during May and June, when he sent some ten thousand Confederates to Coxey's Landing, Virginia, as a result of his first stroke against Lee—though their arms have been taken from them, though their uniforms are anything but "uniform," their hats partly the regulation felt of the Army of Northern Virginia, partly captured Federal caps, and partly nondescript—yet these ragged veterans stand and sit with the dignity of accomplishment. To them, "Marse Robert" is still the general unconquerable, under whom inferior numbers again and again have held their own, and more; the brilliant leader under whom every man gladly rushes to any assault, however impossible it seems, knowing that every order will be made to count.

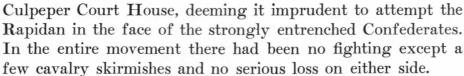

Culpeper Court House, deeming it imprudent to attempt the Rapidan in the face of the strongly entrenched Confederates. In the entire movement there had been no fighting except a few cavalry skirmishes and no serious loss on either side.

On the 9th of September, Lee sent Longstreet and his corps to assist Bragg in the great conflict that was seen to be inevitable around Chattanooga. In spite of reduced strength, Lee proceeded to assume a threatening attitude toward Meade, and in October and early November there were several small but severe engagements as the Confederate leader attempted to turn Meade's flank and force him back to the old line of Bull Run. On the 7th of November, Sedgwick made a brilliant capture of the redoubts on the Rappahannock, and Lee returned once more to his old position on the south side of the Rapidan. This lay between Barnett's Ford, near Orange Court House (Lee's headquarters), and Morton's Ford, twenty miles below. Its right was also protected by entrenchments along the course of Mine Run. Against these, in the last days of November, Meade sent French, Sedgwick, and Warren. It was found impossible to carry the Confederate position, and on December 1st the Federal troops were ordered to recross the Rapidan. In this short campaign the Union lost sixteen hundred men and the Confederacy half that number. With the exception of an unsuccessful cavalry raid against Richmond, in February, nothing disturbed the existence of the two armies until the coming of Grant.

In the early months of 1864, the Army of the Potomac lay between the Rapidan and the Rappahannock, most of it in the vicinity of Culpeper Court House, although some of the troops were guarding the railroad to Washington as far as Bristoe Station, close to Manassas Junction. On the south side of the Rapidan, the Army of Northern Virginia was, as has been seen, securely entrenched. The Confederates' ranks were thin and their supplies were scarce; but the valiant spirit which had characterized the Southern hosts in former battles

THE COMING OF THE STRANGER GRANT

Hither, to Meade's headquarters at Brandy Station, came Grant on March 10, 1864. The day before, in Washington, President Lincoln handed him his commission, appointing him Lieutenant-General in command of all the Federal forces. His visit to Washington convinced him of the wisdom of remaining in the East to direct affairs, and his first interview with Meade decided him to retain that efficient general in command of the Army of the Potomac. The two men had known each other but slightly from casual meetings during the Mexican War. "I was a stranger to most of the Army of the Potomac," said Grant, "but Meade's modesty and willingness to serve in any capacity impressed me even more than had his victory at Gettysburg." The only prominent officers Grant brought on from the West were Sheridan and Rawlins.

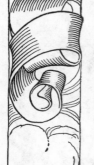

still burned fiercely within their breasts, presaging many desperate battles before the heel of the invader should tread upon their cherished capital, Richmond, and their loved cause, the Confederacy.

Within the camp religious services had been held for weeks in succession, resulting in the conversion of large numbers of the soldiers. General Lee was a religious man. The influence of the awakening among the men in the army during this revival was manifest after the war was over, when the soldiers had gone back to civil life, under conditions most trying and severe. To this spiritual frame of mind may be credited, perhaps, some of the remarkable feats accomplished in subsequent battles by the Confederate army.

On February 29, 1864, the United States Congress passed a law reviving the grade of lieutenant-general, the title being intended for Grant, who was made general-in-chief of the armies of the United States. Grant had come from his victorious battle-grounds in the West, and all eyes turned to him as the chieftain who should lead the Union army to success. On the 9th of March he received his commission. He now planned the final great double movement of the war. Taking control of the whole campaign against Lee, but leaving the Army of the Potomac under Meade's direct command, he chose the strongest of his corps commanders, W. T. Sherman, for the head of affairs in the West. Grant's immediate objects were to defeat Lee's army and to capture Richmond, the latter to be accomplished by General Butler and the Army of the James; Sherman's object was to crush Johnston, to seize that important railroad center, Atlanta, Georgia, and, with Banks' assistance, to open a way between the Atlantic coast and Mobile, on the Gulf, thus dividing the Confederacy north and south, as the conquest of the Mississippi had parted it east and west. It was believed that if either or both of these campaigns were successful, the downfall of the Confederacy would be assured.

SIGNALING ORDERS FROM GENERAL MEADE'S HEADQUARTERS, JUST BEFORE THE WILDERNESS

In April, 1864, General Meade's headquarters lay north of the Rapidan. The Signal Corps was kept busy transmitting the orders preliminary to the Wilderness campaign, which was to begin May 5th. The headquarters are below the brow of the hill. A most important part of the Signal Corps' duty was the interception and translation of messages interchanged between the Confederate signal-men. A veteran of Sheridan's army tells of his impressions as follows: "On the evening of the 18th of October, 1864, the soldiers of Sheridan's army lay in their lines at Cedar Creek. Our attention was suddenly directed to the ridge of Massanutten, or Three Top Mountain, the slope of which covered the left wing of the army—the Eighth Corps. A lively series of signals was being flashed out from the peak, and it was evident that messages were being sent both eastward and westward of the ridge. I can recall now the feeling with which we looked up at those flashes going over our heads, knowing that they must be Confederate messages. It was only later that we learned that a keen-eyed Union officer had been able to read the message: 'To Lieutenant-General Early. Be ready to move as soon as my forces join you, and we will crush Sheridan. Longstreet, Lieutenant-General.' The sturdiness of Sheridan's veterans and the fresh spirit put into the hearts of the men by the return of Sheridan himself from 'Winchester, twenty miles away,' a ride rendered immortal by Read's poem, proved too much at last for the pluck and persistency of Early's worn-out troops."

On a recommendation of General Meade's, the Army of the Potomac was reorganized into three corps instead of the previous five. The Second, Fifth, and Sixth corps were retained, absorbing the First and Third.

Hancock was in command of the Second; Warren, the Fifth; and Sedgwick, the Sixth. Sheridan was at the head of the cavalry. The Ninth Corps acted as a separate army under Burnside, and was now protecting the Orange and Alexandria Railroad. As soon as Meade had crossed the Rapidan, Burnside was ordered to move promptly, and he reached the battlefield of the Wilderness on the morning of May 6th. On May 24th his corps was assigned to the Army of the Potomac. The Union forces, including the Ninth Corps, numbered about one hundred and eighteen thousand men.

The Army of Northern Virginia consisted of three corps of infantry, the First under Longstreet, the Second under Ewell, and the Third under A. P. Hill, and a cavalry corps commanded by Stuart. A notable fact in the organization of the Confederate army was the few changes made in commanders. The total forces under Lee were about sixty-two thousand.

After assuming command, Grant established his headquarters at Culpeper Court House, whence he visited Washington once a week to consult with President Lincoln and the Secretary of War. He was given full authority, however, as to men and movements, and worked out a plan of campaign which resulted in a series of battles in Virginia unparalleled in history. The first of these was precipitated in a dense forest, a wilderness, from which the battle takes its name.

Grant decided on a general advance of the Army of the Potomac upon Lee, and early on the morning of May 4th the movement began by crossing the Rapidan at several fords below Lee's entrenched position, and moving by his right flank. The crossing was effected successfully, the line of march taking part of the Federal troops over a scene of defeat in the

ON THE WAY TO THE FRONT

The Streets of Culpeper, Virginia, in March, 1864. After Grant's arrival, the Army of the Potomac awoke to the activity of the spring campaign. One of the first essentials was to get the vast transport trains in readiness to cross the Rapidan. Wagons were massed by thousands at Culpeper, near where Meade's troops had spent the winter. The work of the teamsters was most arduous; wearied by long night marches—nodding, reins in hand, for lack of sleep—they might at any moment be suddenly attacked in a bold attempt to capture or destroy their precious freight. When the arrangements were completed, each wagon bore the corps badge, division color, and number of the brigade it was to serve. Its contents were also designated, together with the branch of the service for which it was intended. While loaded, the wagons must keep pace with the army movements whenever possible in order to be parked at night near the brigades to which they belonged.

previous spring. One year before, the magnificent Army of the Potomac, just from a long winter's rest in the encampment at Falmouth on the north bank of the Rappahannock, had met the legions of the South in deadly combat on the battlefield of Chancellorsville. And now Grant was leading the same army, whose ranks had been freshened by new recruits from the North, through the same field of war.

By eight o'clock on the morning of the 4th the various rumors as to the Federal army's crossing the Rapidan received by Lee were fully confirmed, and at once he prepared to set his own army in motion for the Wilderness, and to throw himself across the path of his foe. Two days before he had gathered his corps and division commanders around him at the signal station on Clark's Mountain, a considerable eminence south of the Rapidan, near Robertson's Ford. Here he expressed the opinion that Grant would cross at the lower fords, as he did, but nevertheless Longstreet was kept at Gordonsville in case the Federals should move by the Confederate left.

The day was oppressively hot, and the troops suffered greatly from thirst as they plodded along the forest aisles through the jungle-like region. The Wilderness was a maze of trees, underbrush, and ragged foliage. Low-limbed pines, scrub-oaks, hazels, and chinkapins interlaced their branches on the sides of rough country roads that lead through this labyrinth of desolation. The weary troops looked upon the heavy tangles of fallen timber and dense undergrowth with a sense of isolation. Only the sounds of the birds in the trees, the rustling of the leaves, and the passing of the army relieved the heavy pall of solitude that bore upon the senses of the Federal host.

The forces of the Northern army advanced into the vast no-man's land by the roads leading from the fords. In the afternoon, Hancock was resting at Chancellorsville, while Warren posted his corps near the Wilderness Tavern, in which General Grant established his headquarters. Sedgwick's corps

THE "GRAND CAMPAIGN" UNDER WAY—THE DAY BEFORE THE BATTLE

Pontoon-Bridges at Germanna Ford, on the Rapidan.   Here the Sixth Corps under Sedgwick and Warren's Fifth Corps began crossing on the morning of May 4, 1864.   The Second Corps, under Hancock, crossed at Ely's Ford, farther to the east.   The cavalry, under Sheridan, was in advance.   By night the army, with the exception of Burnside's Ninth Corps, was south of the Rapidan, advancing into the Wilderness.   The Ninth Corps (a reserve of twenty thousand men) remained temporarily north of the Rappahannock, guarding railway communications.   On the wooden pontoon-bridge the rear-guard is crossing while the pontonniers are taking up the canvas bridge beyond.   The movement was magnificently managed; Grant believed it to be a complete surprise, as Lee had offered no opposition. That was yet to come.   In the baffling fighting of the Wilderness and Spotsylvania Court House, Grant was to lose a third of his superior number, arriving a month later on the James with a dispirited army that had left behind 54,926 comrades in a month.

had followed in the track of Warren's veterans, but was ordered to halt near the river crossing, or a little south of it. The cavalry, as much as was not covering the rear wagon trains, was stationed near Chancellorsville and the Wilderness Tavern. That night the men from the North lay in bivouac with little fear of being attacked in this wilderness of waste, where military maneuvers would be very difficult.

Two roads—the old Orange turnpike and the Orange plank road—enter the Wilderness from the southwest. Along these the Confederates moved from their entrenched position to oppose the advancing hosts of the North. Ewell took the old turnpike and Hill the plank road. Longstreet was hastening from Gordonsville. The troops of Longstreet, on the one side, and of Burnside, on the other, arrived on the field after exhausting forced marches.

The locality in which the Federal army found itself on the 5th of May was not one that any commander would choose for a battle-ground. Lee was more familiar with its terrible features than was his opponent, but this gave him little or no advantage. Grant, having decided to move by the Confederate right flank, could only hope to pass through the desolate region and reach more open country before the inevitable clash would come. But this was not to be. General Humphreys, who was Meade's chief of staff, says in his " Virginia Campaign of 1864 and 1865 ": " So far as I know, no great battle ever took place before on such ground. But little of the combatants could be seen, and its progress was known to the senses chiefly by the rising and falling sounds of a vast musketry fire that continually swept along the lines of battle, many miles in length, sounds which at times approached to the sublime."

As Ewell, moving along the old turnpike on the morning of May 5th, came near the Germanna Ford road, Warren's corps was marching down the latter on its way to Parker's store, the destination assigned it by the orders of the day. This meeting precipitated the battle of the Wilderness.

THE TANGLED BATTLEFIELD

The Edge of the Wilderness, May 5, 1864. Stretching away to the westward between Grant's army and Lee's lay no-man's-land—the Wilderness. Covered with a second-growth of thicket, thorny underbrush, and twisted vines, it was an almost impassable labyrinth, with here and there small clearings in which stood deserted barns and houses, reached only by unused and overgrown farm roads. The Federal advance into this region was not a surprise to Lee, as Grant supposed. The Confederate commander had caused the region to be carefully surveyed, hoping for the precise opportunity that Grant was about to give him. At the very outset of the campaign he could strike the Federals in a position where superior numbers counted little. If he could drive Grant beyond the Rappahannock—as he had forced Pope, Burnside and Hooker before him—says George Cary Eggleston (in the "History of the Confederate War"), "loud and almost irresistible would have been the cry for an armistice, supported (as it would have been) by Wall Street and all Europe."

Meade learned the position of Ewell's advance division and ordered an attack. The Confederates were driven back a mile or two, but, re-forming and reenforced, the tide of battle was turned the other way. Sedgwick's marching orders were sending him to the Wilderness Tavern on the turnpike. He was on his way when the battle began, and he now turned to the right from the Germanna Ford road and formed several of his divisions on Warren's right. The presence of Hill on the plank road became known to Meade and Grant, about eight in the morning. Hancock, at Chancellorsville, was too far away to check him, so Getty's division of Sedgwick's corps, on its way to the right, was sent over the Brock road to its junction with the plank road for the purpose of driving Hill back, if possible, beyond Parker's store.

Warren and Sedgwick began to entrench themselves when they realized that Ewell had effectively blocked their progress. Getty, at the junction of the Brock and the Orange plank roads, was likewise throwing up breastworks as fast as he could. Hancock, coming down the Brock road from Chancellorsville, reached him at two in the afternoon and found two of A. P. Hill's divisions in front. After waiting to finish his breastworks, Getty, a little after four o'clock, started, with Hancock supporting him, to carry out his orders to drive Hill back. Hancock says: "The fighting became very fierce at once. The lines of battle were exceedingly close, the musketry continuous and deadly along the entire line. . . . The battle raged with great severity and obstinacy until about 8 P.M. without decided advantage to either party." Here, on the Federal left, and in this desperate engagement, General Alexander Hays, one of Hancock's brigade commanders, was shot through the head and killed.

The afternoon had worn away with heavy skirmishing on the right. About five o'clock Meade made another attempt on Ewell's forces. Both lines were well entrenched, but the Confederate artillery enfiladed the Federal positions. It was after

WHERE EWELL'S CHARGE SURPRISED GRANT

A photograph of Confederate breastworks raised by Ewell's men a few months before, while they fought in the Wilderness, May 5, 1864. In the picture we see some of the customary breastworks which both contending armies threw up to strengthen their positions. These were in a field near the turnpike in front of Ewell's main line. The impracticable nature of the ground tore the lines on both sides into fragments; as they swept back and forth, squads and companies strove fiercely with one another, hand-to-hand. Grant had confidently expressed the belief to one of his staff officers that there was no more advance left in Lee's army. He was surprised to learn on the 5th that Ewell's Corps was marching rapidly down the Orange turnpike to strike at Sedgwick and Warren, while A. P. Hill, with Longstreet close behind, was pushing forward on the Orange plank-road against Hancock.

dark when General Seymour of Sedgwick's corps finally withdrew his brigade, with heavy loss in killed and wounded.

When the battle roar had ceased, the rank and file of the Confederate soldiers learned with sorrow of the death of one of the most dashing brigade leaders in Ewell's corps, General John M. Jones. This fighting was the preliminary struggle for position in the formation of the battle-lines of the two armies, to secure the final hold for the death grapple. The contestants were without advantage on either side when the sanguinary day's work was finished.

Both armies had constructed breastworks and were entrenched very close to each other, front to front, gathered and poised for a deadly spring. Early on the morning of May 6th Hancock was reenforced by Burnside, and Hill by Longstreet.

Grant issued orders, through Meade, for a general attack by Sedgwick, Warren, and Hancock along the entire line, at five o'clock on the morning of the 6th. Fifteen minutes before five the Confederates opened fire on Sedgwick's right, and soon the battle was raging along the whole five-mile front. It became a hand-to-hand contest. The Federals advanced with great difficulty. The combatants came upon each other but a few paces apart. Soldiers on one side became hopelessly mixed with those of the other.

Artillery played but little part in the battle of the Wilderness. The cavalry of the two armies had one indecisive engagement on the 5th. The next day both Custer and Gregg repulsed Hampton and Fitzhugh Lee in two separate encounters, but Sheridan was unable to follow up the advantage. He had been entrusted with the care of the wagon trains and dared not take his cavalry too far from them. The battle was chiefly one of musketry. Volley upon volley was poured out unceasingly; screaming bullets mingled with terrific yells in the dense woods. The noise became deafening, and the wounded and dying lying on the ground among the trees made a scene of indescribable horror. Living men rushed in to take

LEE GIVES BLOW FOR BLOW

Another view of Ewell's advanced entrenchments — the bark still fresh where the Confederates had worked with the logs. In the Wilderness, Lee, ever bold and aggressive, executed one of the most brilliant maneuvers of his career. His advance was a sudden surprise for Grant, and the manner in which he gave battle was another. Grant harbored the notion that his adversary would act on the defensive, and that there would be opportunity to attack the Army of Northern Virginia only behind strong entrenchments. But in the Wilderness, Lee's veterans, the backbone of the South's fighting strength, showed again their unquenchable spirit of aggressiveness. They came forth to meet Grant's men on equal terms in the thorny thickets. About noon, May 5th, the stillness was broken by the rattle of musketry and the roar of artillery, which told that Warren had met with resistance on the turnpike and that the battle had begun. Nearly a mile were Ewell's men driven back, and then they came magnificently on again, fighting furiously in the smoke-filled thickets with Warren's now retreating troops. Sedgwick, coming to the support of Warren, renewed the conflict. To the southward on the plank road, Getty's division, of the Sixth Corps, hard pressed by the forces of A. P. Hill, was succored by Hancock with the Second Corps, and together these commanders achieved what seemed success. It was brief; Longstreet was close at hand to save the day for the Confederates.

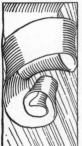

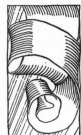

the places of those who had fallen. The missiles cut branches from the trees, and saplings were mowed down as grass in a meadow is cut by a scythe. Bloody remnants of uniforms, blue and gray, hung as weird and uncanny decorations from remaining branches.

The story of the Federal right during the morning is easily told. Persistently and often as he tried, Warren could make no impression on the strongly entrenched Ewell—nor could Sedgwick, who was trying equally hard with Wright's division of his corps. But with Hancock on the left, in his entrenchments on the Brock road, it was different. The gallant and heroic charges here have elicited praise and admiration from friend and foe alike. At first, Hill was forced back in disorder, and driven in confusion a mile and a half from his line. The Confederates seemed on the verge of panic and rout. From the rear of the troops in gray came the beloved leader of the Southern host, General Lee. He was astride his favorite battle-horse, and his face was set in lines of determination. Though the crisis of the battle for the Confederates had arrived, Lee's voice was calm and soft as he commanded, "Follow me," and then urged his charger toward the bristling front of the Federal lines. The Confederate ranks were electrified by the brave example of their commander. A ragged veteran who had followed Lee through many campaigns, leaped forward and caught the bridle-rein of the horse. "We won't go on until you go back," cried the devoted warrior. Instantly the Confederate ranks resounded with the cry, "Lee to the rear! Lee to the rear!" and the great general went back to safety while his soldiers again took up the gage of battle and plunged into the smoke and death-laden storm. But Lee, by his personal presence, and the arrival of Longstreet, had restored order and courage in the ranks, and their original position was soon regained.

The pursuit of the Confederates through the dense forest had caused confusion and disorganization in Hancock's corps.

TREES IN THE TRACK OF THE IRON STORM

The Wilderness to the north of the Orange turnpike. Over ground like this, where men had seldom trod before, ebbed and flowed the tide of trampling thousands on May 5 and 6, 1864. Artillery, of which Grant had a superabundance, was well-nigh useless, wreaking its impotent fury upon the defenseless trees. Even the efficacy of musketry fire was hampered. Men tripping and falling in the tangled underbrush arose bleeding from the briars to struggle with an adversary whose every movement was impeded also. The cold steel of the bayonet finished the work which rifles had begun. In the terrible turmoil of death the hopes of both Grant and Lee were doomed to disappointment. The result was a victory for neither. Lee, disregarding his own safety, endeavored to rally the disordered ranks of A. P. Hill, and could only be persuaded to retire by the pledge of Longstreet that his advancing force would win the coveted victory. Falling upon Hancock's flank, the fresh troops seemed about to crush the Second Corps, as Jackson's men had crushed the Eleventh the previous year at Chancellorsville. But now, as Jackson, at the critical moment, had fallen by the fire of his own men, so Longstreet and his staff, galloping along the plank road, were mistaken by their own soldiers for Federals and fired upon. A minie-ball struck Longstreet in the shoulder, and he was carried from the field, feebly waving his hat that his men might know that he was not killed. With him departed from the field the **life of the attack.**

That cohesion and strength in a battle-line of soldiers, where the men can " feel the touch," shoulder to shoulder, was wanting, and the usual form and regular alignment was broken. It was two hours before the lines were re-formed. That short time had been well utilized by the Confederates. Gregg's eight hundred Texans made a desperate charge through the thicket of the pine against Webb's brigade of Hancock's corps, cutting through the growth, and wildly shouting amid the crash and roar of the battle. Half of their number were left on the field, but the blow had effectually checked the Federal advance.

While the battle was raging Grant's general demeanor was imperturbable. He remained with Meade nearly the whole day at headquarters at the Lacy house. He sat upon a stump most of the time, or at the foot of a tree, leaning against its trunk, whittling sticks with his pocket-knife and smoking big black cigars—twenty during the day. He received reports of the progress of the battle and gave orders without the least evidence of excitement or emotion. " His orders," said one of his staff, " were given with a spur," implying instant action. On one occasion, when an officer, in great excitement, brought him the report of Hancock's misfortune and expressed apprehension as to Lee's purpose, Grant exclaimed with some warmth: " Oh, I am heartily tired of hearing what Lee is going to do. Go back to your command and try to think what we are going to do ourselves."

Several brigades of Longstreet's troops, though weary from their forced march, were sent on a flanking movement against Hancock's left, which demoralized Mott's division and caused it to fall back three-quarters of a mile. Longstreet now advanced with the rest of his corps. The dashing leader, while riding with Generals Kershaw and Jenkins at the head of Jenkins' brigade on the right of the Southern battle array, was screened by the tangled thickets from the view of his own troops, flushed with the success of brilliant flank movement.

A LOSS IN "EFFECTIVE STRENGTH"—WOUNDED AT FREDERICKSBURG

Federal wounded in the Wilderness campaign, at Fredericksburg.   Grant lost 17.3 per cent. of his numbers engaged in the two days' battles of the Wilderness alone.   Lee's loss was 18.1 per cent.   More than 24,000 of the Army of the Potomac and of the Army of Northern Virginia lay suffering in those uninhabited thickets.   There many of them died alone, and some perished in the horror of a forest fire on the night of May 5th.   The Federals lost many gallant officers, among them the veteran Wadsworth.   The Confederates lost Generals Jenkins and Jones, killed, and suffered a staggering blow in the disabling of Longstreet.   The series of battles of the Wilderness and Spotsylvania campaigns were more costly to the Federals than Antietam and Gettysburg combined.

Suddenly the passing column was seen indistinctly through an opening and a volley burst forth and struck the officers. When the smoke lifted Longstreet and Jenkins were down— the former seriously wounded, and the latter killed outright. As at Chancellorsville a year before and on the same battle-ground, a great captain of the Confederacy was shot down by his own men, and by accident, at the crisis of a battle. Jackson lingered several days after Chancellorsville, while Longstreet recovered and lived to fight for the Confederacy till the surrender at Appomattox. General Wadsworth, of Hancock's corps, was mortally wounded during the day, while making a daring assault on the Confederate works, at the head of his men.

During the afternoon, the Confederate attack upon Hancock's and Burnside's forces, which constituted nearly half the entire army, was so severe that the Federal lines began to give way. The combatants swayed back and forth; the Confederates seized the Federal breastworks repeatedly, only to be repulsed again and again. Once, the Southern colors were placed on the Union battlements. A fire in the forest, which had been burning for hours, and in which, it is estimated, about two hundred of the Federal wounded perished, was communicated to the timber entrenchments, the heat and smoke driving into the faces of the men on the Union side, and compelling them in some places to abandon the works. Hancock made a gallant and heroic effort to re-form his lines and push the attack, and, as he rode along the lines, his inspiring presence elicited cheer upon cheer from the men, but the troops had exhausted their ammunition, the wagons were in the rear, and as night was approaching, further attack was abandoned. The contest ended on the lines where it began.

Later in the evening consternation swept the Federal camp when heavy firing was heard in the direction of Sedgwick's corps, on the right. The report was current that the entire Sixth Corps had been attacked and broken. What had happened was a surprise attack by the Confederates,

ONE OF GRANT'S FIELD-TELEGRAPH STATIONS IN 1864

This photograph, taken at Wilcox Landing, near City Point, gives an excellent idea of the difficulties under which telegraphing was done at the front or on the march. With a tent-fly for shelter and a hard-tack box for a table, the resourceful operator mounted his "relay," tested his wire, and brought the commanding general into direct communication with separated brigades or divisions. The U. S. Military Telegraph Corps, through its Superintendent of Construction, Dennis Doren, kept Meade and both wings of his army in communication from the crossing of the Rapidan in May, 1864, till the siege of Petersburg. Over this field-line Grant received daily reports from four separate armies, numbering a quarter of a million men, and replied with daily directions for their operations over an area of seven hundred and fifty thousand square miles. Though every corps of Meade's army moved daily, Doren kept them in touch with headquarters. The field-line was built of seven twisted, rubber-coated wires which were hastily strung on trees or fences.

commanded by General John B. Gordon, on Sedgwick's right flank, Generals Seymour and Shaler with six hundred men being captured. When a message was received from Sedgwick that the Sixth Corps was safe in an entirely new line, there was great rejoicing in the Union camp.

Thus ended the two days' fighting of the battle of the Wilderness, one of the greatest struggles in history. It was Grant's first experience in the East, and his trial measure of arms with his great antagonist, General Lee. The latter returned to his entrenchments and the Federals remained in their position. The first clash had been undecisive. While Grant had been defeated in his plan to pass around Lee, yet he had made a new record for the Army of the Potomac, and he was not turned from his purpose of putting himself between the Army of Northern Virginia and the capital of the Confederacy. During the two days' engagement, there were ten hours of actual fighting, with a loss in killed and wounded of about seventeen thousand Union and nearly twelve thousand Confederates, nearly three thousand men sacrificed each hour. It is the belief of some military writers that Lee deliberately chose the Wilderness as a battle-ground, as it would effectually conceal great inferiority of force, but if this be so he seems to have come to share the unanimous opinions of the generals of both sides that its difficulties were unsurmountable, and within his entrenchments he awaited further attack. It did not come.

The next night, May 7th, Grant's march by the Confederate right flank was resumed, but only to be blocked again by the dogged determination of the tenacious antagonist, a few miles beyond, at Spotsylvania. Lee again anticipated Grant's move. It is not strange that the minds of these two men moved along the same lines in military strategy, when we remember they were both military experts of the highest order, and were now working out the same problem. The results obtained by each are told in the story of the battle of Spotsylvania.

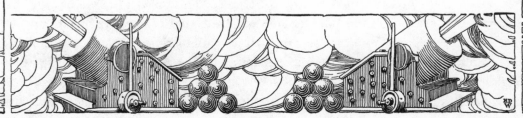

TELEGRAPHING FOR THE ARMIES

ANDREW CARNEGIE

ANDREW CARNEGIE SUPERINTENDED MILITARY RAILWAYS AND GOVERNMENT TELEGRAPH LINES IN 1861

The man who established the Federal military telegraph system amid the first horrors of war was to become one of the world's foremost advocates of peace. As the right hand man of Thomas A. Scott, Assistant Secretary of War, he came to Washington in '61, and was immediately put in charge of the field work of reestablishing communication between the Capital and the North, cut off by the Maryland mobs. A telegraph operator himself, he inaugurated the system of cipher despatches for the War Department and secured the trusted operators with whom the service was begun. A young man of twenty-four at the time, he was one of the last to leave the battlefield of Bull Run, and his duties of general superintendence over the network of railroads and telegraph lines made him a witness of war's cruelties on other fields until he with his chief left the government service June 1, 1862.

THE MILITARY FIELD TELEGRAPH

"No orders ever had to be given to establish the telegraph." Thus wrote General Grant in his memoirs. "The moment troops were in position to go into camp, the men would put up their wires." Grant pays a glowing tribute to "the organization and discipline of this body of brave and intelligent men."

THE MILITARY TELEGRAPH IN THE FIELD

THE ARMY SAVING THE NAVY IN MAY, 1864

Here the army is saving the navy by a brilliant piece of engineering that prevented the loss of a fleet worth $2,000,000. The Red River expedition was one of the most humiliating ever undertaken by the Federals. Porter's fleet, which had so boldly advanced above the falls at Alexandria, was ordered back, only to find that the river was so low as to imprison twelve vessels. Lieut.-Colonel Joseph Bailey, acting engineer of the Nineteenth Corps, obtained permission to build a dam in order to make possible the passage of the fleet. Begun on April 30, 1864, the work was finished on the 8th of May, almost entirely by the soldiers, working incessantly day and night, often up to their necks in water and under the broiling sun. Bailey succeeded in turning the whole current into one channel and the squadron passed below to safety. Not often have inland lumbermen been the means of saving a navy.

The army engineers laughed at this wide-browed, unassuming man when he suggested building a dam so as to release Admiral Porter's fleet imprisoned by low water above the Falls at Alexandria at the close of the futile Red River expedition in 1864. Bailey had been a lumberman in Wisconsin and had there gained the practical experience which taught him that the plan was feasible. He was Acting Chief Engineer of the Nineteenth Army Corps at this time, and obtained permission to go ahead and build his dam. In the undertaking he had the approval and earnest support of Admiral Porter, who refused to consider for a moment the abandonment of any of his vessels even though the Red River expedition had been ordered to return and General Banks was chafing at delay and sending messages to Porter that his troops must be got in motion at once.

Bailey pushed on with his work and in eleven days he succeeded in so raising the water in the channel that all the Federal vessels were able to pass down below the Falls. "Words are inadequate," said Admiral Porter, in his report, "to express the admiration I feel for the ability of Lieut. Colonel Bailey. This is without doubt the best engineering feat ever performed. . . . The highest honors the Government can bestow on Colonel Bailey can never repay him for the service he has rendered the country." For this achievement Bailey was promoted to colonel, brevetted brigadier general, voted the thanks of Congress, and presented with a sword and a purse of $3,000 by the officers of Porter's fleet. He settled in Missouri after the war and was a formidable enemy of the "Bushwhackers" till he was shot by them on March 21, 1867. He was born at Salem, Ohio, April 28, 1827.

COLONEL JOSEPH BAILEY IN 1864.

THE MAN WHO SAVED THE FLEET.

READY FOR HER BAPTISM.

This powerful gunboat, the *Lafayette*, though accompanying Admiral Porter on the Red River expedition, was not one of those entrapped at Alexandria. Her heavy draft precluded her being taken above the Falls. Here we see her lying above Vicksburg in the spring of 1863. She and her sister ship, the *Choctaw*, were side-wheel steamers altered into casemate ironclads with rams. The *Lafayette* had the stronger armament, carrying two 11-inch Dahlgrens forward, four 9-inch guns in the broadside, and two 24-pound howitzers, with two 100-pound Parrott guns astern. She and the *Choctaw* were the most important acquisitions to Porter's fleet toward the end of 1862. The *Lafayette* was built and armed for heavy fighting. She got her first taste of it on the night of April 16, 1863, when Porter took part of his fleet past the Vicksburg batteries to support Grant's crossing of the river in an advance on Vicksburg from below. The *Lafayette*, with a barge and a transport lashed to her, held her course with difficulty through the tornado of shot and shell which poured from the Confederate batteries on the river front in Vicksburg as soon as the movement was discovered. The *Lafayette* stood up to this fiery christening and successfully ran the gantlet, as did all the other vessels save one transport. She was commanded during the Red River expedition by Lieutenant-Commander J. P. Foster.

FARRAGUT AT THE PINNACLE OF HIS FAME

Leaning on the cannon, Commander David Glasgow Farragut and Captain Percival Drayton, chief of staff, stand on the deck of the "Hartford," after the victory in Mobile Bay, of August, 1864. When Gustavus V. Fox, Assistant Secretary of the Navy, proposed the capture of New Orleans from the southward he was regarded as utterly foolhardy. All that was needed, however, to make Fox's plan successful was the man with spirit enough to undertake it and judgment sufficient to carry it out. Here on the deck of the fine new sloop-of-war that had been assigned to him as flagship, stands the man who had just accomplished a greater feat that made him a world figure as famous as Nelson. The Confederacy had found its great general among its own people, but the great admiral of the war, although of Southern birth, had refused to fight against the flag for which, as a boy in the War of 1812, he had seen men die. Full of the fighting spirit of the old navy, he was able to achieve the first great victory that gave new hope to the Federal cause. Percival Drayton was also a Southerner, a South Carolinian, whose brothers and uncles were fighting for the South.

"FAR BY GRAY MORGAN'S WALLS"—THE MOBILE BAY FORT, BATTERED BY FARRAGUT'S GUNS

How formidable was Farragut's undertaking in forcing his way into Mobile Bay is apparent from these photographs. For wooden vessels to pass Morgan and Gaines, two of the strongest forts on the coast, was pronounced by experts most foolhardy. Besides, the channel was planted with torpedoes that might blow the ships to atoms, and within the bay was the Confederate ram *Tennessee*, thought to be the most powerful ironclad ever put afloat. In the arrangements for the attack, Farragut's flagship, the *Hartford*, was placed second, the *Brooklyn* leading the line of battleships, which were preceded by four monitors. At a quarter before six, on the morning of August 5th, the fleet moved. Half an hour later it came within range of Fort Morgan. The whole undertaking was then threatened with disaster. The monitor *Tecumseh*, eager to engage the Confederate ram *Tennessee* behind the line of torpedoes, ran straight ahead, struck a torpedo, and in a few minutes went down with most of the crew. As the monitor sank, the *Brooklyn* recoiled. Farragut signaled: "What's the trouble?" "Torpedoes," was the answer.

WHERE BROADSIDES STRUCK

"Damn the torpedoes!" shouted Farragut. "Go ahead, Captain Drayton. Four bells." Finding that the smoke from the guns obstructed the view from the deck, Farragut ascended to the rigging of the main mast, where he was in great danger of being struck and of falling to the deck. The captain accordingly ordered a quartermaster to tie him in the shrouds. The *Hartford*, under a full head of steam, rushed over the torpedo ground far in advance of the fleet. The battle was not yet over. The Confederate ram, invulnerable to the broadsides of the Union guns, steamed alone for the ships, while the ramparts of the two forts were crowded with spectators of the coming conflict. The ironclad monster made straight for the flagship, attempting to ram it and paying no attention to the fire or the ramming of the other vessels. Its first effort was unsuccessful, but a second came near proving fatal. It then became a target for the whole Union fleet; finally its rudder-chain was shot away and it became unmanageable; in a few minutes it raised the white flag. No wonder Americans call Farragut the greatest of naval commanders.

THE "HARTFORD" JUST AFTER THE BATTLE OF MOBILE BAY

This vivid photograph, taken in Mobile Bay by a war-time photographer from New Orleans, was presented by Captain Drayton of the "Hartford" to T. W. Eastman, U. S. N., whose family has courteously allowed its reproduction here. Never was exhibited a more superb morale than on the "Hartford" as she steamed in line to the attack of Fort Morgan at Mobile Bay on the morning of August 5, 1864. Every man was at his station thinking his own thoughts in the suspense of that moment. On the quarterdeck stood Captain Percival Drayton and his staff. Near them was the chief-quartermaster, John H. Knowles, ready to hoist the signals that would convey Farragut's orders to the fleet. The admiral himself was in the port main shrouds twenty-five feet above the deck. All was silence aboard till the "Hartford" was in easy range of the fort. Then the great broadsides of the old ship began to take their part in the awful cannonade. During the early part of the action Captain Drayton, fearing that some damage to the rigging might pitch Farragut overboard, sent Knowles on his famous mission. "I went up," said the old sailor, "with a piece of lead line and made it fast to one of the forward shrouds, and then took it around the admiral to the after shroud, making it fast there. The admiral said, 'Never mind, I'm all right,' but I went ahead and obeyed orders." Later Farragut, undoing the lashing with his own hands, climbed higher still.

QUARTERMASTER KNOWLES

FORT MORGAN—A BOMBARDMENT BRAVELY ANSWERED

The battered walls of Fort Morgan, in 1864, tell of a terrific smashing by the Federal navy.   But the gallant Confederates returned the blows with amazing courage and skill; the rapidity and accuracy of their fire was rarely equalled in the war.   In the terrible conflict the "Hartford" was struck twenty times, the "Brooklyn" thirty, the "Octorora" seventeen, the "Metacomet" eleven, the "Lacka-wanna" five, the "Ossipee" four, the "Monongahela" five, the "Kennebec" two, and the "Galena" seven.   Of the monitors the "Chickasaw" was struck three times, the "Manhattan" nine, and the "Winnebago" nineteen.   The total loss in the Federal fleet was 52 killed and 170 wounded, while on the Confederate gunboats 12 were killed and 20 wounded.   The night after the battle the "Meta-comet" was turned into a hospital-ship and the wounded of both sides were taken to Pensacola.   The pilot of the captured "Tennessee" guided the Federal ship through the torpedoes, and as she was leaving Pensacola on her return trip Midshipman Carter of the "Tennessee," who also was on the "Metacomet," called out from the wharf: "Don't attempt to fire No. 2 gun (of the "Tennessee"), as there is a shell jammed in the bore, and the gun will burst and kill some one."   All felt there had been enough bloodshed.

THE BRAVEST OF THE BRAVE—THE CONFEDERATE IRONCLAD RAM "TENNESSEE"

Mobile Bay, on the morning of August 5, 1864, was the arena of more conspicuous heroism than marked any naval battle-ground of the entire war. Among all the daring deeds of that day stands out superlatively the gallant manner in which Admiral Franklin Buchanan, C. S. N., fought his vessel, the "Tennessee." "You shall not have it to say when you leave this vessel that you were not near enough to the enemy, for I will meet them, and then you can fight them alongside of their own ships; and if I fall, lay me on one side and go on with the fight." Thus Buchanan addressed his men, and then, taking his station in the pilot-house, he took his vessel into action. The Federal fleet carried more power for destruction than the combined English, French, and Spanish fleets at Trafalgar, and yet Buchanan made good his boast that he would fight alongside. No sooner had Farragut crossed the torpedoes than Buchanan matched that deed, running through the entire line of Federal vessels, braving their broadsides, and coming to close quarters with most of them. Then the "Tennessee" ran under the guns of Fort Morgan for a breathing space. In half an hour she was steaming up the bay to fight the entire squadron single-handed. Such boldness was scarce believable, for Buchanan had now not alone wooden ships to contend with, as when in the "Merrimac" he had dismayed the Federals in Hampton Roads. Three powerful monitors were to oppose him at point-blank range. For nearly an hour the gunners in the "Tennessee" fought, breathing powder-smoke amid an atmosphere superheated to 120 degrees. Buchanan was serving a gun himself when he was wounded and carried to the surgeon's table below. Captain Johnston fought on for another twenty minutes, and then the "Tennessee," with her rudder and engines useless and unable to fire a gun, was surrendered, after a reluctant consent had been wrung from Buchanan, as he lay on the operating table.

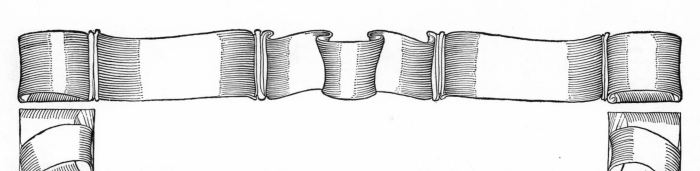

THE BATTLE OF SPOTSYLVANIA COURT HOUSE

But to Spotsylvania history will accord the palm, I am sure, for having furnished an unexampled muzzle-to-muzzle fire; the longest roll of incessant, unbroken musketry; the most splendid exhibition of individual heroism and personal daring by large numbers, who, standing in the freshly spilt blood of their fellows, faced for so long a period and at so short a range the flaming rifles as they heralded the decrees of death. This heroism was confined to neither side. It was exhibited by both armies, and in that hand-to-hand struggle for the possession of the breast-works it seemed almost universal. It would be commonplace truism to say that such examples will not be lost to the Republic.—*General John B. Gordon, C.S.A., in "Reminiscences of the Civil War."*

IMMEDIATELY after the cessation of hostilities on the 6th of May in the Wilderness, Grant determined to move his army to Spotsylvania Court House, and to start the wagon trains on the afternoon of the 7th. Grant's object was, by a flank move, to get between Lee and Richmond. Lee foresaw Grant's purpose and also moved his cavalry, under Stuart, across the opponent's path. As an illustration of the exact science of war we see the two great military leaders racing for position at Spotsylvania Court House. It was revealed later that Lee had already made preparations on this field a year before, in anticipation of its being a possible battle-ground.

Apprised of the movement of the Federal trains, Lee, with his usual sagacious foresight, surmised their destination. He therefore ordered General R. H. Anderson, now in command of Longstreet's corps, to march to Spotsylvania Court House at three o'clock on the morning of the 8th. But the smoke and flames from the burning forests that surrounded

Anderson's camp in the Wilderness made the position untenable, and the march was begun at eleven o'clock on the night of the 7th. This early start proved of inestimable value to the Confederates. Anderson's right, in the Wilderness, rested opposite Hancock's left, and the Confederates secured a more direct line of march to Spotsylvania, several miles shorter than that of the Federals. The same night General Ewell at the extreme Confederate left was ordered to follow Anderson at daylight, if he found no large force in his front. This order was followed out, there being no opposing troops, and the corps took the longest route of any of Lee's troops. General Ewell found the march exhausting and distressing on account of the intense heat and dust and smoke from the burning forests.

The Federal move toward Spotsylvania Court House was begun after dark on the 7th. Warren's corps, in the lead, took the Brock road behind Hancock's position and was followed by Sedgwick, who marched by way of Chancellorsville. Burnside came next, but he was halted to guard the trains. Hancock, covering the move, did not start the head of his command until some time after daylight. When Warren reached Todd's Tavern he found the Union cavalry under Merritt in conflict with Fitzhugh Lee's division of Stuart's cavalry. Warren sent Robinson's division ahead; it drove Fitzhugh Lee back, and, advancing rapidly, met the head of Anderson's troops. The leading brigades came to the assistance of the cavalry; Warren was finally repulsed and began entrenching. The Confederates gained Spotsylvania Court House.

Throughout the day there was continual skirmishing between the troops, as the Northerners attempted to break the line of the Confederates. But the men in gray stood firm. Every advance of the blue was repulsed. Lee again blocked the way of Grant's move. The Federal loss during the day had been about thirteen hundred, while the Confederates lost fewer men than their opponents.

IN THE AUTUMN OF 1863—GRANT'S CHANGING EXPRESSIONS

Although secure in his fame as the conqueror of Vicksburg, Grant still has the greater part of his destiny to fulfil as he faces the camera. Before him lie the Wilderness, Spotsylvania, Cold Harbor, and the slow investment of Petersburg. This series forms a particularly interesting study in expression. At the left hand, the face looks almost amused. In the next the expression is graver, the mouth close set. The third picture looks plainly obstinate, and in the last the stern fighter might have been declaring, as in the following spring: "I propose to fight it out on this line if it takes all summer." The eyes, first unveiled fully in this fourth view, are the unmistakable index to Grant's stern inflexibility, once his decision was made.

IN THE AUTUMN OF 1864—AFTER THE STRAIN OF THE WILDERNESS CAMPAIGN

Here is a furrowed brow above eyes worn by pain. In the pictures of the previous year the forehead is more smooth, the expression grave yet confident. Here the expression is that of a man who has won, but won at a bitter cost. It is the memory of the 50,000 men whom he left in the Wilderness campaign and at Cold Harbor that has lined this brow, and closed still tighter this inflexible mouth. Again, as in the series above, the eyes are not revealed until the last picture. Then again flashes the determination of a hero. The great general's biographers say that Grant was a man of sympathy and infinite pity. It was the more difficult for him, spurred on to the duty by grim necessity, to order forward the lines in blue that withered, again and again, before the Confederate fire, but each time weakened the attenuated line which confronted them.

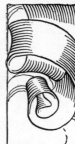

The work of both was now the construction of entrenchments, which consisted of earthworks sloping to either side, with logs as a parapet, and between these works and the opposing army were constructed what are known as abatis, felled trees, with the branches cut off, the sharp ends projecting toward the approaching forces.

Lee's entrenchments were of such character as to increase the efficiency of his force. They were formed in the shape of a huge V with the apex flattened, forming a salient angle against the center of the Federal line. The Confederate lines were facing north, northwest, and northeast, the corps commanded by Anderson on the left, Ewell in the center, and Early on the right, the latter temporarily replacing A. P. Hill, who was ill. The Federals confronting them were Burnside on the left, Sedgwick and Warren in the center, and Hancock on the right.

The day of the 9th was spent in placing the lines of troops, with no fighting except skirmishing and some sharpshooting. While placing some field-pieces, General Sedgwick was hit by a sharpshooter's bullet and instantly killed. He was a man of high character, a most competent commander, of fearless courage, loved and lamented by the army. General Horatio G. Wright succeeded to the command of the Sixth Corps.

Early on the morning of the 10th, the Confederates discovered that Hancock had crossed the Po River in front of his position of the day before and was threatening their rear. Grant had suspected that Lee was about to move north toward Fredericksburg, and Hancock had been ordered to make a reconnaissance with a view to attacking and turning the Confederate left. But difficulties stood in the way of Hancock's performance, and before he had accomplished much, Meade directed him to send two of his divisions to assist Warren in making an attack on the Southern lines. The Second Corps started to recross the Po. Before all were over Early made

MEADE AND SEDGWICK—BEFORE THE ADVANCE THAT BROUGHT SEDGWICK'S
DEATH AT SPOTSYLVANIA

To the right of General Meade, his chief and friend, stands Major-General John Sedgwick, commanding the Sixth Army Corps. He wears his familiar round hat and is smiling. He was a great tease; evidently the performances of the civilian who had brought his new-fangled photographic apparatus into camp suggested a joke. A couple of months later, on the 9th of May, Sedgwick again was jesting—before Spotsylvania Court House. McMahon of his staff had begged him to avoid passing some artillery exposed to the Confederate fire, to which Sedgwick had playfully replied, "McMahon, I would like to know who commands this corps, you or I?" Then he ordered some infantry before him to shift toward the right. Their movement drew the fire of the Confederates. The lines were close together; the situation tense. A sharpshooter's bullet whistled—Sedgwick fell. He was taken to Meade's headquarters. The Army of the Potomac had lost another corps commander, and the Union a brilliant and courageous soldier.

a vigorous assault on the rear division, which did not escape without heavy loss. In this engagement the corps lost the first gun in its most honorable career, a misfortune deeply lamented by every man in the corps, since up to this moment it had long been the only one in the entire army which could make the proud claim of never having lost a gun or a color.

But the great event of the 10th was the direct assault upon the Confederate front. Meade had arranged for Hancock to take charge of this, and the appointed hour was five in the afternoon. But Warren reported earlier that the opportunity was most favorable, and he was ordered to start at once. Wearing his full uniform, the leader of the Fifth Corps advanced at a quarter to four with the greater portion of his troops. The progress of the valiant Northerners was one of the greatest difficulty, owing to the dense wood of low cedar-trees through which they had to make their way. Longstreet's corps behind their entrenchments acknowledged the advance with very heavy artillery and musket fire. But Warren's troops did not falter or pause until some had reached the abatis and others the very crest of the parapet. A few, indeed, were actually killed inside the works. All, however, who survived the terrible ordeal were finally driven back with heavy loss. General James C. Rice was mortally wounded.

To the left of Warren, General Wright had observed what he believed to be a vulnerable spot in the Confederate entrenchments. Behind this particular place was stationed Doles' brigade of Georgia regiments, and Colonel Emory Upton was ordered to charge Doles with a column of twelve regiments in four lines. The ceasing of the Federal artillery at six o'clock was the signal for the charge, and twenty minutes later, as Upton tells us, " at command, the lines rose, moved noiselessly to the edge of the wood, and then, with a wild cheer and faces averted, rushed for the works. Through a terrible front and flank fire the column advanced quickly, gaining the parapet. Here occurred a deadly hand-to-hand

SPOTSYLVANIA COURT HOUSE

WHERE GRANT WANTED TO "FIGHT IT OUT"

For miles around this quaint old village-pump surged the lines of two vast contending armies, May 8–12, 1864. In this picture of only a few months later, the inhabitants have returned to their accustomed quiet, although the reverberations of battle have hardly died away. But on May 7th Generals Grant and Meade, with their staffs, had started toward the little courthouse. As they passed along the Brock Road in the rear of Hancock's lines, the men broke into loud hurrahs. They saw that the movement was still to be southward. But chance had caused Lee to choose the same objective. Misinterpreting Grant's movement as a retreat upon Fredericksburg, he sent Longstreet's corps, now commanded by Anderson, to Spotsylvania. Chance again, in the form of a forest fire, drove Anderson to make, on the night of May 7th, the march from the Wilderness that he had been ordered to commence on the morning of the 8th. On that day, while Warren was contending with the forces of Anderson, Lee's whole army was entrenching on a ridge around Spotsylvania Court House. "Accident," says Grant, "often decides the fate of battle." But this "accident" was one of Lee's master moves.

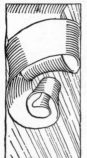

conflict. The enemy, sitting in their pits with pieces upright, loaded, and with bayonets fixed ready to impale the first who should leap over, absolutely refused to yield the ground. The first of our men who tried to surmount the works fell, pierced through the head by musket-balls. Others, seeing the fate of their comrades, held their pieces at arm's length and fired downward, while others, poising their pieces vertically, hurled them down upon their enemy, pinning them to the ground. . . . The struggle lasted but a few seconds. Numbers prevailed, and like a resistless wave, the column poured over the works, quickly putting *hors de combat* those who resisted and sending to the rear those who surrendered. Pressing forward and expanding to the right and left, the second line of entrenchments, its line of battle, and a battery fell into our hands. The column of assault had accomplished its task."

The Confederate line had been shattered and an opening made for expected support. This, however, failed to arrive. General Mott, on the left, did not bring his division forward as had been planned and as General Wright had ordered. The Confederates were reenforced, and Upton could do no more than hold the captured entrenchments until ordered to retire. He brought twelve hundred prisoners and several stands of colors back to the Union lines; but over a thousand of his own men were killed or wounded. For gallantry displayed in this charge, Colonel Upton was made brigadier-general.

The losses to the Union army in this engagement at Spotsylvania were over four thousand. The loss to the Confederates was probably two thousand.

During the 11th there was a pause. The two giant antagonists took a breathing spell. It was on the morning of this date that Grant penned the sentence, " I propose to fight it out on this line if it takes all summer," to his chief of staff, General Halleck.

During this time Sheridan, who had brought the cavalry

THE APEX OF THE BATTLEFIELD

McCool's house, within the "Bloody Angle." The photographs were taken in 1864, shortly after the struggle of Spotsylvania Court House, and show the old dwelling as it was on May 12th, when the fighting was at flood tide all round it; and below, the Confederate entrenchments near that blood-drenched spot. At a point in these Confederate lines in advance of the McCool house, the entrenchments had been thrown forward like the salient of a fort, and the wedge-shaped space within them was destined to become renowned as the "Bloody Angle." The position was defended by the famous "Stonewall Division" of the Confederates under command of General Edward Johnson. It was near the scene of Upton's gallant charge on the 10th. Here at daybreak on May 12th the divisions of the intrepid Barlow and Birney, sent forward by Hancock, stole a march upon the unsuspecting Confederates. Leaping over the breastworks the Federals were upon them and the first of the terrific hand-to-hand conflicts that marked the day began. It ended in victory for Hancock's men, into whose hands fell 20 cannon, 30 standards and 4,000 prisoners, "the best division in the Confederate army."

CONFEDERATE ENTRENCHMENTS NEAR "BLOODY ANGLE"

Flushed with success, the Federals pressed on to Lee's second line of works, where Wilcox's division of the Confederates held them until reënforcements sent by Lee from Hill and Anderson drove them back. On the Federal side the Sixth Corps, with Upton's brigade in the advance, was hurried forward to hold the advantage gained. But Lee himself was on the scene, and the men of the gallant Gordon's division, pausing long enough to seize and turn his horse, with shouts of "General Lee in the rear," hurtled forward into the conflict. In five separate charges by the Confederates the fighting came to close quarters. With bayonets, clubbed muskets, swords and pistols, men fought within two feet of one another on either side of the entrenchments at "Bloody Angle" till night at last left it in possession of the Federals. None of the fighting near Spotsylvania Court House was inglorious. On the 10th, after a day of strengthening positions on both sides, young Colonel Emory Upton of the 121st New York, led a storming party of twelve regiments into the strongest of the Confederate entrenchments. For his bravery Grant made him a brigadier-general on the field.

up to a state of great efficiency, was making an expedition to the vicinity of Richmond. He had said that if he were permitted to operate independently of the army he would draw Stuart after him. Grant at once gave the order, and Sheridan made a detour around Lee's army, engaging and defeating the Confederate cavalry, which he greatly outnumbered, on the 11th of May, at Yellow Tavern, where General Stuart, the brilliant commander of the Confederate cavalry, was mortally wounded.

Grant carefully went over the ground and decided upon another attack on the 12th. About four hundred yards of clear ground lay in front of the sharp angle, or salient, of Lee's lines. After the battle this point was known as the "Bloody Angle," and also as "Hell's Hole." Here Hancock was ordered to make an attack at daybreak on the 12th. Lee had been expecting a move on the part of Grant. On the evening of the 10th he sent to Ewell this message: "It will be necessary for you to reestablish your whole line to-night. . . . Perhaps Grant will make a night attack, as it was a favorite amusement of his at Vicksburg."

Through rain and mud Hancock's force was gotten into position within a few hundred yards of the Confederate breastworks. He was now between Burnside and Wright. At the first approach of dawn the four divisions of the Second Corps, under Birney, Mott, Barlow, and Gibbon (in reserve) moved noiselessly to the designated point of attack. Without a shot being fired they reached the Confederate entrenchments, and struck with fury and impetuosity a mortal blow at the point where least expected, on the salient, held by General Edward Johnson of Ewell's corps. The movement of the Federals was so swift and the surprise so complete, that the Confederates could make practically no resistance, and were forced to surrender.

The artillery had been withdrawn from the earthworks occupied by Johnson's troops on the previous night, but

COPYRIGHT, 1911, PATRIOT PUB. CO.

UNION ARTILLERY MASSING
FOR THE ADVANCE THAT
EWELL'S ATTACK DELAYED
THAT SAME AFTERNOON

BEVERLY HOUSE, MAY 18, 1864

The artillery massing in the meadow gives to this view the interest of an impending tragedy. In the foreground the officers, servants, and orderlies of the headquarters mess camp are waiting for the command to strike their tents, pack the wagons, and move on. But at the very time this photograph was taken they should have been miles away. Grant had issued orders the day before that should have set these troops in motion. However, the Confederate General Ewell had chosen the 18th to make an attack on the right flank. It not only delayed the departure but forced a change in the intended positions of the division as they had been contemplated by the commander-in-chief. Beverly House is where General Warren pitched his headquarters after Spotsylvania, and the spectator is looking toward the battlefield that lies beyond the distant woods. After Ewell's attack, Warren again found himself on the right flank, and at this very moment the main body of the Federal army is passing in the rear of him. The costly check at Spotsylvania, with its wonderful display of fighting on both sides, had in its apparently fruitless results called for the display of all Grant's gifts as a military leader. It takes but little imagination to supply color to this photograph; it is full of it—full of the movement and detail of war also. It is springtime; blossoms have just left the trees and the whole country is green and smiling, but the earth is scarred by thousands of trampling feet and hoof-prints. Ugly ditches cross the landscape; the débris of an army marks its onsweep from one battlefield to another.

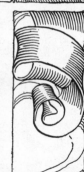

developments had led to an order to have it returned early in the morning. It was approaching as the attack was made. Before the artillerymen could escape or turn the guns upon the Federals, every cannon had been captured. General Johnson with almost his whole division, numbering about three thousand, and General Steuart, were captured, between twenty and thirty colors, and several thousand stands of arms were taken. Hancock had already distinguished himself as a leader of his soldiers, and from his magnificent appearance, noble bearing, and courage had been called "Hancock the Superb," but this was the most brilliant of his military achievements.

Pressing onward across the first defensive line of the Confederates, Hancock's men advanced against the second series of trenches, nearly half a mile beyond. As the Federals pushed through the muddy fields they lost all formation. They reached close to the Confederate line. The Southerners were prepared for the attack. A volley poured into the throng of blue, and General Gordon with his reserve division rushed forward, fighting desperately to drive the Northerners back. As they did so General Lee rode up, evidently intending to go forward with Gordon. His horse was seized by one of the soldiers, and for the second time in the campaign the cry arose from the ranks, "Lee to the rear!" The beloved commander was led back from the range of fire, while the men, under the inspiration of his example, rushed forward in a charge that drove the Federals back until they had reached the outer line of works. Here they fought stubbornly at deadly range. Neither side was able to force the other back. But Gordon was not able to cope with the entire attack. Wright and Warren both sent some of their divisions to reenforce Hancock, and Lee sent all the assistance possible to the troops struggling so desperately to restore his line at the salient.

Many vivid and picturesque descriptions of this fighting at the angle have been written, some by eye-witnesses, others by able historians, but no printed page, no cold type can

THE ONES WHO NEVER CAME BACK

These are some of the men for whom waiting women wept—the ones who never came back. They belonged to Ewell's Corps, who attacked the Federal lines so gallantly on May 18th. There may be some who will turn from this picture with a shudder of horror, but it is no morbid curiosity that will cause them to study it closely. If pictures such as this were familiar everywhere there would soon be an end of war. We can realize money by seeing it expressed in figures; we can realize distances by miles, but some things in their true meaning can only be grasped and impressions formed with the seeing eye. Visualizing only this small item of the awful cost—the cost beside which money cuts no figure—an idea can be gained of what war is. Here is a sermon in the cause of universal peace. The handsome lad lying with outstretched arms and clinched fingers is a mute plea. Death has not disfigured him—he lies in an attitude of relaxation and composure. Perhaps in some Southern home this same face is pictured in the old family album, alert and full of life and hope, and here is the end. Does there not come to the mind the insistent question, "Why?" The Federal soldiers standing in the picture are not thinking of all this, it may be true, but had they meditated in the way that some may, as they gaze at this record of death, it would be worth their while. One of the men is apparently holding a sprig of blossoms in his hand. It is a strange note here.

convey to the mind the realities of that terrible conflict. The
results were appalling. The whole engagement was practically a hand-to-hand contest. The dead lay beneath the feet
of the living, three and four layers deep. This hitherto quiet
spot of earth was devastated and covered with the slain, wel-
tering in their own blood, mangled and shattered into scarcely
a semblance of human form. Dying men were crushed by
horses and many, buried beneath the mire and mud, still lived.
Some artillery was posted on high ground not far from the
apex of the salient, and an incessant fire was poured into the
Confederate works over the Union lines, while other guns kept
up an enfilade of canister along the west of the salient.

The contest from the right of the Sixth to the left of the
Second Corps was kept up throughout the day along the
whole line. Repeatedly the trenches had to be cleared of the
dead. An oak tree twenty-two inches in diameter was cut
down by musket-balls. Men leaped upon the breastworks,
firing until shot down.

The battle of the " angle " is said to have been the most
awful in duration and intensity in modern times. Battle-line
after battle-line, bravely obeying orders, was annihilated. The
entrenchments were shivered and shattered, trunks of trees
carved into split brooms. Sometimes the contestants came so
close together that their muskets met, muzzle to muzzle, and
their flags almost intertwined with each other as they waved
in the breeze. As they fought with the desperation of madmen,
the living would stand on the bodies of the dead to reach over
the breastworks with their weapons of slaughter. Lee hurled
his army with unparalleled vigor against his opponent five
times during the day, but each time was repulsed. Until three
o'clock the next morning the slaughter continued, when the
Confederates sank back into their second line of entrenchments,
leaving their opponents where they had stood in the morning.

All the fighting on the 12th was not done at the " Bloody
Angle." Burnside on the left of Hancock engaged Early's

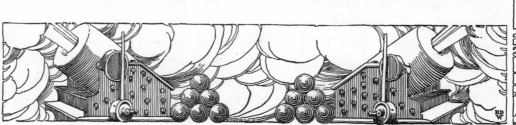

IN ONE LONG BURIAL TRENCH

It fell to the duty of the First Massachusetts Heavy Artillery of General Tyler's division to put under ground the men they slew in the sharp battle of May 18th, and here they are near Mrs. Allsop's barn digging the trench to hide the dreadful work of bullet and shot and shell. No feeling of bitterness exists in moments such as these. What soldier in the party knows but what it may be his turn next to lie beside other lumps of clay and join his earth-mother in this same fashion in his turn. But men become used to work of any kind, and these men digging up the warm spring soil, when their labor is concluded, are neither oppressed nor nerve-shattered by what they have seen and done. They have lost the power of experiencing sensation. Senses become numbed in a measure; the value of life itself from close and constant association with death is minimized almost to the vanishing point. In half an hour these very men may be singing and laughing as if war and death were only things to be expected, not reasoned over in the least.

ONE OF THE FEARLESS CONFEDERATES

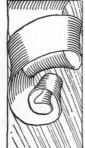

troops and was defeated, while on the other side of the salient Wright succeeded in driving Anderson back.

The question has naturally arisen why that " salient " was regarded of such vital importance as to induce the two chief commanders to force their armies into such a hand-to-hand contest that must inevitably result in unparalleled and wholesale slaughter. It was manifest, however, that Grant had shown generalship in finding the weak point in Lee's line for attack. It was imperative that he hold the gain made by his troops. Lee could ill afford the loss resistance would entail, but he could not withdraw his army during the day without disaster.

The men on both sides seemed to comprehend the gravity of the situation, that it was a battle to the death for that little point of entrenchment. Without urging by officers, and sometimes without officers, they fell into line and fought and bled and died in myriads as though inspired by some unseen power. Here men rushed to their doom with shouts of courage and eagerness.

The pity of it all was manifested by the shocking scene on that battlefield the next day. Piles of dead lay around the " Bloody Angle," a veritable " Hell's Hole " on both sides of the entrenchments, four layers deep in places, shattered and torn by bullets and hoofs and clubbed muskets, while beneath the layers of dead, it is said, there could be seen quivering limbs of those who still lived.

General Grant was deeply moved at the terrible loss of life. When he expressed his regret for the heavy sacrifice of men to General Meade, the latter replied, " General, we can't do these little tricks without heavy losses." The total loss to the Union army in killed, wounded, and missing at Spotsylvania was nearly eighteen thousand. The Confederate losses have never been positively known, but from the best available sources of information the number has been placed at not less than nine thousand men. Lee's loss in high officers was very

THE REDOUBT THAT LEE LET GO

This redoubt covered Taylor's Bridge, but its flanks were swept by artillery and an enfilading fire from rifle-pits across the river. Late in the evening of the 23d, Hancock's corps, arriving before the redoubt, had assaulted it with two brigades and easily carried it. During the night the Confederates from the other side made two attacks upon the bridge and finally succeeded in setting it afire. The flames were extinguished by the Federals, and on the 24th Hancock's troops crossed over without opposition. The easy crossing of the Federals here was but another example of Lee's favorite rule to let his antagonist attack him on the further side of a stream. Taylor's Bridge could easily have been held by Lee for a much longer time, but its ready abandonment was part of the tactics by which Grant was being led into a military dilemma. In the picture the Federal soldiers confidently hold the captured redoubt, convinced that the possession of it meant that they had driven Lee to his last corner.

severe, the killed including General Daniel and General Perrin, while Generals Walker, Ramseur, R. D. Johnston, and McGowan were severely wounded. In addition to the loss of these important commanders, Lee was further crippled in efficient commanders by the capture of Generals Edward Johnson and Steuart. The Union loss in high officers was light, excepting General Sedgwick on the 9th. General Webb was wounded, and Colonel Coon, of the Second Corps, was killed.

Lee's forces had been handled with such consummate skill as to make them count one almost for two, and there was the spirit of devotion for Lee among his soldiers which was indeed practically hero-worship. All in all, he had an army, though shattered and worn, that was almost unconquerable. Grant found that ordinary methods of war, even such as he had experienced in the West, were not applicable to the Army of Northern Virginia. The only hope for the Union army was a long-drawn-out process, and with larger numbers, better kept, and more often relieved, Grant's army would ultimately make that of Lee's succumb, from sheer exhaustion and disintegration.

The battle was not terminated on the 12th. During the next five days there was a continuous movement of the Union corps to the east which was met by a corresponding readjustment of the Confederate lines. After various maneuvers, Hancock was ordered to the point where the battle was fought on the 12th, and on the 18th and 19th, the last effort was made to break the lines of the Confederates. Ewell, however, drove the Federals back and the next day he had a severe engagement with the Union left wing, while endeavoring to find out something of Grant's plans.

Twelve days of active effort were thus spent in skirmishing, fighting, and countermarching. In the last two engagements the Union losses were nearly two thousand, which are included in those before stated. It was decided to abandon the attempt to dislodge Lee from his entrenchments, and to move

"WALK YOUR HORSES"

ONE OF THE GRIM JOKES OF WAR

AS PLAYED AT

CHESTERFIELD BRIDGE, NORTH ANNA

The sign posted by the local authorities at Taylor's bridge, where the Telegraph Road crosses the North Anna, was "Walk your horses." The wooden structure was referred to by the military as Chesterfield bridge. Here Hancock's Corps arrived toward evening of May 23d, and the Confederate entrenchments, showing in the foreground, were seized by the old "Berry Brigade." In the heat of the charge the Ninety-third New York carried their colors to the middle of the bridge, driving off the Confederates before they could destroy it. When the Federals began crossing next day they had to run the gantlet of musketry and artillery fire from the opposite bank. Several regiments of New York heavy artillery poured across the structure at the double-quick with the hostile shells bursting about their heads. When Captain Sleeper's Eighteenth Massachusetts battery began crossing, the Confederate cannoneers redoubled their efforts to blow up the ammunition by well-aimed shots. Sleeper passed over only one piece at a time in order to diminish the target and enforce the observance of the local law by walking his horses! The Second Corps got no further than the ridge beyond, where Lee's strong V formation held it from further advance.

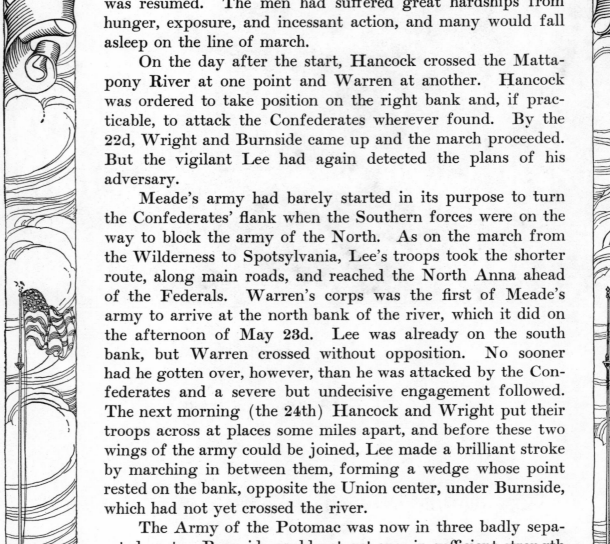

to the North Anna River. On the 20th of May the march was resumed. The men had suffered great hardships from hunger, exposure, and incessant action, and many would fall asleep on the line of march.

On the day after the start, Hancock crossed the Mattapony River at one point and Warren at another. Hancock was ordered to take position on the right bank and, if practicable, to attack the Confederates wherever found. By the 22d, Wright and Burnside came up and the march proceeded. But the vigilant Lee had again detected the plans of his adversary.

Meade's army had barely started in its purpose to turn the Confederates' flank when the Southern forces were on the way to block the army of the North. As on the march from the Wilderness to Spotsylvania, Lee's troops took the shorter route, along main roads, and reached the North Anna ahead of the Federals. Warren's corps was the first of Meade's army to arrive at the north bank of the river, which it did on the afternoon of May 23d. Lee was already on the south bank, but Warren crossed without opposition. No sooner had he gotten over, however, than he was attacked by the Confederates and a severe but undecisive engagement followed. The next morning (the 24th) Hancock and Wright put their troops across at places some miles apart, and before these two wings of the army could be joined, Lee made a brilliant stroke by marching in between them, forming a wedge whose point rested on the bank, opposite the Union center, under Burnside, which had not yet crossed the river.

The Army of the Potomac was now in three badly separated parts. Burnside could not get over in sufficient strength to reenforce the wings, and all attempts by the latter to aid him in so doing met with considerable disaster. The loss in these engagements approximated two thousand on each side.

On the 25th, Sheridan and his cavalry rejoined the army. They had been gone since the 9th and their raid was most

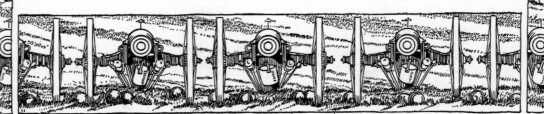

A SANITARY–COMMISSION NURSE AND HER PATIENTS AT FREDERICKSBURG,
MAY, 1864

More of the awful toll of 36,000 taken from the Union army during the terrible Wilderness campaign. The Sanitary Commission is visiting the field hospital established near the Rappahannock River, a mile or so from the heights, where lay at the same time the wounded from these terrific conflicts. Although the work of this Commission was only supplementary after 1862, they continued to supply many delicacies, and luxuries such as crutches, which did not form part of the regular medical corps paraphernalia. The effect of their work can be seen here, and also the appearance of men after the shock of gunshot wounds. All injuries during the war practically fell under three headings: incised and punctured wounds, comprising saber cuts, bayonet stabs, and sword thrusts; miscellaneous, from falls, blows from blunt weapons, and various accidents; lastly, and chiefly, gunshot wounds. The war came prior to the demonstration of the fact that the causes of disease and suppurative conditions are living organisms of microscopic size. Septicemia, erysipelas, lockjaw, and gangrene were variously attributed to dampness and a multitude of other conditions.

successful. Besides the decisive victory over the Confederate cavalry at Yellow Tavern, they had destroyed several depots of supplies, four trains of cars, and many miles of railroad track. Nearly four hundred Federal prisoners on their way to Richmond had been rescued from their captors. The dashing cavalrymen had even carried the first line of work around Richmond, and had made a detour down the James to communicate with General Butler. Grant was highly satisfied with Sheridan's performance. It had been of the greatest assistance to him, as it had drawn off the whole of the Confederate cavalry, and made the guarding of the wagon trains an easy matter.

But here, on the banks of the North Anna, Grant had been completely checkmated by Lee. He realized this and decided on a new move, although he still clung to his idea of turning the Confederate right. The Federal wings were withdrawn to the north side of the river during the night of May 26th and the whole set in motion for the Pamunkey River at Hanovertown. Two divisions of Sheridan's cavalry and Warren's corps were in advance. Lee lost no time in pursuing his great antagonist, but for the first time the latter was able to hold his lead. Along the Totopotomoy, on the afternoon of May 28th, infantry and cavalry of both armies met in a severe engagement in which the strong position of Lee's troops again foiled Grant's purpose. The Union would have to try at some other point, and on the 31st Sheridan's cavalry took possession of Cold Harbor. This was to be the next battleground.

A CHANGE OF BASE—THE CAVALRY SCREEN

This photograph of May 30, 1864, shows the Federal cavalry in actual operation of a most important func-
tion—the "screening" of the army's movements. The troopers are guarding the evacuation of Port Royal
on the Rappahannock, May 30, 1864. After the reverse to the Union arms at Spottsylvania, Grant ordered the change of base from the Rappahannock to McClellan's former starting-point, White House on
the Pamunkey. The control of the waterways, combined with Sheridan's efficient use of the cavalry, made
this an easy matter. Torbert's division encountered Gordon's brigade of Confederate cavalry at Hanovertown and drove it in the direction of Hanover Court House. Gregg's division moved up to this line; Russell's division of infantry encamped near the river-crossing in support, and behind the mask thus formed
the Army of the Potomac crossed the Pamunkey on May 28th unimpeded. Gregg was then ordered to reconnoiter towards Mechanicsville, and after a severe fight at Hawes' shop he succeeded (with the assistance of
Custer's brigade) in driving Hampton's and Fitzhugh Lee's cavalry divisions and Butler's brigade from the
field. Although the battle took place immediately in front of the Federal infantry, General Meade declined
to put the latter into action, and the battle was won by the cavalry alone. It was not to be the last time.

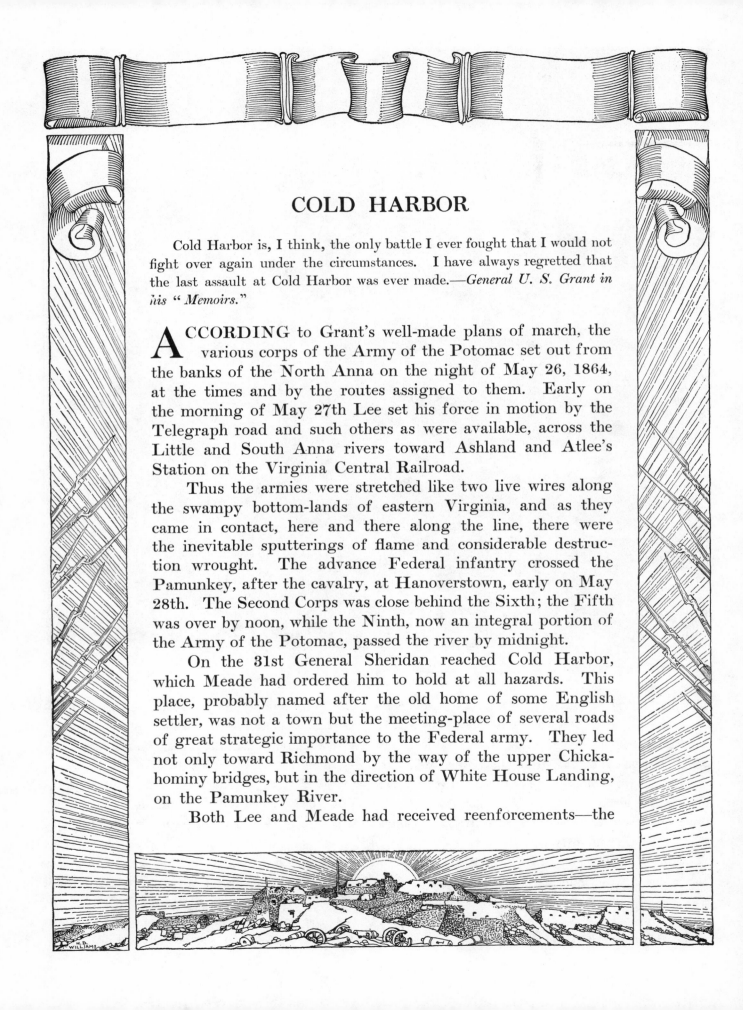

COLD HARBOR

Cold Harbor is, I think, the only battle I ever fought that I would not fight over again under the circumstances. I have always regretted that the last assault at Cold Harbor was ever made.—General U. S. Grant in his "Memoirs."

ACCORDING to Grant's well-made plans of march, the various corps of the Army of the Potomac set out from the banks of the North Anna on the night of May 26, 1864, at the times and by the routes assigned to them. Early on the morning of May 27th Lee set his force in motion by the Telegraph road and such others as were available, across the Little and South Anna rivers toward Ashland and Atlee's Station on the Virginia Central Railroad.

Thus the armies were stretched like two live wires along the swampy bottom-lands of eastern Virginia, and as they came in contact, here and there along the line, there were the inevitable sputterings of flame and considerable destruction wrought. The advance Federal infantry crossed the Pamunkey, after the cavalry, at Hanoverstown, early on May 28th. The Second Corps was close behind the Sixth; the Fifth was over by noon, while the Ninth, now an integral portion of the Army of the Potomac, passed the river by midnight.

On the 31st General Sheridan reached Cold Harbor, which Meade had ordered him to hold at all hazards. This place, probably named after the old home of some English settler, was not a town but the meeting-place of several roads of great strategic importance to the Federal army. They led not only toward Richmond by the way of the upper Chickahominy bridges, but in the direction of White House Landing, on the Pamunkey River.

Both Lee and Meade had received reenforcements—the

READY FOR THE ADVANCE THAT LEE DROVE BACK

Between these luxuriant banks stretch the pontoons and bridges to facilitate the rapid crossing of the North Anna by Hancock's Corps on May 24th. Thus was completed the passage to the south of the stream of the two wings of the Army of the Potomac. But when the center under Burnside was driven back and severely handled at Ox Ford, Grant immediately detached a brigade each from Hancock and Warren to attack the apex of Lee's wedge on the south bank of the river, but the position was too strong to justify the attempt. Then it dawned upon the Federal general-in-chief that Lee had cleaved the Army of the Potomac into two separated bodies. To reënforce either wing would require two crossings of the river, while Lee could quickly march troops from one side to the other within his impregnable wedge. As Grant put it in his report, "To make a direct attack from either wing would cause a slaughter of our men that even success would not justify."

former by Breckinridge, and the scattered forces in western Virginia, and by Pickett and Hoke from North Carolina. From Bermuda Hundred where General Butler was "bottled up "—to use a phrase which Grant employed and afterward regretted—General W. F. Smith was ordered to bring the Eighteenth Corps of the Army of the James to the assistance of Meade, since Butler could defend his position perfectly well with a small force, and could make no headway against Beauregard with a large one. Grant had now nearly one hundred and fourteen thousand troops and Lee about eighty thousand.

Sheridan's appearance at Cold Harbor was resented in vain by Fitzhugh Lee, and the next morning, June 1st, the Sixth Corps arrived, followed by General Smith and ten thousand men of the Eighteenth, who had hastened from the landing-place at White House. These took position on the right of the Sixth, and the Federal line was promptly faced by Longstreet's corps, a part of A. P. Hill's, and the divisions of Hoke and Breckinridge. At six o'clock in the afternoon Wright and Smith advanced to the attack, which Hoke and Kershaw received with courage and determination. The Confederate line was broken in several places, but before night checked the struggle the Southerners had in some degree regained their position. The short contest was a severe one for the Federal side. Wright lost about twelve hundred men and Smith one thousand.

The following day the final dispositions were made for the mighty struggle that would decide Grant's last chance to interpose between Lee and Richmond. Hancock and the Second Corps arrived at Cold Harbor and took position on the left of General Wright. Burnside, with the Ninth Corps, was placed near Bethesda Church on the road to Mechanicsville, while Warren, with the Fifth, came to his left and connected with Smith's right. Sheridan was sent to hold the lower Chickahominy bridges and to cover the road to White House,

IMPROVISED BREASTWORKS

The End of the Gray Line at Cold Harbor. Here at the extreme left of the Confederate lines at Cold Harbor is an example of the crude protection resorted to by the soldiers on both sides in advance or retreat. A momentary lull in the battle was invariably employed in strengthening each position. Trees were felled under fire, and fence rails gathered quickly were piled up to make possible another stand. The space between the lines at Cold Harbor was so narrow at many points as to resemble a road, encumbered with the dead and wounded. This extraordinary proximity induced a nervous alertness which made the troops peculiarly sensitive to night alarms; even small parties searching quietly for wounded comrades might begin a panic. A few scattering shots were often enough to start a heavy and continuous musketry fire and a roar of artillery along the entire line. It was a favorite ruse of the Federal soldiers to aim their muskets carefully to clear the top of the Confederate breastworks and then set up a great shout. The Confederates, deceived into the belief that an attack was coming, would spring up and expose themselves to the well-directed volley which thinned their ranks.

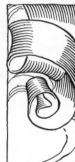

which was now the base of supplies. On the Southern side Ewell's corps, now commanded by General Early, faced Burnside's and Warren's. Longstreet's corps, still under Anderson, was opposite Wright and Smith, while A. P. Hill, on the extreme right, confronted Hancock. There was sharp fighting during the entire day, but Early did not succeed in getting upon the Federal right flank, as he attempted to do.

Both armies lay very close to each other and were well entrenched. Lee was naturally strong on his right, and his left was difficult of access, since it must be approached through wooded swamps. Well-placed batteries made artillery fire from front and both flanks possible, but Grant decided to attack the whole Confederate front, and word was sent to the corps commanders to assault at half-past four the following morning.

The hot sultry weather of the preceding days had brought much suffering. The movement of troops and wagons raised clouds of dust which settled down upon the sweltering men and beasts. But five o'clock on the afternoon of June 2d brought the grateful rain, and this continued during the night, giving great relief to the exhausted troops.

At the hour designated the Federal lines moved promptly from their shallow rifle-pits toward the Confederate works. The main assault was made by the Second, Sixth, and Eighteenth corps. With determined and firm step they started to cross the space between the opposing entrenchments. The silence of the dawning summer morning was broken by the screams of musket-ball and canister and shell. That move of the Federal battle-line opened the fiery furnace across the intervening space, which was, in the next instant, a Vesuvius, pouring tons and tons of steel and lead into the moving human mass. From front, from right and left, artillery crashed and swept the field, musketry and grape hewed and mangled and mowed down the line of blue as it moved on its approach.

COLD HARBOR

The battle of Cold Harbor on June 3d was the third tremendous engagement of Grant's campaign against Richmond within a month. It was also his costliest onset on Lee's veteran army. Grant had risked much in his change of base to the James in order to bring him nearer to Richmond and to the friendly hand which Butler with the Army of the James was in a position to reach out to him. Lee had again confronted him, entrenching himself but six miles from the outworks of Richmond, while the Chickahominy cut off any further flanking movement. There was nothing to do but fight it out, and Grant ordered an attack all along the line. On June 3d he hurled the Army of the Potomac against the inferior numbers of Lee, and in a brave assault upon the Confederate entrenchments, lost ten thousand men in twenty minutes.

Grant's assault at Cold Harbor was marked by the gallantry of General Hancock's division and of the brigades of Gibbon and Barlow, who

WHERE TEN THOUSAND FELL

FEDERAL CAMP AT COLD HARBOR AFTER THE BATTLE

on the left of the Federal line charged up the ascent in their front upon the concentrated artillery of the Confederates; they took the position and held it for a moment under a galling fire, which finally drove them back, but not until they had captured a flag and three hundred prisoners. The battle was substantially over by half-past seven in the morning, but sullen fighting continued throughout the day. About noontime General Grant, who had visited all the corps commanders to see for himself the positions gained and what could be done, concluded that the Confederates were too strongly entrenched to be dislodged and ordered that further offensive action should cease. All the next day the dead and wounded lay on the field uncared for while both armies warily watched each other. The lower picture was taken during this weary wait. Not till the 7th was a satisfactory truce arranged, and then all but two of the wounded Federals had died. No wonder that Grant wrote, "I have always regretted that the last assault at Cold Harbor was ever made."

THE BUSIEST PLACE IN DIXIE

City Point, just after its capture by Butler. From June, 1864, until April, 1865, City Point, at the juncture of the Appomattox and the James, was a point of entry and departure for more vessels than any city of the South including even New Orleans in times of peace. Here landed supplies that kept an army numbering, with fighting force and supernumeraries, nearly one hundred and twenty thousand well-supplied, well-fed, well-contented, and well-munitioned men in the field. This was the marvelous base —safe from attack, secure from molestation. It was meals and money that won at Petersburg, the bravery of full stomachs and warm-clothed bodies against the desperation of starved and shivering out-numbered men. A glance at this picture tells the story. There is no need of rehearsing charges, counter-charges, mines, and counter-mines. Here lies the reason—Petersburg had to fall. As we look back with a retro- spective eye on this scene of plenty and abundance, well may the American heart be proud that only a few miles away were men of their own blood enduring the hardships that the defenders of Petersburg suffered in the last campaign of starvation against numbers and plenty.

THE FORCES AT LAST JOIN HANDS

Charles City Court House on the James River, June 14, 1864. It was with infinite relief that Grant saw the advance of the Army of the Potomac reach this point on June 14th. His last flanking movement was an extremely hazardous one. More than fifty miles intervened between him and Butler by the roads he would have to travel, and he had to cross both the Chickahominy and the James, which were unbridged. The paramount difficulty was to get the Army of the Potomac out of its position before Lee, who confronted it at Cold Harbor. Lee had the shorter line and better roads to move over and meet Grant at the Chickahominy, or he might, if he chose, descend rapidly on Butler and crush him before Grant could unite with him. "But," says Grant, "the move had to be made, and I relied upon Lee's not seeing my danger as I saw it." Near the old Charles City Court House the crossing of the James was successfully accomplished, and on the 14th Grant took steamer and ran up the river to Bermuda Hundred to see General Butler and direct the movement against Petersburg, that began the final investment of that city.

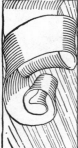

Meade issued orders for the suspension of all further offensive operations.

A word remains to be said as to fortunes of Burnside's and Warren's forces, which were on the Federal right. Generals Potter and Willcox of the Ninth Corps made a quick capture of Early's advanced rifle-pits and were waiting for the order to advance on his main entrenchments, when the order of suspension arrived. Early fell upon him later in the day but was repulsed. Warren, on the left of Burnside, drove Rodes' division back and repulsed Gordon's brigade, which had attacked him. The commander of the Fifth Corps reported that his line was too extended for further operations and Birney's division was sent from the Second Corps to his left. But by the time this got into position the battle of Cold Harbor was practically over.

The losses to the Federal army in this battle and the engagements which preceded it were over seventeen thousand, while the Confederate loss did not exceed one-fifth of that number. Grant had failed in his plan to destroy Lee north of the James River, and saw that he must now cross it.

Thirty days had passed in the campaign since the Wilderness and the grand total in losses to Grant's army in killed, wounded, and missing was 54,929. The losses in Lee's army were never accurately given, but they were very much less in proportion to the numerical strength of the two armies. If Grant had inflicted punishment upon his foe equal to that suffered by the Federal forces, Lee's army would have been practically annihilated.

The Federal general-in-chief had decided to secure Petersburg and confront Lee once more. General Gillmore was sent by Butler, with cavalry and infantry, on June 10th to make the capture, but was unsuccessful. Thereupon General Smith and the Eighteenth Corps were despatched to White House Landing to go forward by water and reach Petersburg before Lee had time to reenforce it.

[Part XII]

TO ATLANTA

Johnston was an officer who, by the common consent of the military men of both sides, was reckoned second only to Lee, if second, in the qualities which fit an officer for the responsibility of great commands. . . . He practised a lynx-eyed watchfulness of his adversary, tempting him constantly to assault his entrenchments, holding his fortified positions to the last moment, but choosing that last moment so well as to save nearly every gun and wagon in the final withdrawal, and always presenting a front covered by such defenses that one man in the line was, by all sound military rules, equal to three or four in the attack. In this way he constantly neutralized the superiority of force his opponent wielded, and made his campaign from Dalton to the Chattahoochee a model of defensive warfare. It is Sherman's glory that, with a totally different temperament, he accepted his adversary's game, and played it with a skill that was finally successful, as we shall see.—*Major-General Jacob D. Cox, U.S.V., in "Atlanta."*

THE two leading Federal generals of the war, Grant and Sherman, met at Nashville, Tennessee, on March 17, 1864, and arranged for a great concerted double movement against the two main Southern armies, the Army of Northern Virginia and the Army of Tennessee. Grant, who had been made commander of all the Federal armies, was to take personal charge of the Army of the Potomac and move against Lee, while to Sherman, whom, at Grant's request, President Lincoln had placed at the head of the Military Division of the Mississippi, he turned over the Western army, which was to proceed against Johnston.

It was decided, moreover, that the two movements were to be simultaneous and that they were to begin early in May. Sherman concentrated his forces around Chattanooga on the Tennessee River, where the Army of the Cumberland had

spent the winter, and where a decisive battle had been fought some months before, in the autumn of 1863. His army was composed of three parts, or, more properly, of three armies operating in concert. These were the Army of the Tennessee, led by General James B. McPherson; the Army of Ohio, under General John M. Schofield, and the Army of the Cumberland, commanded by General George H. Thomas. The last named was much larger than the other two combined. The triple army aggregated the grand total of ninety-nine thousand men, six thousand of whom were cavalrymen, while four thousand four hundred and sixty belonged to the artillery. There were two hundred and fifty-four heavy guns.

Soon to be pitted against Sherman's army was that of General Joseph E. Johnston, which had spent the winter at Dalton, in the State of Georgia, some thirty miles southeast of Chattanooga. It was by chance that Dalton became the winter quarters of the Confederate army. In the preceding autumn, when General Bragg had been defeated on Missionary Ridge and driven from the vicinity of Chattanooga, he retreated to Dalton and stopped for a night's rest. Discovering the next morning that he was not pursued, he there remained. Some time later he was superseded by General Johnston.

By telegraph, General Sherman was apprised of the time when Grant was to move upon Lee on the banks of the Rapidan, in Virginia, and he prepared to move his own army at the same time. But he was two days behind Grant, who began his Virginia campaign on May 4th. Sherman broke camp on the 6th and led his legions across hill and valley, forest and stream, toward the Confederate stronghold. Nature was all abloom with the opening of a Southern spring and the soldiers, who had long chafed under their enforced idleness, now rejoiced at the exhilarating journey before them, though their mission was to be one of strife and bloodshed.

Johnston's army numbered about fifty-three thousand,

SHERMAN IN 1865

If Sherman was deemed merciless in war, he was superbly generous when the fighting was over. To Joseph E. Johnston he offered most liberal terms of surrender for the Southern armies. Their acceptance would have gone far to prevent the worst of the reconstruction enormities. Unfortunately his first convention with Johnston was disapproved. The death of Lincoln had removed the guiding hand that would have meant so much to the nation. To those who have read his published correspondence and his memoirs Sherman appears in a very human light. He was fluent and frequently reckless in speech and writing, but his kindly humanity is seen in both.

and was divided into two corps, under the respective commands of Generals John B. Hood and William J. Hardee. But General Polk was on his way to join them, and in a few days Johnston had in the neighborhood of seventy thousand men. His position at Dalton was too strong to be carried by a front attack, and Sherman was too wise to attempt it. Leaving Thomas and Schofield to make a feint at Johnston's front, Sherman sent McPherson on a flanking movement by the right to occupy Snake Creek Gap, a mountain pass near Resaca, which is about eighteen miles below Dalton.

Sherman, with the main part of the army, soon occupied Tunnel Hill, which faces Rocky Face Ridge, an eastern range of the Cumberland Mountains, north of Dalton, on which a large part of Johnston's army was posted. The Federal leader had little or no hope of dislodging his great antagonist from this impregnable position, fortified by rocks and cliffs which no army could scale while under fire. But he ordered that demonstrations be made at several places, especially at a pass known as Rocky Face Gap. This was done with great spirit and bravery, the men clambering over rocks and across ravines in the face of showers of bullets and even of masses of stone hurled down from the heights above them. On the whole they won but little advantage.

During the 8th and 9th of May, these operations were continued, the Federals making but little impression on the Confederate stronghold. Meanwhile, on the Dalton road there was a sharp cavalry fight, the Federal commander, General E. M. McCook, having encountered General Wheeler. McCook's advance brigade under Colonel La Grange was defeated and La Grange was made prisoner.

Sherman's chief object in these demonstrations, it will be seen, was so to engage Johnston as to prevent his intercepting McPherson in the latter's movement upon Resaca. In this Sherman was successful, and by the 11th he was giving his whole energy to moving the remainder of his forces by the

In the upper picture rises the precipitous height of Rocky Face as Sherman saw it on May 7, 1864. His troops under Thomas had moved forward along the line of the railroad, opening the great Atlanta campaign on schedule time. Looking down into the gorge called Buzzard's Roost, through which the railroad passes, Sherman could see swarms of Confederate troops, the road filled with obstructions, and hostile batteries crowning the cliffs on either side. He knew that his antagonist, Joe Johnston, here confronted him in force. But it was to be a campaign of brilliant flanking movements, and Sherman sat quietly down to wait till the trusty McPherson should execute the first one.

BUZZARD'S ROOST, GEORGIA, MAY 7, 1864

In the lower picture, drawn up on dress parade, stands one of the finest fighting organizations in the Atlanta campaign. This regiment won its spurs in the first Union victory in the West at Mill Springs, Kentucky, January 19, 1862. There, according to the muster-out roll, "William Blake, musician, threw away his drum and took a gun." The spirit of this drummer boy of Company F was the spirit of all the troops from Minnesota. A Georgian noticed an unusually fine body of men marching by, and when told that they were a Minnesota regiment, said, "I didn't know they had any troops up there." But the world was to learn the superlative fighting qualities of the men from the Northwest. Sherman was glad to have all he could get of them in this great army of one hundred thousand veterans.

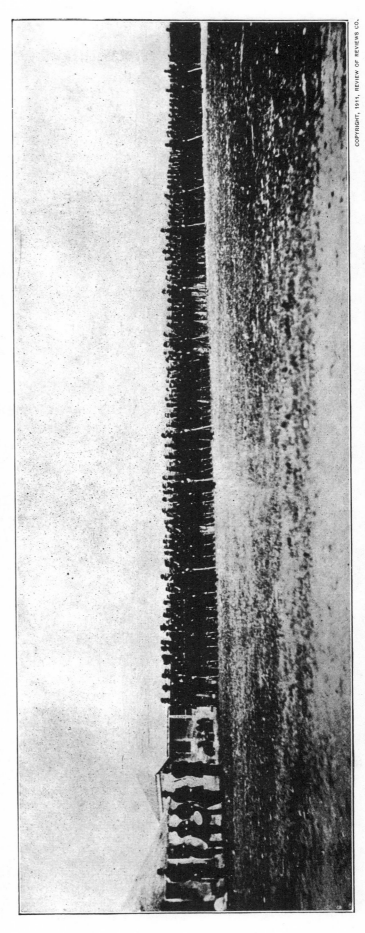

THE SECOND MINNESOTA INFANTRY—ENGAGED AT ROCKY FACE RIDGE, MAY 8-11, 1864

right flank, as McPherson had done, to Resaca, leaving a detachment of General O. O. Howard's Fourth Corps to occupy Dalton when evacuated. When Johnston discovered this, he was quick to see that he must abandon his entrenchments and intercept Sherman. Moving by the only two good roads, Johnston beat Sherman in the race to Resaca. The town had been fortified, owing to Johnston's foresight, and McPherson had failed to dislodge the garrison and capture it. The Confederate army was now settled behind its entrenchments, occupying a semicircle of low wooded hills, both flanks of the army resting on the banks of the Oostenaula River.

On the morning of May 14th, the Confederate works were invested by the greater part of Sherman's army and it was evident that a battle was imminent. The attack was begun about noon, chiefly by the Fourteenth Army Corps under Palmer, of Thomas' army, and Judah's division of Schofield's. General Hindman's division of Hood's corps bore the brunt of this attack and there was heavy loss on both sides. Later in the day, a portion of Hood's corps was massed in a heavy column and hurled against the Federal left, driving it back. But at this point the Twentieth Army Corps under Hooker, of Thomas' army, dashed against the advancing Confederates and pushed them back to their former lines.

The forenoon of the next day was spent in heavy skirmishing, which grew to the dignity of a battle. During the day's operations a hard fight for a Confederate lunette on the top of a low hill occurred. At length, General Butterfield, in the face of a galling fire, succeeded in capturing the position. But so deadly was the fire from Hardee's corps that Butterfield was unable to hold it or to remove the four guns the lunette contained.

With the coming of night, General Johnston determined to withdraw his army from Resaca. The battle had cost each army nearly three thousand men. While it was in progress, McPherson, sent by Sherman, had deftly marched around

IN THE FOREFRONT—GENERAL RICHARD W. JOHNSON AT GRAYSVILLE

On the balcony of this little cottage at Graysville, Georgia, stands General Richard W. Johnson, ready to advance with his cavalry division in the vanguard of the direct movement upon the Confederates strongly posted at Dalton. Sherman's cavalry forces under Stoneman and Garrard were not yet fully equipped and joined the army after the campaign had opened. General Richard W. Johnson's division of Thomas' command, with General Palmer's division, was given the honor of heading the line of march when the Federals got in motion on May 5th. The same troops (Palmer's division) had made the same march in February, sent by Grant to engage Johnston at Dalton during Sherman's Meridian campaign. Johnson was a West Pointer; he had gained his cavalry training in the Mexican War, and had fought the Indians on the Texas border. He distinguished himself at Corinth, and rapidly rose to the command of a division in Buell's army. Fresh from a Confederate prison, he joined the Army of the Cumberland in the summer of 1862 to win new laurels at Stone's River, Chickamauga, and Missionary Ridge. His sabers were conspicuously active in the Atlanta campaign; and at the battle of New Hope Church on May 28th Johnson himself was wounded, but recovered in time to join Schofield after the fall of Atlanta and to assist him in driving Hood and Forrest out of Tennessee. For his bravery at the battle of Nashville he was brevetted brigadier-general, U. S. A., December 16, 1864, and after the war he was retired with the brevet of major-general.

Johnston's left with the view of cutting off his retreat south by seizing the bridges across the Oostenaula, and at the same time the Federal cavalry was threatening the railroad to Atlanta which ran beyond the river. It was the knowledge of these facts that determined the Confederate commander to abandon Resaca. Withdrawing during the night, he led his army southward to the banks of the Etowah River. Sherman followed but a few miles behind him. At the same time Sherman sent a division of the Army of the Cumberland, under General Jeff. C. Davis, to Rome, at the junction of the Etowah and the Oostenaula, where there were important machine-shops and factories. Davis captured the town and several heavy guns, destroyed the factories, and left a garrison to hold it.

Sherman was eager for a battle in the open with Johnston and on the 17th, near the town of Adairsville, it seemed as if the latter would gratify him. Johnston chose a good position, posted his cavalry, deployed his infantry, and awaited combat. The Union army was at hand. The skirmishing for some hours almost amounted to a battle. But suddenly Johnston decided to defer a conclusive contest to another time.

Again at Cassville, a few days later, Johnston drew up the Confederate legions in battle array, evidently having decided on a general engagement at this point. He issued a spirited address to the army: "By your courage and skill you have repulsed every assault of the enemy. . . . You will now turn and march to meet his advancing columns. . . . I lead you to battle." But, when his right flank had been turned by a Federal attack, and when two of his corps commanders, Hood and Polk, advised against a general battle, Johnston again decided on postponement. He retreated in the night across the Etowah, destroyed the bridges, and took a strong position among the rugged hills about Allatoona Pass, extending south to Kenesaw Mountain.

Johnston's decision to fight and then not to fight was a

RESACA—FIELD OF THE FIRST HEAVY FIGHTING

The chips are still bright and the earth fresh turned, in the foreground where are the Confederate earthworks such as General Joseph E. Johnston had caused to be thrown up by the Negro laborers all along his line of possible retreat. McPherson, sent by Sherman to strike the railroad in Johnston's rear, got his head of column through Snake Creek Gap on May 9th, and drove off a Confederate cavalry brigade which retreated toward Dalton, bringing to Johnston the first news that a heavy force of Federals was already in his rear. McPherson, within a mile and a half of Resaca, could have walked into the town with his twenty-three thousand men, but concluded that the Confederate entrenchments were too strongly held to assault. When Sherman arrived he found that Johnston, having the shorter route, was there ahead of him with his entire army strongly posted. On May 15th, "without attempting to assault the fortified works," says Sherman, "we pressed at all points, and the sound of cannon and musketry rose all day to the dignity of a battle." Its havoc is seen in the shattered trees and torn ground in the lower picture.

THE WORK OF THE FIRING AT RESACA

cause for grumbling both on the part of his army and of the inhabitants of the region through which he was passing. His men were eager to defend their country, and they could not understand this Fabian policy. They would have preferred defeat to these repeated retreats with no opportunity to show what they could do.

Johnston, however, was wiser than his critics. The Union army was larger by far and better equipped than his own, and Sherman was a master-strategist. His hopes rested on two or three contingencies—that he might catch a portion of Sherman's army separated from the rest; that Sherman would be so weakened by the necessity of guarding the long line of railroad to his base of supplies at Chattanooga, Nashville, and even far-away Louisville, as to make it possible to defeat him in open battle, or, finally, that Sherman might fall into the trap of making a direct attack while Johnston was in an impregnable position, and in such a situation he now was.

Not yet, however, was Sherman inclined to fall into such a trap, and when Johnston took his strong position at and beyond Allatoona Pass, the Northern commander decided, after resting his army for a few days, to move toward Atlanta by way of Dallas, southwest of the pass. Rations for a twenty days' absence from direct railroad communication were issued to the Federal army. In fact, Sherman's railroad connection with the North was the one delicate problem of the whole movement. The Confederates had destroyed the iron way as they moved southward; but the Federal engineers, following the army, repaired the line and rebuilt the bridges almost as fast as the army could march.

Sherman's movement toward Dallas drew Johnston from the slopes of the Allatoona Hills. From Kingston, the Federal leader wrote on May 23d, " I am already within fifty miles of Atlanta." But he was not to enter that city for many weeks, not before he had measured swords again and again with his great antagonist. On the 25th of May, the two great

ANOTHER RETROGRADE MOVEMENT OVER THE ETOWAH BRIDGE

The strong works in the pictures, commanding the railroad bridge over the Etowah River, were the fourth fortified position to be abandoned by Johnston within a month. Pursued by Thomas from Resaca, he had made a brief stand at Kingston and then fallen back steadily and in superb order into Cassville. There he issued an address to his army announcing his purpose to retreat no more but to accept battle. His troops were all drawn up in preparation for a struggle, but that night at supper with Generals Hood and Polk he was convinced by them that the ground occupied by their troops was untenable, being enfiladed by the Federal artillery. Johnston, therefore, gave up his purpose of battle, and on the night of May 20th put the Etowah River between himself and Sherman and retreated to Allatoona Pass, shown in the lower picture.

In taking this the camera was planted inside the breastworks seen on the eminence in the upper picture. Sherman's army now rested after its rapid advance and waited a few days for the railroad to be repaired in their rear so that supplies could be brought up. Meanwhile Johnston was being severely criticized at the South for his continual falling back without risking a battle. His friends stoutly maintained that it was all strategic, while some of the Southern newspapers quoted the Federal General Scott's remark, "Beware of Lee advancing, and watch Johnston at a stand; for the devil himself would be defeated in the attempt to whip him retreating." But General Jeff C. Davis, sent by Sherman, took Rome on May 17th and destroyed valuable mills and foundries. Thus began the accomplishment of one of the main objects of Sherman's march.

ALLATOONA PASS IN THE DISTANCE

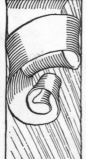

armies were facing each other near New Hope Church, about four miles north of Dallas. Here, for three or four days, there was almost incessant fighting, though there was not what might be called a pitched battle.

Late in the afternoon of the first day, Hooker made a vicious attack on Stewart's division of Hood's corps. For two hours the battle raged without a moment's cessation, Hooker being pressed back with heavy loss. During those two hours he had held his ground against sixteen field-pieces and five thousand infantry at close range. The name " Hell Hole " was applied to this spot by the Union soldiers.

On the next day there was considerable skirmishing in different places along the line that divided the two armies. But the chief labor of the day was throwing up entrenchments, preparatory to a general engagement. The country, however, was ill fitted for such a contest. The continuous succession of hills, covered with primeval forests, presented little opportunity for two great armies, stretched out almost from Dallas to Marietta, a distance of about ten miles, to come together simultaneously at all points.

A severe contest occurred on the 27th, near the center of the battle-lines, between General O. O. Howard on the Federal side and General Patrick Cleburne on the part of the South. Dense and almost impenetrable was the undergrowth through which Howard led his troops to make the attack. The fight was at close range and was fierce and bloody, the Confederates gaining the greater advantage.

The next day Johnston made a terrific attack on the Union right, under McPherson, near Dallas. But McPherson was well entrenched and the Confederates were repulsed with a serious loss. In the three or four days' fighting the Federal loss was probably twenty-four hundred men and the Confederate somewhat greater.

In the early days of June, Sherman took possession of the town of Allatoona and made it a second base of supplies,

PINE MOUNTAIN, WHERE POLK, THE FIGHTING BISHOP OF THE CONFEDERACY, WAS KILLED

The blasted pine rears its gaunt height above the mountain slope, covered with trees slashed down to hold the Federals at bay; and here, on June 14, 1864, the Confederacy lost a commander, a bishop, and a hero. Lieut.-General Leonidas Polk, commanding one of Johnston's army corps, with Johnston himself and Hardee, another corps commander, was studying Sherman's position at a tense moment of the latter's advance around Pine Mountain. The three Confederates stood upon the rolling height, where the center of Johnston's army awaited the Federal attack. They could see the columns in blue pushing east of them; the smoke and rattle of musketry as the pickets were driven in; and the bustle with which the Federal advance guard felled trees and constructed trenches at their very feet. On the lonely height the three figures stood conspicuous. A Federal order was given the artillery to open upon any men in gray who looked like officers reconnoitering the new position. So, while Hardee was pointing to his comrade and his chief the danger of one of his divisions which the Federal advance was cutting off, the bishop-general was struck in the chest by a cannon shot. Thus the Confederacy lost a leader of unusual influence. Although a bishop of the Episcopal Church, Polk was educated at West Point. When he threw in his lot with the Confederacy, thousands of his fellow-Louisianians followed him. A few days before the battle of Pine Mountain, as he and General Hood were riding together, the bishop was told by his companion that he had never been received into the communion of a church and was begged that the rite might be performed. Immediately Polk arranged the ceremony. At Hood's headquarters, by the light of a tallow candle, with a tin basin on the mess table for a baptismal font, and with Hood's staff present as witnesses, all was ready. Hood, "with a face like that of an old crusader," stood before the bishop. Crippled by wounds at Gaines' Mill, Gettysburg, and Chickamauga, he could not kneel, but bent forward on his crutches. The bishop, in full uniform of the Confederate army, administered the rite. A few days later, by a strange coincidence, he was approached by General Johnston on the same errand, and the man whom Hood was soon to succeed was baptized in the same simple manner. Polk, as Bishop, had administered his last baptism, and as soldier had fought his last battle; for Pine Mountain was near.

LIEUT.-GEN. LEONIDAS POLK, C.S.A.

after repairing the railroad bridge across the Etowah River. Johnston swung his left around to Lost Mountain and his right extended beyond the railroad—a line ten miles in length and much too long for its numbers. Johnston's army, however, had been reenforced, and it now numbered about seventy-five thousand men. Sherman, on June 1st, had nearly one hundred and thirteen thousand men and on the 8th he received the addition of a cavalry brigade and two divisions of the Seventeenth Corps, under General Frank P. Blair, which had marched from Alabama.

So multifarious were the movements of the two great armies among the hills and forests of that part of Georgia that it is impossible for us to follow them all. On the 14th of June, Generals Johnston, Hardee, and Polk rode up the slope of Pine Mountain to reconnoiter. As they were standing, making observations, a Federal battery in the distance opened on them and General Polk was struck in the chest with a Parrot shell. He was killed instantly.

General Polk was greatly beloved, and his death caused a shock to the whole Confederate army. He was a graduate of West Point; but after being graduated he took orders in the church and for twenty years before the war was Episcopal Bishop of Louisiana. At the outbreak of the war he entered the field and served with distinction to the moment of his death.

During the next two weeks there was almost incessant fighting, heavy skirmishing, sparring for position. It was a wonderful game of military strategy, played among the hills and mountains and forests by two masters in the art of war. On June 23d, Sherman wrote, "The whole country is one vast fort, and Johnston must have full fifty miles of connected trenches. . . . Our lines are now in close contact, and the fighting incessant. . . . As fast as we gain one position, the enemy has another all ready."

Sherman, conscious of superior strength, was now anxious for a real battle, a fight to the finish with his antagonist.

IN THE HARDEST FIGHT OF THE CAMPAIGN—THE ONE-HUNDRED-AND-TWENTY-FIFTH OHIO

During the dark days before Kenesaw it rained continually, and Sherman speaks of the peculiarly depressing effect that the weather had upon his troops in the wooded country. Nevertheless he must either assault Johnston's strong position on the mountain or begin again his flanking tactics. He decided upon the former, and on June 27th, after three days' preparation, the assault was made. At nine in the morning along the Federal lines the furious fire of musketry and artillery was begun, but at all points the Confederates met it with determined courage and in great force. McPherson's attacking column, under General Blair, fought its way up the face of little Kenesaw but could not reach the summit. Then the courageous troops of Thomas charged up the face of the mountain and planted their colors on the very parapet of the Confederate works. Here General Harker, commanding the brigade in which fought the 125th Ohio, fell mortally wounded, as did Brigadier-General Daniel McCook, and also General Wagner.

FEDERAL ENTRENCHMENTS AT THE FOOT OF KENESAW MOUNTAIN

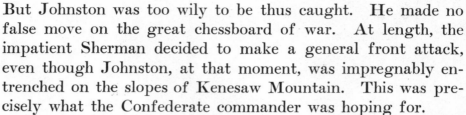

To Atlanta—Sherman vs. Johnston ❖ ❖

But Johnston was too wily to be thus caught. He made no false move on the great chessboard of war. At length, the impatient Sherman decided to make a general front attack, even though Johnston, at that moment, was impregnably entrenched on the slopes of Kenesaw Mountain. This was precisely what the Confederate commander was hoping for.

The desperate battle of Kenesaw Mountain occurred on the 27th of June. In the early morning hours, the boom of Federal cannon announced the opening of a bloody day's struggle. It was soon answered by the Confederate batteries in the entrenchments along the mountain side, and the deafening roar of the giant conflict reverberated from the surrounding hills. About nine o'clock the Union infantry advance began. On the left was McPherson, who sent the Fifteenth Army Corps, led by General John A. Logan, directly against the mountain. The artillery from the Confederate trenches in front of Logan cut down his men by hundreds. The Federals charged courageously and captured the lower works, but failed to take the higher ridges.

The chief assault of the day was by the Army of the Cumberland, under Thomas. Most conspicuous in the attack were the divisions of Newton and Davis, advancing against General Loring, successor of the lamented Polk. Far up on a ridge at one point, General Cleburne held a line of breastworks, supported by the flanking fire of artillery. Against this a vain and costly assault was made.

When the word was given to charge, the Federals sprang forward and, in the face of a deadly hail of musket-balls and shells, they dashed up the slope, firing as they went. Stunned and bleeding, they were checked again and again by the withering fire from the mountain slope; but they re-formed and pressed on with dauntless valor. Some of them reached the parapets and were instantly shot down, their bodies rolling into the Confederate trenches among the men who had slain them, or back down the hill whence they had come. General

A VETERAN BATTERY FROM ILLINOIS, NEAR MARIETTA IN THE ATLANTA

CAMPAIGN

Battery B of the First Illinois Light Artillery followed Sherman in the Atlanta campaign.   It took part in the demonstrations against Resaca, Georgia, May 8 to 15, 1864, and in the battle of Resaca on the 14th and 15th. It was in the battles about Dallas from May 25th to June 5th, and took part in the operations about Marietta and against Kenesaw Mountain in June and July.   During the latter period this photograph was taken. The battery did not go into this campaign without previous experience.   It had already fought as one of the eight batteries at Fort Henry and Fort Donelson, heard the roar of the battle of Shiloh, and participated in the sieges of Corinth and Vicksburg.   The artillery in the West was not a whit less necessary to the armies than that in the East.   Pope's brilliant feat of arms in the capture of Island No. 10 added to the growing respect in which the artillery was held by the other arms of the service.   The effective fire of the massed batteries at Murfreesboro turned the tide of battle.   At Chickamauga the Union artillery inflicted fearful losses upon the Confederates.   At Atlanta again they counted their dead by the hundreds, and at Franklin and Nashville the guns maintained the best traditions of the Western armies.   They played no small part in winning battles.

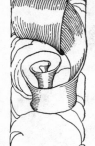

Harker, leading a charge against Cleburne, was mortally wounded. His men were swept back by a galling fire, though many fell with their brave leader.

This assault on Kenesaw Mountain cost Sherman three thousand men and won him nothing. Johnston's loss probably exceeded five hundred. The battle continued but two and a half hours. It was one of the most recklessly daring assaults during the whole war period, but did not greatly affect the final result of the campaign.

Under a flag of truce, on the day after the battle, the men of the North and of the South met on the gory field to bury their dead and to minister to the wounded. They met as friends for the moment, and not as foes. It was said that there were instances of father and son, one in blue and the other in gray, and brothers on opposite sides, meeting one another on the bloody slopes of Kenesaw. Tennessee and Kentucky had sent thousands of men to each side in the fratricidal struggle and not infrequently families had been divided.

Three weeks of almost incessant rain fell upon the struggling armies during this time, rendering their operations disagreeable and unsatisfactory. The camp equipage, the men's uniforms and accouterments were thoroughly saturated with rain and mud. Still the warriors of the North and of the South lived and fought on the slopes of the mountain range, intent on destroying each other.

Sherman was convinced by his drastic repulse at Kenesaw Mountain that success lay not in attacking his great antagonist in a strong position, and he resumed his old tactics. He would flank Johnston from Kenesaw as he had flanked him out of Dalton and Allatoona Pass. He thereupon turned upon Johnston's line of communication with Atlanta, whence the latter received his supplies. The movement was successful, and in a few days Kenesaw Mountain was deserted.

Johnston moved to the banks of the Chattahoochee,

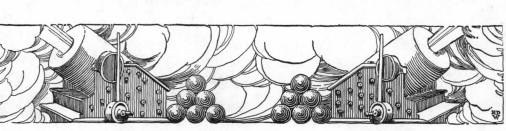

THOMAS' HEADQUARTERS NEAR MARIETTA DURING THE FIGHTING OF
THE FOURTH OF JULY

This is a photograph of Independence Day, 1864. As the sentries and staff officers stand outside the sheltered tents, General Thomas, commanding the Army of the Cumberland, is busy; for the fighting is fierce to-day. Johnston has been outflanked from Kenesaw and has fallen back eastward until he is actually farther from Atlanta than Sherman's right flank. Who will reach the Chattahoochee first? There, if anywhere, Johnston must make his stand; he must hold the fords and ferries, and the fortifications that, with the wisdom of a far-seeing commander, he has for a long time been preparing. The rustic work in the photograph, which embowers the tents of the commanding general and his staff, is the sort of thing that Civil War soldiers had learned to throw up within an hour after pitching camp.

PALISADES AND *CHEVAUX–DE–FRISE* GUARDING ATLANTA

At last Sherman is before Atlanta.   The photograph shows one of the keypoints in the Confederate defense, the fort at the head of Marietta Street, toward which the Federal lines were advancing from the northwest.   The old Potter house in the background, once a quiet, handsome country seat, is now surrounded by bristling fortifications, palisades, and double lines of *chevaux-de-frise*.   Atlanta was engaged in the final grapple with the force that was to overcome her.   Sherman has fought his way past Kenesaw and across the Chattahoochee, through a country which he describes as "one vast fort," saying that "Johnston must have at least fifty miles of connected trenches with abatis and finished batteries."   Anticipating that Sherman might drive him back upon Atlanta, Johnston had constructed, during the winter, heavily fortified positions all the way from Dalton.   During his two months in retreat the fortifications at Atlanta had been strengthened to the utmost.   What he might have done behind them was never to be known.

THE CHATTAHOOCHEE BRIDGE

"One of the strongest pieces of field fortification I ever saw"—this was Sherman's characterization of the entrenchments that guarded the railroad bridge over the Chattahoochee on July 5th. A glimpse of the bridge and the freshly-turned earth in 1864 is given by the upper picture. At this river Johnston made his final effort to hold back Sherman from a direct attack upon Atlanta. If Sherman could get successfully across that river, the Confederates would be compelled to fall back behind the defenses of the city, which was the objective of the campaign. Sherman perceived at once the futility of trying to carry by assault this strongly garrisoned position. Instead, he made a feint at crossing the river lower down, and simultaneously went to work in earnest eight miles north of the bridge. The lower picture shows the canvas pontoon boats as perfected by Union engineers in 1864. A number of these were stealthily set up and launched by Sherman's Twenty-third Corps near the mouth of Soap Creek, behind a ridge. Byrd's brigade took the defenders of the southern bank completely by surprise. It was short work for the Federals to throw pontoon bridges across and to occupy the coveted spot in force.

INFANTRY AND ARTILLERY CROSSING ON BOATS MADE OF PONTOONS.

Sherman following in the hope of catching him while crossing the river. But the wary Confederate had again, as at Resaca, prepared entrenchments in advance, and these were on the north bank of the river. He hastened to them, then turned on the approaching Federals and defiantly awaited attack. But Sherman remembered Kenesaw and there was no battle.

The feints, the sparring, the flanking movements among the hills and forests continued day after day. The immediate aim in the early days of July was to cross the Chattahoochee. On the 8th, Sherman sent Schofield and McPherson across, ten miles or more above the Confederate position. Johnston crossed the next day. Thomas followed later.

Sherman's position was by no means reassuring. It is true he had, in the space of two months, pressed his antagonist back inch by inch for more than a hundred miles and was now almost within sight of the goal of the campaign— the city of Atlanta. But the single line of railroad that connected him with the North and brought supplies from Louisville, five hundred miles away, for a hundred thousand men and twenty-three thousand animals, might at any moment be destroyed by Confederate raiders.

The necessity of guarding the Western and Atlantic Railroad was an ever-present concern with Sherman. Forrest and his cavalry force were in northern Mississippi waiting for him to get far enough on the way to Atlanta for them to pounce upon the iron way and tear it to ruins. To prevent this General Samuel D. Sturgis, with eight thousand troops, was sent from Memphis against Forrest. He met him on the 10th of June near Guntown, Mississippi, but was sadly beaten and driven back to Memphis, one hundred miles away. The affair, nevertheless, delayed Forrest in his operations against the railroad, and meanwhile General Smith's troops returned to Memphis from the Red River expedition, somewhat late according to the schedule but eager to join Sherman in the advance on Atlanta. Smith, however, was directed to

Johnston's parrying of Sherman's mighty strokes was "a model of defensive warfare," declares one of Sherman's own division commanders, Jacob D. Cox. There was not a man in the Federal army from Sherman down that did not rejoice to hear that Johnston had been superseded by Hood on July 18th. Johnston, whose mother was a niece of Patrick Henry, was fifty-seven years old, cold in manner, measured and accurate in speech. His dark firm face, surmounted by a splendidly intellectual forehead, betokened the experienced and cautious soldier. His dismissal was one of the political mistakes which too often hampered capable leaders on both sides. His Fabian policy in Georgia was precisely the same as that which was winning fame against heavy odds for Lee in Virginia.

GENERAL JOSEPH EGGLESTON
JOHNSTON, C. S. A.
BORN 1809; WEST POINT 1829; DIED 1891

LIEUTENANT–GENERAL
JOHN B. HOOD, C. S. A.
BORN 1831; WEST POINT 1853; DIED 1879

The countenance of Hood, on the other hand, indicates an eager, restless energy, an impetuosity that lacked the poise of Sherman, whose every gesture showed the alertness of mind and soundness of judgment that in him were so exactly balanced. Both Schofield and McPherson were classmates of Hood at West Point, and characterized him to Sherman as "bold even to rashness and courageous in the extreme." He struck the first offensive blow at Sherman advancing on Atlanta, and wisely adhered to the plan of the battle as it had been worked out by Johnston just before his removal. But the policy of attacking was certain to be finally disastrous to the Confederates.

take the offensive against Forrest, and with fourteen thousand troops, and in a three days' fight, demoralized him badly at Tupelo, Mississippi, July 14th–17th. Smith returned to Memphis and made another start for Sherman, when he was suddenly turned back and sent to Missouri, where the Confederate General Price was extremely active, to help Rosecrans.

To avoid final defeat and to win the ground he had gained had taxed Sherman's powers to the last degree and was made possible only through his superior numbers. Even this degree of success could not be expected to continue if the railroad to the North should be destroyed. But Sherman must do more than he had done; he must capture Atlanta, this Richmond of the far South, with its cannon foundries and its great machine-shops, its military factories, and extensive army supplies. He must divide the Confederacy north and south as Grant's capture of Vicksburg had split it east and west.

Sherman must have Atlanta, for political reasons as well as for military purposes. The country was in the midst of a presidential campaign. The opposition to Lincoln's re-election was strong, and for many weeks it was believed on all sides that his defeat was inevitable. At least, the success of the Union arms in the field was deemed essential to Lincoln's success at the polls. Grant had made little progress in Virginia and his terrible repulse at Cold Harbor, in June, had cast a gloom over every Northern State. Farragut was operating in Mobile Bay; but his success was still in the future.

The eyes of the supporters of the great war-president turned longingly, expectantly, toward General Sherman and his hundred thousand men before Atlanta. "Do something—something spectacular—save the party and save the country thereby from permanent disruption!" This was the cry of the millions, and Sherman understood it. But withal, the capture of the Georgia city may have been doubtful but for the fact that at the critical moment the Confederate President made a decision that resulted, unconsciously, in a decided

PEACH–TREE CREEK, WHERE HOOD HIT HARD

Counting these closely clustered Federal graves gives one an idea of the overwhelming onset with Hood become the aggressor on July 20th. Beyond the graves are some of the trenches from which the Federals were at first irresistibly driven. In the background flows Peach-Tree Creek, the little stream that gives its name to the battlefield. Hood, impatient to signalize his new responsibility by a stroke that would at once dispel the gloom at Richmond, had posted his troops behind strongly fortified works on a ridge commanding the valley of Peach-Tree Creek about five miles to the north of Atlanta. Here he awaited the approach of Sherman. As the Federals were disposing their lines and entrenching before this position, Hood's eager eyes detected a gap in their formation and at four o'clock in the afternoon hurled a heavy force against it. Thus he proved his reputation for courage, but the outcome showed the mistake. For a brief interval Sherman's forces were in great peril. But the Federals under Newton and Geary rallied and held their ground, till Ward's division in a brave counter-charge drove the Confederates back. This first effort cost Hood dear. He abandoned his entrenchments that night, leaving on the field five hundred dead, one thousand wounded, and many prisoners. Sherman estimated the total Confederate loss at no less than five thousand. That of the Federals was fifteen hundred.

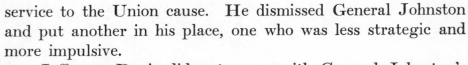

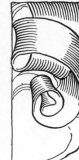
service to the Union cause. He dismissed General Johnston and put another in his place, one who was less strategic and more impulsive.

Jefferson Davis did not agree with General Johnston's military judgment, and he seized on the fact that Johnston had so steadily retreated before the Northern army as an excuse for his removal. On the 18th of July, Davis turned the Confederate Army of Tennessee over to General John B. Hood. A graduate of West Point of the class of 1853, a classmate of McPherson, Schofield, and Sheridan, Hood had faithfully served the cause of the South since the opening of the war. He was known as a fighter, and it was believed that he would change the policy of Johnston to one of open battle with Sherman's army. And so it proved.

Johnston had lost, since the opening of the campaign at Dalton, about fifteen thousand men, and the army that he now delivered to Hood consisted of about sixty thousand in all.

While Hood was no match for Sherman as a strategist, he was not a weakling. His policy of aggression, however, was not suited to the circumstances—to the nature of the country—in view of the fact that Sherman's army was far stronger than his own.

Two days after Hood took command of the Confederate army he offered battle. Sherman's forces had crossed Peach Tree Creek, a small stream flowing into the Chattahoochee, but a few miles from Atlanta, and were approaching the city. They had thrown up slight breastworks, as was their custom, but were not expecting an attack. Suddenly, however, about four o'clock in the afternoon of July 20th, an imposing column of Confederates burst from the woods near the position of the Union right center, under Thomas. The Federals were soon at their guns. The battle was short, fierce, and bloody. The Confederates made a gallant assault, but were pressed back to their entrenchments, leaving the ground covered with dead and wounded. The Federal loss in the battle

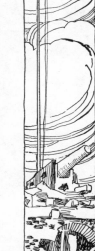

THE ARMY'S FINGER–TIPS—PICKETS BEFORE ATLANTA

A Federal picket post on the lines before Atlanta. This picture was taken shortly before the battle of July 22d. The soldiers are idling about unconcerned at exposing themselves; this is on the "reserve post." Somewhat in advance of this lay the outer line of pickets, and it would be time enough to seek cover if they were driven in. Thus armies feel for each other, stretching out first their sensitive fingers—the pickets. If these recoil, the skirmishers are sent forward while the strong arm, the line of battle, gathers itself to meet the foe. As this was an inner line, it was more strongly fortified than was customary with the pickets. But the men of both sides had become very expert in improvising field-works at this stage of the war. Hard campaigning had taught the veterans the importance to themselves of providing such protection, and no orders had to be given for their construction. As soon as a regiment gained a position desirable to hold, the soldiers would throw up a strong parapet of dirt and logs in a single night. In order to spare the men as much as possible, Sherman ordered his division commanders to organize pioneer detachments out of the Negroes that escaped to the Federals. These could work at night.

of Peach Tree Creek was placed at over seventeen hundred, the Confederate loss being much greater. This battle had been planned by Johnston before his removal, but he had been waiting for the strategic moment to fight it.

Two days later, July 22d, occurred the greatest engagement of the entire campaign—the battle of Atlanta. The Federal army was closing in on the entrenchments of Atlanta, and was now within two or three miles of the city. On the night of the 21st, General Blair, of McPherson's army, had gained possession of a high hill on the left, which commanded a view of the heart of the city. Hood thereupon planned to recapture this hill, and make a general attack on the morning of the 22d. He sent General Hardee on a long night march around the extreme flank of McPherson's army, the attack to be made at daybreak. Meantime, General Cheatham, who had succeeded to the command of Hood's former corps, and General A. P. Stewart, who now had Polk's corps, were to engage Thomas and Schofield in front and thus prevent them from sending aid to McPherson.

Hardee was delayed in his fifteen-mile night march, and it was noon before he attacked. At about that hour Generals Sherman and McPherson sat talking near the Howard house, which was the Federal headquarters, when the sudden boom of artillery from beyond the hill that Blair had captured announced the opening of the coming battle. McPherson quickly leaped upon his horse and galloped away toward the sound of the guns. Meeting Logan and Blair near the railroad, he conferred with them for a moment, when they separated, and each hastened to his place in the battle-line. McPherson sent aides and orderlies in various directions with despatches, until but two were still with him. He then rode into a forest and was suddenly confronted by a portion of the Confederate army under General Cheatham. "Surrender," was the call that rang out. But he wheeled his horse as if to flee, when he was instantly shot dead, and the horse galloped back riderless.

THE FINAL BLOW TO THE CONFEDERACY'S SOUTHERN STRONGHOLD

It was Sherman's experienced railroad wreckers that finally drove Hood out of Atlanta. In the picture the rails heating red-hot amid the flaming bonfires of the ties, and the piles of twisted débris show vividly what Sherman meant when he said their "work was done with a will." Sherman saw that in order to take Atlanta without terrific loss he must cut off all its rail communications. This he did by "taking the field with our main force and using it against the communications of Atlanta instead of against its intrench-ments." On the night of August 25th he moved with practically his entire army and wagon-trains loaded with fifteen days' rations. By the morning of the 27th the whole front of the city was deserted. The Confederates concluded that Sherman was in retreat. Next day they found out their mistake, for the Federal army lay across the West Point Railroad while the soldiers began wrecking it. Next day they were in motion toward the railroad to Macon, and General Hood began to understand that a colossal raid was in progress. After the occupation, when this picture was taken, Sherman's men completed the work of destruction.

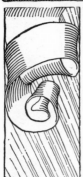
The death of the brilliant, dashing young leader, James B. McPherson, was a great blow to the Union army. But thirty-six years of age, one of the most promising men in the country, and already the commander of a military department, McPherson was the only man in all the Western armies whom Grant, on going to the East, placed in the same military class with Sherman.

Logan succeeded the fallen commander, and the battle raged on. The Confederates were gaining headway. They captured several guns. Cheatham was pressing on, pouring volley after volley into the ranks of the Army of the Tennessee, which seemed about to be cut in twain. A gap was opening. The Confederates were pouring through. General Sherman was present and saw the danger. Calling for Schofield to send several batteries, he placed them and poured a concentrated artillery fire through the gap and mowed down the advancing men in swaths. At the same time, Logan pressed forward and Schofield's infantry was called up. The Confederates were hurled back with great loss. The shadows of night fell—and the battle of Atlanta was over. Hood's losses exceeded eight thousand of his brave men, whom he could ill spare. Sherman lost about thirty-seven hundred.

The Confederate army recuperated within the defenses of Atlanta—behind an almost impregnable barricade. Sherman had no hope of carrying the city by assault, while to surround and invest it was impossible with his numbers. He determined, therefore, to strike Hood's lines of supplies. On July 28th, Hood again sent Hardee out from his entrenchments to attack the Army of the Tennessee, now under the command of General Howard. A fierce battle at Ezra Church on the west side of the city ensued, and again the Confederates were defeated with heavy loss.

A month passed and Sherman had made little progress toward capturing Atlanta. Two cavalry raids which he organized resulted in defeat, but the two railroads from the

THE RUIN OF HOOD'S RETREAT—DEMOLISHED CARS AND ROLLING-MILL

On the night of August 31st, in his headquarters near Jonesboro, Sherman could not sleep. That day he had defeated the force sent against him at Jonesboro and cut them off from returning to Atlanta. This was Hood's last effort to save his communications. About midnight sounds of exploding shells and what seemed like volleys of musketry arose in the direction of Atlanta. The day had been exciting in that city. Supplies and ammunition that Hood could carry with him were being removed; large quantities of provisions were being distributed among the citizens, and as the troops marched out they were allowed to take what they could from the public stores. All that remained was destroyed. The noise that Sherman heard that night was the blowing up of the rolling-mill and of about a hundred cars and six engines loaded with Hood's abandoned ammunition. The picture shows the Georgia Central Railroad east of the town.

BLAIR, OF MISSOURI

Although remaining politically neutral throughout the war, Missouri contributed four hundred and forty-seven separate military organizations to the Federal armies, and over one hundred to the Confederacy. The Union sentiment in the State is said to have been due to Frank P. Blair, who, early in 1861, began organizing home guards. Blair subsequently joined Grant's command and served with that leader until Sherman took the helm in the West. With Sherman Major-General Blair fought in Georgia and through the Carolinas.

BAKER, OF CALIFORNIA

California contributed twelve military organizations to the Federal forces, but none of them took part in the campaigns east of the Mississippi. Its Senator, Edward D. Baker, was in his place in Washington when the war broke out, and, being a close friend of Lincoln, promptly organized a regiment of Pennsylvanians which was best known by its synonym "First California." Colonel Baker was killed at the head of it at the battle of Ball's Bluff, Virginia, October 21, 1861. Baker had been appointed brigadier-general but declined.

KELLEY, OF WEST VIRGINIA

West Virginia counties had already supplied soldiers for the Confederates when the new State was organized in 1861. As early as May, 1861, Colonel B. F. Kelley was in the field with the First West Virginia Infantry marshalled under the Stars and Stripes. He served to the end of the war and was brevetted major-general. West Virginia furnished thirty-seven organizations of all arms to the Federal armies, chiefly for local defense and for service in contiguous territory. General Kelley was prominent in the Shenandoah campaigns.

REPRESENTATIVE SOLDIERS FROM A DOZEN STATES

SMYTH, OF DELAWARE

Little Delaware furnished to the Federal armies fifteen separate military organizations. First in the field was Colonel Thomas A. Smyth, with the First Delaware Infantry. Early promoted to the command of a brigade, he led it at Gettysburg, where it received the full force of Pickett's charge on Cemetery Ridge, July 3, 1863. He was brevetted major-general and fell at Farmville, on Appomattox River, Va., April 7, 1865, two days before the surrender at Appomattox. General Smyth was a noted leader in the Second Corps.

MITCHELL, OF KANSAS

The virgin State of Kansas sent fifty regiments, battalions, and batteries into the Federal camps. Its Second Infantry was organized and led to the field by Colonel R. B. Mitchell, a veteran of the Mexican War. At the first battle in the West, Wilson's Creek, Mo. (August 10, 1861), he was wounded. At the battle of Perryville, Brigadier-General Mitchell commanded a division in McCook's Corps and fought desperately to hold the Federal left flank against a sudden and desperate assault by General Bragg's Confederates.

CROSS, OF NEW HAMPSHIRE

New Hampshire supplied twenty-nine military organizations to the Federal armies. To the Granite State belongs the grim distinction of furnishing the regiment which had the heaviest mortality roll of any infantry organization in the army. This was the Fifth New Hampshire, commanded by Colonel E. E. Cross. The Fifth served in the Army of the Potomac. At Gettysburg, Colonel Cross commanded a brigade, which included the Fifth New Hampshire, and was killed at the head of it near Devil's Den, on July 2, 1863.

PEARCE, OF ARKANSAS

Arkansas entered into the war with enthusiasm, and had a large contingent of Confederate troops ready for the field in the summer of 1861. At Wilson's Creek, Missouri, August 10, 1861, there were four regiments and two batteries of Arkansans under command of Brigadier-General N. B. Pearce. Arkansas furnished seventy separate military organizations to the Confederate armies and seventeen to the Federals. The State was gallantly represented in the Army of Northern Virginia, notably at Antietam and Gettysburg.

STEUART, OF MARYLAND

Maryland quickly responded to the Southern call to arms, and among its first contribution of soldiers was George H. Steuart, who led a battalion across the Potomac early in 1861. These Marylanders fought at First Bull Run, or Manassas, and Lee's army at Petersburg included Maryland troops under Brigadier-General Steuart. During the war this little border State, politically neutral, sent six separate organizations to the Confederates in Virginia, and mustered thirty-five for the Federal camps and for local defense.

CRITTENDEN, THE CONFEDERATE

Kentucky is notable as a State which sent brothers to both the Federal and Confederate armies. Major-General George B. Crittenden, C. S. A., was the brother of Major-General Thomas L. Crittenden, U. S. A. Although remaining politically neutral throughout the war, the Blue Grass State sent forty-nine regiments, battalions, and batteries across the border to uphold the Stars and Bars, and mustered eighty of all arms to battle around the Stars and Stripes and protect the State from Confederate incursions.

LEADERS IN SECURING VOLUNTEERS FOR NORTH AND SOUTH

RANSOM, OF NORTH CAROLINA

The last of the Southern States to cast its fortunes in with the Confederacy, North Carolina vied with the pioneers in the spirit with which it entered the war. With the First North Carolina, Lieut.-Col. Matt W. Ransom was on the firing-line early in 1861. Under his leadership as brigadier-general, North Carolinians carried the Stars and Bars on all the great battlefields of the Army of Northern Virginia. The State furnished ninety organizations for the Confederate armies, and sent eight to the Federal camps.

FINEGAN, OF FLORIDA

Florida was one of the first to follow South Carolina's example in dissolving the Federal compact. It furnished twenty-one military organizations to the Confederate forces, and throughout the war maintained a vigorous home defense. Its foremost soldier to take the field when the State was menaced by a strong Federal expedition in February, 1864, was Brigadier-General Joseph Finegan. Hastily gathering scattered detachments, he defeated and checked the expedition at the battle of Olustee, or Ocean Pond, on February 20.

CLEBURNE, OF TENNESSEE

Cleburne was of foreign birth, but before the war was one year old he became the leader of Tennesseeans, fighting heroically on Tennessee soil. At Shiloh, Cleburne's brigade, and at Murfreesboro, Chattanooga, and Franklin, Major-General P. R. Cleburne's division found the post of honor. At Franklin this gallant Irishman "The 'Stonewall' Jackson of the West," led Tennesseeans for the last time and fell close to the breastworks. Tennessee sent the Confederate armies 129 organizations, and the Federal fifty-six,

south into Atlanta were considerably damaged. But, late in August, the Northern commander made a daring move that proved successful. Leaving his base of supplies, as Grant had done before Vicksburg, and marching toward Jonesboro, Sherman destroyed the Macon and Western Railroad, the only remaining line of supplies to the Confederate army.

Hood attempted to block the march on Jonesboro, and Hardee was sent with his and S. D. Lee's Corps to attack the Federals, while he himself sought an opportunity to move upon Sherman's right flank. Hardee's attack failed, and this necessitated the evacuation of Atlanta. After blowing up his magazines and destroying the supplies which his men could not carry with them, Hood abandoned the city, and the next day, September 2d, General Slocum, having succeeded Hooker, led the Twentieth Corps of the Federal army within its earthen walls. Hood had made his escape, saving his army from capture. His chief desire would have been to march directly north on Marietta and destroy the depots of Federal supplies, but a matter of more importance prevented. Thirty-four thousand Union prisoners were confined at Andersonville, and a small body of cavalry could have released them. So Hood placed himself between Andersonville and Sherman.

In the early days of September the Federal hosts occupied the city toward which they had toiled all the summer long. At East Point, Atlanta, and Decatur, the three armies settled for a brief rest, while the cavalry, stretched for many miles along the Chattahoochee, protected their flanks and rear. Since May their ranks had been depleted by some twenty-eight thousand killed and wounded, while nearly four thousand had fallen prisoners, into the Confederates' hands.

It was a great price, but whatever else the capture of Atlanta did, it ensured the reelection of Abraham Lincoln to the presidency of the United States. The total Confederate losses were in the neighborhood of thirty-five thousand, of which thirteen thousand were prisoners.

[Part XIII]

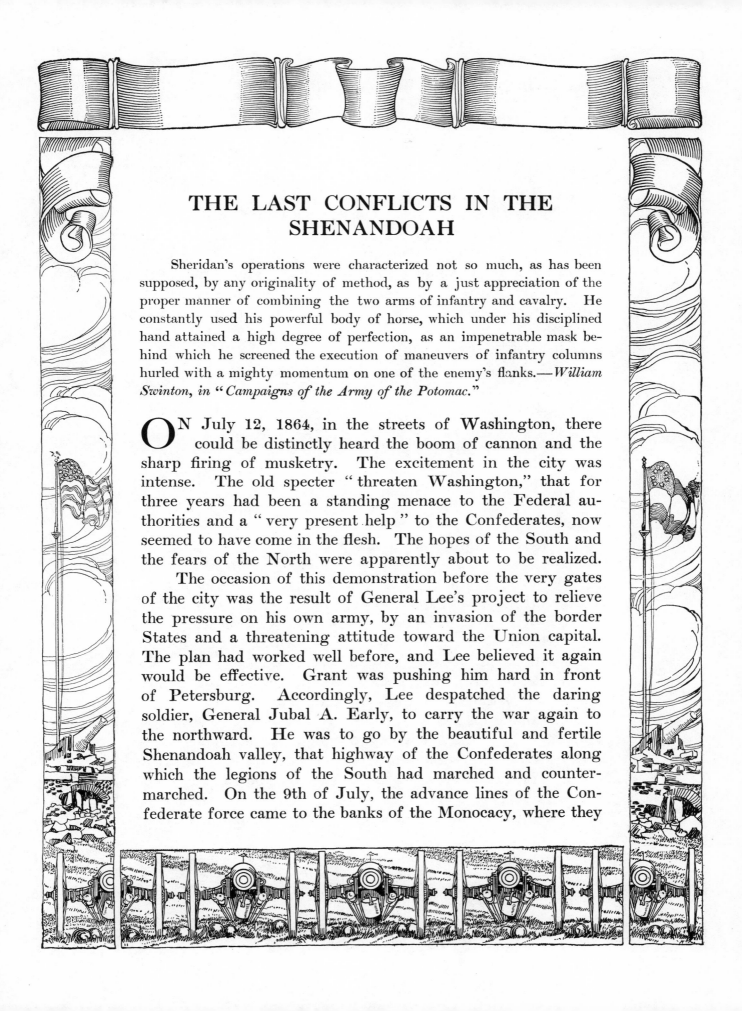

THE LAST CONFLICTS IN THE SHENANDOAH

Sheridan's operations were characterized not so much, as has been supposed, by any originality of method, as by a just appreciation of the proper manner of combining the two arms of infantry and cavalry. He constantly used his powerful body of horse, which under his disciplined hand attained a high degree of perfection, as an impenetrable mask behind which he screened the execution of maneuvers of infantry columns hurled with a mighty momentum on one of the enemy's flanks.—*William Swinton, in "Campaigns of the Army of the Potomac."*

ON July 12, 1864, in the streets of Washington, there could be distinctly heard the boom of cannon and the sharp firing of musketry. The excitement in the city was intense. The old specter "threaten Washington," that for three years had been a standing menace to the Federal authorities and a "very present help" to the Confederates, now seemed to have come in the flesh. The hopes of the South and the fears of the North were apparently about to be realized.

The occasion of this demonstration before the very gates of the city was the result of General Lee's project to relieve the pressure on his own army, by an invasion of the border States and a threatening attitude toward the Union capital. The plan had worked well before, and Lee believed it again would be effective. Grant was pushing him hard in front of Petersburg. Accordingly, Lee despatched the daring soldier, General Jubal A. Early, to carry the war again to the northward. He was to go by the beautiful and fertile Shenandoah valley, that highway of the Confederates along which the legions of the South had marched and counter-marched. On the 9th of July, the advance lines of the Confederate force came to the banks of the Monocacy, where they

found General Lew Wallace posted, with eight thousand men, half of Early's numbers, on the eastern side of that stream, to contest the approach of the Southern troops.

The battle was brief but bloody; the Confederates, crossing the stream and climbing its slippery banks, hurled their lines of gray against the compact ranks of blue. The attack was impetuous; the repulse was stubborn. A wail of musketry rent the air and the Northern soldiers fell back to their second position. Between the opposing forces was a narrow ravine through which flowed a small brook. Across this stream the tide of battle rose and fell. Its limpid current was soon crimsoned by the blood of the dead and wounded. Wallace's columns, as did those of Early, bled, but they stood. The result of the battle for a time hung in the balance. Then the Federal lines began to crumble. The retreat began, some of the troops in order but the greater portion in confusion, and the victorious Confederates found again an open way to Washington.

Now within half a dozen miles of the city, with the dome of the Capitol in full view, the Southern general pushed his lines so close to Fort Stevens that he was ready to train his forty pieces of artillery upon its walls.

General Augur, in command of the capital's defenses, hastily collected what strength in men and guns he could. Heavy artillery, militia, sailors from the navy yard, convalescents, Government employees of all kinds were rushed to the forts around the city. General Wright, with two divisions of the Sixth Corps, arrived from the camp at Petersburg, and Emory's division of the Nineteenth Corps came just in time from New Orleans. This was on July 11th, the very day on which Early appeared in front of Fort Stevens. The Confederate had determined to make an assault, but the knowledge of the arrival of Wright and Emory caused him to change his mind. He realized that, if unsuccessful, his whole force would be lost, and he concluded to return. Nevertheless, he spent the 12th of July in threatening the city. In the middle of

GENERAL JUBAL A. EARLY, THE CONFED-ERATE RAIDER WHO THREATENED WASHINGTON

"My bad old man," as General Lee playfully called him, was forty-eight years of age when he made the brilliant Valley campaign of the summer of 1864, which was halted only by the superior forces of Sheridan. A West Point graduate and a veteran of the Mexican War, Early became, after the death of Jackson, one of Lee's most efficient subordinates. He was alert, aggressive, resourceful. His very eccentricities, perhaps, made him all the more successful as a commander of troops in the field. "Old Jube's" caustic wit and austere ways made him a terror to stragglers, and who shall say that his fluent, forcible profanity did not endear him to men who were accustomed to like roughness of speech?

the afternoon General Wright sent out General Wheaton with Bidwell's brigade of Getty's division, and Early's pickets and skirmishers were driven back a mile.

This small engagement had many distinguished spectators. Pond in " The Shenandoah Valley " thus describes the scene: " On the parapet of Fort Stevens stood the tall form of Abraham Lincoln by the side of General Wright, who in vain warned the eager President that his position was swept by the bullets of sharpshooters, until an officer was shot down within three feet of him, when he reluctantly stepped below. Sheltered from the line of fire, Cabinet officers and a group of citizens and ladies, breathless with excitement, watched the fortunes of the flight."

Under cover of night the Confederates began to retrace their steps and made their way to the Shenandoah, with General Wright in pursuit. As the Confederate army was crossing that stream, at Snicker's Ferry, on the 18th, the pursuing Federals came upon them. Early turned, repulsed them, and continued on his way to Winchester, where General Averell, from Hunter's forces, now at Harper's Ferry, attacked them with his cavalry and took several hundred prisoners.

The Federal authorities were looking for a " man of the hour "—one whom they might pit against the able and strategic Early. Such a one was found in General Philip Henry Sheridan, whom some have called the " Marshal Ney of America." He was selected by General Grant, and his instructions were to drive the Confederates out of the Valley once for all.

The middle of September found the Confederate forces centered about Winchester, and the Union army was ten miles distant, with the Opequon between them. At two o'clock on the morning of September 19th, the Union camp was in motion, preparing for marching orders. At three o'clock the forward movement was begun, and by daylight the Federal advance had driven in the Confederate pickets. Emptying into the Opequon from the west are two converging streams,

THE CAPITOL AT WASHINGTON IN 1863

When the Capitol at Washington was threatened by the Confederate armies, it was still an unfinished structure, betraying its incompleteness to every beholder. This picture shows the derrick on the dome. It is a view of the east front of the building and was taken on July 11, 1863. Washington society had not been wholly free from occasional "war scares" since the withdrawal of most of the troops whose duty it had been to guard the city. Early's approach in July, 1864, found the Nation's capital entirely unprotected. Naturally there was a flutter throughout the peaceable groups of non-combatants that made up the population of Washington at that time, as well as in official circles. There were less than seventy thousand people living in the city in 1864, a large proportion of whom were in some way connected with the Government.

forming a triangle with the Winchester and Martinsburg pike as a base.

The town of Winchester is situated on this road, and was therefore at the bottom of the triangle. Before the town, the Confederate army stretched its lines between the two streams. The Union army would have to advance from the apex of the triangle, through a narrow ravine, shut in by thickly wooded hills and gradually emerging into an undulating valley. At the end of the gorge was a Confederate outwork, guarding the approach to Winchester. Both generals had the same plan of battle in mind. Sheridan would strike the Confederate center and right. Early was willing he should do this, for he planned to strike the Union right, double it back, get between Sheridan's army and the gorge, and thus cut off its retreat.

It took time for the Union troops to pass through the ravine, and it was late in the forenoon before the line of battle was formed. The attack and defense were alike obstinate. Upon the Sixth Corps and Grover's division of the Nineteenth Corps fell the brunt of the battle, since they were to hold the center while the Army of West Virginia, under General Crook, would sweep around them and turn the position of the opposing forces. The Confederate General Ramseur, with his troops, drove back the Federal center, held his ground for two hours, while the opposing lines were swept by musketry and artillery from the front, and enfiladed by artillery. Many Federal prisoners were taken.

By this time, Russell's division of the Sixth Corps emerged from the ravine. Forming in two lines, it marched quickly to the front. About the same time the Confederates were also being reenforced. General Rodes plunged into the fight, making a gallant attack and losing his life. General Gordon, with his columns of gray, swept across the summit of the hills and through the murky clouds of smoke saw the steady advance of the lines of blue. One of Russell's brigades struck the Confederate flank, and the Federal line was reestablished. As the

PROTECTING LOCOMOTIVES FROM THE CONFEDERATE RAIDER

The United States railroad photographer, Captain A. J. Russell, labeled this picture of 1864: "Engines stored in Washington to prevent their falling into Rebel hands in case of a raid on Alexandria." Here they are, almost under the shadow of the Capitol dome (which had just been completed). This was one of the precautions taken by the authorities at Washington, of which the general public knew little or nothing at the time. These photographs are only now revealing official secrets recorded fifty years ago.

ONE OF WASHINGTON'S DEFENDERS

Heavy artillery like this was of comparatively little use in repulsing such an attack as Early might be expected to make. Not only were these guns hard to move to points of danger, but in the summer of '64 there were no trained artillerists to man them. Big as they were, they gave Early no occasion for alarm.

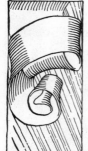
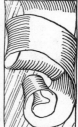

division moved forward to do this General Russell fell, pierced through the heart by a piece of shell.

The Fifth Maine battery, galloping into the field, unlimbered and with an enfilading storm of canister aided in turning the tide. Piece by piece the shattered Union line was picked up and reunited. Early sent the last of his reserves into the conflict to turn the Union right. Now ensued the fiercest fighting of the day. Regiment after regiment advanced to the wood only to be hurled back again. Here it was that the One hundred and fourteenth New York left its dreadful toll of men. Its position after the battle could be told by the long, straight line of one hundred and eighty-five of its dead and wounded.

It was three o'clock in the afternoon; the hour of Early's repulse had struck. To the right of the Union lines could be heard a mighty yell. The Confederates seemed to redouble their fire. The shivering lightning bolts shot through the air and the volleys of musketry increased in intensity. Then, across the shell-plowed field, came the reserves under General Crook. Breasting the Confederate torrent of lead, which cut down nine hundred of the reserves while crossing the open space, they rushed toward the embattled lines of the South.

At the same moment, coming out of the woods in the rear of the Federals, were seen the men of the Nineteenth Corps under General Emory, who had for three hours been lying in the grass awaiting their opportunity. The Confederate bullets had been falling thick in their midst with fatal certainty. They were eager for action. Rushing into the contest like madmen, they stopped at nothing. From two sides of the wood the men of Emory and Crook charged simultaneously. The Union line overlapped the Confederate at every point and doubled around the unprotected flanks. The day for the Southerners was irretrievably lost. They fell back toward Winchester in confusion. As they did so, a great uproar was heard on the pike road. It was the Federal cavalry under

ENTRANCE TO WASHINGTON FROM THE SOUTH—THE FAMOUS "CHAIN BRIDGE"

The sentry and vedette guarding the approach to Washington suggest one reason why Early did not make his approach to the capital from the Virginia side of the Potomac. A chain of more than twenty forts protected the roads to Long Bridge (shown below), and there was no way of marching troops into the city from the south, excepting over such exposed passages. Most of the troops left for the defense of the city were on the Virginia side. Therefore Early wisely picked out the northern outposts as the more vulnerable. Long Bridge was closely guarded at all times, like Chain Bridge and the other approaches, and at night the planks of its floor were removed.

LONG BRIDGE AND THE CAPITOL ACROSS THE BROAD POTOMAC

General Torbert sweeping up the road, driving the Confederate troopers before them. The surprised mass was pressed into its own lines. The infantry was charged and many prisoners and battle-flags captured.

The sun was now sinking upon the horizon, and on the ascending slopes in the direction of the town could be seen the long, dark lines of men following at the heels of the routed army. Along the crest of the embattled summit galloped a force of cavalrymen, which, falling upon the disorganized regiments of Early, aided, in the language of Sheridan, "to send them whirling through Winchester." The Union pursuit continued until the twilight had come and the shadows of night screened the scattered forces of Early from the pursuing cavalrymen. The battle of Winchester, or the Opequon, had been a bloody one—a loss of five thousand on the Federal side, and about four thousand on the Confederate.

By daylight of the following morning the victorious army was again in pursuit. On the afternoon of that day, it caught up with the Confederates, who now turned at bay at Fisher's Hill to resist the further approach of their pursuers. The position selected by General Early was a strong one, and his antagonist at once recognized it as such. The valley of the Shenandoah at this point is about four miles wide, lying between Fisher's Hill and Little North Mountain. General Early's line extended across the entire valley, and he had greatly increased his already naturally strong position. His army seemed safe from attack. From the summit of Three Top Mountain, his signal corps informed him of every movement of the Union army in the valley below. General Sheridan's actions indicated a purpose to assault the center of the Confederate line. For two days he continued massing his regiments in that direction, at times even skirmishing for position. General Wright pushed his men to within seven hundred yards of the Southern battle-line. While this was going on in full view of the Confederate general and his army, another movement was being executed

INSIDE
FORT TOTTEN—THREE
SHIFTING SCENES IN A BIG–GUN DRILL

Constant drill at the guns went on in the defenses of Washington throughout the war. At its close in April, 1865, there were 68 enclosed forts and batteries, whose aggregate perimeter was thirteen miles, 807 guns and 98 mortars mounted, and emplacements for 1,120 guns, ninety-three unarmed batteries for field-guns, 35,711 yards of rifle-trenches, and three block-houses encircling the Northern capital. The entire extent of front of the lines was thirty-seven miles; and thirty-two miles of military roads, besides those previously existing in the District of Columbia, formed the means of interior communication. In all these forts constant preparation was made for a possible onslaught of the Confederates, and many of the troops were trained which later went to take part in the siege of Petersburg where the heavy artillery fought bravely as infantry.

which even the vigilant signal officers on Three Top Mountain had not observed.

On the night of September 20th, the troops of General Crook were moved into the timber on the north bank of Cedar Creek. All during the next day, they lay concealed. That night they crossed the stream and the next morning were again hidden by the woods and ravines. At five o'clock on the morning of the 22d, Crook's men were nearly opposite the Confederate center. Marching his men in perfect silence, by one o'clock he had arrived at the left and front of the unsuspecting Early. By four o'clock he had reached the east face of Little North Mountain, to the left and rear of the Confederates. While the movement was being made, the main body of the Federal army was engaging the attention of the Confederates in front. Just before sundown, Crook's men plunged down the mountain side, from out of the timbered cover. The Confederates were quick to see that they had been trapped. They had been caught in a pocket and there was nothing for them to do except to retreat or surrender. They preferred the former, which was, according to General Gordon, " first stubborn and slow, then rapid, then—a rout."

After the battle of Fisher's Hill the pursuit still continued. The Confederate regiments re-formed, and at times would stop and contest the approach of the advancing cavalrymen. By the time the Union infantry would reach the place, the retreating army would have vanished. Torbert had been sent down Luray Valley in pursuit of the Confederate cavalry, with the hope of scattering it and seizing New Market in time to cut off the Confederate retreat from Fisher's Hill. But at Milford, in a narrow gorge, General Wickham held Torbert and prevented the fulfilment of his plan; and General Early's whole force was able to escape. Day after day this continued until Early had taken refuge in the Blue Ridge in front of Brown's Gap. Here he received reenforcements. Sheridan in the mean time had gone into camp at Harrisonburg, and for

WHERE LINCOLN WAS UNDER FIRE

This is Fort Stevens (originally known as Fort Massachusetts), north of Washington, near the Soldiers' Home, where President Lincoln had his summer residence. It was to this outpost that Early's troops advanced on July 12, 1864. In the fighting of that day Lincoln himself stood on the ramparts, and a surgeon who stood by his side was wounded. These works were feebly garrisoned, and General Gordon declared in his memoirs that when the Confederate troops reached Fort Stevens they found it untenanted. This photograph was taken after the occupation of the fort by Company F of the Third Massachusetts Artillery.

some time the two armies lay watching each other. The Federals were having difficulty in holding their lines of supply.

With the Valley practically given up by Early, Sheridan was anxious to stop here. He wrote to Grant, " I think the best policy will be to let the burning of the crops in the Valley be the end of the campaign, and let some of this army go somewhere else." He had the Petersburg line in mind. Grant's consent to this plan reached him on October 5th, and the following day he started on his return march down the Shenandoah. His cavalry extended across the entire valley. With the unsparing severity of war, his men began to make a barren waste of the region. The October sky was overcast with clouds of smoke and sheets of flame from the burning barns and mills.

As the army of Sheridan proceeded down the Valley, the undaunted cavaliers of Early came in pursuit. His horsemen kept close to the rear of the Union columns. On the morning of October 9th, the cavalry leader, Rosser, who had succeeded Wickham, found himself confronted by General Custer's division, at Tom's Brook. At the same time the Federal general, Wesley Merritt, fell upon the cavalry of Lomax and Johnson on an adjacent road. The two Union forces were soon united and a mounted battle ensued. The fight continued for two hours. There were charges and countercharges. The ground being level, the maneuvering of the squadrons was easy. The clink of the sabers rang out in the morning air. Both sides fought with tenacity. The Confederate center held together, but its flanks gave way. The Federals charged along the whole front, with a momentum that forced the Southern cavalrymen to flee from the field. They left in the hands of the Federal troopers over three hundred prisoners, all their artillery, except one piece, and nearly every wagon the Confederate cavalry had with them.

The Northern army continued its retrograde movement, and on the 10th crossed to the north side of Cedar Creek. Early's army in the mean time had taken a position at the

MEN OF THE THIRD MASSACHUSETTS HEAVY ARTILLERY IN FORT STEVENS

Fort Stevens, on the north line of the defenses of Washington, bore the brunt of the Confederate attack in the action of July 12, 1864, when Early threatened Washington. The smooth-bore guns in its armament were two 8-inch siege-howitzers *en embrasure*, six 24-pounder siege-guns *en embrasure*, two 24-pounder sea-coast guns *en barbette*. It was also armed with five 30-pounder Parrott rifled guns, one 10-inch siege-mortar and one 24-pounder Coehorn mortar. Three of the platforms for siege-guns remained vacant.

COMPANY K, THIRD MASSACHUSETTS HEAVY ARTILLERY, IN FORT STEVENS, 1865

Washington was no longer in danger when this photograph was taken, and the company is taking its ease with small arms stacked— three rifles held together by engaging the shanks of the bayonets. This is the usual way of disposing of rifles when the company is temporarily dismissed for any purpose. If the men are to leave the immediate vicinity of the stacks, a sentinel is detailed to guard the arms. The Third Massachusetts Heavy Artillery was organized for one year in August, 1864, and remained in the defenses of Washington throughout their service, except for Company I, which went to the siege of Petersburg and maintained the pontoon bridges.

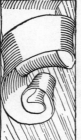

wooded base of Fisher's Hill, four miles away. The Sixth Corps started for Washington, but the news of Early at Fisher's Hill led to its recall. The Union forces occupied ground that was considered practically unassailable, especially on the left, where the deep gorge of the Shenandoah, along whose front rose the bold Massanutten Mountain, gave it natural protection.

The movements of the Confederate army were screened by the wooded ravines in front of Fisher's Hill, while, from the summit of the neighboring Three Top Mountain, its officers could view, as in a panorama, the entire Union camp. Seemingly secure, the corps of Crook on the left of the Union line was not well protected. The keen-eyed Gordon saw the weak point in the Union position. Ingenious plans to break it down were quickly made.

Meanwhile, Sheridan was summoned to Washington to consult with Secretary Stanton. He did not believe that Early proposed an immediate attack, and started on the 15th, escorted by the cavalry, and leaving General Wright in command. At Front Royal the next day word came from Wright enclosing a message taken for the Confederate signal-flag on Three Top Mountain. It was from Longstreet, advising Early that he would join him and crush Sheridan. The latter sent the cavalry back to Wright, and continued on to Washington, whence he returned at once by special train, reaching Winchester on the evening of the 18th.

Just after dark on October 18th, a part of Early's army under the command of General John B. Gordon, with noiseless steps, moved out from their camp, through the misty, autumn night. The men had been stripped of their canteens, in fear that the striking of them against some object might reveal their movements. Orders were given in low whispers. Their path followed along the base of the mountain—a dim and narrow trail, upon which but one man might pass at a time. For seven miles this sinuous line made its way through the dark

A HOUSE NEAR WASHINGTON STRUCK BY ONE OF EARLY'S SHELLS

The arrival of Grant's trained veterans in July, 1864, restored security to the capital city after a week of fright. The fact that shells had been thrown into the outskirts of the city gave the inhabitants for the first time a realizing sense of immediate danger. This scene is the neighborhood of Fort Stevens, on the Seventh Street road, not far from the Soldiers' Home, where President Lincoln was spending the summer. The campaign for his reëlection had begun and the outlook for his success and that of his party seemed at this moment as dubious as that for the conclusion of the war. Grant had weakened his lines about Richmond in order to protect Washington, while Lee had been able to detach Early's Corps for the brilliant Valley Campaign, which saved his Shenandoah supplies.

gorge, crossing the Shenandoah, and at times passing within four hundred yards of the Union pickets.

It arrived at the appointed place, opposite Crook's camp on the Federal right, an hour before the attack was to be made. In the shivering air of the early morning, the men crouched on the river bank, waiting for the coming of the order to move forward. At last, at five o'clock, it came. They plunged into the frosty water of the river, emerged on the other side, marched in " double quick," and were soon sounding a reveille to the sleeping troops of Sheridan. The minie balls whizzed and sang through the tents. In the gray mists of the dawn the legions of the South looked like phantom warriors, as they poured through the unmanned gaps. The Northerners sprang to arms. There was a bloody struggle in the trenches. Their eyes saw the flames from the Southern muskets; the men felt the breath of the hot muzzles in their faces, while the Confederate bayonets were at their breasts. There was a brief struggle, then panic and disorganization. Only a quarter of an hour of this yelling and struggling, and two-thirds of the Union army broke like a mill-dam and poured across the fields, leaving their accouterments of war and the stiffening bodies of their comrades. Rosser, with the cavalry, attacked Custer and assisted Gordon.

Meanwhile, during these same early morning hours, General Early had himself advanced to Cedar Creek by a more direct route. At half-past three o'clock his men had come in sight of the Union camp-fires. They waited under cover for the approach of day. At the first blush of dawn and before the charge of Gordon, Early hurled his men across the stream, swept over the breastworks, captured the batteries and turned them upon the unsuspecting Northerners. The Federal generals tried to stem the impending disaster. From the east of the battlefield the solid lines of Gordon were now driving the fugitives of Crook's corps by the mere force of momentum. Aides were darting hither and thither, trying to reassemble the

GENERAL SHERIDAN'S "WINCHESTER"

"Winchester" wore no such gaudy trappings when he sprang "up from the South, at break of day" on that famous ride of October 19, 1864, which has been immortalized in Thomas Buchanan Read's poem. The silver-mounted saddle was presented later by admiring friends of his owner. The sleek neck then was dark with sweat, and the quivering nostrils were flecked with foam at the end of the twenty-mile dash that brought hope and courage to an army and turned defeat into the overwhelming victory of Cedar Creek. Sheridan himself was as careful of his appearance as Custer was irregular in his field dress. He was always careful of his horse, but in the field decked him in nothing more elaborate than a plain McClellan saddle and army blanket.

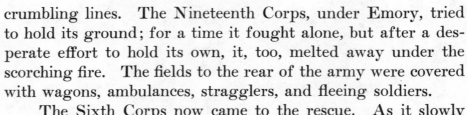
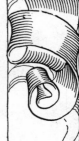

crumbling lines. The Nineteenth Corps, under Emory, tried
to hold its ground; for a time it fought alone, but after a desperate effort to hold its own, it, too, melted away under the
scorching fire. The fields to the rear of the army were covered
with wagons, ambulances, stragglers, and fleeing soldiers.

The Sixth Corps now came to the rescue. As it slowly
fell to the rear it would, at times, turn to fight. At last it
found a place where it again stood at bay. The men hastily
gathered rails and constructed rude field-works. At the same
time the Confederates paused in their advance. The rattle of
musketry ceased. There was scarcely any firing except for the
occasional roar of a long-range artillery gun. The Southerners seemed willing to rest on their well-earned laurels of the
morning. In the language of the successful commander, it was
" glory enough for one day."

But the brilliant morning victory was about to be changed
to a singular afternoon defeat. During the morning's fight,
when the Union troops were being rapidly overwhelmed with
panic, Rienzi, the beautiful jet-black war-charger, was bearing
his master, the commander of the Federal army, to the field of
disaster. Along the broad valley highway that leads from
Winchester, General Sheridan had galloped to where his embattled lines had been reduced to a flying mob. While riding
leisurely away from Winchester about nine o'clock he had
heard unmistakable thunder-peals of artillery. Realizing that
a battle was on in the front, he hastened forward, soon to be
met, as he crossed Mill Creek, by the trains and men of his
routed army, coming to the rear with appalling rapidity.

News from the field told him of the crushing defeat of
his hitherto invincible regiments. The road was blocked by
the retreating crowds as they pressed toward the rear. The
commander was forced to take to the fields, and as his steed,
flecked with foam, bore him onward, the disheartened refugees
greeted him with cheers. Taking off his hat as he rode, he
cried, " We will go back and recover our camps." The words

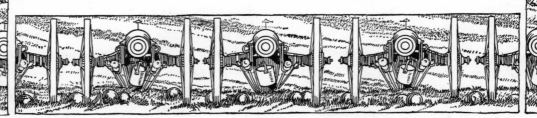

GENERAL PHILIP H. SHERIDAN IN THE SHENANDOAH CAMPAIGN

Two generations of schoolboys in the Northern States have learned the lines beginning, "Up from the south at break of day." This picture represents Sheridan in 1864, wearing the same hat that he waved to rally his soldiers on that famous ride from "Winchester, twenty miles away." As he reined up his panting horse on the turnpike at Cedar Creek, he received salutes from two future Presidents of the United States. The position on the left of the road was held by Colonel Rutherford B. Hayes, who had succeeded, after the rout of the Eighth Corps in the darkness of the early morning, in rallying some fighting groups of his own brigade; while on the right stood Major William McKinley, gallantly commanding the remnant of his fighting regiment—the Twenty-third Ohio.

seemed to inspire the demoralized soldiers. Stragglers fell into line behind him; men turned to follow their magnetic leader back to the fight.

Vaulting his horse over the low barricade of rails, he dashed to the crest of the field. There was a flutter along the battle-line. The men from behind their protecting wall broke into thunderous cheers. From the rear of the soldiers there suddenly arose, as from the earth, a line of the regimental flags, which waved recognition to their leader. Color-bearers reassembled. The straggling lines re-formed. Early made another assault after one o'clock, but was easily repulsed.

It was nearly four o'clock when the order for the Federal advance was given. General Sheridan, hat in hand, rode in front of his infantry line that his men might see him. The Confederate forces now occupied a series of wooded crests. From out of the shadow of one of these timbered coverts, a column of gray was emerging. The Union lines stood waiting for the impending crash. It came in a devouring succession of volleys that reverberated into a deep and sullen roar. The Union infantry rose as one man and passed in among the trees. Not a shot was heard. Then, suddenly, there came a screaming, humming rush of shell, a roar of musketry mingling with the yells of a successful charge. Again the firing ceased, except for occasional outbursts. The Confederates had taken a new position and reopened with a galling fire. General Sheridan dashed along the front of his lines in personal charge of the attack. Again his men moved toward the lines of Early's fast thinning ranks. It was the final charge. The Union cavalry swept in behind the fleeing troops of Early and sent, again, his veteran army "whirling up the Valley."

The battle of Cedar Creek was ended; the tumult died away. The Federal loss had been about fifty-seven hundred; the Confederate over three thousand. Fourteen hundred Union prisoners were sent to Richmond. Never again would the gaunt specter of war hover over Washington.

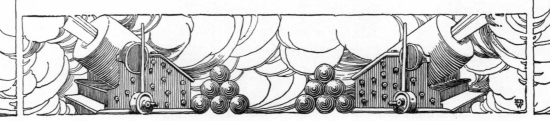

FROM THE ARMY TO THE WHITE HOUSE

War-time portraits of six soldiers whose military records assisted them to the Presidential Chair.

Garfield in '63—(left to right) Thomas, Wiles, Tyler, Simmons, Drillard, Ducat, Barnett, Goddard, Rosecrans, Garfield, Porter, Bond, Thompson, Sheridan.

Brig.-Gen. Andrew Johnson,
President, 1865–69.

General Ulysses S. Grant,
President, 1869–77.

Bvt. Maj.-Gen. Rutherford B. Hayes,
President, 1877–81.

Maj.-Gen. James A. Garfield,
President, March to September, 1881.

Bvt. Brig.-Gen. Benjamin Harrison,
President, 1889–93.

Brevet Major William McKinley,
President, 1897–1901.

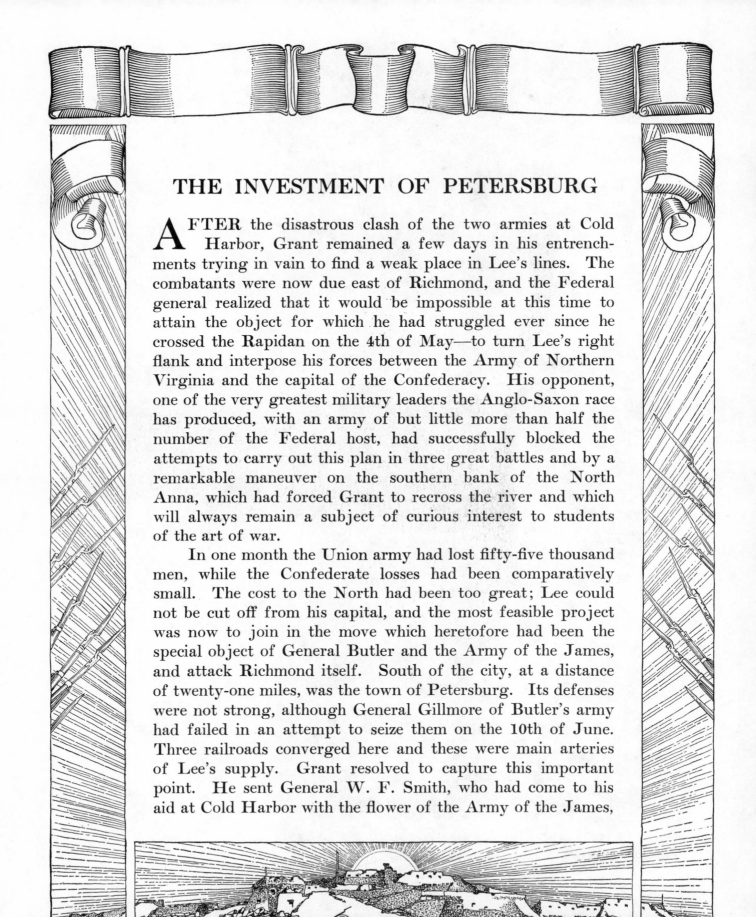

THE INVESTMENT OF PETERSBURG

AFTER the disastrous clash of the two armies at Cold Harbor, Grant remained a few days in his entrenchments trying in vain to find a weak place in Lee's lines. The combatants were now due east of Richmond, and the Federal general realized that it would be impossible at this time to attain the object for which he had struggled ever since he crossed the Rapidan on the 4th of May—to turn Lee's right flank and interpose his forces between the Army of Northern Virginia and the capital of the Confederacy. His opponent, one of the very greatest military leaders the Anglo-Saxon race has produced, with an army of but little more than half the number of the Federal host, had successfully blocked the attempts to carry out this plan in three great battles and by a remarkable maneuver on the southern bank of the North Anna, which had forced Grant to recross the river and which will always remain a subject of curious interest to students of the art of war.

In one month the Union army had lost fifty-five thousand men, while the Confederate losses had been comparatively small. The cost to the North had been too great; Lee could not be cut off from his capital, and the most feasible project was now to join in the move which heretofore had been the special object of General Butler and the Army of the James, and attack Richmond itself. South of the city, at a distance of twenty-one miles, was the town of Petersburg. Its defenses were not strong, although General Gillmore of Butler's army had failed in an attempt to seize them on the 10th of June. Three railroads converged here and these were main arteries of Lee's supply. Grant resolved to capture this important point. He sent General W. F. Smith, who had come to his aid at Cold Harbor with the flower of the Army of the James,

MAHONE, "THE HERO OF THE CRATER"

General William Mahone, C. S. A. It was through the promptness and valor of General Mahone that the Southerners, on July 30, 1864, were enabled to turn back upon the Federals the disaster threatened by the hidden mine. On the morning of the explosion there were but eighteen thousand Confederates left to hold the ten miles of lines about Petersburg. Everything seemed to favor Grant's plans for the crushing of this force. Immediately after the mine was sprung, a terrific cannonade was opened from one hundred and fifty guns and mortars to drive back the Confederates from the breach, while fifty thousand Federals stood ready to charge upon the panic-stricken foe. But the foe was not panic-stricken long. Colonel McMaster, of the Seventeenth South Carolina, gathered the remnants of General Elliott's brigade and held back the Federals massing at the Crater until General Mahone arrived at the head of three brigades. At once he prepared to attack the Federals, who at that moment were advancing to the left of the Crater. Mahone ordered a counter-charge. In his inspiring presence it swept with such vigor that the Federals were driven back and dared not risk another assault. At the Crater, Lee had what Grant lacked—a man able to direct the entire engagement.

The Investment of Petersburg ❖ ❖ ❖ ❖

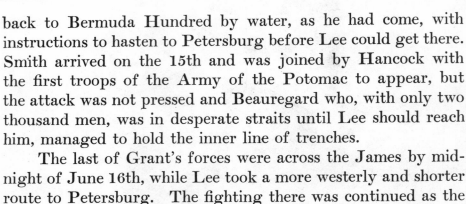

back to Bermuda Hundred by water, as he had come, with instructions to hasten to Petersburg before Lee could get there. Smith arrived on the 15th and was joined by Hancock with the first troops of the Army of the Potomac to appear, but the attack was not pressed and Beauregard who, with only two thousand men, was in desperate straits until Lee should reach him, managed to hold the inner line of trenches.

The last of Grant's forces were across the James by midnight of June 16th, while Lee took a more westerly and shorter route to Petersburg. The fighting there was continued as the two armies came up, but each Union attack was successfully repulsed. At the close of day on the 18th both opponents were in full strength and the greatest struggle of modern times was begun. Impregnable bastioned works began to show themselves around Petersburg. More than thirty miles of frowning redoubts connected extensive breastworks and were strengthened by mortar batteries and field-works which lined the fields near the Appomattox River. It was a vast net of fortifications, but there was no formal siege of Lee's position, which was a new entrenched line selected by Beauregard some distance behind the rifle-pits where he had held out at such great odds against Hancock and Smith.

Grant, as soon as the army was safely protected, started to extend his lines on the west and south, in order to envelop the Confederate right flank. He also bent his energies to destroying the railroads upon which Lee depended for supplies. Attempts to do this were made without delay. On June 22d two corps of the Union army set out for the Weldon Railroad, but they became separated and were put to flight by A. P. Hill. The Federal cavalry also joined in the work, but the vigilant Confederate horsemen under W. H. F. Lee prevented any serious damage to the iron way, and by July 2d the last of the raiders were back in the Federal lines, much the worse for the rough treatment they had received.

Now ensued some weeks of quiet during which both armies

WHAT EIGHT THOUSAND POUNDS OF POWDER DID

The Crater, torn by the mine within Elliott's Salient. At dawn of July 30, 1864, the fifty thousand Federal troops waiting to make a charge saw a great mass of earth hurled skyward like a water-spout. As it spread out into an immense cloud, scattering guns, carriages, timbers, and what were once human beings, the front ranks broke in panic; it looked as if the mass were descending upon their own heads. The men were quickly rallied; across the narrow plain they charged, through the awful breach, and up the heights beyond to gain Cemetery Ridge. But there were brave fighters on the other side still left, and delay among the Federals enabled the Confederates to rally and re-form in time to drive the Federals back down the steep sides of the Crater. There, as they struggled amidst the horrible débris, one disaster after another fell upon them. Huddled together, the mass of men was cut to pieces by the canister poured upon them from well-planted Confederate batteries. At last, as a forlorn hope, the colored troops were sent forward; and they, too, were hurled back into the Crater and piled upon their white comrades.

were strengthening their fortifications. On June 25th Sheridan returned from his cavalry raid on the Virginia Central Railroad running north from Richmond. He had encountered Hampton and Fitzhugh Lee at Trevilian Station on June 11th, and turned back after doing great damage to the railway. Ammunition was running short and he did not dare risk another engagement. Sheridan was destined not to remain long with the army in front of Petersburg. Lee had detached a corps from his forces and, under Early, it had been doing great damage in Maryland and Pennsylvania. So Grant's cavalry leader was put at the head of an army and sent to the Shenandoah valley to drive Early's troops from the base of their operations.

Meanwhile the Federals were covertly engaged in an undertaking which was fated to result in conspicuous failure. Some skilled miners from the upper Schuylkill coal regions in the Forty-eighth Pennsylvania attached to the Ninth Corps were boring a tunnel from the rear of the Union works underneath the Confederate fortifications. Eight thousand pounds of gunpowder were placed in lateral galleries at the end of the tunnel. At twenty minutes to five on the morning of July 30th, the mine was exploded. A solid mass of earth and all manner of material shot two hundred feet into the air. Three hundred human beings were buried in the débris as it fell back into the gaping crater. The smoke had barely cleared away when General Ledlie led his waiting troops into the vast opening. The horror of the sight sickened the assailants, and in crowding into the pit they became completely demoralized. In the confusion officers lost power to reorganize, much less to control, their troops.

The stunned and paralyzed Confederates were not long in recovering their wits. Batteries opened upon the approach to the crater, and presently a stream of fire was poured into the pit itself. General Mahone hastened up with his Georgia and Virginia troops, and there were several desperate charges

FORT MAHONE—"FORT DAMNATION"

RIVES' SALIENT

TRAVERSES AGAINST CROSS–FIRE

GRACIE'S SALIENT, AND OTHER FORTS ALONG THE TEN MILES OF DEFENSES

Dotted with formidable fortifications such as these, Confederate works stretched for ten miles around Petersburg. Fort Mahone was situated opposite the Federal Fort Sedgwick at the point where the hostile lines converged most closely after the battle of the Crater. Owing to the constant cannonade which it kept up, the Federals named it Fort Damnation, while Fort Sedgwick, which was no less active in reply, was known to the Confederates as Fort Hell. Gracie's salient, further north on the Confederate line, is notable as the point in front of which General John B. Gordon's gallant troops moved to the attack on Fort Stedman, the last desperate effort of the Confederates to break through the Federal cordon. The views of Gracie's salient show the French form of *chevaux-de-frise*, a favorite protection against attack much employed by the Confederates.

before the Federals withdrew at Burnside's order. Grant had had great expectations that the mine would result in his capturing Petersburg and he was much disappointed. In order to get a part of Lee's army away from the scene of what he hoped would be the final struggle, Hancock's troops and a large force of cavalry had been sent north of the James, as if a move on Richmond had been planned. In the mine fiasco on that fatal July 30th, thirty-nine hundred men (nearly all from Burnside's corps) were lost to the Union side. The Confederate loss was about one thousand.

In the torrid days of mid-August Grant renewed his attacks upon the Weldon Railroad, and General Warren was sent to capture it. He reached Globe Tavern, about four miles from Petersburg, when he encountered General Heth, who drove him back. Warren did not return to the Federal lines but entrenched along the iron way. The next day he was fiercely attacked by the Confederate force now strongly reenforced by Mahone. The assault was most sudden. Mahone forced his way through the skirmish line and then turned and fought his opponents from their rear. Another of his divisions struck the Union right wing. In this extremity two thousand of Warren's troops were captured and all would have been lost but for the timely arrival of Burnside's men.

Two days later the Southerners renewed the battle and now thirty cannon poured volley after volley upon the Fifth and Ninth corps. The dashing Mahone again came forward with his usual impetuousness, but the blue line finally drove Lee's men back. And so the Weldon Railroad fell into the hands of General Grant. Hancock, with the Second Corps, returned from the north bank of the James and set to work to assist in destroying the railway, whose loss was a hard blow to General Lee. It was not to be expected that the latter would permit this work to continue unmolested and on the 25th of August, A. P. Hill suddenly confronted Hancock, who entrenched himself in haste at Ream's Station. This did not

AN AFTERNOON CONCERT AT THE OFFICERS' QUARTERS, HAREWOOD HOSPITAL, NEAR WASHINGTON

Hospital life for those well enough to enjoy it was far from dull. Witness the white-clad nurse with her prim apron and hoopskirt on the right of the photograph, and the band on the left. Most hospitals had excellent libraries and a full supply of current newspapers and periodicals, usually presented gratuitously. Many of the larger ones organized and maintained bands for the amusement of the patients; they also provided lectures, concerts, and theatrical and other entertainments. A hospital near the front receiving cases of the most severe character might have a death-rate as high as twelve per cent., while those farther in the rear might have a very much lower death-rate of but six, four, or even two

LOUISA M. ALCOTT,
THE AUTHOR OF "LITTLE WOMEN,"
AS A NURSE IN 1862

per cent. The portrait accompanying shows Louisa M. Alcott, the author of "Little Men," "Little Women," "An Old Fashioned Girl," and the other books that have endeared her to millions of readers. Her diary of 1862 contains this characteristic note: "November. Thirty years old. Decided to go to Washington as a nurse if I could find a place. Help needed, and I love nursing and must let out my pent-up energy in some new way." She had not yet attained fame as a writer, but it was during this time that she wrote for a newspaper the letters afterwards collected as "Hospital Sketches." It is due to the courtesy of Messrs. Little, Brown & Company of Boston that the wartime portrait is here reproduced.

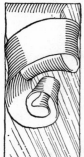

save the Second Corps, which for the first time in its glorious career was put to rout. Their very guns were captured and turned upon them.

In the following weeks there were no actions of importance except that in the last days of September Generals Ord and Birney, with the Army of the James, captured Fort Harrison, on the north bank of that river, from Generals Ewell and Anderson. The Federals were anxious to have it, since it was an excellent vantage point from which to threaten Richmond. Meanwhile Grant was constantly extending his line to the west and by the end of October it was very close to the South Side Railroad. On the 27th there was a hard fight at Hatcher's Run, but the Confederates saved the railway and the Federals returned to their entrenchments in front of Petersburg.

The active struggle now ceased, but Lee found himself each day in more desperate straits. Sheridan had played sad havoc with such sources of supply as existed in the rich country to the northwest. The Weldon Railroad was gone and the South Side line was in imminent danger. The Southerners were losing heart. Many went home for the winter on a promise to return when the spring planting was done. Lee was loath to let them go, but he could ill afford to maintain them, and the very life of their families depended upon it. Those who remained at Petersburg suffered cruelly from hunger and cold. They looked forward to the spring, although it meant renewal of the mighty struggle. The Confederate line had been stretched to oppose Grant's westward progress until it had become the thinnest of screens. A man lost to Lee was almost impossible to replace, while the bounties offered in the North kept Grant's ranks full.

[Part XIV]

SHERMAN'S FINAL CAMPAIGNS

I only regarded the march from Atlanta to Savannah as a "shift of base," as the transfer of a strong army, which had no opponent, and had finished its then work, from the interior to a point on the sea coast, from which it could achieve other important results. I considered this march as a means to an end, and not as an essential act of war. Still, then as now, the march to the sea was generally regarded as something extraordinary, something anomalous, something out of the usual order of events; whereas, in fact, I simply moved from Atlanta to Savannah, as one step in the direction of Richmond, a movement that had to be met and defeated, or the war was necessarily at an end.—General W. T. Sherman, in his "Memoirs."

THE march to the sea, in which General William T. Sherman won undying fame in the Civil War, is one of the greatest pageants in the world's warfare—as fearful in its destruction as it is historic in its import. But this was not Sherman's chief achievement; it was an easy task compared with the great campaign between Chattanooga and Atlanta through which he had just passed. "As a military accomplishment it was little more than a grand picnic," declared one of his division commanders, in speaking of the march through Georgia and the Carolinas.

Almost immediately after the capture of Atlanta, Sherman, deciding to remain there for some time and to make it a Federal military center, ordered all the inhabitants to be removed. General Hood pronounced the act one of ingenious cruelty, transcending any that had ever before come to his notice in the dark history of the war. Sherman insisted that his act was one of kindness, and that Johnston and Hood themselves had done the same—removed families from their homes—in other places. The decision was fully carried out.

Many of the people of Atlanta chose to go southward, others to the north, the latter being transported free, by Sherman's order, as far as Chattanooga.

Shortly after the middle of September, Hood moved his army from Lovejoy's Station, just south of Atlanta, to the vicinity of Macon. Here Jefferson Davis visited the encampment, and on the 22d he made a speech to the homesick Army of Tennessee, which, reported in the Southern newspapers, disclosed to Sherman the new plans of the Confederate leaders. These involved nothing less than a fresh invasion of Tennessee, which, in the opinion of President Davis, would put Sherman in a predicament worse than that in which Napoleon found himself at Moscow. But, forewarned, the Federal leader prepared to thwart his antagonists. The line of the Western and Atlantic Railroad was more closely guarded. Divisions were sent to Rome and to Chattanooga. Thomas was ordered to Nashville, and Schofield to Knoxville. Recruits were hastened from the North to these points, in order that Sherman himself might not be weakened by the return of too many troops to these places.

Hood, in the hope of leading Sherman away from Atlanta, crossed the Chattahoochee on the 1st of October, destroyed the railroad above Marietta and sent General French against Allatoona. It was the brave defense of this place by General John M. Corse that brought forth Sherman's famous message, "Hold out; relief is coming," sent by his signal officers from the heights of Kenesaw Mountain, and which thrilled the North and inspired its poets to eulogize Corse's bravery in verse. Corse had been ordered from Rome to Allatoona by signals from mountain to mountain, over the heads of the Confederate troops, who occupied the valley between. Reaching the mountain pass soon after midnight, on October 5th, Corse added his thousand men to the nine hundred already there, and soon after daylight the battle began. General French, in command of the Confederates, first

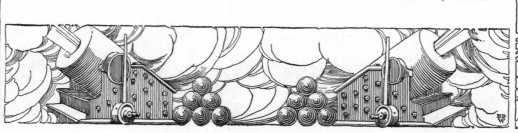

BEFORE THE MARCH TO THE SEA

These two photographs of General Sherman were taken in 1864—the year that made him an inter-
national figure, before his march to the sea which electrified the civilized world, and exposed once for
all the crippled condition of the Confederacy. After that autumn expedition, the problem of the
Union generals was merely to contend with detached armies, no longer with the combined States of the
Confederacy. The latter had no means of extending further support to the dwindling troops in the
field. Sherman was the chief Union exponent of the tactical gift that makes marches count as much
as fighting. In the early part of 1864 he made his famous raid across Mississippi from Jackson to
Meridian and back again, destroying the railroads, Confederate stores, and other property, and des-
olating the country along the line of march. In May he set out from Chattanooga for the invasion of
Georgia. For his success in this campaign he was appointed, on August 12th, a major-general in the
regular army. On November 12th, he started with the pick of his men on his march to the sea.
After the capture of Savannah, December 21st, Sherman's fame was secure; yet he was one of the
most heartily execrated leaders of the war. There is a hint of a smile in the right-hand picture. The
left-hand portrait reveals all the sternness and determination of a leader surrounded by dangers,
about to penetrate an enemy's country against the advice of accepted military authorities.

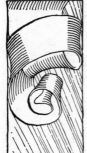

summoned Corse to surrender, and, receiving a defiant answer, opened with his guns. Nearly all the day the fire was terrific from besieged and besiegers, and the losses on both sides were very heavy.

During the battle Sherman was on Kenesaw Mountain, eighteen miles away, from which he could see the cloud of smoke and hear the faint reverberation of the cannons' boom. When he learned by signal that Corse was there and in command, he said, "If Corse is there, he will hold out; I know the man." And he did hold out, and saved the stores at Alla-toona, at a loss of seven hundred of his men, he himself being among the wounded, while French lost about eight hundred.

General Hood continued to move northward to Resaca and Dalton, passing over the same ground on which the two great armies had fought during the spring and summer. He destroyed the railroads, burned the ties, and twisted the rails, leaving greater havoc, if possible, in a country that was already a wilderness of desolation. For some weeks Sherman followed Hood in the hope that a general engagement would result. But Hood had no intention to fight. He went on to the banks of the Tennessee opposite Florence, Alabama. His army was lightly equipped, and Sherman, with his heavily burdened troops, was unable to catch him. Sherman halted at Gaylesville and ordered Schofield, with the Twenty-third Corps, and Stanley, with the Fourth Corps, to Thomas at Nashville.

Sherman thereupon determined to return to Atlanta, leaving General Thomas to meet Hood's appearance in Tennessee. It was about this time that Sherman fully decided to march to the sea. Some time before this he had telegraphed to Grant: "Hood . . . can constantly break my roads. I would infinitely prefer to make a wreck of the road . . . send back all my wounded and worthless, and, with my effective army, move through Georgia, smashing things to the sea." Grant thought it best for Sherman to destroy Hood's army

THE ATLANTA BANK BEFORE THE MARCH TO THE SEA

As this photograph was taken, the wagons stood in the street of Atlanta ready to accompany the Federals in their impending march to the sea.   The most interesting thing is the bank building on the corner, completely destroyed, although around it stand the stores of merchants entirely untouched.   Evidently there had been here faithful execution of Sherman's orders to his engineers—to destroy all buildings and property of a public nature, such as factories, foundries, railroad stations, and the like; but to protect as far as possible strictly private dwellings and enterprises.   Those of a later generation who witnessed the growth of Atlanta within less than half a century after this photograph was taken, and saw tall office-buildings and streets humming with industry around the location in this photograph, will find in it an added fascination.

first, but Sherman insisted that his plan would put him on the offensive rather than the defensive. He also believed that Hood would be forced to follow him. Grant was finally won to the view that if Hood moved on Tennessee, Thomas would be able to check him. He had, on the 11th of October, given permission for the march. Now, on the 2d of November, he telegraphed Sherman at Rome: "I do not really see that you can withdraw from where you are to follow Hood without giving up all we have gained in territory. I say, then, go on as you propose." It was Sherman, and not Grant or Lincoln, that conceived the great march, and while the march itself was not seriously opposed or difficult to carry out, the conception and purpose were masterly.

Sherman moved his army by slow and easy stages back to Atlanta. He sent the vast army stores that had collected at Atlanta, which he could not take with him, as well as his sick and wounded, to Chattanooga, destroyed the railroad to that place, also the machine-shops at Rome and other places, and on November 12th, after receiving a final despatch from Thomas and answering simply, "Despatch received—all right," the last telegraph line was severed, and Sherman had deliberately cut himself off from all communication with the Northern States. There is no incident like it in the annals of war. A strange event it was, as Sherman observes in his memoirs. "Two hostile armies marching in opposite directions, each in the full belief that it was achieving a final and conclusive result in a great war."

For the next two days all was astir in Atlanta. The great depot, round-house, and machine-shops were destroyed. Walls were battered down; chimneys pulled over; machinery smashed to pieces, and boilers punched full of holes. Heaps of rubbish covered the spots where these fine buildings had stood, and on the night of November 15th the vast débris was set on fire. The torch was also applied to many places in the business part of the city, in defiance of the strict orders of

"TUNING UP"—A DAILY DRILL IN THE CAPTURED FORT

Here Sherman's men are seen at daily drill in Atlanta. This photograph has an interest beyond most war pictures, for it gives a clear idea of the soldierly bearing of the men that were to march to the sea. There was an easy carelessness in their appearance copied from their great commander, but they were never allowed to become slouchy. Sherman was the antithesis of a martinet, but he had, in the Atlanta campaign, molded his army into the "mobile machine" that he desired it to be, and he was anxious to keep the men up to this high pitch of efficiency for the performance of still greater deeds. No better disciplined army existed in the world at the time Sherman's "bummers" set out for the sea.

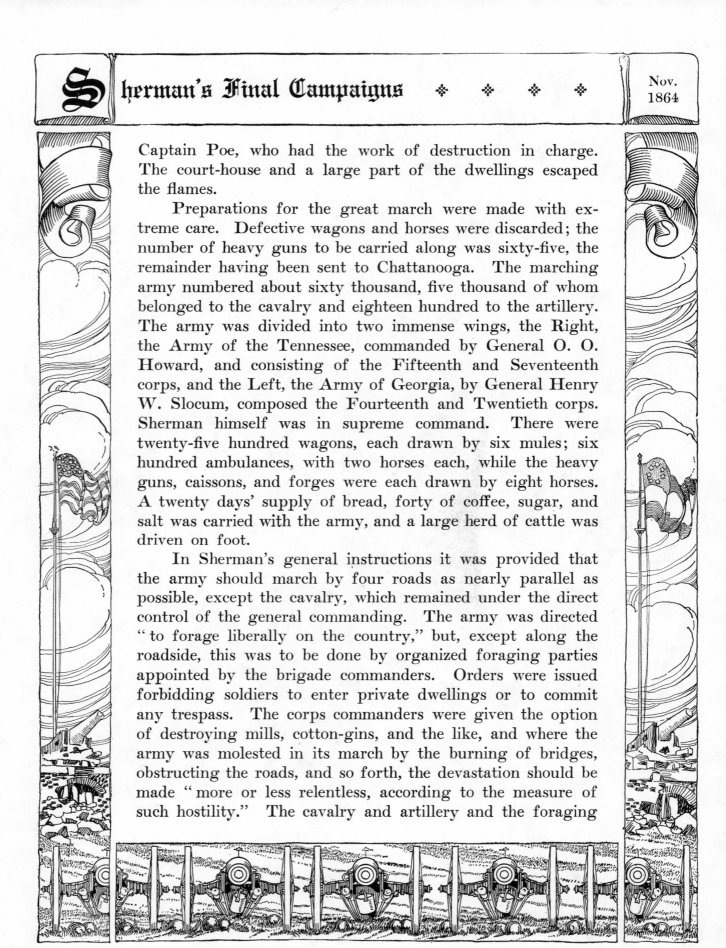

Captain Poe, who had the work of destruction in charge. The court-house and a large part of the dwellings escaped the flames.

Preparations for the great march were made with extreme care. Defective wagons and horses were discarded; the number of heavy guns to be carried along was sixty-five, the remainder having been sent to Chattanooga. The marching army numbered about sixty thousand, five thousand of whom belonged to the cavalry and eighteen hundred to the artillery. The army was divided into two immense wings, the Right, the Army of the Tennessee, commanded by General O. O. Howard, and consisting of the Fifteenth and Seventeenth corps, and the Left, the Army of Georgia, by General Henry W. Slocum, composed the Fourteenth and Twentieth corps. Sherman himself was in supreme command. There were twenty-five hundred wagons, each drawn by six mules; six hundred ambulances, with two horses each, while the heavy guns, caissons, and forges were each drawn by eight horses. A twenty days' supply of bread, forty of coffee, sugar, and salt was carried with the army, and a large herd of cattle was driven on foot.

In Sherman's general instructions it was provided that the army should march by four roads as nearly parallel as possible, except the cavalry, which remained under the direct control of the general commanding. The army was directed "to forage liberally on the country," but, except along the roadside, this was to be done by organized foraging parties appointed by the brigade commanders. Orders were issued forbidding soldiers to enter private dwellings or to commit any trespass. The corps commanders were given the option of destroying mills, cotton-gins, and the like, and where the army was molested in its march by the burning of bridges, obstructing the roads, and so forth, the devastation should be made "more or less relentless, according to the measure of such hostility." The cavalry and artillery and the foraging

CUTTING LOOSE FROM THE BASE, NOVEMBER 12TH

"On the 12th of November the railroad and telegraph communications with the rear were broken and the army stood detached from all friends, dependent on its own resources and supplies," writes Sherman. Meanwhile all detachments were marching rapidly to Atlanta with orders to break up the railroad en route and "generally to so damage the country as to make it untenable to the enemy." This was a necessary war measure. Sherman, in a home letter written from Grand Gulf, Mississippi, May 6, 1863, stated clearly his views regarding the destruction of property. Speaking of the wanton havoc wrought on a fine plantation in the path of the army, he added: "It is done, of course, by the accursed stragglers who won't fight but hang behind and disgrace our cause and country. Dr. Bowie had fled, leaving everything on the approach of our troops. Of course, devastation marked the whole path of the army, and I know all the principal officers detest the infamous practice as much as I do. Of course, I expect and do take corn, bacon, ham, mules, and everything to support an army, and don't object much to the using of fences for firewood, but this universal burning and wanton destruction of private property is not justified in war."

parties were permitted to take horses, mules, and wagons from the inhabitants without limit, except that they were to discriminate in favor of the poor. It was a remarkable military undertaking, in which it was intended to remove restrictions only to a sufficient extent to meet the requirements of the march. The cavalry was commanded by General Judson Kilpatrick, who, after receiving a severe wound at Resaca, in May, had gone to his home on the banks of the Hudson, in New York, to recuperate, and, against the advice of his physician, had joined the army again at Atlanta.

On November 15th, most of the great army was started on its march, Sherman himself riding out from the city next morning. As he rode near the spot where General McPherson had fallen, he paused and looked back at the receding city with its smoking ruins, its blackened walls, and its lonely, tenantless houses. The vision of the desperate battles, of the hope and fear of the past few months, rose before him, as he tells us, "like the memory of a dream." The day was as perfect as Nature ever gives. The men were hilarious. They sang and shouted and waved their banners in the autumn breeze. Most of them supposed they were going directly toward Richmond, nearly a thousand miles away. As Sherman rode past them they would call out, "Uncle Billy, I guess Grant is waiting for us at Richmond." Only the commanders of the wings and Kilpatrick were entrusted with the secret of Sherman's intentions. But even Sherman was not fully decided as to his objective—Savannah, Georgia, or Port Royal, South Carolina—until well on the march.

There was one certainty, however—he was fully decided to keep the Confederates in suspense as to his intentions. To do this the more effectually he divided his army at the start, Howard leading his wing to Gordon by way of McDonough as if to threaten Macon, while Slocum proceeded to Covington and Madison, with Milledgeville as his goal. Both were secretly instructed to halt, seven days after starting, at Gor-

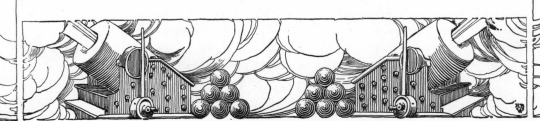

THE BUSTLE OF DEPARTURE FROM ATLANTA

Sherman's men worked like beavers during their last few days in Atlanta. There was no time to be lost; the army was gotten under way with that precision which marked all Sherman's movements. In the upper picture, finishing touches are being put to the railroad, and in the lower is seen the short work that was made of such public buildings as might be of the slightest use in case the Confederates should recapture the town. As far back as Chattanooga, while plans for the Atlanta campaign were being formed, Sherman had been revolving a subsequent march to the sea in case he was successful. He had not then made up his mind whether it should be in the direction of Mobile or Savannah, but his Meridian campaign, in Mississippi, had convinced him that the march was entirely feasible, and gradually he worked out in his mind its masterly details. At seven in the morning on November 16th, Sherman rode out along the Decatur road, passed his marching troops, and near the spot where his beloved McPherson had fallen, paused for a last look at the city. "Behind us," he says, "lay Atlanta, smouldering and in

RUINS IN ATLANTA

ruins, the black smoke rising high in air and hanging like a pall over the ruined city." All about could be seen the glistening gun-barrels and white-topped wagons, "and the men marching steadily and rapidly with a cheery look and swinging pace." Some regimental band struck up "John Brown," and the thousands of voices of the vast army joined with a mighty chorus in song. A feeling of exhilaration pervaded the troops. This marching into the unknown held for them the allurement of adventure, as none but Sherman knew their destination. But as he worked his way past them on the road, many a group called out, "Uncle Billy, I guess Grant is waiting for us at Richmond." The devil-may-care spirit of the troops brought to Sherman's mind grave thoughts of his own responsibility. He knew that success would be regarded as a matter of course, but should he fail the march would be set down as "the wild adventure of a crazy fool." He had no intention of marching directly to Richmond, but from the first his objective was the seacoast, at Savannah or Port Royal, or even Pensacola, Florida.

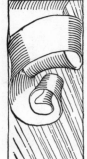

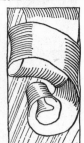

don and Milledgeville, the latter the capital of Georgia, about a hundred miles to the southeast. These two towns were about fifteen miles apart.

General Hood and General Beauregard, who had come from the East to assist him, were in Tennessee, and it was some days after Sherman had left Atlanta that they heard of his movements. They realized that to follow him would now be futile. He was nearly three hundred miles away, and not only were the railroads destroyed, but a large part of the intervening country was utterly laid waste and incapable of supporting an army. The Confederates thereupon turned their attention to Thomas, who was also in Tennessee, and was the barrier between Hood and the Northern States.

General Sherman accompanied first one corps of his army and then another. The first few days he spent with Davis' corps of Slocum's wing. When they reached Covington, the negroes met the troops in great numbers, shouting and thanking the Lord that "deliverance" had come at last. As Sherman rode along the streets they would gather around his horse and exhibit every evidence of adoration.

The foraging parties consisted of companies of fifty men. Their route for the day in which they obtained supplies was usually parallel to that of the army, five or six miles from it. They would start out before daylight in the morning, many of them on foot; but when they rejoined the column in the evening they were no longer afoot. They were astride mules, horses, in family carriages, farm wagons, and mule carts, which they packed with hams, bacon, vegetables, chickens, ducks, and every imaginable product of a Southern farm that could be useful to an army.

In the general orders, Sherman had forbidden the soldiers to enter private houses; but the order was not strictly adhered to, as many Southern people have since testified. Sherman declares in his memoirs that these acts of pillage and violence were exceptional and incidental. On one occasion Sherman

THE GUNS THAT SHERMAN TOOK ALONG

In Hood's hasty evacuation of Atlanta many of his guns were left behind. These 12-pounder Napoleon bronze field-pieces have been gathered by the Federals from the abandoned fortifications, which had been equipped entirely with field artillery, such as these. It was an extremely useful capture for Sherman's army, whose supply of artillery had been somewhat limited during the siege, and still further reduced by the necessity to fortify Atlanta. On the march to the sea Sherman took with him only sixty-five field-pieces. The Negro refugees in the lower picture recall an embarrassment of the march to the sea. "Negroes of all sizes" flocked in the army's path and stayed there, a picturesque procession, holding tightly to the skirts of the army which they believed had come for the sole purpose of setting them free. The cavalcade of Negroes soon became so numerous that Sherman became anxious for his army's sustenance, and finding an old gray-haired black at Covington, Sherman explained to him carefully that if the Negroes continued to swarm after the army it would fail in its purpose and they would not get their freedom. Sherman believed that the old man spread this news to the slaves along the line of march, and in part saved the army from being overwhelmed by the contrabands.

NEGROES FLOCKING IN THE ARMY'S PATH

saw a man with a ham on his musket, a jug of molasses under his arm, and a big piece of honey in his hand. As the man saw that he was observed by the commander, he quoted audibly to a comrade, from the general order, "forage liberally on the country." But the general reproved him and explained that foraging must be carried on only by regularly designated parties.

It is a part of military history that Sherman's sole purpose was to weaken the Confederacy by recognized means of honorable warfare; but it cannot be denied that there were a great many instances, unknown to him, undoubtedly, of cowardly hold-ups of the helpless inhabitants, or ransacking of private boxes and drawers in search of jewelry and other family treasure. This is one of the misfortunes of war—one of war's injustices. Such practices always exist even under the most rigid discipline in great armies, and the jubilation of this march was such that human nature asserted itself in the license of warfare more than on most other occasions. General Washington met with similar situations in the American Revolution. The practice is never confined to either army in warfare.

Opposed to Sherman were Wheeler's cavalry, and a large portion of the Georgia State troops which were turned over by General G. W. Smith to General Howell Cobb. Kilpatrick and his horsemen, proceeding toward Macon, were confronted by Wheeler and Cobb, but the Federal troopers drove them back into the town. However, they issued forth again, and on November 21st there was a sharp engagement with Kilpatrick at Griswoldville. The following day the Confederates were definitely checked and retreated.

The night of November 22d, Sherman spent in the home of General Cobb, who had been a member of the United States Congress and of Buchanan's Cabinet. Thousands of soldiers encamped that night on Cobb's plantation, using his fences for camp-fire fuel. By Sherman's order, everything on the

The task of General Hardee in defending Savannah was one of peculiar difficulty. He had only eighteen thousand men, and he was uncertain where Sherman would strike. Some supposed that Sherman would move at once upon Charleston, but Hardee argued that the Union army would have to establish a new base of supplies on the seacoast before attempting to cross the numerous deep rivers and swamps of South Carolina. Hardee's task therefore was to hold Savannah just as long as possible, and then to withdraw northward to unite with the troops which General Bragg was assembling, and with the detachments scattered at this time over the Carolinas. In protecting his position around Savannah, Fort McAllister was of prime importance, since it commanded the Great Ogeechee River in such a way as to prevent the approach of the Federal fleet,

THE DEFENDER OF SAVANNAH

Sherman's dependence for supplies. It was accordingly manned by a force of two hundred under command of Major G. W. Anderson, provided with fifty days' rations for use in case the work became isolated. This contingency did not arrive. About noon of December 13th, Major Anderson's men saw troops in blue moving about in the woods. The number increased. The artillery on the land side of the fort was turned upon them as they advanced from one position to another, and sharpshooters picked off some of their officers. At half-past four o'clock, however, the long-expected charge was made from three different directions, so that the defenders, too few in number to hold the whole line, were soon overpowered. Hardee now had to consider more narrowly the best time for withdrawing from the lines at Savannah.

FORT McALLISTER—THE LAST BARRIER TO THE SEA

plantation movable or destructible was carried away next day, or destroyed. Such is the price of war.

By the next night both corps of the Left Wing were at Milledgeville, and on the 24th started for Sandersville. Howard's wing was at Gordon, and it left there on the day that Slocum moved from Milledgeville for Irwin's Crossroads. A hundred miles below Milledgeville was a place called Millen, and here were many Federal prisoners which Sherman greatly desired to release. With this in view he sent Kilpatrick toward Augusta to give the impression that the army was marching thither, lest the Confederates should remove the prisoners from Millen. Kilpatrick had reached Waynesboro when he learned that the prisoners had been taken away. Here he again encountered the Confederate cavalry under General Wheeler. A sharp fight ensued and Kilpatrick drove Wheeler through the town toward Augusta. As there was no further need of making a feint on Augusta, Kilpatrick turned back toward the Left Wing. Wheeler quickly followed and at Thomas' Station nearly surrounded him, but Kilpatrick cut his way out. Wheeler still pressed on and Kilpatrick chose a good position at Buck Head Creek, dismounted, and threw up breastworks. Wheeler attacked desperately, but was repulsed, and Kilpatrick, after being reenforced by a brigade from Davis' corps, joined the Left Wing at Louisville.

On the whole, the great march was but little disturbed by the Confederates. The Georgia militia, probably ten thousand in all, did what they could to defend their homes and their firesides; but their endeavors were futile against the vast hosts that were sweeping through the country. In the skirmishes that took place between Atlanta and the sea the militia was soon brushed aside. Even their destroying of bridges and supplies in front of the invading army checked its progress but for a moment, as it was prepared for every such emergency. Wheeler, with his cavalry, caused more trouble, and engaged Kilpatrick's attention a large part of the time. But even he

WATERFRONT AT SAVANNAH, 1865

Savannah was better protected by nature from attack by land or water than any other city near the Atlantic seaboard. Stretching to the north, east, and southward lay swamps and morasses through which ran the river-approach of twelve miles to the town. Innumerable small creeks separated the marshes into islands over which it was out of the question for an army to march without first building roads and bridging miles of waterways. The Federal fleet had for months been on the blockade off the mouth of the river, and Savannah had been closed to blockade runners since the fall of Fort Pulaski in April, 1862. But obstructions and powerful batteries held the river, and Fort McAllister, ten miles to the south, on the Ogeechee, still held the city safe in its guardianship.

FORT McALLISTER, THAT HELD THE FLEET AT BAY

did not seriously retard the irresistible progress of the legions of the North.

The great army kept on its way by various routes, covering about fifteen miles a day, and leaving a swath of destruction, from forty to sixty miles wide, in its wake. Among the details attendant upon the march to the sea was that of scientifically destroying the railroads that traversed the region. Battalions of engineers had received special instruction in the art, together with the necessary implements to facilitate rapid work. But the infantry soon entered this service, too, and it was a common sight to see a thousand soldiers in blue standing beside a stretch of railway, and, when commanded, bend as one man and grasp the rail, and at a second command to raise in unison, which brought a thousand railroad ties up on end. Then the men fell upon them, ripping rail and tie apart, the rails to be heated to a white heat and bent in fantastic shapes about some convenient tree or other upright column, the ties being used as the fuel with which to make the fires. All public buildings that might have a military use were burned, together with a great number of private dwellings and barns, some by accident, others wantonly. This fertile and prosperous region, after the army had passed, was a scene of ruin and desolation.

As the army progressed, throngs of escaped slaves followed in its trail, "from the baby in arms to the old negro hobbling painfully along," says General Howard, "negroes of all sizes, in all sorts of patched costumes, with carts and broken-down horses and mules to match." Many of the old negroes found it impossible to keep pace with the army for many days, and having abandoned their homes and masters who could have cared for them, they were left to die of hunger and exposure in that naked land.

After the Ogeechee River was crossed, the character of the country was greatly changed from that of central Georgia. No longer were there fertile farms, laden with their Southern

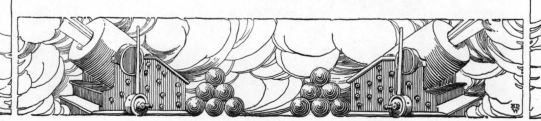

THE FIFTEEN MINUTES' FIGHT

Across these ditches at Fort McAllister, through entangling abatis, over palisading, the Federals had to fight every inch of their way against the Confederate garrison up to the very doors of their bomb-proofs, before the defenders yielded on December 13th. Sherman had at once perceived that the position could be carried only by a land assault. The fort was strongly protected by ditches, palisades, and plentiful abatis; marshes and streams covered its flanks, but Sherman's troops knew that shoes and clothing and abundant rations were waiting for them just beyond it, and had any of them been asked if they could take the fort their reply would have been in the words of the poem: "Ain't we simply got to take it?" Sherman selected for the honor of the assault General Hazen's second division of the Fifteenth Corps, the same which he himself had commanded at Shiloh and Vicksburg. Gaily the troops crossed the bridge on the morning of the 13th. Sherman was watching anxiously through his glass late in the afternoon when a Federal steamer came up the river and signaled the query: "Is Fort McAllister taken?" To which Sherman sent reply: "Not yet, but it will be in a minute." At that instant Sherman saw Hazen's troops emerge from the woods before the fort, "the lines dressed as on parade, with colors flying." Immediately dense clouds of smoke belching from the fort enveloped the Federals. There was a pause; the smoke cleared away, and, says Sherman, "the parapets were blue with our men." Fort McAllister was taken.

harvests of corn and vegetables, but rather rice plantations and great pine forests, the solemn stillness of which was broken by the tread of thousands of troops, the rumbling of wagon-trains, and by the shouts and music of the marching men and of the motley crowd of negroes that followed.

Day by day Sherman issued orders for the progress of the wings, but on December 2d they contained the decisive words, "Savannah." What a tempting prize was this fine Southern city, and how the Northern commander would add to his laurels could he effect its capture! The memories clinging about the historic old town, with its beautiful parks and its magnolia-lined streets, are part of the inheritance of not only the South, but of all America. Here Oglethorpe had bartered with the wild men of the forest, and here, in the days of the Revolution, Count Pulaski and Sergeant Jasper had given up their lives in the cause of liberty.

Sherman had partially invested the city before the middle of December; but it was well fortified and he refrained from assault. General Hardee, sent by Hood from Tennessee, had command of the defenses, with about eighteen thousand men. And there was Fort McAllister on the Ogeechee, protecting the city on the south. But this obstruction to the Federals was soon removed. General Hazen's division of the Fifteenth Corps was sent to capture the fort. At five o'clock in the afternoon of the 13th Hazen's men rushed through a shower of grape, over abatis and hidden torpedoes, scaled the parapet and captured the garrison. That night Sherman boarded the *Dandelion*, a Union vessel, in the river, and sent a message to the outside world, the first since he had left Atlanta.

Henceforth there was communication between the army and the Federal squadron, under the command of Admiral Dahlgren. Among the vessels that came up the river there was one that was received with great enthusiasm by the soldiers. It brought mail, tons of it, for Sherman's army, the accumulation of two months. One can imagine the eagerness

A BIG GUN AT FORT McALLISTER

Fort McAllister is at last in complete possession of the Federals, and a group of the men who had charged over these ramparts has arranged itself before the camera as if in the very act of firing the great gun that points seaward across the marshes, toward Ossabaw Sound.　There is one very peculiar thing proved by this photograph—the gun itself is almost in a fixed position as regards range and sweep of fire.　Instead of the elevating screw to raise or depress the muzzle, there has been substituted a block of wood wedged with a heavy spike, and the narrow pit in which the gun carriage is sunk admits of it being turned but a foot or so to right or left.　It evidently controlled one critical point in the river, but could not have been used in lending any aid to the repelling of General Hazen's attack.　The officer pointing with outstretched arm is indicating the very spot at which a shell fired from his gun would fall.　The men in the trench are artillerymen of General Hazen's division of the Fifteenth Corps; their appearance in their fine uniforms, polished breastplates and buttons, proves that Sherman's men could not have presented the ragged appearance that they are often pictured as doing in the war-time sketches.　That Army and Navy have come together is proved also by the figure of a marine from the fleet, who is standing at "Attention" just above the breach of the gun.　Next, leaning on his saber, is a cavalryman, in short jacket and chin-strap.

with which these war-stained veterans opened the longed-for letters and sought the answer to the ever-recurring question, " How are things at home? "

Sherman had set his heart on capturing Savannah; but, on December 15th, he received a letter from Grant which greatly disturbed him. Grant ordered him to leave his artillery and cavalry, with infantry enough to support them, and with the remainder of his army to come by sea to Virginia and join the forces before Richmond. Sherman prepared to obey, but hoped that he would be able to capture the city before the transports would be ready to carry him northward.

He first called on Hardee to surrender the city, with a threat of bombardment. Hardee refused. Sherman hesitated to open with his guns because of the bloodshed it would occasion, and on December 21st he was greatly relieved to discover that Hardee had decided not to defend the city, that he had escaped with his army the night before, by the one road that was still open to him, which led across the Savannah River into the Carolinas. The stream had been spanned by an improvised pontoon bridge, consisting of river-boats, with planks from city wharves for flooring and with old car-wheels for anchors. Sherman immediately took possession of the city, and on December 22d he sent to President Lincoln this message: " I beg to present to you, as a Christmas gift, the city of Savannah, with one hundred and fifty heavy guns and plenty of ammunition, and also about twenty-five thousand bales of cotton." As a matter of fact, over two hundred and fifty guns were captured, and thirty-one thousand bales of cotton. General Hardee retreated to Charleston.

Events in the West now changed Grant's views as to Sherman's joining him immediately in Virginia. On the 16th of December, General Thomas accomplished the defeat and utter rout of Hood's army at Nashville. In addition, it was found that, owing to lack of transports, it would take at least two months to transfer Sherman's whole army by sea. There-

THE SPOILS OF VICTORY

Here are the men that marched to the sea doing their turn as day-laborers, gleefully trundling their wheelbarrows, gathering up everything of value in Fort McAllister to swell the size of Sherman's "Christmas present." Brigadier-General W. B. Hazen, after his men had successfully stormed the stubbornly defended fort, reported the capture of twenty-four pieces of ordnance, with their equipment, forty tons of ammunition, a month's supply of food for the garrison, and the small arms of the command. In the upper picture the army engineers are busily at work removing a great 48-pounder 8-inch Columbiad that had so long repelled the Federal fleet. There is always work enough and to spare for the engineers both before and after the capture of a fortified position. In the wheelbarrows is a harvest of shells and torpedoes. These deadly instruments of destruction had been relied upon by the Confederates to protect the land approach to Fort McAllister, which was much less strongly defensible on that side than at the waterfront. While Sherman's army was approaching Savannah one of his officers had his leg blown off by a torpedo buried in the road and stepped on by his horse. After that Sherman set a line of Confederate prisoners across the road to march ahead of the army, and no more torpedoes were found. After the capture of Fort McAllister the troops set to work gingerly scraping about wherever the ground seemed to have been disturbed, trying to find and remove the dangerous hidden menaces to life. At last the ground was rendered safe and the troops settled down to the occupation of Fort McAllister where the bravely fighting little Confederate garrison had held the key to Savannah. The city was the first to fall of the Confederacy's Atlantic seaports, now almost locked from the outside world by the blockade. By the capture of Fort McAllister, which crowned the march to the sea, Sherman had numbered the days of the war. The fall of the remaining ports was to follow in quick succession, and by Washington's Birthday, 1865, the entire coast-line was to be in possession of the Federals.

SHERMAN'S TROOPS DISMANTLING FORT McALLISTER

fore, it was decided that Sherman should march through the Carolinas, destroying the railroads in both States as he went. A little more than a month Sherman remained in Savannah. Then he began another great march, compared with which, as Sherman himself declared, the march to the sea was as child's play. The size of his army on leaving Savannah was practically the same as when he left Atlanta—sixty thousand. It was divided into two wings, under the same commanders, Howard and Slocum, and was to be governed by the same rules. Kilpatrick still commanded the cavalry. The march from Savannah averaged ten miles a day, which, in view of the conditions, was a very high average. The weather in the early part of the journey was exceedingly wet and the roads were well-nigh impassable. Where they were not actually under water the mud rendered them impassable until corduroyed. Moreover, the troops had to wade streams, to drag themselves through swamps and quagmires, and to remove great trees that had been felled across their pathway.

The city of Savannah was left under the control of General J. G. Foster, and the Left Wing of Sherman's army under Slocum moved up the Savannah River, accompanied by Kilpatrick, and crossed it at Sister's Ferry. The river was overflowing its banks and the crossing, by means of a pontoon bridge, was effected with the greatest difficulty. The Right Wing, under Howard, embarked for Beaufort, South Carolina, and moved thence to Pocotaligo, near the Broad River, whither Sherman had preceded it, and the great march northward was fairly begun by February 1, 1865.

Sherman had given out the word that he expected to go to Charleston or Augusta, his purpose being to deceive the Confederates, since he had made up his mind to march straight to Columbia, the capital of South Carolina.

The two wings of the army were soon united and they continued their great march from one end of the State of South Carolina to the other. The men felt less restraint in devas-

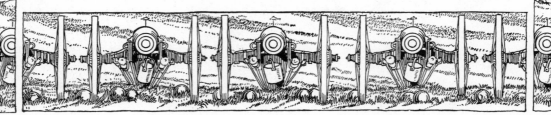

COLOR–GUARD OF THE EIGHTH MINNESOTA—WITH SHERMAN WHEN JOHNSTON SURRENDERED

The Eighth Minnesota Regiment, which had joined Sherman on his second march, was with him when Johnston's surrender wrote "Finis" to the last chapter of the war, April 26, 1865. In Bennett's little farmhouse, near Durham's Station, N. C., were begun the negotiations between Johnston and Sherman which finally led to that event. The two generals met there on April 17th; it was a highly dramatic moment, for Sherman had in his pocket the cipher message just received telling of the assassination of Lincoln.

THE END OF THE MARCH—BENNETT'S FARMHOUSE

tating the country and despoiling the people than they had felt in Georgia. The reason for this, given by Sherman and others, was that there was a feeling of bitterness against South Carolina as against no other State. It was this State that had led the procession of seceding States and that had fired on Fort Sumter and brought on the great war. No doubt this feeling, which pervaded the army, will account in part for the reckless dealing with the inhabitants by the Federal soldiery. The superior officers, however, made a sincere effort to restrain lawlessness.

On February 17th, Sherman entered Columbia, the mayor having come out and surrendered the city. The Fifteenth Corps marched through the city and out on the Camden road, the remainder of the army not having come within two miles of the city. On that night Columbia was in flames. The conflagration spread and ere the coming of the morning the best part of the city had been laid in ashes.

Before Sherman left Columbia he destroyed the machine-shops and everything else which might aid the Confederacy. He left with the mayor one hundred stand of arms with which to keep order, and five hundred head of cattle for the destitute.

As Columbia was approached by the Federals, the occupation of Charleston by the Confederates became more and more untenable. In vain had the governor of South Carolina pleaded with President Davis to reenforce General Hardee, who occupied the city. Hardee thereupon evacuated the historic old city—much of which was burned, whether by design or accident is not known—and its defenses, including Fort Sumter, the bombardment of which, nearly four years before, had precipitated the mighty conflict, were occupied by Colonel Bennett, who came over from Morris Island.

On March 11th, Sherman reached Fayetteville, North Carolina, where he destroyed a fine arsenal. Hitherto, Sherman's march, except for the annoyance of Wheeler's cavalry, had been but slightly impeded by the Confederates. But

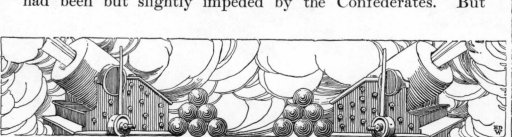

AN EMERGENCY GUNBOAT FROM THE NEW YORK FERRY SERVICE

This craft, the "Commodore Perry," was an old New York ferryboat purchased and hastily pressed into service by the Federal navy to help solve the problem of patrolling the three thousand miles of coast, along which the blockade must be made effective. In order to penetrate the intricate inlets and rivers, light-draft fighting-vessels were required, and the most immediate means of securing these was to purchase every sort of merchant craft that could possibly be adapted to the purposes of war, either as a fighting-vessel or as a transport. The ferryboat in the picture has been provided with guns and her pilot-houses armored. A casemate of iron plates has been provided for the gunners. The Navy Department purchased and equipped in all one hundred and thirty-six vessels in 1861, and by the end of the year had increased the number of seamen in the service from 7,600 to over 22,000. Many of these new recruits saw their first active service aboard the converted ferryboats, tugboats, and other frail and unfamiliar vessels making up the nondescript fleet that undertook to cut off the commerce of the South. The experience thus gained under very unusual circumstances placed them of necessity among the bravest sailors of the navy.

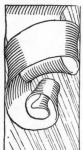

henceforth this was changed. General Joseph B. Johnston, his old foe of Resaca and Kenesaw Mountain, had been recalled and was now in command of the troops in the Carolinas. No longer would the streams and the swamps furnish the only resistance to the progress of the Union army.

The first engagement came at Averysboro on March 16th. General Hardee, having taken a strong position, made a determined stand; but a division of Slocum's wing, aided by Kilpatrick, soon put him to flight, with the loss of several guns and over two hundred prisoners.

The battle of Bentonville, which took place three days after that of Averysboro, was more serious. Johnston had placed his whole army, probably thirty-five thousand men, in the form of a V, the sides embracing the village of Bentonville. Slocum engaged the Confederates while Howard was hurried to the scene. On two days, the 19th and 20th of March, Sherman's army fought its last battle in the Civil War. But Johnston, after making several attacks, resulting in considerable losses on both sides, withdrew his army during the night, and the Union army moved to Goldsboro. The losses at Bentonville were: Federal, 1,527; Confederate, 2,606.

At Goldsboro the Union army was reenforced by its junction with Schofield, who had come out of the West with over twenty-two thousand men from the army of Thomas in Tennessee. But there was little need of reenforcement. Sherman's third great march was practically over. As to the relative importance of the second and third, Sherman declares in his memoirs, he would place that from Atlanta to the sea at one, and that from Savannah through the Carolinas at ten.

Leaving his army in charge of Schofield, Sherman went to City Point, in Virginia, where he had a conference with General Grant and President Lincoln, and plans for the final campaign were definitely arranged. He returned to Goldsboro late in March, and, pursuing Johnston, received, finally, on April 26th the surrender of his army.

THE LAST PORT CLOSED

Fort Fisher, captured January 15, 1865. With the capture of Fort Fisher, Wilmington, the great importing depot of the South, on which General Lee said the subsistence of his army depended, was finally closed to all blockade runners. The Federal navy concentrated against the fortifications of this port the most powerful naval force ever assembled up to that time—fifty-five ships of war, including five ironclads, altogether carrying six hundred guns. The upper picture shows the nature of the palisade, nine feet high, over which some two thousand marines attempted to pass; the lower shows interior of the works after the destructive bombardment.

INSIDE FORT FISHER—WORK OF THE UNION FLEET

CAUGHT BY HER OWN KIND

The blockade-runner "A. D. Vance." It frequently took a blockade-runner to catch a blockade-runner, and as the Federal navy captured ship after ship of this character they began to acquire a numerous fleet of swift steamers from which it was difficult for any vessel to get away. The "Vance" brought many a cargo to the hungry Southern ports, slipping safely by the blockading fleet and back again till her shrewd Captain Willie felt that he could give the slip to anything afloat. On her last trip she had safely gotten by the Federal vessels lying off the harbor of Wilmington, North Carolina, and was dancing gleefully on her way with a bountiful cargo of cotton and turpentine when, on September 10, 1864, in latitude 34° N., longitude 76° W., a vessel was sighted which rapidly bore down upon her. It proved to be the "Santiago de Cuba," Captain O. S. Glisson. The rapidity with which the approaching vessel overhauled him was enough to convince Captain Willie that she was in his own class. The "Santiago de Cuba" carried eleven guns, and the "Vance" humbly hove to, to receive the prize-crew which took her to Boston, where she was condemned. In the picture we see her lying high out of the water, her valuable cargo having been removed and sold to enrich by prize-money the officers and men of her fleet captor.

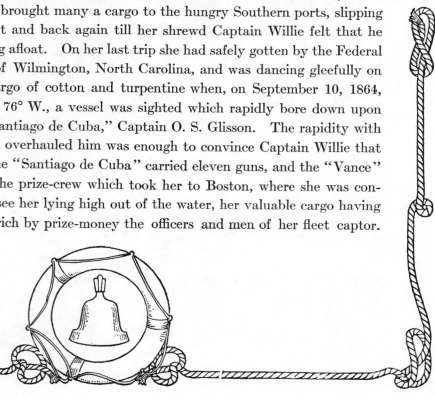

A GREYHOUND CAUGHT—WRECK OF THE BLOCKADE–RUNNER "COLT"

The wreck of this blockade-runner, the "Colt," lies off Sullivan's Island, Charleston Harbor, in 1865. The coast of the Carolinas, before the war was over, was strewn with just such sights as this. The bones of former "greyhounds" became landmarks by which the still uncaptured block-ade-runners could get their bearings and lay a course to safety. If one of these vessels were cut off from making port and surrounded by Federal pursuers, the next best thing was to run her ashore in shallow water, where the gunboats could not follow and where her valuable cargo could be se-cured by the Confederates. A single cargo at war-time prices was enough to pay more than the cost of the vessel. Regular auctions were held in Charleston or Wilmington, where prices for goods not needed by the Confederate Government were run up to fabulous figures. The business of blockade-running was well organized abroad, especially in England. One successful trip was enough to start the enterprise with a handsome profit. A blockade-runner like the "Kate," which made forty trips or more, would enrich her owners almost beyond the dreams of avarice.

THE CONFEDERATE RAM "STONEWALL"

Here are two striking views in the Port Royal dry-dock of the Confederate ram "Stonewall." When this powerful fighting-ship sailed from Copenhagen, Jan. 6, 1865, under command of Capt. T. J. Page, C.S.N., the Federal navy became confronted by its most formidable antagonist during the war. In March, 1863, the Confederacy had negotiated a loan of £3,000,000, and being thus at last in possession of the necessary funds, Captain Bulloch and Mr. Slidell arranged with M. Arman, who was a member of the *Corps-Legislatif* and proprietor of a large shipyard at Bordeaux, for the construction of ironclad ships of war. Mr. Slidell had already received assurances from persons in the confidence of Napoleon III that the building of the ships in the French yards would not be interfered with, and that getting them to sea would be connived at by the Government. Owing to the indubitable proof laid before the Emperor by the Federal diplomats at Paris, he was compelled to revoke the guarantee that had been given to Slidell and Bulloch. A plan was arranged, however, by which M. Arman should sell the vessels to various European powers; and he disposed of the ironclad ram "Sphinx" to the Danish Government, then at war with Prussia. Delivery of the ship at Copenhagen was not made, however, till after the war had ceased, and no trouble was experienced by the Confederates in arranging for the purchase of the vessel. On January 24, 1865, she rendezvoused off Quiberon, on the French coast; the remainder of her officers, crew, and supplies were put aboard of her;

the Confederate flag was hoisted over her, and she was christened the "Stonewall." Already the vessel was discovered to have sprung a leak, and Captain Page ran into Ferrol, Spain. Here dock-yard facilities were at first granted, but were withdrawn at the protest of the American Minister. While Captain Page was repairing his vessel as best he could, the "Niagara" and the "Sacramento" appeared, and after some weeks the "Stonewall" offered battle in vain.

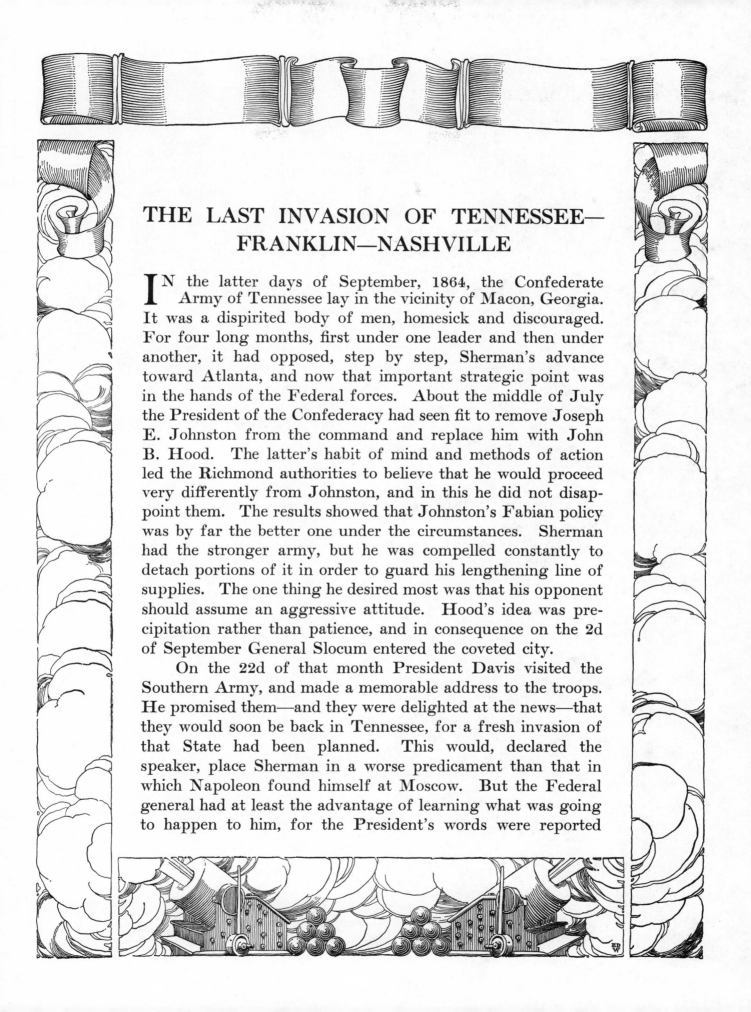

THE LAST INVASION OF TENNESSEE—
FRANKLIN—NASHVILLE

IN the latter days of September, 1864, the Confederate
Army of Tennessee lay in the vicinity of Macon, Georgia.
It was a dispirited body of men, homesick and discouraged.
For four long months, first under one leader and then under
another, it had opposed, step by step, Sherman's advance
toward Atlanta, and now that important strategic point was
in the hands of the Federal forces. About the middle of July
the President of the Confederacy had seen fit to remove Joseph
E. Johnston from the command and replace him with John
B. Hood. The latter's habit of mind and methods of action
led the Richmond authorities to believe that he would proceed
very differently from Johnston, and in this he did not disap-
point them. The results showed that Johnston's Fabian policy
was by far the better one under the circumstances. Sherman
had the stronger army, but he was compelled constantly to
detach portions of it in order to guard his lengthening line of
supplies. The one thing he desired most was that his opponent
should assume an aggressive attitude. Hood's idea was pre-
cipitation rather than patience, and in consequence on the 2d
of September General Slocum entered the coveted city.

On the 22d of that month President Davis visited the
Southern Army, and made a memorable address to the troops.
He promised them—and they were delighted at the news—that
they would soon be back in Tennessee, for a fresh invasion of
that State had been planned. This would, declared the
speaker, place Sherman in a worse predicament than that in
which Napoleon found himself at Moscow. But the Federal
general had at least the advantage of learning what was going
to happen to him, for the President's words were reported

verbatim in the Southern papers, and he prepared to meet his antagonists. Thomas, with the Army of the Cumberland, was sent to Nashville while Schofield, with his smaller force known as the Army of the Ohio, returned to Knoxville where he had spent the previous winter, to await Hood's advance. By the 1st of October the latter was across the Chattahoochee in the hope of drawing Sherman from Atlanta. There was a brave fight at Allatoona where General Corse "held the fort," but Sherman, although he followed the Confederate army, was unable to bring on a general engagement.

His great plan of a march through Georgia to the sea was now fully formed in his mind. He had not yet obtained Grant's sanction to the scheme, but he ordered Schofield to cooperate with Thomas and sent the Fourth Corps as further assistance. He himself ceased the pursuit of Hood at Gaylesville and turned back to Atlanta, confident that the fate of Tennessee was safe in the hands of his ablest lieutenant, George H. Thomas. Hood appeared on the 26th of October at Decatur on the south bank of the Tennessee River. Lack of supplies had delayed his advance, but even so his performances had greatly alarmed the North. Twice had he interposed between Sherman and the Federal base and had destroyed many miles of railway, but what in other circumstances would have placed the Union leader in a dangerous predicament was now of little moment, since the latter was rapidly making preparations to cut himself off from all communication with the source of his supplies. It was necessary that Hood should have the assistance of Forrest, whose dauntless cavalry had been playing great havoc with the Federal stores in western Tennessee, so he moved to Florence before crossing the river, and here Forrest joined him on November 14th. In the meantime, Schofield, with about twenty-eight thousand men, had reached Pulaski on the way to encounter the Southern advance.

Now began a series of brilliant strategic moves, kept up for a fortnight before the two small armies—they were of

RUSHING A FEDERAL BATTERY OUT OF JOHNSONVILLE

When Thomas began to draw together his forces to meet Hood at Nashville, he ordered the garrison at Johnsonville, on the Tennessee, eighty miles due west of Nashville, to leave that place and hasten north. It was the garrison at this same Johnsonville that, a month earlier, had been frightened into panic and flight when the bold Confederate raider, Forrest, appeared on the west bank of the river and began a noisy cannonade. New troops had been sent to the post. They appear well coated and equipped. The day after the photograph was taken (November 23d) the encampment in the picture was broken.

almost equal strength—met in one awful clash. Hood's efforts were bent toward cutting Schofield off from Thomas at Nashville. There was a mad race for the Duck River, and the Federals got over at Columbia in the very nick of time. The Southern leader, by a skilful piece of strategy and a forced march, pushed on to Spring Hill ahead of his opponent. He was in an excellent position to annihilate General Stanley who was in advance, and then crush the remainder of the Federals who were moving with the slow wagon-trains. But owing to a number of strange mishaps, which brought forth much recrimination but no satisfactory explanation, the Union army slipped by with little damage and entrenched itself at Franklin on the Harpeth River. Of all the dark days of Confederate history—and they were many—the 29th of November, 1864, has been mourned as that of "lost opportunities."

Schofield did not expect, or desire, a battle at Franklin, but he was treated to one the following afternoon when the Confederates came up, and it was of the most severe nature. The first attack was made as the light began to wane, and the Federal troops stood their ground although the orders had been to withdraw, because through some blunder two brigades in blue had been stationed, unsupported, directly in front of Hood's approach. The stubborn resistance of Schofield's army only increased the ardor of the opponents. It is said that thirteen separate assaults were made upon the Union entrenchments, and the fearful carnage was finally carried into the streets and among the dooryards of the little town. At nine o'clock the fury of the iron storm was quelled. Five Confederate generals, including the gallant Cleburne, lay dead upon the field. In two of the Southern brigades all the general officers were either killed or wounded. Hood's loss was about sixty-three hundred, nearly three times that of Schofield. By midnight the latter was on his way, uninterrupted, to Nashville.

Meanwhile Thomas was performing a herculean task within the fortifications of that capital city. He had received

FORT NEGLEY, LOOKING TOWARD THE CONFEDERATE CENTER AND LEFT, AS HOOD'S VETERANS THREATENED THE CITY

It was Hood's hope that, when he had advanced his line to the left of the position shown in this photograph, he might catch a weak spot in Thomas' forces. But Thomas had no weak spots. From the casemate, armored with railroad iron, shown here, the hills might be easily seen on which the Confederate center and left were posted at the opening of the great battle of Nashville.

THE PRIZE OF THE NASHVILLE CAMPAIGN—THE STATE CAPITOL

a large number of raw recruits and a motley collection of troops from garrisons in the West. These had to be drilled into an efficient army, and not one move to fight would Thomas make until this had been done. Grant, in Virginia, grew impatient and the Northern papers clamored for an attack on Hood, who had now arrived with thirty-eight thousand men before the city. Finally Grant took action, and General Logan was hurrying to assume the Federal command. But by the time he reached Louisville there was no need for his services.

Thomas had for some days been ready with his force of forty-five thousand, but to increase the difficulties of his position, a severe storm of freezing rain made action impossible until the morning of December 15th. The Union lines of defense were in a semi-circle and Hood was on the southeast, lightly entrenched. The first assault on his right wing followed by one on his left, forced the Confederates back to a second position two miles to the south, and that was the first day's work. Hood had detached a part of his forces and he did all he could to gain time until he might recover his full strength. But he had respite only until Thomas was ready on the morrow, which was about noon. The Union army deployed in front of the Southerners and overlapped their left wing. An attack on the front was bravely met and repulsed by the Confederates, and the Federal leader, extending his right, compelled his opponent to stretch his own lines more and more. Finally they broke just to the left of the center, and a general forward movement on the Union side ended in the utter rout of the splendid and courageous Army of Tennessee.

It melted away in disorder; the pursuit was vigorous, and only a small portion reassembled at Columbia and fell back with a poor show of order behind the Tennessee.

Many military historians have seen in the battle of Nashville the most crushing defeat of the war. Certainly no other brought such complete ruin upon a large and well-organized body of troops.

THOMAS ADVANCING HIS OUTER LINE AT NASHVILLE, DECEMBER 16TH

Camp-fires were still smouldering along the side of the abatis where the lens caught the field of Nashville, while Thomas' concentric forward movement was in progress. Note the abatis to the right of the picture, the wagons moving and ready to move in the background, and the artillery on the left. White tents gleam from the distant hills. A few straggling soldiers remain. The Federals are closing with Hood's army a couple of miles to the right of the scene in the picture.

GUARDING THE LINE DURING THE ADVANCE

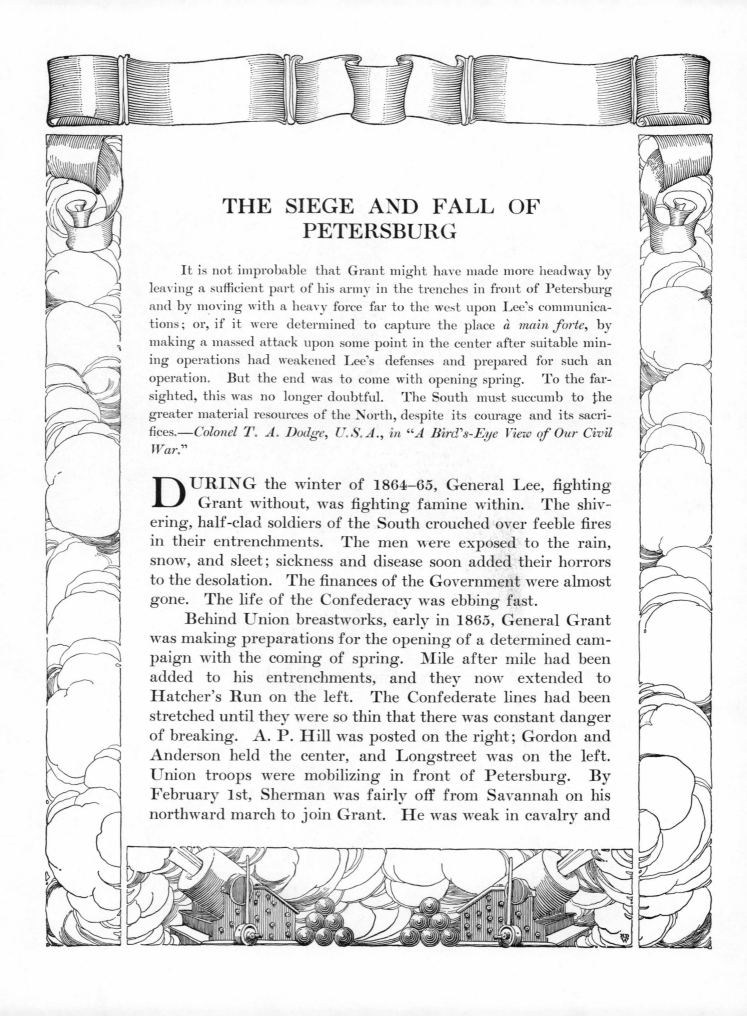

THE SIEGE AND FALL OF PETERSBURG

It is not improbable that Grant might have made more headway by leaving a sufficient part of his army in the trenches in front of Petersburg and by moving with a heavy force far to the west upon Lee's communications; or, if it were determined to capture the place *à main forte*, by making a massed attack upon some point in the center after suitable mining operations had weakened Lee's defenses and prepared for such an operation. But the end was to come with opening spring. To the far-sighted, this was no longer doubtful. The South must succumb to the greater material resources of the North, despite its courage and its sacrifices.—*Colonel T. A. Dodge, U.S.A., in "A Bird's-Eye View of Our Civil War."*

DURING the winter of 1864–65, General Lee, fighting Grant without, was fighting famine within. The shivering, half-clad soldiers of the South crouched over feeble fires in their entrenchments. The men were exposed to the rain, snow, and sleet; sickness and disease soon added their horrors to the desolation. The finances of the Government were almost gone. The life of the Confederacy was ebbing fast.

Behind Union breastworks, early in 1865, General Grant was making preparations for the opening of a determined campaign with the coming of spring. Mile after mile had been added to his entrenchments, and they now extended to Hatcher's Run on the left. The Confederate lines had been stretched until they were so thin that there was constant danger of breaking. A. P. Hill was posted on the right; Gordon and Anderson held the center, and Longstreet was on the left. Union troops were mobilizing in front of Petersburg. By February 1st, Sherman was fairly off from Savannah on his northward march to join Grant. He was weak in cavalry and

A BATTERED RELIC OF COLONIAL DAYS IN PETERSBURG

This beautiful old mansion on Bolingbroke Street could look back to the days of buckles and small clothes; it wears an aggrieved and surprised look, as if wondering why it should have received such buffetings as its pierced walls, its shattered windows and doorway show. Yet it was more fortunate than some of its near-by neighbors, which were never again after the visitation of the falling shells fit habitations for mankind. Many of these handsome residences were utterly destroyed, their fixtures shattered beyond repair; their wainscoting, built when the Commonwealth of Virginia was

THE SHATTERED DOORWAY

ruled over by the representative of King George, was torn from the walls and, bursting into flames, made a funeral pyre of past comforts and magnificence. The havoc wrought upon the dwellings of the town was heavy; certain localities suffered more than others, and those residents who seemed to dwell in the safest zones had been ever ready to open their houses to the sick and wounded of Lee's army. As Grant's troops marched in, many pale faces gazed out at them from the windows, and at the doorsteps stood men whose wounds exempted them from ever bearing arms again.

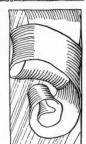

Grant determined to bring Sheridan from the Shenandoah, whence the bulk of Early's forces had been withdrawn, and send him to assist Sherman. Sheridan left Winchester February 27th, wreaking much destruction as he advanced, but circumstances compelled him to seek a new base at White House. On March 27th he formed a junction with the armies of the Potomac and the James. Such were the happenings that prompted Lee to prepare for the evacuation of Petersburg. And he might be able, in his rapid marches, to outdistance Grant, join his forces with those of Johnston, fall on Sherman, destroy one wing of the Union army and arouse the hopes of his soldiers, and prolong the life of his Government.

General Grant knew the condition of Lee's army and, with the unerring instinct of a military leader, surmised what the plan of the Southern general must be. He decided to move on the left, destroy both the Danville and South Side railroads, and put his army in better condition to pursue. The move was ordered for March 29th.

General Lee, in order to get Grant to look another way for a while, decided to attack Grant's line on the right, and gain some of the works. This would compel Grant to draw some of his force from his left and secure a way of escape to the west. This bold plan was left for execution to the gallant Georgian, General John B. Gordon, who had successfully led the reverse attack at Cedar Creek, in the Shenandoah, in October, 1864. Near the crater stood Fort Stedman. Between it and the Confederate front, a distance of about one hundred and fifty yards, was a strip of firm earth, in full view of both picket lines. Across this space some deserters had passed to the Union entrenchments. General Gordon took advantage of this fact and accordingly selected his men, who, at the sound of the signal gun, should disarm the Federal pickets, while fifty more men were to cross the open space quickly with axes and cut away the abatis, and three hundred others were to rush through the opening, and capture the fort and guns.

APPROACHING THE POST OF DANGER—PETERSBURG, 1865

A FEW STEPS NEARER THE PICKET LINE

IN BEHIND THE SHELTER

For nine months of '64–'65 the musket-balls sang past these Federal picket posts, in advance of Federal Fort Sedgwick, called by the Confederates "Fort Hell." Directly opposite was the Confederate Fort Mahone, which the Federals, returning the compliment, had dubbed "Fort Damnation." Between the two lines, separated by only fifty yards, sallies and counter-sallies were continual occurrences after dark. In stealthy sorties one side or the other frequently captured the opposing pickets before alarm could be given. No night was without its special hazard. During the day the pastime here was sharp-shooting with muskets and rifled cannon.

At four o'clock on the morning of March 25, 1865, Gordon had everything in readiness. His chosen band wore white strips of cloth across the breast, that they might distinguish each other in the hand-to-hand fight that would doubtless ensue. Behind these men half of Lee's army was massed to support the attack. In the silence of the early morning, a gunshot rang out from the Confederate works. Not a Federal picket-shot was heard. The axemen rushed across the open and soon the thuds of their axes told of the cutting away of the abatis. The three hundred surged through the entrance, overpowered the gunners, captured batteries to the right and to the left, and were in control of the situation. Gordon's corps of about five thousand was on hand to sustain the attack but the remaining reserves, through failure of the guides, did not come, and the general found himself cut off with a rapidly increasing army surrounding him.

Fort Haskell, on the left, began to throw its shells. Under its cover, heavy columns of Federals sent by General Parke, now commanding the Ninth Corps, pressed forward. The Confederates resisted the charge, and from the captured Fort Stedman and the adjoining batteries poured volley after volley on Willcox's advancing lines of blue. The Northerners fell back, only to re-form and renew the attack. This time they secured a footing, and for twenty minutes the fighting was terrific. Again they were repulsed. Then across the brow of the hill swept the command of Hartranft. The blue masses literally poured onto the field. The furious musketry, and artillery directed by General Tidball, shrivelled up the ranks of Gordon until they fled from the fort and its neighboring batteries in the midst of withering fire, and those who did not were captured. This was the last aggressive effort of the expiring Confederacy in front of Petersburg, and it cost three thousand men. The Federal loss was not half that number.

The affair at Fort Stedman did not turn Grant from his plans against the Confederate right. With the railroads here

SECURITY FROM SURPRISE

THE MOLE–HILL RAMPARTS, NEAR THE CRATER

These well-made protections of sharpened spikes, as formidable as the pointed spears of a Roman legion, are *chevaux-de-frise* of the Confederates before their main works at Petersburg. They were built after European models, the same as employed in the Napoleonic wars, and were used by both besiegers and besieged along the lines south of the Appomattox. Those shown in this picture were in front of the entrenchments near Elliott's salient and show how effectually it was protected from any attempt to storm the works by rushing tactics on the part of the Federal infantry. Not far from here lies the excavation of the Crater.

destroyed, Richmond would be completely cut off. On the morning of the 29th, as previously arranged, the movement began. Sheridan swept to the south with his cavalry, as if he were to fall upon the railroads. General Warren, with fifteen thousand men, was working his way through the tangled woods and low swamps in the direction of Lee's right. At the same time, Lee stripped his entrenchments at Petersburg as much as he dared and hurried General Anderson, with infantry, and Fitzhugh Lee, with cavalry, forward to hold the roads over which he hoped to escape. On Friday morning, March 31st, the opposing forces, the Confederates much reenforced, found themselves at Dinwiddie Court House. The woods and swamps prevented the formation of a regular line of battle. Lee made his accustomed flank movement, with heavy loss to the Federals as they tried to move in the swampy forests. The Northerners finally were ready to advance when it was found that Lee had fallen back. During the day and night, reenforcements were coming in from all sides. The Confederates had taken their position at Five Forks.

Early the next afternoon, the 1st of April, Sheridan, reenforced by Warren, was arranging his troops for battle. The day was nearly spent when all was in readiness. The sun was not more than two hours high when the Northern army moved toward that of the South, defended by a breastwork behind a dense undergrowth of pines. Through this mass of timber the Federals crept with bayonets fixed. They charged upon the Confederates, but, at the same time, a galling fire poured into them from the left, spreading dismay and destruction in their midst. The intrepid Sheridan urged his black battlecharger, the famous Rienzi, now known as Winchester, up and down the lines, cheering his men on in the fight. He seemed to be everywhere at once. The Confederate left was streaming down the White Oak Road. But General Crawford had reached a cross-road, by taking a circuitous route, and the Southern army was thus shut off from retreat. The Federal

[Concluded on page 294]

To this gallant young Georgia officer, just turned thirty-three at the time, Lee entrusted the last desperate effort to break through the tightening Federal lines, March 25, 1865. Lee was confronted by the dilemma of either being starved out of Petersburg and Richmond, or of getting out himself and uniting his army to that of Johnston in North Carolina, to crush Sherman before Grant could reach him. Gordon was to begin this latter, almost impossible, task by an attack on Fort Stedman, which the Confederates believed to be the weakest point in the Federal fortifications. The position had been captured from them in the beginning, and they knew that the nature of the ground and its nearness to their own lines had made it difficult to strengthen it very much. It was planned to surprise the fort before daylight. Below are seen the rabbit-like burrows of Gracie's Salient, past which Gordon led his famished men. When the order came to go forward, they did not flinch, but hurled themselves bravely against fortifications far stronger than their own. Three columns of a hundred picked men each moved down the slope shown on the left and advanced in the darkness against

GENERAL JOHN B. GORDON,
C. S. A.

Stedman. They were to be followed by a division. Through the gap which the storming parties were expected to open in the Federal lines, Gordon's columns would rush in both directions and a cavalry force was to sweep on and destroy the pontoon bridges across the Appomattox and to raid City Point, breaking up the Federal base. It was no light task, for although Fort Stedman itself was weak, it was flanked by Battery No. 10 on the right and by Battery No. 11 on the left. An attacking party on the right would be exposed to an enfilading fire in crossing the plain; while on the left the approach was difficult because of ravines, one of which the Confederate engineers had turned into a pond by damming a creek. All night long General Gordon's wife, with the brave women of Petersburg, sat up tearing strips of white cloth, to be tied on the arms of the men in the storming parties so that they could tell friend from foe in the darkness and confusion of the assault. Before the sleep-dazed Federals could offer effective resistance, Gordon's men had possession of the fort and the batteries. Only after one of the severest engagements of the siege were the Confederates driven back.

GRACIE'S SALIENT—AFTER GORDON'S FORLORN HOPE HAD CHARGED

cavalry had dismounted and was doing its full share of work. The Confederates soon found themselves trapped, and the part of their army in action that day was nearly annihilated. About five thousand prisoners were taken.

With night came the news of the crushing blow to Lee. General Grant was seated by his camp-fire surrounded by his staff, when a courier dashed into his presence with the message of victory. Soon from every great gun along the Union line belched forth the sheets of flame. The earth shook with the awful cannonade. Mortar shells made huge parabolas through the air. The Union batteries crept closer and closer to the Confederate lines and the balls crashed into the streets of the doomed city. The bombardment of Petersburg was on.

At dawn of the 2nd of April the grand assault began. The Federal troops sprang forward with a rush. Despite the storms of grape and canister, the Sixth Corps plunged through the battery smoke, and across the walls, pushing the brave defenders to the inner works. The whole corps penetrated the lines and swept everything before it toward Hatcher's Run. Some of the troops even reached the South Side Railroad, where the brave General A. P. Hill fell mortally wounded.

Everywhere, the blue masses poured into the works. General Ord, on the right of the Sixth Corps, helped to shut the Confederate right into the city. General Parke, with the Ninth Corps, carried the main line. The thin gray line could no longer stem the tide that was engulfing it. The Confederate troops south of Hatcher's Run fled to the west, and fought General Miles until General Sheridan and a division from Meade appeared on the scene. By noon the Federals held the line of the outer works from Fort Gregg to the Appomattox. The last stronghold carried was Fort Gregg, at which the men of Gibbon's corps had one of the most desperate struggles of the war. The Confederates now fell back to the inner fortifications and the siege of Petersburg came to an end.

APRIL SECOND—"THIS IS A SAD BUSINESS"

As his general watched, this boy fought to stem the Federal rush—but fell, his breast pierced by a bayonet, in the trenches of Fort Mahone. It is heart-rending to look at a picture such as this; it is sad to think of it and to write about it. Here is a boy of only fourteen years, his face innocent of a razor, his feet unshod and stockingless in the bitter April weather. It is to be hoped that the man who slew him has forgotten it, for this face would haunt him surely. Many who fought in the blue ranks were young, but in the South there were whole companies made up of such boys as this. At the battle of Newmarket the scholars of the Virgina Military Institute, the eldest seventeen and the youngest twelve, marched from the classrooms under arms, joined the forces of General Breckinridge, and aided by their historic charge to gain a brilliant victory over the Federal General Sigel. The never-give-in spirit was implanted in the youth of the Confederacy, as well as in the hearts of the grizzled veterans. Lee had inspired them, but in addition to this inspiration, as General Gordon writes, "every man of them was supported by their extraordinary consecration, resulting from the conviction that he was fighting in the defense of home and the rights of his State. Hence their unfaltering faith in the justice of the cause, their fortitude in the extremest privations, their readiness to stand shoeless and shivering in the trenches at night and to face any danger at their leader's call."

APPOMATTOX

I now come to what I have always regarded—shall ever regard—as the most creditable episode in all American history—an episode without a blemish, imposing, dignified, simple, heroic. I refer to Appomattox. Two men met that day, representative of American civilization, the whole world looking on. The two were Grant and Lee—types each. Both rose, and rose unconsciously, to the full height of the occasion—and than that occasion there has been none greater. About it, and them, there was no theatrical display, no self-consciousness, no effort at effect. A great crisis was to be met; and they met that crisis as great countrymen should. Consider the possibilities; think for a moment of what that day might have been; you will then see cause to thank God for much.—*General Charles Francis Adams, U.S.V., in Phi Beta Kappa Address delivered at the University of Chicago, June 17, 1902.*

WE are now to witness the closing scene of one of the greatest tragedies ever enacted on the world's stage. Many and varied had been the scenes during the war; the actors and their parts had been real. The wounds of the South were bleeding; the North was awaiting the decisive blow. Thousands of homes were ruined. Fortunes, great and small, had melted away by the hundreds of millions. In Richmond, the citadel of the waning Confederacy, the people were starving. The Southern army, half clad and without food, was but a shadow of its once proud self. Bravely and long the men in gray had followed their adored leader. Now the limit of endurance had been reached.

It was the second day of April, 1865. Lee realized that after Petersburg his beloved Richmond must fall. The order was given for the movement to begin at eight o'clock that night. The darkness of the early morning of the 3d was suddenly transformed into a lurid light overcasting the heavens

MEN ABOUT TO WITNESS APPOMATTOX

No photographer was present at Appomattox, that supreme moment in our national history, when Americans met for the last time as foes on the field. Nothing but fanciful sketches exist of the scene inside the McLean home. But here is a photograph that shows most of the Union officers present at the conference. Nine of the twelve men standing above stood also at the signing of Lee's surrender, a few days later. The scene is City Point, in March, 1865. Grant is surrounded by a group of the officers who had served him so faithfully. At the surrender, it was Colonel T. S. Bowers (third from left) upon whom Grant called to make a copy of the terms of surrender in ink. Colonel E. S. Parker, the full-blooded Indian on Grant's staff, an excellent penman, wrote out the final copy. Nineteen years later, General Horace Porter recorded with pride that he loaned General Lee a pencil to make a correction in the terms. Colonels William Duff and J. D. Webster, and General M. R. Patrick, are the three men who were not present at the interview. All of the remaining officers were formally presented to Lee. General Seth Williams had been Lee's adjutant when the latter was superintendent at West Point some years before the war. In the lower photograph General Grant stands between General Rawlins and Colonel Bowers. The veins standing out on the back of his hand are plainly visible. No one but he could have told how calmly the blood coursed through them during the four tremendous years.

GRANT BETWEEN RAWLINS AND BOWERS

for miles around the famous city whose name had become a household word over the civilized world. Richmond was in flames! The capital of the Confederacy, the pride of the South, toward which the Army of the Potomac had fought its way, leaving a trail of blood for four weary years, had at last succumbed to the overwhelming power of Grant's indomitable armies.

President Davis had received a despatch while attending services at St. Paul's church, Sunday morning, the 2d, advising him that the city must be evacuated that night, and, leaving the church at once, he hastened the preparations for flight with his personal papers and the archives of the Confederate Government. During that Sabbath day and night Richmond was in a state of riot. There had been an unwarranted feeling of security in the city, and the unwelcome news, spreading like an electric flash, was paralyzing and disastrous in its effect. Prisoners were released from their toils, a lawless mob overran the thoroughfares, and civic government was nullified. One explosion after another, on the morning of the 3d, rent the air with deafening roar, as the magazines took fire. The scene was one of terror and grandeur.

The flames spread to the city from the ships, bridges, and arsenal, which had been set on fire, and hundreds of buildings, including the best residential section of the capital of the Confederacy, were destroyed.

When the Union army entered the city in the morning, thousands of the inhabitants, men, women, and children, were gathered at street corners and in the parks, in wildest confusion. The commissary depot had been broken open by the starving mob, and rifled of its contents, until the place was reached by the spreading flames. The Federal soldiers stacked arms, and heroically battled with the fire, drafting into the work all able-bodied men found in the city. The invaders extinguished the flames, and soon restored the city to a state of order and safety. The invalid wife of General Lee, who was

IN PETERSBURG—AFTER NINE MONTHS OF BATTERING

This fine mansion on Bolingbroke Street, the residential section of Petersburg, has now, on the 3d of April, fallen into the hands of straggling Union soldiers. Its windows have long since been shattered by shells from distant Federal mortars; one has even burst through the wall. But it was not till the night of April 2d, when the retreat of the Confederate forces started, that the citizens began to leave their homes. At 9 o'clock in the morning General Grant, surrounded by his staff, rode quietly into the city. The streets were deserted. At length they arrived at a comfortable home standing back in a yard. There he dismounted and sat for a while on the piazza. Soon a group of curious citizens gathered on the sidewalk to gaze at the commander of the Yankee armies. But the Union troops did not remain long in the deserted homes. Sheridan was already in pursuit south of the Appomattox, and Grant, after a short conference with Lincoln, rode to the west in the rear of the hastily marching troops. Bolingbroke Street and Petersburg soon returned to the ordinary occupations of peace in an effort to repair the ravages of the historic nine months' siege.

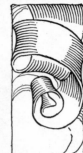

exposed to danger, was furnished with an ambulance and corporal's guard until the danger was past.

President Lincoln, who had visited Grant at Petersburg, entered Richmond on the 4th of April. He visited President Davis' house, and Libby Prison, then deserted, and held a conference with prominent citizens and army officers of the Confederacy. The President seemed deeply concerned and weighted down with the realization of the great responsibilities that would fall upon him after the war. Only ten days later the nation was shaken from ocean to ocean by the tragic news of his assassination.

General Lee had started on his last march by eight o'clock on the night of the 2d. By midnight the evacuation of both Petersburg and Richmond was completed. For nine months the invincible forces of Lee had kept a foe of more than twice their numerical strength from invading their stronghold, and only after a long and harassing siege were they forced to retreat. They saw the burning city as their line of march was illuminated by the conflagration, and emotions too deep for words overcame them. The woods and fields, in their fresh, bright colors of spring, were in sharp contrast to the travel-worn, weather-beaten, ragged veterans passing over the verdant plain. Lee hastened the march of his troops to Amelia Court House, where he had ordered supplies, but by mistake the train of supplies had been sent on to Richmond. This was a crushing blow to the hungry men, who had been stimulated on their tiresome march by the anticipation of much-needed food. The fatality of war was now hovering over them like a huge black specter.

General Grant did not proceed to Richmond, but leaving General Weitzel to invest the city, he hastened in pursuit of Lee to intercept the retreating army. This pursuit was started early on the 3d. On the evening of that date there was some firing between the pursuing army and Lee's rear guard. It was Lee's design to concentrate his force at Amelia Court

APPOMATTOX STATION—LEE'S LAST ATTEMPT TO PROVISION HIS RETREATING ARMY

At this railroad point, three miles from the Court House, a Confederate provision train arrived on the morning of April 8th. The supplies were being loaded into wagons and ambulances by a detail of about four thousand men, many of them unarmed, when suddenly a body of Federal cavalry charged upon them, having reached the spot by a by-road leading from the Red House. After a few shots the Confederates fled in confusion. The cavalry drove them on in the direction of Appomattox Court House, capturing many prisoners, twenty-five pieces of artillery, a hospital train, and a large park of wagons. This was Lee's last effort to obtain food for his army.

FEDERAL SOLDIERS WHO PERFORMED ONE OF THE LAST DUTIES AT APPOMATTOX

A detail of the Twenty-sixth Michigan handed out paroles to the surrendered Confederates.

House, but this was not to be accomplished by the night of the 4th. Not until the 5th was the whole army up, and then it was discovered that no adequate supplies were within less than fifty miles. Subsistence could be obtained only by foraging parties. No word of complaint from the suffering men reached their commander, and on the evening of that disappointing day they patiently and silently began the sad march anew. Their course was through unfavorable territory and necessarily slow. The Federals were gaining upon their retreating columns. Sheridan's cavalry had reached their flank, and on the 6th there was heavy skirmishing. In the afternoon the Federals had arrived in force sufficient to bring on an engagement with Ewell's corps in the rear, at Sailor's Creek, a tributary of the Appomattox River. Ewell was surrounded by the Federals and the entire corps captured. General Anderson, commanding the divisions of Pickett and Johnson, was attacked and fought bravely, losing many men. In all about six thousand Confederate soldiers were left in the hands of the pursuing army.

On the night of the 6th, the remainder of the Confederate army continued the retreat and arrived at Farmville, where the men received two days' rations, the first food except raw or parched corn that had been given them for two days. Again the tedious journey was resumed, in the hope of breaking through the rapidly-enmeshing net and forming a junction with Johnston at Danville, or of gaining the protected region of the mountains near Lynchburg. But the progress of the weak and weary marchers was slow and the Federal cavalry had swept around to Lee's front, and a halt was necessary to check the pursuing Federals. On the evening of the 8th, Lee reached Appomattox Court House. Here ended the last march of the Army of Northern Virginia.

General Lee and his officers held a council of war on the night of the 8th and it was decided to make an effort to cut their way through the Union lines on the morning of the next day. On the 7th, while at Farmville, on the south side of the

EMPTY VAULTS—THE EXCHANGE BANK, RICHMOND, 1865

The sad significance of these photographs is all too apparent. Not only the bank buildings were in ruins, but the financial system of the entire South. All available capital had been consumed by the demands of the war, and a system of paper currency had destroyed credit completely. Worse still was the demoralization of all industry. Through large areas of the South all mills and factories were reduced to ashes, and everywhere the industrial system was turned topsy-turvy. Truly the problem that confronted the South was stupendous.

WRECK OF THE GALLEGO FLOUR MILLS

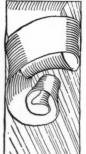

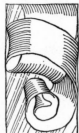

Appomattox River, Grant sent to Lee a courteous request for the surrender of the Army of Northern Virginia, based on the hopelessness of further resistance on the part of that army. In reply, Lee expressed sympathy with Grant's desire to avoid useless effusion of blood and asked the terms of surrender.

The next morning General Grant replied to Lee, urging that a meeting be designated by Lee, and specifying the terms of surrender, to which Lee replied promptly, rejecting those terms, which were, that the Confederates lay down their arms, and the men and officers be disqualified for taking up arms against the Government of the United States until properly exchanged. When Grant read Lee's letter he shook his head in disappointment and said, "It looks as if Lee still means to fight; I will reply in the morning."

On the 9th Grant addressed another communication to Lee, repeating the terms of surrender, and closed by saying, "The terms upon which peace can be had are well understood. By the South laying down their arms they will hasten that most desirable event, save thousands of human lives, and hundreds of millions of property not yet destroyed. Sincerely hoping that all our difficulties may be settled without the loss of another life, I subscribe myself, etc."

There remained for Lee the bare possibility, by desperate fighting, of breaking through the Federal lines in his rear. To Gordon's corps was assigned the task of advancing on Sheridan's strongly supported front. Since Pickett's charge at Gettysburg there had been no more hopeless movement in the annals of the war. It was not merely that Gordon was overwhelmingly outnumbered by the opposing forces, but his hunger-enfeebled soldiers, even if successful in the first onslaught, could count on no effective support, for Longstreet's corps was in even worse condition than his own. Nevertheless, on the morning of Sunday, the 9th, the attempt was made. Gordon was fighting his corps, as he said, "to a frazzle," when Lee came at last to a realizing sense of the futility of it all and

SIGNS OF PEACE—CONFEDERATE ARTILLERY CAPTURED AT RICHMOND AND WAITING SHIPMENT

Never again to be used by brother against brother, these Confederate guns captured in the defenses about Richmond are parked near the wharves on the James River ready for shipment to the national arsenal at Washington, once more the capital of a united country. The reflection of these instruments of destruction on the peaceful surface of the canal is not more clear than was the purpose of the South to accept the issues of the war and to restore as far as in them lay the bases for an enduring prosperity. The same devotion which manned these guns so bravely and prolonged the contest as long as it was possible for human powers to endure, was now directed to the new problems which the cessation of hostilities had provided. The restored Union came with the years to possess for the South a significance to be measured only by the thankfulness that the outcome had been what it was and by the pride in the common traditions and common blood of the whole American people. These captured guns are a memory therefore, not of regret, but of recognition, gratitude, that the highest earthly tribunal settled all strife in 1865.

COEHORNS, MORTARS, LIGHT AND HEAVY GUNS

ordered a truce. A meeting with Grant was soon arranged on the basis of the letters already exchanged. The conference of the two world-famous commanders took place at Appomattox, a small settlement with only one street, but to be made historic by this meeting. Lee was awaiting Grant's arrival at the house of Wilmer McLean. It was here, surrounded by staff-officers, that the terms were written by Grant for the final surrender of the Army of Northern Virginia. The terms, and their acceptance, were embodied in the following letters, written and signed in the famous " brick house " on that memorable Sunday:

APPOMATTOX COURT HOUSE, VIRGINIA,
APRIL 9, 1865.

GENERAL: In accordance with the substance of my letter to you of the 8th instant, I propose to receive the surrender of the Army of Northern Virginia on the following terms, to wit: Rolls of all the officers and men to be made in duplicate, one copy to be given to an officer to be designated by me, the other to be retained by such officer or officers as you may designate. The officers to give their individual paroles not to take up arms against the Government of the United States until properly exchanged; and each company or regimental commander to sign a like parole for the men of their commands. The arms, artillery, and public property to be parked and stacked, and turned over to the officers appointed by me to receive them. This will not embrace the side-arms of the officers, nor their private horses or baggage. This done, each officer and man will be allowed to return to his home, not to be disturbed by the United States authority so long as they observe their paroles and the laws in force where they may reside.

U. S. GRANT, *Lieutenant-General.*

General R. E. Lee.

HEADQUARTERS ARMY OF NORTHERN VIRGINIA,
APRIL 9, 1865.

GENERAL: I have received your letter of this date containing the terms of the surrender of the Army of Northern Virginia as proposed by you. As they are substantially the same as those expressed in your

LINCOLN

THE LAST SITTING—ON THE DAY OF LEE'S SURRENDER

On April 9, 1865, the very day of the surrender of Lee at Appomattox, Lincoln, for the last time, went to the photographer's gallery.   As he sits in simple fashion sharpening his pencil, the man of sorrows cannot forget the sense of weariness and pain that for four years has been unbroken.   No elation of triumph lights the features. One task is ended—the Nation is saved.   But another, scarcely less exacting, confronts him.   The States which lay "out of their proper practical relation to the Union," in his own phrase, must be brought back into a proper practical relation.   But this task was not for him.   Only five days later the sad eyes reflected upon this page closed forever upon scenes of earthly turmoil. Bereft of Lincoln's heart and head, leaders attacked problems of reconstruction in ways that proved unwise.   As the mists of passion and prejudice cleared away, both North and South came to feel that this patient, wise, and sympathetic ruler was one of the few really great men in history, and that he would live forever in the hearts of men made better by his presence during those four years of storm.

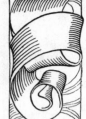

letter of the 8th instant, they are accepted. I will proceed to designate the proper officers to carry the stipulation into effect.

R. E. LEE, *General.*

Lieutenant-General U. S. Grant.

When Federal officers were seen galloping toward the Union lines from Appomattox Court House it was quickly surmised that Lee had surrendered. Cheer after cheer was sent up by the long lines throughout their entire length; caps and tattered colors were waved in the air. Officers and men alike joined in the enthusiastic outburst. It was glad tidings, indeed, to these men, who had fought and hoped and suffered through the long bloody years.

When Grant returned to his headquarters and heard salutes being fired he ordered it stopped at once, saying, "The war is over; the rebels are our countrymen again; and the best sign of rejoicing after the victory will be to abstain from all demonstration in the field."

Details of the surrender were arranged on the next day by staff-officers of the respective armies. The parole officers were instructed by General Grant to permit the Confederate soldiers to retain their own horses—a concession that was most welcome to many of the men, who had with them animals brought from the home farm early in the war.

There were only twenty-eight thousand men to be paroled, and of these fewer than one-third were actually bearing arms on the day of the surrender. The Confederate losses of the last ten days of fighting probably exceeded ten thousand.

The Confederate supplies had been captured by Sheridan, and Lee's army was almost at the point of starvation. An order from Grant caused the rations of the Federal soldiers to be shared with the "Johnnies," and the victorious "Yanks" were only too glad to tender such hospitality as was within their power. These acts of kindness were slight in themselves, but they helped immeasurably to restore good feeling and to

One of the proudest days of the nation—May 24, 1865—here lives again. The true greatness of the American people was not displayed till the close of the war. The citizen from the walks of humble life had during the contest become a veteran soldier, equal in courage and fighting capacity to the best drilled infantry of Marlborough, Frederick the Great, or Napoleon. But it remained to be seen whether he would return peacefully to the occupations of peace. European nations made dark predictions. "Would nearly a million men," they asked, "one of the mightiest military organizations ever trained in war, quietly lay aside this resistless power and disappear into the unnoted walks of civil life?" Europe with its standing armies thought not. Europe was mistaken. The disbanded veterans lent the effectiveness of military order and discipline to the industrial and commercial development of the land they had come to love with an increased devotion. The pictures are of Sherman's troops marching

THE RETURN OF THE SOLDIERS—THE GRAND REVIEW

THE SAME SCENE, A FEW SECONDS LATER

down Pennsylvania Avenue. The horsemen in the lead are General Francis P. Blair and his staff, and the infantry in flashing new uniforms are part of the Seventeenth Corps in the Army of Tennessee. Little over a year before, they had started with Sherman on his series of battles and flanking marches in the struggle for Atlanta. They had taken a conspicuous and important part in the battle of July 22d east of Atlanta, receiving and finally repulsing attacks in both front and rear. They had marched with Sherman to the sea and participated in the capture of Savannah. They had joined in the campaign through the Carolinas, part of the time leading the advance and tearing up many miles of railway track, and operating on the extreme right after the battle of Bentonville. After the negotiations for Johnston's surrender were completed in April, they set out on the march for the last time with flying colors and martial music, to enter the memorable review at Washington in May, here preserved.

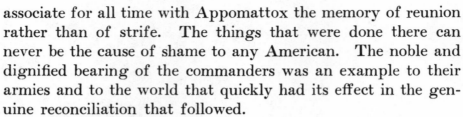

associate for all time with Appomattox the memory of reunion rather than of strife. The things that were done there can never be the cause of shame to any American. The noble and dignified bearing of the commanders was an example to their armies and to the world that quickly had its effect in the genuine reconciliation that followed.

The scene between Lee and his devoted army was profoundly touching. General Long in his "Memoirs of Lee" says: "It is impossible to describe the anguish of the troops when it was known that the surrender of the army was inevitable. Of all their trials, this was the greatest and hardest to endure." As Lee rode along the lines of the tried and faithful men who had been with him at the Wilderness, at Spotsylvania, and at Cold Harbor, it was not strange that those ragged, weather-beaten heroes were moved by deep emotion and that tears streamed down their bronzed and scarred faces. Their general in broken accents admonished them to go to their homes and be as brave citizens as they had been soldiers.

Thus ended the greatest civil war in history, for soon after the fall of the Confederate capital and the surrender of Lee's army, there followed in quick succession the surrender of all the remaining Southern forces.

While these stirring events were taking place in Virginia, Sherman, who had swept up through the Carolinas with the same dramatic brilliancy that marked his march to the sea, accomplishing most effective work against Johnston, was at Goldsboro. When Johnston learned of the fall of Richmond and Lee's surrender he knew the end had come and he soon arranged for the surrender of his army on the terms agreed upon at Appomattox. In the first week of May General "Dick" Taylor surrendered his command near Mobile, and on the 10th of the same month, President Jefferson Davis, who had been for nearly six weeks a fugitive, was overtaken and made a prisoner near Irwinsville, Georgia. The Southern Confederacy was a thing of the past.